From Little London to Little Bengal

From Little London to Little Bengal

Religion, Print, and Modernity in Early British India, 1793–1835

DANIEL E. WHITE

The Johns Hopkins University Press

Baltimore

© 2013 The Johns Hopkins University Press
All rights reserved. Published 2013
Printed in the United States of America on acid-free paper
2 4 6 8 9 7 5 3 1

The Johns Hopkins University Press
2715 North Charles Street
Baltimore, Maryland 21218-4363
www.press.jhu.edu

Library of Congress Cataloging-in-Publication Data
White, Daniel E.
From Little London to Little Bengal : religion, print, and modernity in early
British India, 1793–1835 / Daniel E. White.
pages cm
Includes bibliographical references and index.
ISBN 978-1-4214-1164-4 (hardcover : alk. paper)
ISBN 978-1-4214-1165-1 (electronic)
ISBN 1-4214-1164-4 (hardcover : alk. paper)
ISBN 1-4214-1165-2 (electronic)
1. English literature—19th century—History and criticism. 2. Romanticism—England.
3. Religion and literature. 4. Imperialism in literature. 5. Books and reading—England—
History. 6. Books and reading—India—History. 7. Printing—England—History—
19th century. 8. Printing—India—History—19th century. I. Title.
PR468.R44W48 2013
820.9'382—dc23   2013010183

A catalog record for this book is available from the British Library.

Special discounts are available for bulk purchases of this book. For more information,
please contact Special Sales at 410-516-6936 or specialsales@press.jhu.edu.

The Johns Hopkins University Press uses environmentally friendly
book materials, including recycled text paper that is composed of at least
30 percent post-consumer waste, whenever possible.

*For Family
and Friends the World O'er*

CONTENTS

Each page of this book reminds me of someone who helped along the way. I owe more than I can say to a group of colleagues and friends in the field of British Romanticism: Jeffrey Cox, Michael Gamer, Julie Kipp, Gregory Kucich, Mark Lussier, Tilar Mazzeo, the late Jane Moody, and Paul Youngquist, among others. We miss you, Jane. Although I've often wanted to escape from Southey, I've seldom wanted to escape from the Southeyans: Tim Fulford, Lynda Pratt, Carol Bolton, and Diego Saglia. My most fruitful and energizing intellectual exchanges have been with Rosinka Chaudhuri, Michael Franklin, and Mary Ellis Gibson, who have read and responded to individual chapters or the entirety of the manuscript, as have Jeannine DeLombard, Markman Ellis, Humberto Garcia, James Masland, Norbert Schürer, David Taylor, and James Wood.

Opportunities to present parts of this book as lectures to various audiences have been invaluable; for their invitations I would like to thank Angela Esterhammer and Tilottama Rajan (London, Ontario), Michael Franklin (Gregynog), Tim Fulford (Keswick and Nottingham), Kevin Gilmartin (San Marino), Jill Heydt-Stevenson (Boulder), Kurt Johnson (York), Anne Mellor (Los Angeles), Tom Mole and Andrew Piper (Montreal), Malabika Sarkar (Kolkata), Peter Stallybrass (Philadelphia), and Sarah Zimmerman (New York). To my hosts in Kolkata, Malabika and Sudipto Sarkar, to the members of the Centre for Studies in Romantic Literature at Jadavpur University, and to Abir Lal Mitra, for his subsequent correspondence, I am particularly grateful. One of the fondest memories of my research in India will always be the guided tour of the Carey Library at Serampore College given to me by the late Sunil K. Chatterjee. For volunteering thoughts, suggesting sources, and/or fielding so many questions, sometimes simple and sometimes not, I thank Rosinka Chaudhuri, Jeffrey Cox, Nora Crook, Andrew Davis, Markman Ellis, Máire ní Fhlathúin, Neil Fraistat, Michael Franklin, Anindita Ghosh, Mary Ellis Gibson, Heather Jackson, Anne

Janowitz, Peter Kitson, Jeremy Knight, Saree Makdisi, Michael Paoli, Nicholas Roe, Sara Salih, Norbert Schürer, Sakti Sadhan Mukhopadhyay, Padma Rangarajan, and Timothy Whelan. Lynn Festa, Betty Joseph, Peter Kitson, and Daniel O'Quinn have been consistent supporters of my work.

Librarians and archivists make research possible, and I sincerely appreciate the assistance I have received from the staffs of the following institutions: the British Library (London), the London Metropolitan Archives, the National Archives (Kew), the Bodleian Library (Oxford), the Angus Library of Regent's Park College (Oxford), the Bristol Baptist College Library and Archives (especially Roger Hayden), the Bristol Central Library, the Oriental Club (London), the New York Public Library, the National Library of India (Kolkata), the National Archives of India (New Delhi), the Carey Library at Serampore College (Srirampur), the Huntington Library (San Marino), and the Thomas Fisher Rare Book Library, the E. J. Pratt Library, and Robarts Library at the University of Toronto.

My colleagues in English and the Book History and Print Culture Program in Toronto have been an unfailing source of inspiration and support, both personal and professional, especially Alan Bewell, Christian Campbell, Jeannine DeLombard, Alexandra Gillespie, Heather Jackson, the late Robin Jackson, Thomas Keymer, Marie Korey, the late Richard Landon, Jeremy Lopez, Deidre Lynch, William Robins, Mari Ruti, Sara Salih, David Taylor, Leslie Thomson, Holger Syme, and Christopher Warley. My gratitude is also due to many graduate students, but especially to the following four, who worked with me as research assistants at the British Library: Lindsey Eckert, Tara McDonald, Muhammad Sid-Ahmad, and Alexander Willis. Matthew McAdam, Melissa Solarz, Joanne Allen, and Mary Lou Kenney of the Johns Hopkins University Press have been extremely reliable and helpful. Without the material support provided by the University of Toronto and a Standard Research Grant from the Social Sciences and Humanities Research Council of Canada, the research for this book would not have been possible.

Parts of several chapters have appeared in print in earlier versions: " 'Mysterious Sanctity': Sectarianism and Syncretism from Volney to Hemans," *European Romantic Review* 15, no. 2 (June 2004): 269–76; " 'A little God whom they had just sent over': Robert Southey's *The Curse of Kehama* and the Museum of the Bristol Baptist College," *Nineteenth-Century Contexts* 32, no. 2 (June 2010): 99–120; "Imperial Spectacles, Imperial Publics: Panoramas in and of Calcutta," *Wordsworth Circle* 41, no. 2 (Spring 2010): 71–81; and "Idolatry, Evangelicalism, and the Intense Objectivism of Robert Southey," *Romanticism* 17, no. 1 (2011): 39–51. I am grateful for permission to reprint these materials here. Every effort has been made to secure the necessary permissions to reproduce copyright material in this work. If any omissions are brought to my notice, I will be happy to include appropriate acknowledgments in any subsequent editions.

This book is dedicated to my family—to my mother, Nancy White, and the late Robert Hirschfeld, and to my father, Mitchell White, and Janet Birnkrant—as well as to the friends whose lives have become intertwined with my own: Dan Beale, Sophie Carter, Michael Paoli, Joshua Satin, Olivia Trench, Kate Tyler, Richard Warlow, James Wood, and Pascal Wyse. To my beautiful Jeannine De-Lombard, thank you for making the past seventeen years so full of joy, adventure, and love.

AJ	*Asiatic Journal*
AR	*Annual Review*
BL	British Library
CG	*Calcutta Gazette*
CJ	*Calcutta Journal*
CMP	*Calcutta Morning Post*
ER	*Edinburgh Review*
LMA	London Metropolitan Archives
PA	*Periodical Accounts Relative to the Baptist Missionary Society*
QR	*Quarterly Review*

For Indian personal names, I use the Anglicization adopted by the individual whenever possible. For place names, when deemed necessary I provide contemporary spellings parenthetically, but in general I follow nineteenth-century conventions—for instance, "Seringapatam (Srirangapatna)" but simply "Calcutta"—unless I am explicitly referring to a city today, in which case it would be "Kolkata." Throughout, I italicize words from Indian languages, with the exception of proper nouns and words commonly used in English. Because diacritics are so irregular in eighteenth- and nineteenth-century sources, I have chosen to omit them, though otherwise I retain idiosyncratic spellings, offering clarifications as needed.

From Little London to Little Bengal

Introduction

As Britain sought to reverse its trade deficit with India in the early nineteenth century by expanding the market for British goods on the subcontinent, evangelicals and utilitarians were avidly promoting the export not of Lancashire cottons but of Christianity and improvement—in a word, of "civilization." So at the height of the debate over the renewal of the East India Company charter in 1813, when one of the burning questions involved whether missionary activity should for the first time be permitted within Company territory, Governor of Madras Sir Thomas Munro's panegyric on India would have been particularly inflammatory: "If civilisation were to become an article of trade between the two countries, he was convinced that England would greatly benefit by the import cargo."[1] Since Raymond Schwab's *The Oriental Renaissance: Europe's Rediscovery of India and the East, 1680–1880* (1950; trans. 1984), British Romanticism has rightly appeared to be a movement shaped as much by the import cargo of classical Indian culture, both religious and secular, as by the new dawn and terrible days of the French Revolution, the regional nature and "common" language of the Lake District, alpine sublimity, or the urban public spheres of London or Edinburgh. This book shifts the focus away from influence and the relations it implies, building instead on different ways of understanding the cultural, political, economic, and religious lives of individuals and groups, their ties and tensions, in early nineteenth-century Britain and Bengal.

The "new imperial history," which examines how individual and collective identities, spaces, and temporalities are mutually constituted across national, protonational, or other boundaries, replaces a Eurocentric binary perspective on metropolitan center and imperial periphery, long taken for granted, with attention to circulation and scale.[2] "Europe's colonies were never empty spaces to be made over in Europe's image or fashioned in its interests," write Ann Laura Stoler and Frederick Cooper; "nor, indeed, were European states self-contained entities that at one point projected themselves overseas. Europe was made by its imperial projects, as much as colonial encounters were shaped by conflicts within Europe itself."[3] In spite of the now common premises that "metropole and colony have to be seen in a unitary field of analysis"[4] and that the origins of globalization are to be found in the culture of consumption fostered by eighteenth-century mercantile imperialism, scholars of late eighteenth- and early nineteenth-century Anglophone writing still need literary studies that do not view India primarily through the lens of British Orientalist representations, seeing India essentially as an abstraction, a reflection, and a projection of British imaginations.[5] For that perspective, as I hope to show, is the legacy of a specific Romantic ideology of imperial rule, born in and of the period itself. Anglophone writing not merely about but from India, written by Indians, including the growing numbers of mixed-race "East Indians,"[6] as well as by Europeans, reveals a much wider, more complex, and riven culture of empire. Cultural histories of Western Orientalism, crucial as they have been, need to give way to the stubborn fact that Britons and Indians inhabited the same globe, a material and imagined terrain where unequal relations of power and representation were contested through alliances and conflicts, communication and mistranslation, sympathies and failures of feeling and understanding.

In 1831 the London-based *Asiatic Journal* adapted Munro's still resonant claim and proposed that "if *poetry* were to become an article of trade between the two countries, England would gain by the import-cargo."[7] The work under review that prompted this new, arresting assertion was *The Bengal Annual, a Literary Keepsake for M.DCCCXXXI*, edited by David Lester Richardson and recently arrived from the press of Samuel Smith and Co., Hare Street, Calcutta.[8] And the reviewer's declaration was indeed intended to surprise, for until then Calcutta had been thought of as a capital of commerce, not of literature, and whatever Anglophone poetry did come out of India had been viewed as either an exercise in nostalgia, if written by European exiles in the service of the East India Company, or a servile attempt at mimicry, if written by East Indians or Indians, who had never set foot on British shores. But following the founding of the Hindu College in 1817, the suspension of censorship over newspapers in 1818, the ensuing emergence of new publications in English, Persian, and Bengali, the rise of Rammohun Roy as a major public intellectual, especially after *The Precepts of Jesus* (1820), the coming of age of a generation of young Indians and East Indians educated in English, and the galvanizing of the orthodox Hindu community against the new "Hindu liberals," Calcutta in the 1820s and early 1830s witnessed an explosion of print culture, with poetry at its very center. "Calcutta ought to have its name changed," proposed a satirical piece in the *India Gazette* (1824) on the new "Tank School" of poetry—from the great tank in front of the Writers' Buildings—published by Company servants in the Calcutta papers: "Instead of being called the city of Palaces, it should be denominated the city of Poets. Parnassus is no longer the haunt of the muses. They have fled to Calcutta, and the Hooghly has become the Castalian stream."[9]

With the rise of an active print industry and an ever more autonomous newspaper press and reading public in Calcutta in the early nineteenth century, relationships between the metropolitan and imperial capitals increasingly relied on fluid but unequal movements of people, ideas, books, and other commodities. By the 1820s, many subjects in London and Calcutta experienced imperial culture and space in circulation, defining the two capitals in multidirectional, recursive, or contrapuntal rather than unilinear terms.[10] These metaphors suggest not just new ways for social and cultural historians today to look back upon the past—methods of reading and interpretation—but powerful lenses in the past through which people saw their world differently, and contested one another's visions.

This book is inspired by and organized around the realization that in the early nineteenth century part of Calcutta could be called "Little London," and part of London "Little Bengal." The circular structure of the book, from Little London in Bengal to Little Bengal in London, reflects the recursive movements it traces, for neither the point of departure nor the point of arrival is truly an origin or end.[11] Although the circuits I follow have a long, well-documented, and varied prehistory, from John Mandeville's late fourteenth-century *Travels* and Dryden's "Annus Mirabilis" (1667) up to William Jones's "Third Anniversary Discourse," delivered to the Asiatic Society of Bengal in 1786, these two novel, implicated spaces affirm that the late eighteenth and early nineteenth centuries—which I will call the "Romantic" era only in European contexts—witnessed the rise of new and distinct imperial dynamics. As Catherine Hall and Sonya Rose point out, "The connections between British state formation and empire building stretch back a long way, certainly into the pre-modern period. It was the shift from an empire of commerce and the seas to an empire of conquest, however, that brought the political and economic effects of empire home in new ways."[12] Following the defeat of Tipu Sultan at Seringapatam (Srirangapatna) in 1799, the remaining threat to Britain's military power in India was the Mahratta Confederacy in central and west India (the western Deccan), and by the end of the third Anglo-Mahratta War in 1818, British rule by conquest was largely uncontested. But just because Britons began to think of India as a "possession" did not make it so. The stance obscures the messy reality of ongoing intercultural nego-tiations, alliances, and conflicts that marked the period with which this book is concerned, from the arrival of the Baptist missionaries in 1793 to the 1830s, with the deaths of Henry Derozio and Rammohun[13] in 1831 and 1833, respectively, and Macaulay's "Minute on Indian Education" in 1835.

The period is distinguished by another development. India was not, and never became, a "settler colony," but in the early nineteenth century British civil and military servants passed longer parts of their lives overseas than had their eighteenth-century counterparts, the "nabob" generations.[14] For most "Anglo-Indians," as they were called, it thus became very important to maintain connec-tions to Britain by keeping up with the latest fashions and books, by reproducing home to the best of their abilities. In 1812–13, as I discuss in chapter 1, residents of Calcutta could go to see panoramas of Dover, Edinburgh, and Ramsgate. This replication of home abroad in a medium not invented until 1787 suggests an understanding of distance and scale corresponding to a concurrent public-sphere ideology of imperial rule. For inhabitants of Little London, the miniatur-ization and transportability of culture bring Britain and India into a mimetic kind of proximity, like that between a landscape and its panoramic depiction, between reality and its reduced reflection. All authority lies with the former, the location and source of culture and public opinion, whereas the latter becomes a framed abstraction fit, as if by nature, for the exercise of geographically distant sovereignty, which in other senses was not so distant at all.

At the same time, the fantasy of Little London was constantly challenged and undermined by different ways of life, perspectives, and ideologies, involv-ing relations among Europeans, East Indians, and Indians who tended to favor free trade, liberty of the press, and polyglot education. If Little Londoners saw themselves as surrounded by millions of Indians to be ruled by the authority and civilization emanating from home—from the Company directors at Lead-enhall Street, the Parliamentary Board of Control at Westminster, and British culture and public opinion—in fact they were surrounded by evolving commu-nities with varying degrees of influence struggling for disparate but at times overlapping interests, from the new radical journalists led by James Silk Buck-ingham and Rammohun (discussed in chapter 1) to the elite, conservative Hindu families who maintained the annual Durga Pujas (chapter 1), the Baptist mis-sionaries up the river in Serampore (Srirampur) (chapter 2), and the East Indian Derozio, along with the influential generation of Indian students he taught at the Hindu College (chapter 3). In different ways, these individuals and groups

were creating and insisting on a new print culture and an attendant Indian public with distinct tastes and divergent political, racial, and religious affiliations,
bound together by an unavoidable sense of distance and emergent autonomy
from London, a sense that Calcutta in many ways was not a Little London at all.

If in the early nineteenth century London came to Calcutta, where its presence was contested by competing visions, Calcutta went to London as well. The
eighteenth-century phenomenon of "nabobery" had fostered a fear, capitalized
on so effectively by Edmund Burke and Richard Sheridan in their prosecution
of Warren Hastings before the House of Lords, that Oriental despotism and decadence were infecting the British Constitution, and British constitutions, both
abroad and at home.[15] And by the early nineteenth century, with the appetite
for literary Orientalism whetted by William Jones, William Beckford, Elizabeth
Hamilton, Robert Southey, Sydney Owenson, and others, Byron could famously
advise Thomas Moore, "Stick to the East; the oracle, Staël, told me it was the only
poetical policy."[16] Through fictions in prose and verse and because of the awareness raised by the debate surrounding the renewal of the Company charter in
1813, it appeared to Byron in that same year that the public was "orientalizing."[17]
Less well known but more pertinent to the material presence of Indian culture
in London in the 1820s and 1830s than either nabobery or British Orientalist
imaginative writing are the space and community in Marylebone and Mayfair
known as Little Bengal (discussed in chapter 4), where many families of Anglo-
Indians (or "old Indians," as they would be known back in Britain) settled upon
their return.[18] With its Royal Asiatic Society, Oriental Club, and Hindostanee
Coffee House, its curries, hookahs, and nautches, its ayahs, mixed-race families,
and "Persian princesses," Little Bengal displaced and relocated people, books,
fashions, and tastes, producing a unique space of exile in the very heart of home.

Because many of the terms central to this study have meanings particular
to the circumstances of early British India and because many of the institutions, individuals, and groups discussed will be unfamiliar to some British and
North American readers, I will frame my interests and goals by briefly describing the 1813 Charter Act, which ended the East India Company's monopoly over
the Indian trade, recast the conflict between "Anglicists" and "Orientalists," secured the place of missionaries in Company territories, and led to the founding
of the "secular" Hindu College. The following paragraphs introduce the historical background of evangelicalism and English-language education in early
nineteenth-century Bengal and clarify necessary terminology.

When the East India Company's charter was renewed in 1813, two controversial and consequential articles were included, the "pious" and educational clauses.[19] According to the former, missionary activity would no longer be prohibited within territories administered by the Company. In 1793 the Baptist missionaries had made their way to Bengal as indigo farmers, and even so, they probably would have been turned back had they not sailed on a Danish rather than a Company vessel. According to the educational clause, the substantial sum of 100,000 rupees (approximately £10,000) per year would be committed to "the encouragement of the learned natives of India . . . and promotion of a knowledge of the sciences" among them. It has become something of a truism, which even the most cursory glance at the second and third decades of the nineteenth century complicates, that together these clauses settled the longstanding debate between the Orientalist and Anglicist camps among the Company's servants, governors, and shareholders, its Board of Directors at Leadenhall Street, and its Board of Control in the House of Commons, and that the Anglicists won.

In other words, no longer would colonial administration continue in the Orientalist mode of empire-building established by Robert Clive, Warren Hastings, and Richard Wellesley. In that mode, following its assumption of the *diwani* of Bengal, Bihar, and Orissa in 1765,[20] the Company had nominally operated as part of the Mughal Empire and accordingly adopted Hindu and Muslim political, legal, and social forms while maintaining a policy of religious nonintervention (thus the exclusion of missionaries) and cultivating the study of Sanskrit and Persian, the official language of government, revenue, and law. After 1813, for the first time the Company would enter the business of "civilizing" Indians through religion and education, that is, by encouraging Protestant evangelicals to spread the gospel and by promoting the acquisition of English and the study of Western science. If the trial of Warren Hastings had turned the tide away from the Orientalists, so the story goes, Charles Grant Sr.'s "Observations On the State of Society among the Asiatic Subjects of Great Britain, particularly with respect to Morals; and on the means of improving it" (1813), the new charter in that same year, and James Mill's *The History of British India* (1817) marked the ascendancy of the Anglicists, and it would only be a matter of time until Macaulay's "Minute" finished the job in 1835.[21]

A key moment for this historical assessment was the establishment in 1817 of the ostensibly secular and Western Hindu College, the precursor of today's Presidency University, Kolkata. When a "very respectable meeting of the Hindoos" assembled at the home of Sir Edward Hyde East, chief justice of the Supreme Court of Calcutta, in May 1816 to consider a plan previously put forward by David Hare, Rammohun, and others, a committee was formed that subsequently set forth the "primary object" of the college as "the tuition of the sons of respectable Hindoos, in the English and Indian languages, and in the Literature and Science of Europe and Asia."[22] Although Hare and Rammohun were "progressives" and the latter was always described as a "Hindu reformer," the other Hindu supporters of the college enterprise formed a fundamentally "conservative" group, though as we will see, all of these categories need to be applied with care and caution.

A more appropriate word than "conservative," to start with, would be "orthodox" (*sanatani*). By "orthodoxy" I mean both the acceptance of Vedic authority and the observance of a body of medieval Puranic (Sakta and Vaishnava) customs that had come to seem traditional, even if many of them had changed radically over time and some were of comparatively recent advent, from the performance of elaborate pujas to regulations of marriage and widowhood and the defense of sati. Saktas, who worship the divine energy of Brahman, or God, as identified with the goddess Devi, among Bengalis in her forms as Durga, Kali, and Jaggadhatri, made up the largest religious community in Bengal, followed by the Vaishnavas, who worship Brahman as Vishnu, usually as manifested in the avatars Rama and Krishna.

Although I use the term "orthodoxy" to indicate the embrace and maintenance of religious attitudes thought to be established, I do not mean to dissever beliefs (doctrine) from practices, which inform a range of collective dispositions. Part of the history of Western secularization is the separating of theology from religious culture more broadly conceived (embodied methods of preaching and prayer, writing and speaking styles, reading habits, modes of congregational sociability, etc.), but for Protestant Christianity that separation was very much in process and incomplete in the Romantic era, when Christology, predestination, election, and so forth, were inextricable from the manners and personalities of different kinds of Christians and the interactions among them in ways that for the most part are no longer the case today. For Hindus in the late Mughal and early British periods, as Srinivas Aravamudan points out, "orthopraxies" were as important as orthodoxies, if not more so.[23] For the sake of efficiency, I use the latter term to embrace the two.

In the early nineteenth century the orthodox tended to resist the importation of non-Hindu beliefs and practices, either via Christian evangelicalism or what was perceived to be syncretistic openness to originary truths shared by various religious systems. "Heterodoxy," in this context, signifies the challenge posed by the followers of Rammohun, the future Brahmoists, who sought to reform and refine contemporary Hinduism by returning it to the purity of the Upanishads and an "ancient period of harmony,"[24] while dismissing apparently traditional customs such as idolatry and sati, along with a host of Puranic and Tantric devotional practices, as, in David Kopf's phrase, "medieval excrescences."[25] At the same time, the heterodox in the early nineteenth century often syncretized monotheistic and rationalist tenets of classical Hinduism and Unitarian Christianity with constitutive elements of Islam and other Indian religions into a universal theism. The orthodox would form the so-called conservative Dharma Sabha, whereas the heterodox would form the so-called liberal Brahma Sabha (which later became the Brahmo Samaj), although as Kopf rightly stresses, "Neither group could be classed as 'conservative' or 'liberal' but each looked to a different element in a newly created Hindu consciousness of their own past."[26]

It is thus important not to equate "reformist" with "liberal" or "radical," nor "orthodox" with "conservative"; indeed, all these terms were used quite loosely in the nineteenth century, and more importantly, opposed political and religious categories could overlap. Peary Chand Mittra, for instance, describes Ramkamal Sen as a "strict orthodox Hindoo" who was "liberal in his ideas."[27] And Kopf has provided a thorough complication of all these categories in his comparison of two supposedly paradigmatic figures, the liberal reformer Rammohun and the orthodox and conservative Radhakanta Deb.[28] Thus Brian Pennington writes, "The habit of casting competing groups as either 'reformers' (e.g., the Brahmo Samaj) or 'orthodox' (e.g., the Dharma Sabha) has for too long obscured the modern character of emerging Hindu organizations; their mutually shared goals, interests, and strategies; and their common passion for preserving and embodying the ancient past."[29] While the heterodox reformer Rammohun had been involved in the early stages of planning the Hindu College, he did not join the managing committee or publicly support the enterprise for fear of, in the words of the Presidency College Register, "alarming the prejudices of his orthodox countrymen and thus marring the whole cause."[30] The heterodox, liberal Rammohun could not join the orthodox, conservative managing committee of a Westernizing and secular experiment in progressive education.

And if these were the divisions among the founders, within the first decade of the institution its students would coalesce into a third community, known by the 1830s and 1840s as the protonationalist Young Bengal movement, or, due to the influence of their teacher from 1828 to 1831, the Derozians, whose presumed deracination, Westernization, and secularization I discuss in chapter 3. A close look at the early sociability associated with the college, and especially a close reading of the poetry written *about* that sociability by the college's most famous teacher, the mixed-race poet and prodigy Henry Derozio, master of English literature and history, challenges this clear-cut construal of the Derozians as representative of Macaulay's "class who may be interpreters between us and the millions whom we govern; a class of persons, Indian in blood and colour, but English in taste, in opinions, in morals, and in intellect," in spite of Macaulay's explicit call in the very next paragraph "to give larger encouragement to the Hindoo college at Calcutta."[31] But more importantly, a historically and formally sensitive reading of Derozio's poetry also undermines the equation of modernity with secularity defined in a straightforward manner as "the negation of religion" rather than "a cumulatively and dialectically achieved condition."[32] In broad terms, this book unravels the old story of the Anglicist victory ushering in secular modernity.

◆ ◆

In 1819 E. W. Stillingfleet, vicar of South Cave, a small village in Yorkshire, preached a sermon titled "On the Propagation of Christianity, in the Eastern Colonial Possessions of Britain," in which he told his provincial congregants, "The ocean has changed its character, in the estimate of mankind. It no longer separates; it has become the channel of intercourse, and even of union, between far-distant lands."[33] The message, however, was hardly cosmopolitan: "We are made familiarly acquainted with the manners, the habits, the peculiarities, the opinions, the religion, even of the most barbarous, and most remote people. In their turn, they admire and feel our superiority. May they discover, and understand the basis, on which that superiority rests!"[34] The ocean had indeed changed its character, but not always with the effect the vicar anticipated.

In the pages to follow I will bring a book-historical methodology and a nuanced treatment of religious encounter between Hinduism and Protestant Christianity to bear on early imperial channels of intercourse, exploring how a series of often materialized, ambivalent exchanges shaped understandings of imperial life for Britons and Indians in the early nineteenth century.[35] In an era when for Protestant Christians the doctrine of *sola scriptura* had softened and diffused into a generalized faith in the civilizing effects of print communication, the explosion of print in Bengal and the new traffic in books between London and Calcutta and within Bengal exposed unresolved tensions, even outright contradictions, in the worldviews underpinning hierarchical relationships between the two capitals and their overlapping public spheres. But books were far from the only, or the most important, circulating objects that exerted power over the subjects of early British India. Missionaries, East India Company civil servants and military men, Bengalis both elite and common, and the newly coalesced mixed-race East Indian community lived in a world saturated by circulating commodities *as well as* objects that did not live for the sake of exchange. By attending to the movements of and interactions between diverse people and diverse things, I hope to show how the following imperial phenomena, too often understood as discrete, were mutually constitutive: the traffic in commodities, the production and circulation of *non*commodified objects (such as religious tracts and *murtis*, or "Hindu idols"),[36] the encounter between Calvinist evangelicalism and Hinduism, the interplay between modernity and secularity in early British India, and the new transnational print culture of writers, publishers, and reading publics in London and Calcutta.

Chapter 1, "'Little London': Imperial Publics, Imperial Spectacles," begins with a meditation upon distance and scale, authenticity and imitation, in the idea of Little London. I then locate its first major challenge in Buckingham's and Rammohun's struggles to articulate an Indian public sphere, necessarily hybrid and local yet autonomous, cosmopolitan, assertive, and distinctly "Indian" in a novel sense. Journalism therefore played a role in patterning its own new Indian spirit as a "creole nationalism."[37] But in keeping with Partha Chatterjee's critique of this ultimately Eurocentric narrative, any cultural history of the period needs to add other chapters to the story, not for "sentimental" reasons, as Chatterjee writes, but because the "most powerful as well as the most creative results of the nationalist imagination in Asia and Africa are posited not on an identity but rather on a *difference* with the 'modular' forms of the national society propagated by the modern West."[38] I thus move from print journalism to two spectacular spaces in early nineteenth-century Calcutta that engaged with Little London through identity and difference, the panorama and the annual Durga Puja, which were held in the "White Town" (extending off the Maidan, the fields surrounding Fort William, from Esplanade Row to the north to Alipore to the south and from the river to the west to Chowringhee Road to the east) and the "Black Town" (to the north), respectively (fig. 1).[39] These entertainments, the former secular and the latter sacred, though ambiguously so to Europeans, could simultaneously affirm British authority, augment the symbolic and cultural capital of elite Bengali families, and project new relationships among and between Britons, Indians, and the amusements they enjoyed. At stake in these imitative and self-assertive spectacles was the fortification or erosion of the walls securing Little London and cordoning off Europeans from Indians, public from private, politics from entertainment, modern from traditional, and secular from sacred.

The most controversial imposition of identity upon India, however, and the one that provoked the passions of Company shareholders in London, evangelicals around the world, and Hindus both reformist and orthodox in and around Calcutta was the introduction of Protestant missionaries into Bengal, so it is to

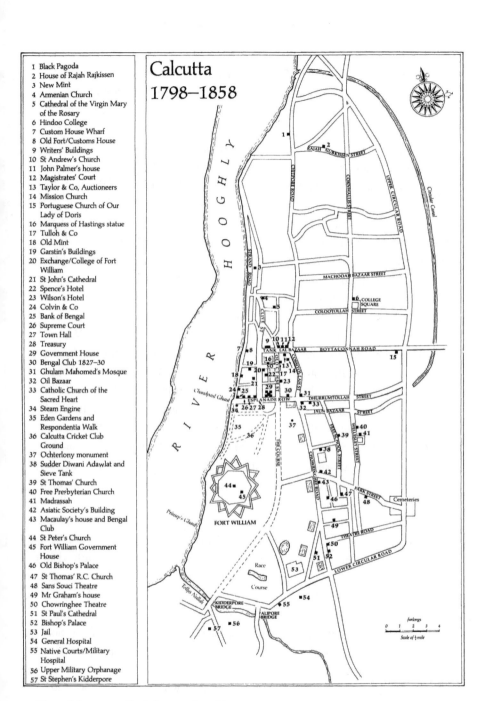

1 Black Pagoda
2 House of Rajah Rajkissen
3 New Mint
4 Armenian Church
5 Cathedral of the Virgin Mary
   of the Rosary
6 Hindoo College
7 Custom House Wharf
8 Old Fort/Customs House
9 Writers' Buildings
10 St Andrew's Church
11 John Palmer's house
12 Magistrates' Court
13 Taylor & Co, Auctioneers
14 Mission Church
15 Portuguese Church of Our
   Lady of Doris
16 Marquess of Hastings statue
17 Tulloh & Co
18 Old Mint
19 Garstin's Buildings
20 Exchange/College of Fort
   William
21 St John's Cathedral
22 Spence's Hotel
23 Wilson's Hotel
24 Colvin & Co
25 Bank of Bengal
26 Supreme Court
27 Town Hall
28 Treasury
29 Government House
30 Bengal Club 1827–30
31 Ghulam Mahomed's Mosque
32 Oil Bazaar
33 Catholic Church of the
   Sacred Heart
34 Steam Engine
35 Eden Gardens and
   Respondentia Walk
36 Calcutta Cricket Club
   Ground
37 Ochterlony monument
38 Sudder Diwani Adawlat and
   Sieve Tank
39 St Thomas' Church
40 Free Presbyterian Church
41 Madrassah
42 Asiatic Society's Building
43 Macaulay's house and Bengal
   Club
44 St Peter's Church
45 Fort William Government
   House
46 Old Bishop's Palace
47 St Thomas' R.C. Church
48 Sans Souci Theatre
49 Mr Graham's house
50 Chowringhee Theatre
51 St Paul's Cathedral
52 Bishop's Palace
53 Jail
54 General Hospital
55 Native Courts/Military
   Hospital
56 Upper Military Orphanage
57 St Stephen's Kidderpore

Calcutta
1798–1858

Fig. 1. *Calcutta, 1798–1858*. Reproduced from Losty, *Calcutta, City of Palaces*, 72.
© The British Library Board.

this subject that I turn in chapter 2. "Secret Sharers and Evangelical Signs: The Idol, the Book, and the Intense Objectivism of Robert Southey" shifts the metropolitan scene from London to Bristol and follows missionaries from the Bristol Baptist College and Missionary Society to the Danish settlement of Serampore, just north of Calcutta on the Hugli River. Almost immediately upon their arrival in Bengal, they began to collect Hindu devotional materials, especially small wood, brass, or bronze "idols," and to ship them back to the Baptist College Museum. They also began printing and circulating Bibles, books of the New Testament, and religious tracts. In the movements of and relations between idols and books, I find an integrated evangelical circuit of communication. If Little London intimately linked transportable European fashions to the circulation of raw materials and commodities, Calvinist missionaries set in motion a different set of values, economic and affective. The British Romantic response most grounded in this material culture of the early empire in India is to be found in Robert Southey's writings about the missionary movement in the *Annual* and *Quarterly* reviews and in his epic poem *The Curse of Kehama* (1810). Whereas idols were subjected to various forms of conversion in the museum of the Baptist College and on itinerant fundraising tours, in Southey's writings they are treated with considerably less iconoclasm than we might expect from an advocate of empire and Christianization. His uncomfortable place within the "high" Romantic movement, on the one hand, and his strangely sympathetic treatment of idolatry, on the other, can be traced to the same root, his intensely objective (the phrase is De Quincey's) imagination, his instinct and insistence that external things are good or bad according to the social relations we project into them and that they in turn mediate.

The third chapter, "'I would not have the day return': Henry Derozio and Rammohun Roy in Cosmopolitan Calcutta," juxtaposes these two figures' perspectives on time and history and joins the research of Rosinka Chaudhuri and Mary Ellis Gibson in introducing Derozio, a major talent who died too young, to a broader audience today.[40] Dismissed for much of the nineteenth and twentieth centuries as an imitative, derivative poet and teacher who sought to foster Indian nationalism by celebrating India's glorious past in the language of Burns, Scott, Byron, Shelley, and Moore, Derozio in fact produced a diverse and experimental range of writings, in poetry and prose, that we can only now begin to appreciate thanks to recent scholarship and editions.[41] In the world of circulation studied in this book, "imitation" takes on various meanings and values under different conditions. After all, it was precisely through imitation that Britons in Little London defined and authorized their own subjectivity and right to rule. From their point of view, however, they weren't imitating, but simply being, a privilege that came with the sense and reality of conquest. When a colonial subject such as Derozio—a mixed-race Christian raised and educated in English with a preternatural mastery for his age of the English canon—imitates, he engages in more than mimicry, even in Homi Bhabha's sense of a "double vision which in disclosing the ambivalence of colonial discourse also disrupts its authority."[42] I instead introduce the term "citation," which I adapt in this chapter from Walter Benjamin's reflections on historical situations in which the past is charged with the time of the now (*Jetztzeit*). Whereas imitation, like influence, is unidirectional, citation is recursive, projecting the self out onto a range of styles and voices that in turn inform and become part of the self that cites. Memory in Derozio's mature poems performs "a process of signification" that, if it does not exactly "erase any prior or originary presence of the nation-people to demonstrate the prodigious, living principles of the people as contemporaneity,"[43] does imagine the national present by inventing the past and investing it with the new and the now. For Derozio the past is thus neither an origin nor an essence. And the agent of this act is a disinherited and alienated form of memory, which paradoxically insists on remembering and echoing events, times, and feelings that the self never knew, just as through citation the "imitative" poet himself remembers and echoes words that were not his own. As Chaudhuri writes, Derozio's nationalism "constructs a notion of indigen[ei]ty ('my native land') that might have borrowed from Scott and Byron its linguistic contours, but was often—and perhaps especially *because* of the distinctive nature of the borrowing—emphatically, and unprecedentedly, Indian in its mooring."[44]

From Little London we thus proceed through two chapters on different forms of circulation, of things and words, before ending in Little Bengal. Whereas exile abroad, with its imitations of life in England, energized Little Londoners to embrace their imperial mission to trade, consume, and acquire useful knowledge about the land and people they ruled, exile at home, with its imitations of life in India, had different effects, which I describe with respect to two related institutions, the Royal Asiatic Society and the Oriental Club. Little Bengal could be seen as part of an imperial circuit, contributing specialized experience and information to the ongoing mission and still connected to global movements of ideas, capital, and commodities. In this light, its residents, although geographically exiled from the location abroad where they had become domesticated, could remain at home with the empire, so to speak, in England. In another light, Little

Bengalis found themselves sealed off, represented from within and without as a race apart, with their own tastes and even language, retired from active service abroad yet without a place in London's social scenes.

This cultural arena provides the context in which to reconsider the most highly publicized crossing of the period, the voyage of Rammohun in 1830 as emissary of the Mughal emperor to the court of Great Britain. A charismatic figure—Coleridge hailed him as the "Luther of Brahmanism"[45]—Rammohun was a source of fascination in London and in Bristol, where he died and was buried in 1833. I close my story with an account and analysis of Rammohun's social life in London, where he was emissary to far more than the court. In drawing rooms and chapels, in coaches and theaters, at soirées and taverns, and especially but by no means exclusively in Unitarian circles, Rammohun's energetic sociability affords an opportunity to complement recent social and political histories that have detailed his contributions to the discourse of liberal imperialism. Integral to rather than separate from the history of his ideas, his friendships and conversations in England, often with women, and their coverage in the popular press reveal an "Orientalization" of London very different from that of Little Bengal. Rammohun connects Britain and India as inextricable yet autonomous participants in a cosmopolitan world more expansive than either, where sympathies distinct to separate cultural traditions can be translated and universalized.

Instead of considering the impact or influence of early imperial India on British literature, or vice versa, therefore, I seek to expose a powerful current of imperial culture—of which a globalized Romanticism was only a part—that projected its values as mobile and its ideals as exceeding the conceptual boundaries of territorial nationalism. Each chapter treats scenarios that mobilized people and things, animating highly contested categories of public opinion and enacting new social, religious, and literary affiliations. In different and often antagonistic ways, the central figures in this story—the radical English travel writer and journalist James Silk Buckingham (1786–1855), the Hindu reformer and journalist Rammohun Roy (1772–1833), the Baptist missionaries of Serampore, the poet and critic Robert Southey (1774–1843), and the mixed-race prodigy Henry Louis Vivian Derozio (1809–31)—contributed to a cosmopolitanism that was neither exported, imported, nor local. In place of discrete national publics and counterpublics, of influence and imitation, the exchanges among these figures and the circuits through which their writings traveled require us to think in terms of different scales of affiliation, communication, and circulation. This is not to say that the spatial scales of a cosmopolitan or transnational imagined community exclude nationalist commitments; rather, as Bruce Robbins suggests, cosmopolitanism is often an integral element of nationalism, as was the case with the Indian protonationalisms of early nineteenth-century Calcutta.[46] We will thus consider the rise of an Anglophone "Indian literature" and the articulation of an "Indian public" as part of an alternative modernity that cannot be reduced to the reactions of groups peripheral to the metropolitan center of power and culture, a model that does not do justice to the complexity or diversity of early nineteenth-century Bengali print or to the circulation of people, things, and ideas between London and Calcutta.

CHAPTER ONE

"Little London"

Imperial Publics, Imperial Spectacles

CALCUTTA lo! as LONDON o'er the THAME,

Lifts her high head above old HOUGLY's stream . . .

—*John Horsford, "The Art of Living in India" (1800)*

At the end of *The Surgeon's Daughter* (1827), Walter Scott's only work set in India, when the surrogate narrator, Mr. Croftangry, has finished the tale and is basking in the applause of his female and almost exclusively young audience, a "merciless old lady" interrupts the chorus of praise by making "a disquisition upon shawls, which she had the impudence to say, arose entirely out of" the story.[1] Her implication is that because Mr. Croftangry has never been to India, his tale is like an imitation Kashmir shawl made at Paisley, which lacks a certain "inimitable cross-stitch in the border" by which the authentic shawl is recognized:

> From the genuine Indian, she made a digression to the imitation shawls now made at Paisley, out of real Thibet wool, not to be known from the actual Country shawl, except by some inimitable cross-stitch in the border. "It is well," said the old lady, wrapping herself up in a rich Kashmire, "that there is some way of knowing a thing that cost fifty guineas from an article that is sold for five; but I venture to say there are not one out of ten thousand that would understand the difference."[2]

From her perspective, the cross-stitch is the only sign of the actual and discernible difference between the genuine Indian manufacture and the British imitation. Yet not one out of ten thousand knows it, and to the rest the distinction, real as it is, remains invisible and intangible. Modernity has erased every sign of difference but this one, in the border, where it is still recognizable to the old woman, while the young, oblivious to its absence, happily applaud the imitative tale as if it were the real thing. Her impudent resistance reminds anyone who will listen that there are still borders, where one thing becomes another, India becomes Britain, real becomes imitation, and fifty guineas become five. Three years before *The Surgeon's Daughter* appeared, an actual surgeon who had been to India, the Persianist and poet James Atkinson, described Calcutta as "little London in Bengal."[3] If Tibetan wool could be shipped to Paisley, where European technology could imitate Indian handicraft, so could English civilization be transported to India, where metropolitan lifestyles, fashions, and commodities could be reproduced, in miniature.

I take the phrase—and the fantasy—"Little London" from Atkinson's poem "The City of Palaces" (1824), whose title cemented Calcutta's imperial nickname:

> Yes, thou'rt a little London in Bengal,
> A microcosm; loose, and yet compact;
> A snug epitome, a capital
> Concentring every folly; brief, abstract,
> The essence of all worldliness, in fact
> A wonder, formed like island on the main
> Amidst a sea of pagans, to exact
> Allegiance from their millions, not in vain,
> For intellect hath power, to bind as with a chain. (15)

According to this consequential imagining of Calcutta, the metropole is coextensive with the cosmos, which the outpost miniaturizes, epitomizes, and abstracts. To reduce London from the world itself to the essence of worldliness, imperial life cuts it down to size and then draws it away, relocating it from one sea to another. If London is the capital of the island nation at the center of the new imperium—"A prodigy of power, transcending all / The conquests, and the governments, of old" (5)—Calcutta replicates London's fashions and authority, its folly and intellect, in order to rule the "sea of pagans" that surrounds the islandlike "White Town" of the city of palaces. In a common figure that we will see repeated, non-European subjects of empire are undistinguished and undifferentiated, a "sea" or "millions" or, a few verses later, "sable swarms" (15). In keeping with the stanza's turn, Little London thus serves a dual function. As an island that reflects Britishness, on the one hand, it forms a kind of convex mirror concentering the Corinthian follies of metropolitan rambles and sprees. In the early 1820s Atkinson's Calcutta looks a lot like Pierce Egan's London: it too is "fashion's fane," the site of "feasts and balls, / Cock-fighting, races, masques, and riot in their halls" (14). As expected, the poem provides a panoramic view of the European commodities with which the recently arrived Company servant, or "griffin," outfits himself for his new life in Little London: "Where bugles, saddles, harness, powder, shot, / And boots, and buck-skins, are in order placed; / . . . / With neckcloth tight and stiff, and body laced, / He sports a Dandy form, uncomfortably braced" (24). On the other hand, Little London is formed in this way in order to "exact / Allegiance." As the turn suggests, folly and the exercise of authority are "in fact" part of the same project; the wonder is that these follies are "not in vain." Calcutta is a "nurse of opulence and vice" (14), yet it is precisely "the giddy whirl of Fashion's sphere" (24), of civilized display and consumption, that demonstrates the superiority of European society over the "pagan customs, pagan rites, / And pagan pleasures" (21) the poem then depicts. European dissipation may lead individual Britons to an early grave, but Little London remains the latest and greatest form of empire that the Hugli River has seen as it "Flows on unchanged, while all is changed beside" (28).

Just as the old woman's recognition of the inimitable cross-stitch has real consequences for her perception of the difference in value between otherwise indistinguishable commodities, the various ways that Britons and Indians alike saw, failed to see, or critiqued the very idea of Little London in Bengal enforced or contested the most significant aspects of imperial culture and authority. For at stake in the existence of Little London was the recognition or denial that new social formations in Calcutta constituted not an undifferentiated "sea of pagans" but rather an Indian public sphere to which the East India Company and its Parliamentary Board of Control were responsible. As a uniform and encompassing image, Little London imposes a vision of Calcutta radically at odds with the dramatic emergence of an Indian literature in English and with the idea of an Indian public during the years when the battle over the freedom of the press in India raged, from Richard Wellesley's Regulations for the Control and Guidance of Newspapers in 1799 to the suspension of newspaper censorship in 1818, its reimposition by the Press Ordinance of 1823, and Charles Metcalfe's Press Act of 1835.

Assessing the applicability of Habermas's vocabulary to early British India, Sandria Freitag begins her introduction to a special issue of *South Asia* on the public sphere with the premise that "definitions of 'the public' frequently rest . . . on delineations of what 'the public' is defined *in contradistinction to.*"[4] Within the framework of European patterns, the classical public sphere was conceived by Habermas as an intermediary realm between the private sphere (the home and the marketplace) and the state. As Freitag bluntly puts it, however, these contradistinctions "do not seem to work for colonial India."[5] And yet, as C. A. Bayly and others have shown, the language of the public was both appropriated and mapped onto "indigenous antecedents"[6] such as the *akhbars*, or manuscript newspapers of Mughal courts, and the *panchayats*, or local civil juries. At once less and more than an explanatory model, the idea of publicity in India for this very reason served as a difficult yet dynamic way of representing cultural activities and associations of individuals across national, religious, and ethnic lines. "While we may establish the *analytical* inaccuracy of the application" of European distinctions between the private and public realms, writes Freitag, "we must nevertheless gauge the powerful appeal they exercised for people at the time."[7]

Building on the work of social historians and anthropologists and keeping in mind both the impossibility of translating European into Indian publicity and the political and cultural stakes of attempts to do so in the early nineteenth century, in this chapter I take a novel approach to the question of the public sphere in India by considering two very different urban spectacles that transformed private individuals, that is, individuals outside the state power of the East India Company's legislative and judicial systems, into collective, authoritative bodies. The panorama, on the one hand, and the annual Durga Puja, the only Hindu religious festival to which Europeans were formally and routinely invited, on the other, engaged in complex and fascinating ways with the ideological fantasy that Calcutta was a Little London in Bengal. Bernard Cohn has described early British India as "an epistemological space," proposing that the "British believed they could explore and conquer this space through translation: establishing correspondence could make the unknown and the strange knowable."[8] As we will see in later chapters, writers as diverse as the Baptist missionaries, Robert Southey, Rammohun Roy, Phebe Gibbes, and Sydney Owenson followed William Jones in applying different traditions of religious, cultural, and linguistic syncretism in order to make India knowable. But the debate over the Indian public sphere presented another kind of translation, with which we will begin.

An often overlooked aspect of the unequal relations of power between the colonial state and metropolitan culture, on the one hand, and the colonized elite of Bengal, on the other, was that translation necessarily went in both directions. If, as Partha Chatterjee and many others have now demonstrated, modernity was not a modular import from the West to the East, similarly the development of public opinion in Bengal was a double act on the part of Indians, mixed-race East Indians, and radical Europeans, double in that it involved both appropriating Western media, forms, and terms and *making recognizable* indigenous practices that were either inherited, hybrid, new, or a combination thereof.[9] By their nature these novel expressions of "Indian" public opinion—Indian in a sense that evades the polarities of authenticity and imitation—disputed the legitimacy of what Sudipta Sen has called "distant sovereignty,"[10] a phrase prefigured in the period by James Silk Buckingham, one of this chapter's key figures, in his attacks on "the East-India company's distant and doubly-delegated rule."[11]

Indian Public Opinion and John Bullism of the Heart

If the power of European intellect is simply to "bind," as Atkinson's model goes, then the enabling condition of that bondage is a starkly hierarchical and binary relationship with respect to intellect itself. In Little London there can be no Indian literature that might engage, assimilate, or answer, let alone challenge, European intellect, just as there can be no Indian public that might read, incorporate, or discuss, let alone review, the products of European culture beside or in dialogue with its own. But Little London was far smaller than the Calcutta of Buckingham, Rammohun, and Prasanna Kumar Tagore; of the Serampore Baptists; of Henry Meredith Parker, Horace Hayman Wilson, and David Lester Richardson; of David Hare, Henry Louis Vivian Derozio, and the "Derozians" or "Hindu liberals" (later called "Young Bengal"), discussed in chapter 3; of Mrtyunjay Vidyalankar, chief pundit of Bengali and Sanskrit at the College of Fort William, and the orthodox managers of the Hindu College Radhakanta Deb, Ramkamal Sen, and Rasamoy Dutt.[12] I cannot hope to provide detailed introductions to all these figures, among many others, in the pages that follow, but if their various contributions to "Romantic-era" histories of modernity, publicity, nationalism, cosmopolitanism, cross-cultural education, translation, spectacle, evangelicalism, secularization, and poetry in English register for students and scholars of these concerns, a comparatist case will have been made, more or less implicitly, for British Romanticism as part of and constituted by a simultaneously divided, contested, and coherent Anglophone culture beyond the borders of the territorial nation.

Until the loosening of censorship under Governor General Hastings (Francis Rawdon, Marquess of Hastings) in 1818, the press had been subject to Wellesley's regulations of 1799, according to which every printer was required to print his name at the bottom of the newspaper, every editor and proprietor of a newspaper needed to register his name and address with the chief secretary of the government, and no paper was to be published at all until it had been inspected by the chief secretary or his proxy, with the sole "penalty for offending against any of" these regulations "to be immediate embarkation for Europe."[13] In April 1818, however, an East Indian named Jacob Heatley, proprietor and editor of the *Calcutta Morning Post*, fell afoul of the acting chief secretary, W. B. Bayley, who objected to passages that Heatley intended to print. When he refused to comply with Bayley's order to expunge them, Bayley realized that the threatened penalty of deportation to England could not apply to a mixed-race native of India such as Heatley and that the office of the chief secretary was therefore without recourse in this instance. Furthermore, the precedent would mean that the office would thereafter be toothless in any situation involving publications by East Indians or Indians.[14] Censorship was accordingly discontinued in August 1818.

General rules were substituted in its place, but the window had been opened for new oppositionist papers and the attendant images of the public that they would fashion and promote. And although this new public first found its material form in newspapers run predominantly by Europeans—the main target of concern soon became Buckingham's radical *Calcutta Journal* (1818–23)—the Court of Directors in London hastened to observe "that a free press cannot be confined to Europeans, that four native newspapers were started on the withdrawal of censorship, and that such a press must be injurious. The half-castes may be made, as they must at no remote period become, a source of great anxiety to Government."[15] These four newspapers were Harihar Dutta's *Jam-i-Jahan Numa* (1822), which appeared first in Urdu and then quickly switched over to Persian, Rammohun's Persian *Mirat al-Akhbar* (1822), and the two opposed Bengali papers, the so-called liberal *Sambad Kaumudi* (1821), edited by Rammohun, and the so-called orthodox *Samachar Chandrika* (1822).[16] And as the Directors feared, over the next decade these were followed by the six (or more) newspapers associated with the Derozians and the "half-caste" East Indian community: the *Hesperus* (1829), the *Kaleidoscope* (1829), the *Parthenon* (1830), the *Enquirer* (1831), the *East Indian* (1831), and the *Gyananneshan* (1831).[17]

When John Adam succeeded to the post of acting governor general in 1823, one of his first priorities was to settle an old score with Buckingham, who in Adam's eyes had taken advantage of the suspension of censorship and the liberal policy toward the press, the "notion of unrestrained intercommunication by printing,"[18] under the regime of the Marquess of Hastings. Buckingham was summarily deported without trial, as a consequence of which, in his own words a year later, the press "began to fall into the hands of Indo-Britons and Natives, who were beyond the reach of any power except that of the King's Court, administering English [libel] law."[19] Before he left for London in April 1823, his parting shot helped to create the very reality he would soon describe: he turned the editorship of the *Calcutta Journal* over to Francis Sandys, an "Indo-Briton." Adam proposed new licensing regulations, which were quickly ratified by a single judge, in order to justify retroactively Buckingham's expulsion and to restrict future criticism of Company authority by a law "which should put down all free printing by *direct* restraint, and should constrain Natives and Indo-Britons equally with Englishmen."[20]

As discussions of this episode on both sides of the ocean suggest, at stake in the question of an Indian public in the early era of global print-capitalism was more than just an ideology of civilizational superiority. Especially during this phase of the debate over the freedom of the press in India, "public opinion" emerged as a crucial counter in a struggle for power that contested the very definition of rule. Here is how the Company's Court of Directors argued that censorship should be reimposed in a letter addressed to the Board of Control. Whereas the press is the organ of "public opinion" under a free government, the Directors proposed,

> in India public opinion cannot be said to exist. The advantages to the governed produced by public opinion in other countries, under a free government, are in some measure secured to the people of India by a chain of responsibility and a gradation of checks, extending from the local government and the constituted authorities at home, to the British Parliament, and through the Parliament to the people of England. . . . The Indian governments thus become amenable, in the last resort, to a public far more enlightened than the Indian public.[21]

The logic is arresting. In nations in which public opinion can be said to exist, the "chain" ascends in a straight vertical line from the first and foundational link, the public, up through the local government and authorities to Parliament, which is responsible to all the bodies below, to which it is bound. In classical Habermasian terms, "private people" have "come together as a public"[22] and defined this new corporate identity as the sphere of rational-critical debate that both regulates and authorizes government. But in the absence of Indian public opinion, the chain instead forms an arch, ascending from the private "people of India," who are not sufficiently enlightened to have public opinion, up through the local government and authorities in India to the government in England (Parliament and the Court of Directors), but the chain then descends not back to the people of India but instead to the English public. Because the government of India is in England and part of the English government, the Directors reasoned, it is "responsible to the English public. . . . It is in this country, therefore, and not in India, that its measures ought to be discussed."[23] The paternalistic relationship of metropole to empire ultimately rests not on the fact that the government of India is in England but rather on the belief that the common government of both is responsible to the English public, and therefore it is the free press in England that secures the responsibility of the government to the governed people of India. The position is summarized by a letter from "An Old Indian" to the editor of the conservative London-based *Asiatic Journal* in 1821: "When a constitution shall be established in India, such as has been the growth of ages in England; when a public shall have been formed in that country corresponding in its nature and composition with a British public; then let the press be free from the controul of the governing power."[24]

The relationship between Buckingham and Rammohun, a friendship we will follow to England in chapter 4, and their respective journalistic activities vividly illustrate the situations described by Freitag and Cohn: within the period itself, Buckingham and Rammohun were aware of the powerful appeal of correspondence, *in spite of* its inaccuracy, between an established British public and a new Indian one. In other words, they well understood that the empire was an "epistemological space" and that "Old Indians" in London and Calcutta would fight against any commercial, legal, and political autonomy from Company rule by maintaining that no correspondence in "nature and composition" existed between print communication in the metropole and in the colony. "The favourite position put forth in all shapes and phrases by the enemies of free discussion, to catch unthinking people in England," wrote Buckingham once back in London, "is this—'There is no Public in India—therefore, no public opinion—therefore, no use for an organ to express it—therefore, a free Press can do no good, and may do harm, &c.'—This is the language of Mr. Adam.—It may be doubted if a more contemptible sophism ever before disgraced the manifesto of any ruler."[25] Citing Rammohun by name along with "Natives . . . of prodigious wealth, acquired in external commerce and interior traffic, Hindoos, Mussulmauns, Parsees, Portuguese, Armenian, and Indo-British, deeply concerned in shipping, ship-building, indigo planting, coffee planting, rum distilling, &c. &c.," he asked, "Is it not then the most contemptible of drivelling, to say, that such men as these are to be considered as political non-entities?"[26] So long as Calcutta remained Little London, a mere microcosm, it would have no need of self-expression in the absence of any self other than a reflection.

In different but complementary and allied ways, Buckingham and Rammohun took up the difficult challenge posed by Little London. Their strategy was to fashion it into something at once larger and new, a public they described as "Indian" in nature and composition, which they then sought to present in recognizable terms to a plural, polyglot audience in Calcutta and to a readership in England fairly ignorant of Indian affairs but upon whose opinion rested the Company's authority. To understand the strategy, it will be helpful to look briefly at the conception of Buckingham's and Rammohun's papers, the *Calcutta Journal* and the *Sambad Kaumudi*, and the relations between the two.

One month after the suspension of censorship, Buckingham raised a lightning rod in the form of the *Calcutta Journal*, the first daily in India. The *Prospectus*, published on 22 September 1818, proclaimed the paper's progressive determination to participate in the invention of a new national print culture, taking its epigraph from Bacon: "A froward retention of custom is as turbulent a thing as innovation, and they that reverence too much old times are but a scorn to the new."[27] According to the *Prospectus*, existing journals "have no sentiment, either of the public or of their own, on the leading features of the times, . . . and no more of original disquisition than has been first echoed from the Prints of Europe to those of India, and then, in sevenfold repetition, from one to the other" (1). In other words, Buckingham tacitly takes the Little London fantasy of echo and repetition for truth and sees himself, in opposition to it, as creating a new reality. Complaining of "this absence of novelty," he declares that a portion of the paper would be "devoted to Original Communications, Literary and Scientific Notices, the progress of the Belles Lettres and the Arts, Extracts of the most interesting portions of New and Popular Works, Original and Selected Poetry, occasional Reviews of Books, and early Notices of the latest and most approved Publications" (1).

Above all, this "novelty"—one of Buckingham's favorite words—would be distinctly Indian. He proposes "the establishment of correspondents at different stations in the interior of India, and at the Presidencies of Bombay and Madras, as well as the ports of Ceylon and the Malabar and Coromandel coasts, extending also to the Eastern Islands and to China" (2). Most remarkably, he announces "a Monthly Compendium . . . to be called THE SPIRIT OF THE INDIAN JOURNALS, to contain only Indian News, whether of Politics, War, commerce, or Literature, omitting altogether the information coming to us from Europe, as well as Advertisements and matters of a merely local interest, and thus adapting it for transmission to any part of the world" (2). The last claim is a crucial part of Buckingham's imagining of an Indian community embracing Anglophone European, East Indian, and elite Indian readers and writers as, in Benedict Anderson's well-known terms, "limited and sovereign."[28] He thus takes the next logical step and declares that although the paper will be Indian, or rather *because* it will be Indian in this novel sense, it will not be of "merely local interest" but rather will take its place among the circulating representatives of established nations: "It is conceived that this would be an eligible Paper to be forwarded to England, America, and the Mediterranean."[29]

On 20 December 1821 the *Calcutta Journal* ran a long article welcoming the "Establishment of a Native Newspaper, Edited by a Learned Hindoo." This new paper was the *Sambad Kaumudi,* and the "Learned Hindoo" was Rammohun.[30] Three issues had already appeared, "but as no English Editor has yet had the liberality to notice this Infant undertaking," Buckingham characteristically wrote, "it falls to us, as usual, to . . . notice this dawning of Free Discussion in the Newspaper Press of Bengal."[31] The *Calcutta Journal* then inserted the English version of the *Sambad Kaumudi*'s "Prospectus" as well as the "Address to the Bengal Public," which had appeared in its first issue. According to the "Address," "the Conductors of the newly established Bengally Newspaper . . . beg leave to state in a brief manner that the object of that Publication is the PUBLIC GOOD." Having pointed out that "a Newspaper conducted *exclusively* by Natives, in the Native Languages *is a novelty at least*," the "Address" went on to claim that "our country-men will readily conclude that although the Paper in question be conducted by us, and may consequently be considered our property, yet *virtually* it is the 'PAPER OF THE PUBLIC,' since in it they can at all times have inserted, any thing that *tends to the public good*, and by a respectful expression of their grievances, be enabled to get them redressed."[32] Whereas the language of representative government was common among the more radical elements of Young Bengal, and even Prasanna Kumar Tagore went so far as to hold out the "example of America" as a model for India in 1831,[33] Rammohun remained a liberal constitutionalist who sought to reform parliamentary control over Company rule, gain admission for Indians into the civil service, and thus ameliorate the British government of India.[34] Buckingham and the *Calcutta Journal* thus make common cause with Rammohun and the *Sambad Kaumudi* in the assertion of an Indian public opinion across religious, racial, and even linguistic lines that would shift power from Company tyranny and "old corruption" to a greater measure of local autonomy for government and free trade under English legislation and law. It was this alliance that threatened to break the chain structuring metropolitan and imperial relations of authority and responsibility.

When this issue of the *Calcutta Journal* arrived in London, the *Asiatic Journal*—the London-based "Oracle of Leaden Hall Street,"[35] as Buckingham called it—immediately responded by mistakenly assuming that the editor of the *Sambad Kaumudi* must be a *"protegé"* of Buckingham: "It is easy to collect from the manner in which this subject is introduced by Mr. Buckingham, what is to be the character of the proposed native newspaper; and we are anxious to draw the public attention to it at home, ere it is too late."[36] The *Asiatic Journal* then gives the following reason why this "native newspaper" could only serve to foment discontent:

> India has no party relation except that of the governor and the governed, no *antique* and loyal opposition, no liberal and generous party spirit, differing as to the means, but united as to the end, *the public good*. The native Indian has no domestic feeling, no permanent interest in common with the European resident, no community of affections, of religion, or of soil, with the stranger under whose sceptre he lives; and above all (if we may be pardoned the expression) he possesses no John Bullism of heart.[37]

It is no coincidence that the conservative mouthpiece of Calcutta, which tarred any criticism of Company rule with the old brush of anti-Jacobinism, was called the *John Bull in the East*. For Little London must be kept an island of strangers surrounded by a sea of millions, a swarm. As the Serampore missionary Joshua Marshman had put it in a passage that would be often cited thereafter, "The Hindoos resemble an immense number of particles of sand, which are incapable of forming a solid mass. There is no bond of union among them, nor any principle capable of effecting it. . . . The brahmans, as well as the nation at large, are a vast number of disconnected atoms, totally incapable of cohesion."[38] Almost a century before John Strachey's *India: Its Administration and Progress* (1903), the *Asiatic Journal* and Marshman had answered Strachey's question "What is India?" in almost the same terms. "The answer that I have sometimes given," replies Strachey, "sounds paradoxical, but it is true. There is no such country, and this is the first and most essential fact about India that can be learned."[39] "There is not, and never was an India," he concludes, "or even any country of India, possessing, according to European ideas, any sort of unity, physical, political, social, or religious; no Indian nation, no 'people of India,' of which we hear so much."[40]

The problem faced in the 1820s by Buckingham, Rammohun, and others, of course, is captured by Strachey's caveat, "according to European ideas." For Buckingham, the *Asiatic Journal* had "stretch[ed] its pigmy optics to a country evidently far beyond its visual ken," and he responded by asking rhetorically, "Is it true that 'the Native Indian has no permanent interest in common with the European resident'?"[41] For a free-trader such as Buckingham, not only did the fact that the Indian empire was funded by Indian, not British, capital bring the interests of wealthy natives and British merchants together but the progress of educational and journalistic collaboration all around him between European and Bengali radicals and liberals gave the lie to Little London. Furthermore, he went on to claim, the new Indian and East Indian newspapers were not simply mimicking the English press, and Rammohun, proprietor of both the *Sambad Kaumudi* and the *Mirat al-Akhbar,* was no mere *"protegé."* "Printing was first introduced into India by the English in their great cities," Buckingham acknowledged, "but the custom of circulating manuscript newspapers in multiplied copies is of considerable antiquity among the Natives, the Mahomedans particularly: and these Ukhbars (as they are called) have always contained political rumours and intelligence, often mixed up with satirical and personal remarks."[42] Buckingham and Rammohun thus represented common interests and a shared, plural vocabulary that did not exclusively affiliate the media and expression of public opinion with Western technology and reason or with the English language.[43]

And the threat of this alliance was clear. As late as 1832 a satirical series titled "Plans for the Government of India" appeared in the *Asiatic Journal.* In the first plan an "original thinker," Sir B. C., is asked, "What is to be done with the East-India question?," to which he replies, "Get rid of it": *"Lord A.* Get rid of the question you mean, of course; that is the very thing I want to do. *Sir B. C.* No; get rid of India. . . . Let the Hindoos and Gentoos, the havildars, and the jemitdars, and the devildars, go about their business."[44] In his confusion of terms, Sir B. C. expresses the fear that there could be coherence in all this baffling pluralism, and that Britons should just leave Indians to it. This is one satirical perspective on the threat posed by the new Indian public. The second plan, on the other hand, seeks to ridicule those who would actually embrace rather than reject the possibility, embodying them in the form of a lecturer who inveighs against the "detestable and tyrannical oligarchy by which that fair region is now disgraced."[45] The lecturer is clearly Buckingham. "My plan is a simple one," he announces:

I propose . . . in the first place, that Raja Ram Mohun Roy be appointed Governor General of India; that all the judicial posts be filled by Mahomedans, all the revenue offices by Hindoos, and the police be executed by East-Indians or Indo-Britons. The beauty of this plan, ladies and gentlemen, consists in this: the raja is neither a Hindoo, a Mahomedan, nor a Christian, so that he can have no bias towards any part of the population of India; and the rest, being antagonistical, . . . they would keep, by their very opposition, the whole machine of government in steady operation, just as an arch is retained firmly together, by contrary pressure on all sides of it.—*(Great applause.)*[46]

At the time, Rammohun was in London, where at a dinner hosted for him by the Royal Asiatic Society in June 1831 Charles Watkins Williams Wynn, president of the society and former president of the Company's Board of Control, had remarked that Rammohun was "as much a British subject as any gentleman present." Almost a year later, in April 1832, Rammohun reminded Wynn of this comment and wrote, "From the high opinion R.R. entertains of Mr. Wynn's constitutional bearing he feels a wish to know from him, confidentially, whether in Mr. Wynn's opinion R.R. is eligible to sit in the Parliament."[47] It is not impossible that the real danger expressed in the *Asiatic Journal*'s satire in the spring of 1832 may have been the prospect of a reformed Parliament including the first Indian MP, some sixty years before Dadabhai Naoroji.[48] In any case, the satire anxiously imagines not just an Indian governor general but a plural Indian nation in which forces of repulsion would operate as forces of counterpoise, like the *Sambad Kaumudi* and *Samachar Chandrika*, "differing as to the means, but united as to the end, *the public good*," and thus sustaining the solid mass of an arch rather than dissolving into particles of sand or disconnected atoms, or, worse, the combustible agents of communalism.

While in Little London the power of intellect was "to bind as with a chain," in the capacious Calcutta of Buckingham and Rammohun intellect had the power to translate, adopt, transform, and/or invent indigenous, European, and new forms of communication in the creation of a liberal and often cosmopolitan culture that, at once diffuse and coherent, was fighting to define itself as a modern, autonomous public. And when this public evoked the language of cosmopolitanism, it presented one Indian alternative—by no means the only or the last—to the "cosmopolitanism of reason" associated by Uday Mehta with James Mill, Bentham, and J. S. Mill, for whom "the repetition, presumption, and assertion of the familiar" denied "the archaic, the premodern, the religious, the Indian— in a word, the unfamiliar, along with the sentiments, feelings, sense of location, and forms of life of which they are a part."[49]

The Panorama and the Fabled Cap of Fortunatus

Benedict Anderson's revised edition (1991) of *Imagined Communities: Reflections on the Origin and Spread of Nationalism*, first published in 1983, added the coordinate of space to his argument that print capitalism forged modern national consciousness by creating the apprehension of time as uniform and empty. As the novel and the newspaper produced ceremonies of reading practices through which individual imaginations synchronized and unified disparate and distant actions, the census, the map, and the museum transformed space, with all of its sacred, local, and specific affiliations, into a homogeneous surface fit for the "logo" of national identity, a serializable expanse characterized by "its emptiness, contextlessness, visual memorableness, and infinite reproducibility in every direction."[50] Still, print has understandably remained central to considerations of the public, the nation, and the modern. One of the contributions of book history has been to expand our understanding of print beyond its legibility to include the individual and social effects of its visibility, tangibility, and reproducibility. As Lynn Hunt has insisted, the "world is not just discursively constructed. It is also built through . . . nonlinguistic modes of communication that have their own logic."[51] Rather than turn from my discussion of the discursive shaping of Indian publicity by Buckingham and Rammohun to the materiality of print culture in early nineteenth-century Bengal—an ongoing field of study energized especially by the work of Anindita Ghosh and Abhijit Gupta[52] and a topic I will take up in the next chapter—I would like to follow Hunt and think instead about "visual forms of communication," with "their potential for collective sharing with other viewers,"[53] as media in which the fantasy of Little London was enforced and contested.

While tracing shipments of books from England to Calcutta in early nineteenth-century newspaper notices, I came across an advertisement for "The Panorama of Dover" on the front page of the *Calcutta Morning Post* for 24 January 1812 (fig. 2). The panorama, I realized, could be considered among other particularly charged spectacles within the early British Empire in India. Below I discuss a religious festival, Durga Puja, and the following chapter addresses two related objects of sight: idols, which were encountered, collected, written about, and often sent back to England by Baptist missionaries and by East India Company servants with an antiquarian bent; and books themselves, both those that arrived in boxes with each fleet and were then sold off at the Calcutta auction houses and those that were printed locally at the Baptist Press and distributed by missionaries as they preached in public. Initiating a pattern of thinking about people, ideas, and things that circulated between Britain and Bengal and that operated in diverse ways because of their location and movement, my treatment of the panorama views the medium as a visual technology that defined, realized, and differentiated the authority of social formations in London and Calcutta. The panorama visually displayed and physically enacted social groups as agents or objects of public opinion, and these contrary modes of representation corresponded to and configured discrepant models of colonial governance. Because of my interest in the ways that practices, objects, and metaphors of vision function in distinct imperial locations, I would like to ask what panoramas in London

Fig. 2. *The Calcutta Morning Post*, 24 January 1812, p. 1. © The British Library Board.

of India and in Calcutta of Britain can reveal about how audiences viewed themselves and the empire from these two very different vantages. These two kinds of panoramas, I think, tell opposite sides of the same story, as the mercantile empire of the eighteenth century gave way to the commercial, colonial empire of the nineteenth and as Little London struggled to defend its borders against new expressions of Indian publicity.[54] Panoramas in London of India and in Calcutta of Britain played a role in reflecting social groups as publics or disaggregated in-

Fig. 3. Section of the Rotunda, Leicester Square, in which is exhibited the Panorama, by Robert Mitchell. R. Mitchell, *Plans and Views in Perspective*, plate 14. © The Trustees of the British Museum.

dividuals, the contrasting definitions of which corresponded to divergent visions of British authority over India.

Invented by Robert Barker in 1787, panoramas by the mid-1790s had taken their place among the fashionable attractions of London, and their popularity soon spread throughout the Continent and the European colonies in North America, India, and Australia (fig. 3).[55] The panorama was first and foremost a visual technology that set both things and people in motion, a moving picture in both senses of the word. Here is how Thomas Dibdin describes his experience of viewing Robert Ker Porter's massive 2,550-square-foot, semicircular (270°) *Storming of Seringapatam* (fig. 4), which opened in the Lyceum Theatre, in the Strand, in April 1800 before touring the provinces and Ireland for two years[56]:

> I can never forget its first impression upon my own mind. It was as a thing dropt from the clouds—all fire, energy, intelligence, and animation. You looked a second time, the figures moved, and were commingled in hot and bloody fight. . . . You longed to be leaping from crag to crag with Sir David Baird, who is hallooing his men on to victory! Then, again, you seemed to be listening to the groans of the wounded and the dying—and more than one female was carried out swooning.

Fig. 4. *The Great Historical Picture of the Storming of Seringapatam, By the British Troops and their Allies, May 4th, 1790,* by Robert Ker Porter. © Victoria and Albert Museum, London.

The accessories . . . rock, earth, and water . . . half choked up with the bodies of the dead, made you look on with a shuddering awe, and retreat as you shuddered. The public poured in by hundreds and by thousands for even a transient gaze—for such a sight was altogether as marvellous as it was novel. You carried it home, and did nothing but think of it, talk of it, and dream of it.[57]

Although the panorama is a "thing . . . all . . . animation" in which "the figures moved," the chief objects animated in this description are the bodies of the viewers themselves: their gaze raises emotions that manifest themselves in actual motions, the swoon and the shudder of awe and retreat. The effect of the medium is to communicate activity—fire, energy, and intelligence—from the objects to the subjects of vision.

In keeping with the direction of this transfer, the critical discussion of panoramas has focused on the central, elevated perspective of the medium, which radically changes the viewing experience from that of traditional landscape painting. But the question of how it changes this experience has led to divergent theories. Following Bernard Comment's claim that the panorama sought to realize the early nineteenth-century "double dream . . . of totality and of possession,"[58] Michael Charlesworth argues that the "panoramic impulse [is] closely complicit with the colonizing process" and that the characteristically Romantic "loss of control over panoramic vision is a *precondition* for the subversive view of colonization."[59] Panoramas are thus complicit with what Charlesworth calls "overlordship": they force viewers to "look at them from a position of identification with the point of view of the rulers. . . . They encourage a sense of identity of outlook between viewer and those in power, and one that excludes, by distancing and superiority of station, the possibility of identification with the subjugated."[60] Gillen D'Arcy Wood, on the other hand, writes that the panorama "represented a radical democratization of landscape art not only by virtue of its subject matter . . . but its very form. Unlike a conventional gallery painting, which presupposed a single optimum viewing-point, the circular panorama offered no privileged vantage and invited a collective circulation by the spectators."[61] The panorama thus becomes one of Wordsworth's "gross and violent stimulants," in which visual details simply accumulate, resulting in a "landscape view" that, unlike the depictions from Wordsworth's own elevated prospects on nature, "is wholly externalized."[62]

In light of these conflicting interpretations, William Galperin concludes, "the Panorama was suddenly all things to all people."[63] The panorama form provided "internal resistance" in that it could draw the viewer in two different directions. "The majority of Panoramas," Galperin shows, "were consumed by details and sufficiently distracting to remove the viewer from an otherwise stable and controlling subject-position," while some panoramas did provide "a vantage in which the viewer would be privileged to 'command.'"[64] When distraction subverts control and privilege, the "previously sovereign subject" is transformed "into a detail among details"; the panorama could thus fascinate viewers "at the cost of the beholder's authority."[65] As we will see, however, overlordship and democratization need not be alternatives, for the question of London's sovereignty over Bengal was always less a matter of knowledge and information than of the perspectives that endowed knowledge and information with authority for particular groups of people and not for others.

As an information technology, the panorama performed this function for individuals and groups by providing views of distant landscapes, cityscapes, and people, but it also served as a metaphor in the popular press and travel writing.

Daniel O'Quinn has called the panorama "an optical and a narrative machine."[66] Panoramic metaphors accordingly suggested that the medium, like newspapers and novels, maps and museums, told stories that could bridge the temporal and spatial distances between agents and objects of imperial power. In October 1806, for instance, the publisher C. Taylor advertised a new periodical called the *Literary Panorama*, explaining the choice of title as follows: "A PANORAMA is an ingenious device in the Art of Painting, wherein a Spectator, from an elevated central situation, by directing his attention to each part successively, inspects the whole." The perspective of the new journal would be similarly all-embracing. "The opulent Metropolis of the United Kingdom is our central station," from where the reader would view the empire around it in a sweeping glance: "The reader who has concerns in AMERICA, the WEST-INDIES, the SOUTHERN HEMISPHERE, or those immense TERRITORIES in INDIA which enjoy the blessings of British protection, may expect intelligence always marked by fidelity. . . . In our Indian department, especially, various communications will appear in this work, exclusively, on which we might safely rest our claim to distinction."[67] The technology that actually provided faithful intelligence by bridging the distance in space and time between England and India—steam power—would not transform communication between the two until the late 1830s, when the mails and passengers began to travel by steam to Alexandria, then overland to Suez, and then again by steam onward to Bombay, Madras, or Calcutta, cutting the journey from approximately six months to roughly two. Describing Malta in 1837, the travel writer Adolphus Slade uses the panorama metaphor in a way that reveals the extent to which steam power actualized a phenomenon that had already been vividly experienced in paint and the imagination: "Without moving, you have the *élite* of the whole world brought to you. A steam-packet every month to and from England; to and from Greece and Corfu; to and from Alexandria; weekly communication with France and Italy, annihilates the distance. You travel in all countries by their means; you gain information and amusement through them. The panorama is ever shifting."[68]

When Buckingham accused the *Asiatic Journal* of "stretching its pigmy optics to a country evidently far beyond its visual ken" in 1823, the spatial and temporal distance had not been annihilated. His point was that London's claim to authority over India on the basis of informed public opinion was undermined by the inability of even the most advanced optics available to reach India, let alone bring its details into focus or convey images of events under six months old. As early as 1787 William Jones had written in very similar terms to Earl Spencer: "We are the best judges here of all that relates to ourselves. In Europe you see

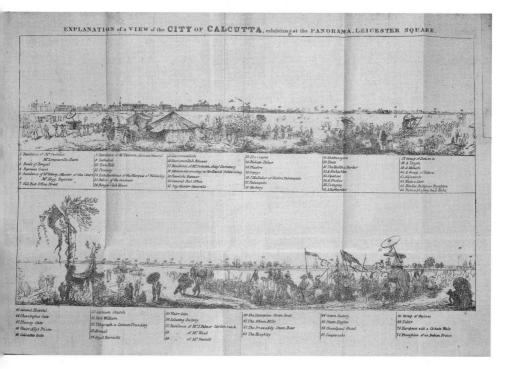

Fig. 5. *Explanation of a View of the City of Calcutta, exhibiting at the Panorama, Leicester Square,* by Robert Burford. © The British Library Board.

India through a glass darkly: here, we are in a strong light; and a thousand little *nuances* are perceptible to us, which are not visible through your best telescopes."[69] Panoramas in London depicting imperial landscapes, cityscapes, and people sought to reinforce metropolitan authority by serving as magnifiers, and in fact to allow for "minute inspection" of the Colosseum in Regent's Park the public was accommodated with "numerous telescopes."[70] On 1 March 1830, in the great circle of the Leicester Square rotunda, opened one such vista on the city of palaces, Robert Burford's Panorama of Calcutta, which was critically acclaimed and had a successful run, to say the least, not closing until the end of May 1831 (fig. 5).[71]

Burford's panorama is fairly unique for the prominent place it gives to individuals and groups—"several thousand Figures," according to the newspaper announcements[72]—at the expense of landscape and architecture in its reproduction of "one of the most magnificent and thickly peopled cities in the world."[73] William Wood's *Series of Twenty-Eight Panoramic Plates of Calcutta* (1833) also depicts individuals, but they are fewer and more scattered than the groups in Burford's panorama, and their main effect is to portray a harmonious and peaceful

Fig. 6. *Chowringhee Road*, by William Wood. W. Wood, *Series of Twenty-Eight Panoramic Plates of Calcutta*, plate 17. © The British Library Board.

aesthetic balance between, on the one hand, various ranks of Indians and, on the other, buildings, land, vegetation, and livestock (fig. 6), none of which is granted visual priority over any other. And to achieve a similar effect by different means, Frederick Fiebig's panoramic paintings of Calcutta, published as lithographs in 1847, view the city from the elevated perspective of the Ochterlony Monument (erected in 1828), depicting people from such a height that they blend into the surrounding scenery (fig. 7).[74] Both of these, especially Fiebig's paintings, present in a fairly straightforward manner the commanding views we expect from the medium and can serve as illustrations of visual overlordship.[75] Burford's panorama, on the other hand, suggests different possibilities. According to the review in the *Examiner*, "The Artist gives to the people of London a power like that possessed by the fabled cap of Fortunatus. He enables you to be present, as it were, in all parts of the world."[76] As we will see, the power given to the people of London by Burford's art was to be present in Leicester Square and Calcutta, and to be so in a specific way.

Although the audience was elevated, the reviews emphasized that the overall effect was one of flatness. As the *Gentleman's Magazine* pointed out, "To relieve the flatness of the view, . . . the artist has introduced groupes of figures, which, though seldom seen at Calcutta, add much to the interest of the picture."[77] The

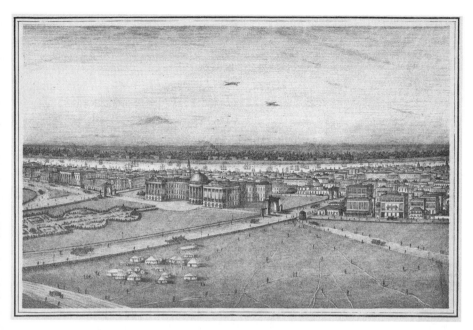

Fig. 7. Town Hall. Government House, by Frederick Fiebig. Fiebig, *Panorama of Calcutta Drawn after Nature,* plate 3. © The British Library Board.

Athenaeum similarly commented that the "foreground is occupied with figures representing the manners of the native Indians in every variety," praising Burford for having "succeeded wonderfully in his elephants" and only complaining that there "is no building or object of importance brought prominently into the foreground."[78] It was these groups of figures, then, not the cityscape, that were the key source of the panorama's effect. Even though such a combination of human beings would seldom, if ever, have been assembled in the center of the Maidan, the reviews agreed that the panorama "affords a correct idea of the place."[79]

Unlike the flat page of the "Explanation," which displays the groups arrayed in two horizontal lines before the reader, the circular panorama itself presented the figures as *surrounding* the spectators. The essential relationship in this panorama was between two groups of people separated by distance and elevation, the viewing public and, in the catalog provided by the *Gentleman's Magazine,* a "magnificent procession of a native prince, mounted on an elephant, and accompanied by three other elephants, camels, several spirited horses, and a numerous retinue of servants in splendid costumes; in another part of the picture, a devotee is undergoing penance, by being swung in the air, suspended by a hook in the muscles of his body; groups of dancers, jugglers, palanquins, and dealers in fruit, agreeably diversify the scene."[80] The fact that the reviews are so ready to acknowledge that the depiction of this diversity assembled all at once is inaccurate, while insisting that the idea of the place is correct, suggests that the panorama was creating expectations as much as it was fulfilling them.

In particular, it was producing relations of power that call for a complication of overlordship and democratization as alternative readings. Three elements of the panorama would have evoked the sublime and thus played with the individual viewer's sense of self and safety: the sheer denseness of the detail overall, which maps the exotic onto the urban crowd and thus threatens to consume the individual viewer's autonomy; the grandeur of Oriental royalty, which reminds the European spectator that the Eastern empire depends on successful negotiations with and subordination of existing political and military powers; and the Charak (or "hook-swinging") Puja, one of the three great Romantic emblems of Hindu enthusiasm, along with sati and the Rath Yatra "chariot-procession" of the Jagannath temple in Puri. The charak tree (center, top frame) is the tallest object portrayed and is therefore positioned in the background so that it is no higher than the viewers' perspective, as it would be were it set in the foreground. As a "young friend, who resided some time in Calcutta," informed the *Lady's Magazine*, "The Fakir swinging is not at all in keeping, the distance is wrong."[81] In Edmund Burke's well-known formulation, "When danger or pain press too nearly, they are incapable of giving any delight . . . but at certain distances . . . they are delightful."[82] The combination of detail, power, and enthusiasm at every turn overwhelms any solitary viewer's sense of autonomy, let alone sovereignty.

But at the same time, the combination forces a juxtaposition between the groups surveyed and the group surveying, and here the effect is different, authorizing not domination but rather public opinion in the appraisal of the effects. "The assemblage of artists, amateurs, critics and nabobs, invited to the private view of Mr. Burford's Panorama of Calcutta, all agree in pronouncing it excellent," began the review in the *Athenaeum*. The nabobs affirm "that the representation was accurate," and the artists "that the picture was well painted," leaving the amateurs with "nothing to do but acquiesce in the opinions, and note the observations of persons so much more *au fait* on the occasion than themselves." The only group yet to pronounce is the critics, who opine, "The exhibition is indeed a splendid one."[83] The scene therefore offers an exotic sublime, but one in which the experience is not based on the relation between an individual viewer and a scene. Whereas Fiebig's panoramic paintings allow the individual viewer to see him- or herself as a metonym for national rule over the imperial capital and therefore over India, Burford's panorama, at the cost of the *individual* beholder's authority, forces viewers to see themselves as part of a British viewing, discriminating public over and against the viewed and judged people of India. The authority of artists, amateurs, critics, and nabobs is grounded in judgment and criticism, and the consequence is not overlordship or democratization but overlordship *and* democratization—elevation over others in which power lies not in lordship but in the *au fait* opinion and taste of a metropolitan public.

And although for the most part the groups displayed comprise the various ranks of "natives," the governed people of India include Europeans, as we have seen in the debate over the existence of an "Indian" public or in Buckingham's use of the word in the phrase "the spirit of the Indian journals." Imagine the spectators, most with the "Explanation" in hand, others perhaps with telescopes, information technologies that turn separation into critical distance. As their gazes shift from the pages to the painted scenes to one another, they experience the elevated platform as an "island on the main / Amidst a sea of pagans." But whereas Atkinson's poem, written from the perspective of a Briton in Calcutta, makes it clear that the sea is populated by millions of Indians, Burford's panorama, painted from the perspective of a Briton in London, imagines the relation between island and ocean differently. Less visible in the "Explanation" but commented on in the press was the presence in the painting of Europeans, especially the "tents of British officers,"[84] as objects of the viewers' gaze and as part of the agreeable diversity. Burford's own *Description of a View of the City of Calcutta*, which was keyed to the "Explanation," describes "within the tents, a party of Europeans . . . taking their evening repast."[85] What the spectator sees, in other words, is a hierarchy not of a privileged individual viewer over an exotic cityscape or of sovereign Britons at home over subject "pagans" abroad but rather of one group of people in London who do form a public over another distant group of people, primarily Indians of every rank but including Britons, who do not. The Panorama of Calcutta in London thus actualizes the metropolitan public-sphere ideology of colonial rule. If this panorama was a telescope, it provided an optics of a very particular kind. For unlike Dibdin, who "longed to be leaping from crag to crag with Sir David Baird" in the *Storming of Seringapatam* at the Lyceum, the audience in Leicester Square was made to feel that distance was necessary and right and that magnification was the suitable means by which Britons in London should literally and figuratively want to view Little London, where the Course, visible in Burford's panorama behind "A Group of Natives" and the "Hindoo Religious Procession," was "frequented by all the fashionables of Calcutta, in carriages or on horseback; in fact, it is their Hyde Park."[86]

The panoramas of Britain in Calcutta tell another side, if not *the* other side, of the same anxious story. When some panoramas closed in London after a usual run of several months, the canvases were rolled up and shipped to Calcutta, where in the first two decades of the nineteenth century panoramas were frequently advertised on the front page of newspapers. As far as I have been able to ascertain, the panoramas deemed suitable for transportation to and exhibition in India depicted exclusively European scenes (although a book of lithographs called *A Panoramic View of the Holy City of Benares* was printed in Calcutta in 1827), including in 1812–13 alone spectacles of Dover, Edinburgh, and Ramsgate, with a panorama of the Battle of Waterloo on display in 1817.[87] These were exhibited for mixed audiences of Britons, other Europeans, and elite Bengalis. On 29 January 1813, for instance, an advertisement for the Panorama of Ramsgate appeared in the *Calcutta Morning Post* in both English and Bengali. In Calcutta between the years 1797 and 1817 the price of a visit to a panorama ranged from two to eight sicca rupees, with children often admitted at a discount. Although affordable for Europeans, the normal price of four rupees meant that bilingual advertisements were also directed at rich Indians, at the nouveau riche "babus," in other words, who would have been reading the *Calcutta Morning Post* in the first place.[88]

Although I have been unable to determine the precise site of "the Rotunda" where, according to the advertisements, most panoramas were mounted, I can conjecture that it refers to the "column-girt rotunda" of the Exchange in Tank Square,[89] for earlier panoramas (in the late 1790s), such as "the Panorama, Exhibiting a grand view of London, [which] will open on the first day of January next in Tank Square . . . Proprietor, Mr. Mathew Isacke, Chief Officer of the Honorable Company's Ship 'Lord Camden,' " were displayed in Tank Square.[90] A manuscript account of Calcutta in 1805 by I. H. T. Roberdeau, who came to India around 1800, includes the following, perhaps referring to Isacke's exhibition: "I arrived in India just time enough to witness the decline and fall of a . . . Panorama," which "failed for want of Patronage."[91] But there was certainly sufficient patronage by early 1808, when, according to the *Calcutta Gazette*, "a Panorama of the City of London" (possibly Robert Barker's) opened "for the gratification of the Public, at Mr. Home's House, Chouringhee . . . Days of Exhibition—Mondays, Wednesdays, and Fridays, from Eight o'Clock in the Morning, till Four in the Afternoon."[92] The *Gazette* then announced that proceeds in the impressive amount of 1,247 rupees from "Mr. Home's Panorama, from January to 31st March 1808" had been donated to the Native Hospital.[93]

Because the sources on panoramas in Calcutta are unfortunately sparse, much of what follows is conjectural, based on theorizations of the panorama form in the context of my own thinking about the relations between the new Indian public sphere, visuality in the early empire, and the permeation of commodity culture throughout every aspect of urban imperial life in the first third of the nineteenth century. According to Stephan Oettermann, the animating action of the panorama corresponds to a specific moment of urbanization and early industrial capitalism. As a technology that disciplines through sight, the panorama does for leisure and amusement what Bentham's panopticon does for criminality and labor: "The panorama is the art form of the Industrial Revolution," Oettermann writes, and "what finds expression in the panorama as art (and its counterpart the panopticon as a form of institution) is the dialectic of the bourgeois mode of seeing."[94] Renzo Dubbini modifies this argument by proposing that the panorama emerged precisely as industrialization was turning the professed object of panoramic vision into a contradiction in terms: "The panorama attempted to provide a total image of the city," yet the new spaces and movements of the industrialized metropolis "shattered the unified vision of the panorama; it was no longer possible to represent a dynamic, continually expanding urban space in one absolute, all-embracing glance."[95] I think that Oettermann is right to connect the panoramic gaze with the disciplining of industrial labor, on the one hand, and leisure as consumption, on the other, but as Ker Porter's panorama makes clear, the animating action of the medium also corresponds to a specific moment of early *imperial* history.

Just as Dubbini finds a contradiction between the medium and its moment, the lines of vision and power that we can imagine were produced by Isacke's or Home's panorama of London or the Panorama of Dover in Calcutta reveal a "locality paradox"[96] particular to Little London's reversed imperial perspective. The "all-embracing glance" of the panorama form depends on the actuality and illusion of centrality—you are actually in the center of the physical space, yet you experience yourself at the center of the scene depicted—a position from which the panorama makes it impossible for any individual viewer to depart. Thus one form of centrality is produced by Ker Porter's metropolitan imperial panorama, which displaces the viewer from London in order to put him or her in the midst of a foreign battle in which Baird's and Britain's troops are victorious over Tipu. The paradox of being in London and Seringapatam at once therefore reinforces authority, and the ultimate effect remains the double centralization of the viewer, who stands in the middle of the panorama, which itself stands in the metropolitan heart of the empire. And Burford's, as we have seen, provides another, more tenuous fortification of the metropolitan perspective by projecting the viewers from London to an elevated point in the middle of a circle of figures on the Esplanade in Calcutta, where the one group's double perspective provides critical distance from and enables public opinion about the other. The panoramas of London or Dover in Calcutta also bestow the power of the fabled cap of Fortunatus, allowing their viewers to be present in two places at once, the perspectival center and periphery of empire, but in a very different context and therefore with other conceivable effects.

In Little London the panorama was one of many kinds of consumption available to displaced Britons, who considered themselves exiles—a phenomenon discussed in later chapters—and thus sought out entertainments and fashions that would let them mirror life at home. The newspaper advertisements among which the notices for panoramas appear regularly proclaim the availability of "Europe Goods," from Manchester counterpanes and Hessian boots to carriages and the *Edinburgh Review* (see fig. 2). In the pages of the newspapers, the panorama is operating according to Benjamin's memorable description of the medium as among the phantasmagoric spectacles of modernity in which consumers effectively saw their world—"the city indoors"—as an endless parade of advertisements, of images of circulating commodities.[97] According to the spatial logic of the front page of the *Calcutta Morning Post*, to visit a panorama of Dover or Edinburgh or Ramsgate in Calcutta is the graphic equivalent of purchasing Europe goods. In this light, the panorama visually realizes and enacts the Little London fantasy: here reflects there, and everything the viewer sees is an image or reproduction in a microcosm, a miniature world where Britons re-create home until they can return to, and rule from, the real thing. The panorama becomes a kind of nostalgic transporter that beams the viewer back to Britain, meaning that the centralized and authorized metropolitan fashions and taste can be lived and experienced in the peripheral trading capital of a commercial and colonial empire.

Thus far we have considered the stakes of articulating a *new* Indian public through print and treated the panorama in London as a visual technology that grants and denies publicity, but when a panorama of London comes to Calcutta, it operates on its spectators by turning them into not a new public but rather a *little* one. Just as Barker's canvases are now in Bengal, through the illusory power of the medium so is Britain, and while the little Indian viewing public is enjoying the panorama, it is interpellated as a social organization whose agreement with metropolitan taste affirms its inseparability from metropolitan life, as one's shadow is inseparable from oneself. In their very lack of autonomous opinion, their inclusion as part of a critical culture of consumption located "at home," members of the little public see themselves as playing an essential role within the British Empire, for their tastes are harmonized with their imperial mission, their active participation in the acquisition, consumption, and exchange of commodities in circulation.

But it is not impossible, as Benjamin's dialectical approach to the logic of the commodity would suggest, that the panorama could have done its work too well. Peter Otto has offered a more extreme alternative to Comment's, Charlesworth's, and Wood's positions in his proposal that the hyperreality of the panorama medium called attention to its status as illusion, as more than or even as independent from the reality it represented, so that the panorama could have left its audience with "a sense of the contingent nature of all perceptual worlds, the *unreality of reality*."[98] In this case, the panorama relocates Britain, both its landscapes and its cityscapes, as well as its metropolitan fashions and commodities, to India, where the evident transportability of the home culture undermines the relativity of scale that distinguishes London from Little London. The panorama would thus interpellate the imperial subject in a different manner by indicating the contingency of borders, revealing the reproducibility of culture, demonstrating the artistic effects that create illusions of motion and scale, and projecting the homogeneous logic of the commodity upon the enjoyment of the scene. Confusing indoors and outdoors, image and object, mobile and static, entertainment and information, exchange value and use value, the iterable panorama transforms landscapes and cityscapes into spectacles that can be endlessly altered and restaged for repeated viewing as a form of consumption. A kind of deconstructive machine, the panorama ultimately subverts the distinction between center and periphery itself, redefining the latter, paradoxically, as a space that *includes* the former. Calcutta then becomes something different from Little London, something other than a "snug epitome" where identity is bound by and subservient to metropolitan tastes, which Little Londoners share, feed, and consume. Perhaps the hyperreality of the Panorama of London in Calcutta displays a fantasy that if London can be so easily and successfully unmoored from England and commodified for export, then Little London is all there is in the new bourgeois empire of global trade, a world of nothing but peripheries.

These conceivable dynamics came together in striking fashion when the Panorama of Dover closed in late January 1812. The papers report that it was replaced by one of Edinburgh, but an advertisement in the *Calcutta Gazette* in February announces that the auction house of

Williams and Hohler Have received Orders to Dispose of by Public Auction, On Monday next,... The Panorama of *Dover*, by the celebrated and well known Mr. Barker, and which has been so justly and highly esteemed here. This painting forms a circle of about 160 feet, and contains upwards of 1000 square yards of Canvas, and can be put up (without a brick building) at a very trifling expence, and is well worth the attention of any Gentleman wishing so pleasing a Picturesque Scene in his Compound.[99]

In its first incarnation, in London in 1809, the spectacle of Dover fashioned its audience as an enlightened public that exercised taste while acquiring information and enjoying the entertainment. In its second incarnation, in Calcutta in 1811–12, the spectacle reminded a new audience of either its "little" public identity or its role in the hyperreality of commercial empire. In its third (and final?) incarnation, the panorama itself finds a home as a commodity in the compound of a private gentleman in Bengal. Assume that the amount has been paid down and the painting put up, either indoors, in a space large enough, or perhaps outdoors, in a garden rotunda or shaded enclosure during the dry winter months.[100] Upon entering the purchaser's compound, the visitors are transported by the scene, and not just any scene but the iconic last sight of England witnessed by the departing voyager.[101] For that illusory moment the actual location, the material, and the artifice all disappear, leaving the private space transformed into the spectacle of an empire in which it is not people who transport things but rather things that transport people, culture, and civilization. The scene thus displays what has been left behind even as it proclaims itself a phantasmagoric illusion whose value resides in the parade of commodities as they are advertised in newspapers and as they circulate through public auctions in the trading capital of a colonial empire. And when the illusion ends, the spectacle in its latest incarnation does not simply bring the viewers back to earth: they look at Dover and, "without a brick building," see or at least recall the Bengali trees and sky over the perspectival plane and recognize the reality that the English "pleasing . . . Picturesque Scene" is perfectly at home in India, as a commodity and thus the essence of worldliness, in this private gentleman's compound.

Inventing Tradition: Durga Puja, Idolatry, and Sympathy

On several fall days each September or October throughout the early nineteenth century, Europeans and elite Bengali men could mingle on the viewing platform of the Rotunda in the morning or afternoon and then meet again in the evening to enjoy another kind of spectacle in a different social space, the mansions of the Black Town to the north. They would have been free to give the whole day to entertainment instead of business because all "the serious affairs of life [had] been suspended"[102] for Europeans and Indians alike. Thus a contributor to *The Orient Pearl, for 1835*, M. Crow, describes the festive atmosphere in his office on the day before "the Durgá Pujá vacation" in late September 1832 as follows: "We all looked forward to the approaching holidays with an infantine anxiety, which forcibly remind me of my school-days on the eve of Christmas vacation."[103] During their days off, many Europeans would take boat trips up the river. And at night they would visit the homes of wealthy Bengalis for the celebration of Durga Puja, the only Hindu religious ritual that Europeans were invited to witness and, to a certain, ambiguous extent, participate in.

If the panorama was very much a European import that turned individuals into spectators distinguished, empowered, and bound by relations to objects perceived and to one another, the annual Durga Puja was one of the *"indigenous bases* onto which western European notions of 'the public' could have become grafted or, perhaps more accurately, transmuted."[104] But as Buckingham and Rammohun anticipated recent revisionist social history by subverting the Eurocentric assumption that the circulation of news brought modernity from the West to the East, here the notion of indigeneity will need to be called into question, for tradition itself, Durga Puja reveals, can be invented.[105] When Atkinson describes Hindu religious festivals in "The City of Palaces"—"Why sound thy streets, CALCUTTA, with the noise / Of multitudes in holiday attire?" (13)— he takes the common European view of idolatry as emblematic of India's unchanging and eternal premodernity. "Thousands of years have seen the same" (16), he writes, depicting the daily worship of "gods, of wood or brass" (17) and, like Burford and many others, the bloody theatricality of the Charak Puja: "Lo! high aloft a frantic zealot swings, / The iron in his body deep and fast, / . . . the fiends below / Whirl him more rapidly, till tired, at last, / The maddened wretch descends, full pleased to shew / The quivering flesh torn up,—the blood devoted, flow" (17). And when challenged by the voice of reason, the "fiends" take refuge in the characteristic defense of superstition: "Yet they can boast antiquity, the vast / Traditions of old Time, of centuries / Gone by, of countless generations past, / And say their rites are sanctified by these! / May they not worship idols as they please!" (18). Here, as in the picture of "the fanatic swinging himself high in air"[106] in Burford's panorama or in typical newspaper accounts of "The Churrick Pooja . . . with all its wonted noise, show and debauchery,"[107] the spectacular ritual easily serves to distinguish the sea of Indian religious enthusiasm from the island of European modernity and thus to divide Indians themselves from the Europeans who would reform and civilize their antique, idolatrous faith.

Distance was necessary to maintain the division, but Durga Puja challenged all of these terms, as well as these borders, obscuring the lines between Black Town and White Town, pagan actors and enlightened audience, and thus threatening the ideology of social separation by which the walls of Little London were secured. Unlike the panoramas of Britain in Calcutta, Durga Puja was not a mirror in which Europeans saw themselves as miniaturized members of metropolitan life, though, like the panorama, it too reflected and defined social organizations, granting or denying them the authority of publicity through the pleasures of sociability and spectacle, in this case in the context of the religious calendar and customs of colonial India.

Over the course of four days each September or October, Bengali Hindus celebrate the puja of the goddess Durga, along with Kali and Jagaddhatri one of the three major Sakta deities worshipped in Bengal and the embodiment of virtue victorious over vice in the form of the demon Mahisasura. During the early colonial era, Durga Puja was distinguished from other religious festivals by the opportunity it provided for public intercommunal mixing. Thus the *Asiatic Journal* describes the puja of 1827 as "a very heterogeneous sort of business" in which "our native friends . . . [throw] their doors open to a promiscuous mob."[108] Open invitations appeared in the newspapers, while Europeans of significant political and social standing received printed Durga Puja cards from the families of prominent Bengalis—members of the *bhadralok*, or monied elite—"inviting ladies and Gentlemen of the christian community to their houses," in the words of "Remarks on Hindoo Festivals," published in the *Kaleidoscope* in 1829.[109] In the middle of the grand mansions of notable Bengali families was "an open area occupying a considerable space, without roof," where "a covering of red or some other coloured cloth is thrown over the ballustrades by means of cross ropes" (fig. 8).[110]

There the puja would involve two main spectacular elements. The first was a familiar form of display, characterized as a secular "entertainment" and often described by the general term *tamasha* (spectacle, show, going-on), including a nautch, or dance accompanied by music, along with other performances, such as devotional and/or satirical songs (*panchalis*), often bawdy poetry or *kobi* recitations, pantomimes (*sawngs*), juggling, and feats of daring.[111] The entertainment would be still more heterogeneous than the audience, featuring both Hindu and Muslim performers, with occasional appearances by Europeans as well. In 1837 Emma Roberts reported the scandal produced by "the assistance accorded by English performers of eminence in the native concerts given at the . . . festival of the dark goddess Durga. . . . The choice of Handel's music completed the profanation."[112] In a letter to the editor of the *East Indian*, to which I will return several times below, an apparently British writer denominated "W." explains, "The Eu-

Fig. 8. Europeans being entertained in Calcutta during Durga Puja, by William Prinsep, ca. 1840. Watercolor on paper. © The British Library Board. All Rights Reserved. The Bridgeman Art Library.

ropeans are specially invited to *this* poojah, not indeed to join in the worship of the goddess, but to *enjoy* the spectacle of nautches and festivities connected with the service."[113] The second, less familiar kind of spectacle, what "W." somewhat misleadingly labels "the worship of the goddess" itself, was called *darshan,* or the reciprocal sight of the goddess annually embodied in the *murti,* which was installed in the recess, or *pandal,* and which typically featured in accounts of the various pujas. At the "dwelling of Mudhoo Soodun Sundul," for instance, in "the recess, the image of the protecting goddess shone forth with unrivalled richness of decoration and brilliancy of colouring."[114] Both kinds of spectacle, *tamasha* and *darshan,* were forms of devotion in that they had become integrated into the holiday. While Europeans occasionally and often vaguely acknowledged the "connection" between the "festivities" and the "service," however, they tended to draw an inordinately rigid distinction between the former as public, social, and secular and the latter as private and sacred, or rather as superstitious and idolatrous.

These intercommunal performances divided Britons along predictable lines. In the late eighteenth century a fictional young Hinduphile and adherent of Warren Hastings's Orientalist regime, Phebe Gibbes's heroine Sophia Goldborne in *Hartly House, Calcutta* (1789), could describe the puja and warmly admire the "idol superbly dressed with silver, gold, pearls, and the richest manufactures."[115] At the opposite end, in 1806 the Baptist missionary William Ward attended a puja at which the "filthy songs" and "indecent attitudes" of the dancers, along with the reflection that he "was standing in an idol temple," produced in his mind "sensations of the greatest horror,"[116] while a mid-nineteenth-century evangelical sermon printed at the Baptist Mission Press, *Hindu Holidays, the Festivals of "Devil-Worship;" Ought Christians to Observe Them?* (1846), lays down the principle "that *Idol-worship is Devil-worship*—that *Idols' Feast-days are Devils' Feast-days*" and refers to a Durga Puja card as "*a devil-worship invitation.*"[117] In the early nineteenth century, many saw nothing wrong with the indulgence of "liberal curiosity,"[118] while evangelicals and utilitarians, who supported a program of Christianization and Anglicization, tended to frown upon the holiday, especially Christians' participation in it, with responses ranging from expressions of horror at licentiousness and idolatry to simple disapproval. "It has been a question which we have heard not unfrequently discussed," an even-handed writer for the *Government Gazette* explained, "whether it is becoming in Europeans and Christians to attend the nautches held annually on this occasion. Of course every one, according to inclination or conviction, will decide for himself; but the general impression appears to be, that there is no great harm in going as mere lookers-on. Others take a graver view of the subject."[119]

In 1829 appeared a four-stanza newspaper poem, "Doorga Poojah. The Nautch," an acrostic in which the first letters of the lines of each stanza spell a different word, capturing these graver views and alternating the targets of satire between native hosts (stanzas 1 and 3) and European spectators (stanzas 2 and 4). The first stanza attacks the puja hosts for SUPERSTITION, for "Offering incense to a *God* / Nothing but a painted clod." The second then indicts Europeans, "Infidels to England's God" who "Doorga's *mysteries* may applaud," for countenancing IDOLATRY by their attendance and approbation. The third reduces native display of "Orient pearls and diamond fair, / Strings of rubies, gems as rare" to mere OSTENTATION. And the last accuses "Petty fops" and "Pert uncivil clerks" in the audience of PUPPYISM, the European counterpart to native ostentation.[120] Ostentation and puppyism, of course, were common subjects for lighthearted satire, and the real tension in the debate over European attendance lay in their combination with and subordination to superstition and idolatry. "As sincere Christians, we cannot but deplore the continuance of these degrading rites," complained a letter to the *Calcutta Journal* that was then reprinted in London, adding, "That Europeans should countenance a crime forbidden in the very front of the Decalogue, and placed by the sacred writers amongst the foulest transgressions, is most lamentable indeed."[121] And the missionary periodical *Friend of India* tried to head off the common distinction between the supposedly secular and largely harmless spectacle, on the one hand, and the degrading pagan ritual, on the other, by reminding its readers "that they cannot attend a nautch at a pooja without giving countenance to the worship of the idol. . . . It is true that the nautch is no act of worship. Very far from it. The songs have no more reference to Doorga than to the Queen of England. But the whole exhibition, nautch, and pooja, and all together, from beginning to end, is got up for the direct purpose of doing honour to Doorga."[122]

Also at stake and, I want to emphasize, inseparable from the anxiety over idolatry was the fact of social mixing itself, especially the potential for conservative "cultural" activities shared between elite Britons and Bengalis to blur the lines between secular and sacred, public and private. In her discussion of the "missionary public" in mid-nineteenth-century Jamaica, Catherine Hall points out that "Habermas's vision of the public sphere is secular in its definition,"[123] but in the colonial context of the "'devotional' idiom," writes Sandria Freitag, the "nomenclature of 'cultural' should not be seen as the same as 'private'," because devotional and cultural activities in early nineteenth-century Bengal "bear little resemblance to the 'private' category identified for western Europe."[124] So long as the *tamasha* could be kept separate from *darshan* as an entertainment that was at once public and secular, a timeless and authentic spectacle that Europeans witnessed as "mere lookers-on," as dispassionate and liberal observers of Oriental culture, attendance at the pujas could be reconciled to the other pleasures of Little London. But if "the whole exhibition, nautch, and pooja, and all together" was understood to be a unified religious ritual and a contemporary rather than timeless performance, then Europeans would be forced to acknowledge themselves as spectators and actors within larger conservative social relations of power and patronage that were Indian *as well as* modern.

Neither imported nor inherited, these relations constituted a kind of publicity that was indigenous in that it was produced in and through, rather than outside of, local historical time and development. The energy with which these categories were fought over and the care and expense lavished on the pujas by powerful orthodox Bengali families such as the Debs of Shovabazar, the Mitras of neighboring Kumartuli, and the Malliks of Pathuriaghata[125] suggest that Durga Puja may have been more of a modern and political indigenous exercise than the unspoken rules of social mixing in Little London could allow. As Swati Chattopadhyay has demonstrated, before the division of Calcutta into administrative units in the 1850s, in fact, the heterogeneous neighborhood structure of the eighteen *paras* and the social organizations *dals* (groups or parties) in part cohered around the houses of wealthy patron families such as these.[126]

In Pathuriaghata elaborate pujas were also held at the home of Gopi Mohun Tagore (1760–1819), father of Prasanna Kumar, who soon after the puja of 1831 found himself at the center of a controversy that broke out among the liberal Hindu and mixed-race communities in the pages of several non-European newspapers. It started when the *East Indian*, edited by Derozio, and the *Enquirer*, the paper of the Hindu liberals edited by Derozio's student Krishna Mohun Banerjea, attacked Prasanna Kumar, another of Derozio's students, who was editor of the *Reformer*, the English-language mouthpiece of the followers of Rammohun, which (like the *East Indian* and the *Enquirer*) was consistently opposed to idolatry and other "superstitions." The reason for the attack was that Prasanna Kumar had celebrated the Durga Puja in his family's house. The case was, as a writer to the *India Gazette* who signed himself "A Native" revealed, that Prasanna Kumar had inherited property from his family on the condition that he celebrate the puja and that his apparent observance in no way changed the fact that "he hates [idolatry] as much as Mr. Derozio . . . or Baboo Krishna Mohona Banerjeah can do."[127]

Anticlimactic as the controversy was, it opened up fault lines, and once it died down "W." wrote his long letter to the editor of the *East Indian* reflecting on "the nature and tendencies" of the Durga Puja and asking what "the numerous pretexts urged" by Christians "for attending these poojahs" were. He listed three: first, "it is politic to cultivate the good opinion of the Hindoo nation; Our security is based upon their good opinion of us"; second, "We do not go to worship the Goddess, but to witness the nautches and to hear the music and singing"; and third, "We are invited as guests, and it would be rude and illiberal to decline an invitation." Expanding on those who urge these pretexts, "W." has them say, "Oh! it is only a '*tumasha*', and as we have never before seen anything so *Oriental*, and yet have read and heard so much about it, we must go."[128] Divided off from *darshan*, the *tamasha* becomes the spectacle of an authentic Orient. Thus in late September 1819 the *Calcutta Journal* had announced that "if the reader be one who has never witnessed the magnificent spectacle of a Doorgah Poojah in Calcutta, we can only assure him that he will find the splendid fiction of the Arabian Nights completely realized in the Fairy Palace of Rajah Ramchunder Roy, on the evenings of the 26th, 27th, and 28th instant."[129]

Realized, or performed? The fact was that far from resurrecting a classical golden age, bringing its timeless traditions to life for European consumption, the pujas were only slightly more authentic, as that word is commonly used, than the Arabian Nights themselves. Although there were rural precedents for the pujas before the colonial era, the expansion of the celebrations by the new urban *bhadralok* coincided with the period of transition from Mughal to British rule in the 1750s and 1760s, as Rachel McDermott has now shown, and "it was during the 1700s that interest in Durgā was greatest."[130] Two historical interpretations are available. The first, fundamentally pro-British, suggests that the stability of British rule simultaneously augmented the wealth of *zamindari* (Hindu landholding) families and removed their former fear of displaying wealth before the local *nawabs* (Mughal representatives) and their agents. The second, a pro-Mughal, or rather anti-British-colonialist position, holds that it was the success of the *zamindari* system under Mughal protection that increased the power of Hindu families, who then adapted the puja in order to consolidate status and display symbolic capital within the new patronage system of the East India Company. Either way, the timeless golden age was really no more than half a century old, and it was thoroughly mediated by recent imperial transformations of Indian political economy. For these reasons, Dermot Killingley refers to the Durga Puja hosts as the "newly-traditional newly-rich."[131] In the early nineteenth century, then, when a European received a Durga Puja card and said "Oh! it is only a *'tumasha'*, and . . . we have never before seen anything so *Oriental*," he or she was talking about something new.[132]

The paradoxical idea of a newly traditional custom defended as ancient by the orthodox hosts and perceived as timeless by the European guests nicely captures the collusion between powerful, conservative Bengali families and the patronage system of the East India Company, which inherited and transformed Mughal rituals of display and respect.[133] But defined and practiced in this manner, the activities of the modern Durga Puja in the early nineteenth century stand in stark contrast to the denial that the "native Indian" had any "domestic feeling" or "permanent interest in common with the European resident," any "community of affections, of religion, or of soil, with the stranger under whose sceptre he lives." The social sympathies enacted at the pujas, to the contrary, indicated a community of affections and therefore of power outside of the British state in Bengal and the British public to which it was responsible. And this is why it became so important not only to separate *tamasha* from *darshan* but also to deny that the spectacle could afford any real pleasure to Europeans of taste and judgment.

The *Government Gazette* offered, "We have no objection to the contemplation of the religious rites of the Hindus, for the gratification of liberal curiosity, nor to a participation in their amusements, . . . if they yield a real entertainment."[134] Struggling to define "real entertainment," the writer can only reiterate that "the vague and undefined mobbing of the Durga Puja can yield, we should fancy, neither information nor diversion" (671). As we saw on the elevated platforms of the panoramas in both London and Calcutta, the combination of information and diversion shared among individuals collected in public spaces could shape social organizations with respect to the authority of other groups and the state. It was thus essential that Durga Puja yield neither information nor diversion, and, as the writer admonishes, "our native friends . . . had much better dispense with European society, until they can offer it something more worthy of acceptance than profusion and antics; and Europeans had better decline that of the native community, until both parties have something mutually instructive or interesting" (671). The fascinating thing about this labored attempt to police the boundaries between the elite European and Indian communities is that in spite of very real social interactions in the past and the present, it concludes by imagining some vague form of sociability between the two in the very near future: "There need be no great delay" in designing mutually instructive and interesting social activities, "for many of the native gentlemen who lend themselves to the public celebration of the Durga Puja, are far from being deficient, either in the intelligence, or information, or command of the English language, requisite to a free and friendly intercourse with their guests at a more propitious season, and under more favourable circumstances" (671–72). That more propitious season, evidently, should not accord with the Hindu religious calendar, and while the more favorable circumstances remain undefined, it is clear that if native gentlemen are qualified by intelligence, information, and command of English to enter the social life of Little London, they will do so on none other than its own microcosmic terms, which are not those of Durga Puja.

So along with and inseparable from countenancing idolatry, sympathy became the flashpoint for opponents of the pujas. "Christians, the avowed enemies of Idolatry, act so inconsistently and so unreasonably as to attend," wrote "W.," while "the more considerate Hindoos must know that the mind of every true Christian revolts at the spectacle of their idolatrous worship, and that therefore the guests on such an occasion can feel no sympathy nor communion with the host."[135] The objection to idolatry went well beyond the first and second commandments, then, but the theological basis of the debate should not be discounted, nor dismissed as cover for something else. The real power of sympathetic feelings at Durga Puja around 1830 was that they could bridge the gap between public authority and religion, which in early British India needed to be relegated to the apolitical realm of private life to an even greater extent than in Britain itself, where these very same years (1828–32) saw serious and successful assaults on the confessional state in the Repeal of the Corporation and Test Acts (1828), Catholic Emancipation (1829), and the Reform Bill itself in 1832. Thus the debate over Durga Puja came to a head in 1830–31 with the attendance at the pujas of Lord Bentinck, the ruler who embodied the program to liberalize and Anglicize India and who was reported to have said to James Mill before departing, "I am going to British India; but I shall not be Governor-General. It is you that will be Governor-General."[136]

When "W." reminds his readers, then, that "the 'Card' invites not to a social party, not to a communion of friendship,—but for the specified purpose 'of celebrating the Durga Poojah holydays,' "[137] he signals the widespread unease in 1831 that the division between public spectacle and private worship could not be sustained. In fact, between and occasionally in the lines of the coverage of the pujas in the European press it is evident that the hosts expected the governor general to participate in both forms of devotional spectatorship. Descriptions of Christians viewing the nautches and other festivities are numerous, but we also get fleeting glimpses of Europeans being explicitly asked "to see the goddess" upon arrival or before departure. Thus we read that in 1830, after "God Save the King" was played upon the entry of the governor general's suite, Lord and Lady Bentinck, "being pleased with the songs and sword-exercise" at the home of "Kaleekishen Bahadur" (i.e., Radhakanta's brother Kalikrishna Deb), "saw the goddess Doorgah out of curiosity, and leaving the Raja after an hour's stay, departed to Baboo Gopeemohun Deb's, where having viewed the goddess, their Lordships, Lady Bentinck, and suite, were conducted up stairs by Baboo Radakant Deb, and entertained by him with due respect."[138] According to another account of this same puja, after "taking a glimpse of the Doorga" the governor general left Kalikrishna's house for "Gopeemohun Deb's, on entering which, his lordship was conducted . . . to the Doorga place, and from thence to the Upper apartments of his house."[139]

Did Bentinck see Durga "out of curiosity" or as part of a religious ritual? The answer depends on perspective and may well be both, for it seems significant that the viewing apparently occurs in these accounts immediately upon his arrival or before his departure. To the hosts, at least, and as Bentinck must have known, it was clearly important that the symbolic head of the British state in India look not just at the nautches but also into the eyes of the goddess, whether or not he believed they could look back. Here we have an orthodox counterpart, if not *the* orthodox counterpart, to the heterodox Rammohun's and the free-trader Buckingham's modernizing agenda for print journalism, which sought to grant autonomy and authority to writers and readers in India, allowing them to regulate or even (for Buckingham) supersede the state power of the East India Company. The Durga Puja thus becomes an important yearly ritual through which, as Freitag writes, "the cultural or local/domestic world was constructed by Indian males primarily as a way to explore the new expressions of power and patronage by focusing, especially, on a range of activities that the British had defined as apolitical," a world including "expressions of cultural patronage, religious activity and connections among people expressed in kin or fictive kin terms."[140]

In Little London it was possible either to say, "Oh! it is only a '*tumasha*', and as we have never before seen anything so *Oriental*, . . . we must go," or, with William Ward, to recede in horror from "sights . . . such as can never be described by the pen of a christian writer."[141] As members of a little audience separate from native actors, Europeans could visit Black Town and see either authenticity in the resurrection of classical India or the equally authentic licentiousness of superstition, idolatry, ostentation, and puppyism. To the puja organizer in newly traditional and religiously conservative Calcutta, however, there was no "inimitable cross-stitch," and a successful performance in which "God Save the King" was played before the governor general enjoyed a nautch and saw the goddess enacted mutual sympathies and conferred authority within new systems of patronage. In the communion of spectacle, the strand distinguishing island from sea eroded, giving way to a city where the political, the public, the modern, and the secular world could not always be secured from, and bind, the apolitical, the private, the traditional, and the sacred. It is no wonder that evangelicals found themselves in an unlikely alliance with Buckingham, Rammohun, Christian East Indians, and liberal and radical Hindus in vigorously opposing the idolatry and ideology of Durga Puja.

Maya Jasanoff, Durba Ghosh, and most recently Partha Chatterjee have challenged the "air of nostalgic celebration" with which stories of intercommunal social mixing, cultural openness, and enlightened curiosity in the early colonial era have been told.[142] In print, in panoramas, and in pujas, Europeans, East Indians, and Indians did interact in ways that would not be possible after the hardening of racist hierarchies in the mid-nineteenth century. But it does not follow that we must choose between nostalgic celebration and suspicious censure in our historical perspective on these forms of sociability. There is no more reason to associate friendship, openness, or curiosity with benign disinterest than to assume that commerce, authority, and law correspond to the selfish or predatory instincts of human nature. Little London and its discursive, spectacular, and sympathetic alternatives represented sites of contest and negotiation where different images of Indian modernity were either rendered invisible or made recognizable.

CHAPTER TWO

Secret Sharers and Evangelical Signs

The Idol, the Book, and the Intense Objectivism
of Robert Southey

One small but influential group of Britons did not come to Bengal to trade or to consume, though they did both. The Baptist missionaries in the Danish settlement of Serampore, on the west bank of the Hugli north of Calcutta, were removed from Little London by more than just fourteen miles of river. While East India Company servants saw themselves as liberating capital and household goods, the Baptists were far more concerned with souls and household gods. As we have seen, there is a unified relationship between the fashions of Little London and the imperial mission of its exiled inhabitants, between the importation and consumption of Europe goods and European entertainments, in other words, and the extraction and exportation of silver, raw cotton, manufactured textiles, indigo, and spices. It was along one integrated circuit that such goods found their way to Britain, where they made themselves "at home" and thus allowed empire to be "lived across everyday practices."[1] On the very same ships, gods set sail too. How their journeys were part of evangelical print culture in Bengal and the ways they made themselves "at home" in England are the questions explored in this chapter.

Robert Southey saw one of them in Bristol in late 1799. On the first of January, 1800, he wrote a letter to S. T. Coleridge after paying a visit to the library and museum of the Bristol Baptist College:

> The Baptist Library here—I have got access to, and the privilege of carrying home its books. This is of importance to me. The books relating to Oriental matters are many and good. Do you know that they have missionaries in the East Indies? Ryland showed me a little God whom they had just sent over—the primitial spoils I suppose—twas an ugly brass epicene-looking God sitting cross-legged upon a peacock. Should not you like to hear a controversy between a Baptist and a Bramin?[2]

Although it is hard to say what became of this "ugly brass epicene-looking God," there is a remarkable amount we can venture about it.[3] The god was almost certainly Karttikeya (also called Skanda, Murukan, and Kumara), whose posture when mounted on his peacock *vahana* (vehicle) is often *lalitasana* (with one leg crossed).[4] By the eighteenth century the cult of Karttikeya as Murukan had long endured primarily in Tamil-speaking areas of South India, but the god did (and still does) play a role in the annual Durga Puja in Bengal, as well as in the Kartik Puja, which follows soon after.[5] It is reasonable to suppose that this particular small brass god was a household *murti* in or near the neighboring villages of Mudnabatty (Madnabati) and Moypaldiggy (Mahipaldighi), just north of Malda and 225 miles north of Calcutta, where in 1797–98 the Baptist missionaries were trying to support themselves as indigo farm managers.[6] It probably came into the hands of the missionary John Fountain, who then could have packed it into a box in the late spring or summer of 1798, for in a letter of May 1798 Fountain wrote from Mudnabatty to John Webster Morris, publisher of the *Periodical Accounts Relative to the Baptist Missionary Society* and member of the society committee, "I . . . intend . . . to send a box by the ships of next season, containing some of the implements, utensils, and idols, of the Hindoos" (*PA* 1:422–23).[7] This box probably made its way by boat from Malda down the Ganges, Bhagirathi, and Hugli Rivers to Calcutta, and from there to Saugor, where it would have been loaded onto an East Indiaman awaiting the sailing of the fleet at some point between October 1798 and January 1799, to coincide with the northeast monsoons. The box would have arrived in London in early to mid-summer, and from there it would have traveled by mail coach to Bristol, where John Ryland, president of both the Missionary Society and the Bristol Education Society, did show the idol to Southey at the end of 1799.[8]

Little more than a year after seeing Karttikeya at the Baptist College, Southey wrote to Coleridge from Lisbon, "I have planned a Hindoo romance of original extravagance."[9] While composing *The Curse of Kehama* (1810) over the ensuing decade, Southey also entered a debate that would change the course of the empire in India. In Britain this same debate shaped the history of periodical literature by providing one of the main topics that brought the *Edinburgh* and *Quarterly* reviews into fierce opposition and clear self-definition. The question of the so-called pious clause proposed by Foreign Secretary Lord Castlereagh for inclusion in the 1813 Company charter concerned whether or not Protestant missionaries should be officially allowed and encouraged to spread the gospel in India and to attempt to convert Hindus and Muslims to Christianity.[10] Under the auspices of the Baptist Missionary Society, in November 1793 William Carey and

John Thomas had arrived together in Bengal, where they were joined by Fountain in 1796 and by William Ward, Daniel Brunsdon, William Grant, and Joshua and Hannah Marshman in 1799.[11] Their activities, together with the print that their activities produced, spurred the debate over Britain's role in fostering "religious and moral improvement" in India. On the evangelical side were Claudius Buchanan, Charles Grant Sr., John Shore, Thomas Babington, Zachary Macaulay, William Wilberforce, and the rest of the Clapham Sect Saints; opposed to missions (and definitely to Dissenting ones) were Thomas Twining, J. Scott Waring, Charles "Hindoo" Stuart, Sydney Smith, and the rest of the editorial board of the *Edinburgh Review*.[12]

The touchstone of the controversy, and, for that matter, the source of knowledge about Indian religious life for many readers in the first decade of the nineteenth century, came in the form of a specific set of texts and the reviews of them: the *Periodical Accounts Relative to the Baptist Missionary Society*, especially the first three volumes, published between 1800 and 1806. Permeating these accounts of the Baptists' lives and labors in India, and the responses they generated, was the discourse of idolatry. The Baptists' project of sending idols back to Bristol reveals the difficulty, or perhaps the impossibility, of substituting the good book, and good books, for what W. J. T. Mitchell has named "the 'bad objects' of empire, the things that produce ambivalence and need to be neutralized, merely tolerated, or destroyed." These are "uncanny things that we should be able to dismiss as naive, superstitious objects of primitive subjectivities, but which at the same time awaken a certain suspicion or doubt about the reliability of our own categories."[13] By reading the missionaries' twinned accounts of transporting idols and of distributing Bibles and printed tracts, I propose that bad idols and good books were secret sharers, not just because they held properties in common but because they needed one another within a unified circuit of communication. I then turn to Southey's writings on the missionary movement in the *Annual* and *Quarterly* reviews[14] and his mythological treatment of idolatry in *The Curse of Kehama*, which scripts new lives for bad objects, developing out of his engagement with evangelicalism and its contradictions an instrumental, "Romantic" vision of conquest and conversion far more amenable to idolatrous ritual practices.

Baptists, Print, and Idolatry

During the early years of the British Empire in India, two unique kinds of objects were crossing each other regularly at sea. Ships leaving England in the winter, aiming to round the Cape and catch the southwest monsoons between

April and September to arrive in Bengal in late summer or fall, would often bear boxes of books. Newspapers would then advertise the invoices of titles "exposed for sale" according to the name of the ship and the ship's captain. Books would be listed by price and categorized under such headings as "Theological Works," "Periodical Works," and "Miscellaneous." Like other Europe goods, their availability would be announced at the major auction houses of Calcutta—Ferris and Co., Tulloh and Co., or Gould and Campbell's "Great Room." But as the sight of Karttikeya at the Bristol Baptist College indicates, a surprising number of ships leaving Calcutta carried a different form of freight, not "goods" per se but not without value either. Letters like Fountain's to Morris mentioned above and entries such as the following from William Ward's journal (on 4 February 1801) appear frequently in the missionary diaries and correspondence: "Yesterday Bro. B. [Brunsdon] was packing up a number of idols for the Bristol Museum."[15] Arjun Appadurai has proposed a "methodological fetishism" that would turn "our attention to the things themselves," while more recently Mitchell has asked, "What happens to objects when they undergo a 'worlding' in their circulation, moving across frontiers, flowing from one part of the globe to another?"[16] In the context of the early empire in India, two intimately related classes of "worlded" objects include books and brass, bronze, clay, stone, wood, or marble *murtis*, typically referred to in early nineteenth-century English as "Hindoo idols."

The story of the first English Protestant missionaries in India involves the circumstances of the Particular (i.e., Calvinistic) Baptist denomination in the late eighteenth century, when many Dissenters of the new middling classes were attempting to embrace polite respectability by distancing themselves from the Calvinism, enthusiasm, and austerity that were among the legacies of seventeenth-century Puritanism. But Calvinism maintained its hold on the working classes, especially among the Particular Baptists—"low-born and low-bred mechanics" (*QR* 1:224), Southey called them in the *Quarterly Review* in 1809—and the Methodists who followed George Whitefield rather than John Wesley. As the name suggests, the defining distinction of the Baptists (originally Anabaptists, or rebaptizers) was their adherence to the practice of adult baptism by immersion. In one sense, this meant that they were not born into their faith in the same way as most members of the Established Church or of the other two old nonconformist denominations, Presbyterians and Independents. Further, adult baptism was more than just a matter of timing; "putting on Christ," as it was commonly called, was not an affair that could simply be scheduled on a calendar. In fact, it altered one's sense of time itself: baptism followed a long process of private introspection and public examination, and the life of a Baptist did not proceed in a progressive or homogeneous trajectory culminating in the acceptance of God's grace on a given day but rather was punctuated by violent, inscrutable, and unpredictable intercessions. The origins of evangelicalism in Bengal lay in just such a one.[17]

In 1781 John Thomas, twenty-four-year-old son of the deacon of a Baptist church in Gloucestershire, realized that his uniform life of hopelessness had changed when "it pleased God to make my sins a heavy burden to me" (*PA* 1:13). Often he would find himself "almost distracted, starting up in my bed, and crying out with fear. One afternoon, I had retired for prayer, and I was so apprehensive, that I thought I felt Satan come and touch my heel, which gave me great fear and mental distress."[18] Soon afterwards, Thomas attended a sermon by Samuel Stennett, which he heard "with new ears": "I beheld a new object in a new light, even Christ crucified" (*PA* 1:14). Thereafter, "days and nights were spent in the enjoyment of believing that Christ had suffered for *me* in particular. ME, ME, so insignificant, so worthless! . . .—this thought attended me for many days, and wherever I was, I had many tears of joy and gladness."[19] Two years later, Thomas sailed for Calcutta as surgeon of the East Indiaman *Oxford*. Upon his arrival, he "sought for religious people, but found none" (*PA* 1:14). Far from thinking of converting Indians, Thomas was horrified by the irreligion of his fellow Europeans. Disappointed, he "advertised for a christian," literally, in the form of a notice in the *India Gazette* on 1 November 1783 seeking "serious persons" who would join in a religious society "for the more effectually spreading the knowledge of Jesus Christ, and his glorious gospel, in and about Bengal" (*PA* 1:15). After the *Oxford* returned to London in 1784, Thomas "put on Christ" on Christmas Day. The *Oxford* sailed again in 1786, and it was during Thomas's second stay in Calcutta that he met the evangelicals Charles Grant Sr. and George Udny, becoming "greatly concerned at heart for the condition of these perishing multitudes of Pagans, in utter darkness; and . . . inflamed with fervent desires to go and declare the glory of Christ among them" (*PA* 1:18).

Meanwhile, at the very same time, in 1786, a twenty-five-year-old shoemaker in Northamptonshire with a prodigious gift for languages, William Carey, was putting to paper his thoughts on "the Obligations of Christians to use Means for the Conversion of the Heathen" (*PA* 1:1–2). Raised in the Established Church but exposed to Dissent by a fellow apprentice, Carey had been baptized in 1783. He accepted the ministry of the Baptist congregation at Olney in 1786, and at a meeting of Baptist ministers at Clipstone in 1791 he proposed the question "Whether it were not practicable, and our bounden duty, to attempt somewhat toward spreading the gospel in the heathen world?"[20] In the following year he published his manuscript as *An Enquiry into the Obligations of Christians, to Use Means for the Conversion of the Heathens. In which the Religious State of the Different Nations of the World, the Success of Former Undertakings, and the Practicability of Further Undertakings, are Considered* (1792). At the next annual meeting of the association, at Nottingham, it was resolved "that a plan be prepared . . . for forming a society among the Baptists for propagating the gospel among the heathen." And then on 2 October 1792 at Kettering "The Particular Baptist Society for Propagating the Gospel amongst the Heathen" was formed (*PA* 1:3). Amongst *which* heathen the gospel would be propagated, however, remained a wide-open question, for in his *Enquiry* Carey had calculated the population of the world as 731 million, divided by religion as follows: pagans, 420 million; Mahometans, 130 million; Catholics, 100 million; Protestants, 44 million; Greek and Armenian churches, 30 million; and Jews, "perhaps" 7 million.[21] But by November 1792 Carey had received a letter from Thomas, who had returned from his second voyage and was at the time "trying to establish a fund in London for a mission to Bengal" (*PA* 1:7). Carey proposed an alliance, and the society, after receiving and considering a narrative of Thomas's life and his labors in India, approved the plan. Under the auspices of the Baptist Missionary Society, the party that set sail on 13 June 1793 included Carey; his wife, Dorothy; their four children, Felix, William, Peter, and the newborn infant Jabez; Dorothy's sister Kitty; and Thomas.[22]

Before the renewal in 1813 of the East India Company's charter, with its pious clause, missionary activity was prohibited within Company territory. Had they not sailed in a Danish ship, the *Kron Princesse Maria*, it is likely that the group would have been turned back immediately upon arrival. Instead, they landed in Calcutta in November and soon departed for Mudnabatty and Moypaldiggy, where, through Udny's patronage, they would try their hand at indigo farming. Their numbers grew when, as I've mentioned, they were joined by Fountain in 1796 and by Ward, Brunsdon, Grant, and the Marshmans in 1799. In 1800 they relocated to the Danish settlement Serampore in "the immediate vicinity of the metropolis, yet beyond the reach of the British authorities."[23]

A Calvinist culture of print drove their endeavors in the two areas this chapter considers, the production and circulation of books and the transportation of idols from Bengal to the museum of the Baptist College in Bristol. The mission was shaped, as Miles Ogborn writes, by an "almost unshakeable belief in the fundamental necessity of creating Christian converts by putting into heathen hands the Scriptures printed in their own languages and teaching them the word of the Lord."[24] In the early years Carey repeatedly emphasized to Ryland, "It will be requisite for the society to send a printing press from England; and if our lives are spared, we will repay them. We can engage native printers, to perform the press and compositor's work" (*PA* 1:125). He eventually acquired a press "just landed from England" for 400 sicca rupees, or £50, in September 1798. In anticipation of this purchase, the previous spring Ward had been chosen to join Carey in large part because he was a printer by trade. After his arrival in 1799, book production became an important part of the mission, involving numerous *pandits*, who assisted in the translation work, along with compositors, pressmen, sweepers, and, after 1809, when the mission started producing its own paper, many laborers to work at the mill. Between 1800 and 1832 the Baptist Mission Press printed and put in circulation 212,000 volumes in forty languages.[25]

While Carey was completing the translation of the New Testament into Bengali, though, Fountain was otherwise employed. His letter to Morris of May 1798 initiates a string of references to an activity that channeled evangelical energies, put a singular kind of object into a particular form of circulation, and brought people in Britain and India into new relations with each other and with things. "We are sending an assortment of Hindu gods to the Bristol Museum, and some other curiosities to different friends," wrote Carey in late December 1800, for instance, requesting in return "a few tulips, daffodils, snowdrops, lilies, and seeds of other things."[26] And while Brunsdon was "packing up a number of idols for the Bristol Museum" on 4 February 1801, a "native observing said it was a very great sin to box them in that way."[27]

In order to understand the interactions between these people and these things, and thus the Particular Baptists' perspectives on materiality in general and print in particular, we should first briefly consider their brand of evangelical Calvinism, which, like all meaningful aspects of religious life, constituted a system of belief as well as practice. As both Sydney Smith and Southey were keenly aware, Calvinism was not just a matter of doctrine but rather informed every thought, action, manner, and gesture of the Baptist missionaries—what Southey labeled "their peculiar language" (*QR* 1:222) and what Smith assaulted under the capacious rubric of "fanaticism,"[28] and to which we could apply Bourdieu's term, their "habitus."[29] In order to qualify to set out for India in 1799, the printer Ward had to answer a set of doctrinal questions posed to him by Andrew Fuller, "that fierce and fiery Calvinist" (*QR* 1:206), as Southey called him. The summary of Ward's responses, before the Broadmead Chapel in Bristol, is as follows: "The being and attributes of God, the total depravity of man, free and full salvation by the grace of God through a mediator, the deity of Christ, the work of the Holy Spirit in regeneration, and the final salvation of believers, are doctrines which I believe, and consider as inclusive of all others" (*PA* 1:510). Thus far the heart of the Westminster Confession, but as Smith wrote in the *Edinburgh Review*, "It is impossible to arrive at any knowledge of a religious sect by merely detailing the settled articles of their belief."[30]

More than settled articles, the doctrines of providence, of total depravity, and especially of irresistible grace through the agency of the Holy Spirit produced a material world that needed to be made legible and accordingly required interpretation. The *Evangelical Magazine* read God's handwriting in even the most common things and occurrences: a young man takes the Lord's name in vain, and a bee stings him on the tongue; a minister plays cards, and when it is his turn to deal, he drops down dead; and so on. Inheritors of the seventeenth-century Calvinistic tradition, which saw a world full of wonders, and of the eighteenth-century Enlightenment view that the universe was a theocentric pattern of intricate order and causality, the Baptists could find providence in catastrophes (such as the fire that consumed the mission press in 1812) as well as the quotidian.[31] It is commonplace to associate these perspectives with an antimaterialism that denigrates sensory vision in favor of the abstract sense that looks through matter to the invisible spirit of God. Materiality in this way becomes fundamentally textual in that it exists in order to be transformed through processes of reading into signs, whether in the form of things, events, systems, scripture, or our own bodies.

And like most zealously held positions, antimaterialism inspired not just repulsion from but also fascination with its contraries. For Carey in particular, divinity was manifest in both wonders and systems, a sense that produced an obsession with the material world, a classificatory zeal, and made him one of the premier botanists and natural historians of the early nineteenth century. According to an account reproduced in George Smith's *Life of William Carey* (1885), "Classification is his grand hobby, and wherever anything can be classified, there you find Dr. Carey; not only does he classify and arrange the roots of plants and words, but visit his dwelling, and you find he has fitted up and classified shelves full of minerals, stones, shells, etc., and cages full of birds."[32] Michael Gaudio has remarked that by the late seventeenth century the "Calvinist impulse to know the true, immaterial nature of divinity by knowing its opposite began to spark an interest in the comparative study of religions—that is, in the treatment of the various religions of the world as so many material practices."[33] Like plants and words, Hindu theological and devotional systems, and the "idolatrous" objects that accompanied them, were subject to the mission's classificatory zeal, be it in the pages of Ward's *Account of the Writings, Religion, and Manners of the Hindoos* (1811) or in the cabinets of the museum in Bristol.[34]

Philosophers of religion Moshe Halbertal and Avishai Margalit foreground a simple but important premise: "different concepts of God create . . . different concepts of idolatry."[35] In the Baptists' relations of their encounters with Hinduism, the concept of God as demanding acceptance of human depravity and the disciplined reading of the self and the world for signs of grace and providence informs their evangelical understanding of idolatry. According to Calvin in *Institutes of the Christian Religion*, the second commandment "restrains our license from daring to subject God, who is incomprehensible, to our sense perceptions. . . . Whatever visible forms of God man devises are diametrically opposed to His nature."[36] For the Particular Baptists, we can and must scan the world and our hearts for signs of grace and providence—indignant bees, fatal decks of cards, plants, fires, tears. Through the work of the Holy Spirit we may see the written words of God all around us and in ourselves, but we do not ever see *him*: as God says to Moses, "Thou canst not see my face: for there shall no man see me, and live" (Exod. 33:20).[37] God's face is not to be seen with the eyes, but his words are to be read in the sights of every thing. The biblical injunctions against "strange worship," Halbertal and Margalit point out, can apply either to the worship of false gods (in which case it is the gods who are "strange") or to the attempt to worship the true God through false means (in which case it is the worship that is "strange"), with the latter usually involving an emphasis on ritual over belief, on the visible over the invisible.[38] More so than Marshman and Ward, let alone Thomas and Fountain, Carey was remarkably open-minded, and he was also sufficiently influenced by the writings of Jones, Wilkins, and the Asiatic Society (of which he became a member) to acknowledge that according to the Hindu "Shasters . . . there is one great God, Omnipotent, Omnipresent, and Omniscient" (*PA* 1:19). But in the missionary writings the strangeness of popular Hindu worship in the second sense elevates ritual over faith, body over spirit, vision over language, and one kind of seeing, *darshan*, over another, reading.

Scholar of comparative religion Diana Eck explains the role of *darshan* in Hindu devotion as follows: "When Hindus go to a temple, they do not commonly say, 'I am going to worship,' but rather, 'I am going for *darśan*.' They go to 'see' the image of the deity. . . . The central act of . . . worship . . . is to . . . behold the image with one's own eyes, to see and be seen by the deity."[39] Before the *darshan* of the god is possible, the *murti* undergoes a ceremony called *pranapratistha*, which endows the image with life (*prana*, literally "breath") and sight, making divinity and agency immanent in materiality. Worshippers at religious festivals are thus described as *darshan*-seekers. This form of seeing is central to the devotion encountered by the missionaries and understood by them as idolatry, seemingly the pure antithesis of reading and reflecting upon scripture.

The Baptists found an ally and an antagonist in another opponent of idolatry, Rammohun Roy. Rammohun agreed that contemporary, popular Hinduism had devolved into idolatrous superstition but differed in his syncretistic and pluralist assertion that all religions contained the seeds of truth and that there were more ways to God than grace through the mediation of Christ. Although the iconoclastic Rammohun and the Baptists coincided in their opposition to idolatry, he saw their Trinitarianism as sheltering the worship of God in material form. He also came to object to their paternalistic dogmatism, especially following Marshman's angry response to Rammohun's attempt to divest the New Testament of "mystery" in *The Precepts of Jesus* (1820). In the third number of the *Brahmunical Magazine, The Missionary and the Brahmun* (1821), he isolates a tension within the orthodox Christian response to idolatry. Missionaries, he argues, advocate the "adoration of Jesus Christ as the very God in the material form" yet at the same time insist that they "worship God in spirit." This spiritual worship, they claim, distinguishes them from idolaters and justifies their evangelicalism. But if "we admit that the worship of spirit possessed of material body is worship in spirit," Rammohun continues, "we must not any longer impute idolatry to any religious sect, for none of them adore mere matter unconnected with spirit. . . . Do the idolaters among Hindoos worship the assumed forms of their incarnations, divested of their spirit? Nothing of the kind! Even in worshipping idols Hindoos do not consider them objects of worship until they have performed Pranpratishtha or communication of divine life."[40] Rammohun's rejection of God's material form bolstered the Baptists' attacks on idol worship, but at the same time it affronted their Christology, undermining any absolute differentiation between idolatry and the spiritual word of God.

A different challenge was articulated by Rammohun's orthodox Hindu opponent and Carey's own former chief *pandit* in the Bengali-Sanskrit Department of the College of Fort William, Mrtyunjay Vidyalankar. It was easy for evangelicals to secure scripture from idol so long as they understood contemporary Hinduism to claim materiality to be the only medium in which spirit could be apprehended. In his *Vedanta Chandrika* (1817), Mrtyunjay agreed with Rammohun "that a stone or piece of wood was certainly not God," as David Kopf writes, but went on to take a position different from that of either Rammohun or "the truly traditional pundit. He did not view image-worship as a necessary evil but as a necessary symbol."[41] Because to the Baptists the word of God is both a legible sign and a visible mark, in the material form of the book as in the incarnate body of Christ, the reciprocal vision accorded by popular Hinduism to either matter connected with spirit or necessary, symbolic objects was deeply threatening to the evangelical habitus, calling for commitments of energy beyond debate and persuasion and ultimately accounting for the new lives gods would lead in England.

In their tracts, preaching, oral and printed debates with interlocutors in Bengal and Britain, and methods of publishing and distributing print, Hinduism could thus serve as the material practice against which the Baptists defined Protestant Christianity according to a distinction between Christian legibility and Hindu visuality. For just as the missionaries attempted to proclaim Christ crucified, their shorthand for the all-inclusive story of grace freely given to sinful human beings through the mediation of divine sacrifice, they also sought to transform the material media and physical practices through which beliefs are communicated and instilled. Although they were well aware of the classical Sanskrit literary tradition—in 1801 Carey was appointed head of Sanskrit, Bengali, and Marathi at the College of Fort William, and after he finished work on the Bengali New Testament, he set out upon *A Grammar of the Sungskrit Language, Composed from the Works of the Most Esteemed Grammarians* (Serampore, 1806) and *The Ramayuna of Valmeeki, in the Original Sungscrit, with a Prose Translation* (Serampore, 1806–10)—they understood contemporary Hinduism as eschewing its own *sastras*, or scriptures, for an idolatry of the eye, which was not the eye of a reader. This is another reason why Rammohun came to pose such a challenge, as a Hindu devoted not just to theological debate in pamphlets and newspapers but also to the free distribution of print: to remind Hindus of their own monotheistic tradition, he wrote in the preface to his *Translation of an Abridgment of the Vedant* (1816), "I have, to the best of my abilities, translated this hitherto unknown work, as well as an abridgment thereof, into the Hindoostanee and Bengalee languages; and distributed them, free of cost, among my own countrymen, as widely as circumstances have possibly allowed."[42] Persisting in their distinction, the Baptists sought to replace idols with books, substituting one kind of object for another, and one form of sight for another. In the replacement of image with print, print serves as both practice and metaphor, to recall Thomas's terms during his conversion experience, for the "new object" beheld, through the intercession of grace, "in a new light."

But the relations between Calvinistic signs and print suggest a more complicated distinction between legibility and visuality than one based on sheer opposition. Baptists typically distributed their tracts while preaching in public, especially at sites of what they saw as idolatrous devotion, where they would attempt to put printed matter into Hindu hands. As Leslie Howsam, Anindita Ghosh, and Leah Price have explored, when print is distributed for free, it produces relationships between and among author, disseminator, text, and reader that are distinct from those produced by a literary market.[43] The movements of both books and idols were part of an integrated evangelical circuit of communication,[44] to apply Robert Darnton's phrase to the practices of the Baptists as publishers and of their prospective converts as "readers" in Bengal, on the one hand, and to the collection and transportation of devotional materials from Bengal to Bristol, on the other.

Descriptions of the process by which Baptists attempted conversion from idolatrous worship reveal the sites and structure of this circuit, upon which their theory of conversion relied. "I need abundance of grace, in order to communicate divine things to others," wrote Carey, for "faith is a communicative principle, and . . . true believers will as naturally speak of the things of God, as a fountain will call forth streams" (*PA* 1:171). From the evangelical perspective, obstructing the "communicative principle" of living faith from flowing between God (as Trinity), Holy Spirit, missionary, missionary press, distributed book at a site of idolatrous worship, prospective convert as "reader," and back to God was the popular Hindu devotional practice of viewing objects similar to the book but with one chief difference: in idols—not "things of God" but things of earth— spirit was supposed to be immanent and actually visible, not just legible, to the eye. The Baptists repeatedly refer to "carnality" as the triumph of the eye over the heart, the thing over the sign, the image over the text, and *darshan* over reading. Within the circuit at the point of distribution, furthermore, the idol did not just need to be removed; while its exportation created an absence to be filled by print distributed for free, its importation, as we will see, introduced a necessary presence in the form of the object's new life in England.

The market for books as commodities was driven by a different set of desires, which it will be helpful to consider briefly before turning to the evangelical circuit in greater detail. Perhaps the most self-consciously commodified form in the early nineteenth century was the literary annual. When D. L. Richardson launched the first such work written and published in India, the *Bengal Annual* (1830–36), he knew that he was competing with imported books, which as Europe goods held the distinct advantage of providing a physical connection to home. Exilic nostalgia became the keynote of the *Bengal Annual.* Although Richardson included works by several writers who were born in India and had never been to Britain (Harachandra Ghose, Kasiprasad Ghosh, Rae Man Kisen, and the East Indian Henry Derozio), the new annual was otherwise accurately described by the *Oriental Literary Observer* as "the production of exiles, written by the sojourners in a foreign land, and filled with remembrances of their native country, sweet, sad, and tender, and with passionate longings after home."[45] The first issue opened with an essay titled "The Literati of British India," in which Richardson acknowledged that such a volume of poetry and some prose would not be standard fare for his market, which was primarily but not exclusively (as I discuss in chapter 4) in Bengal: "There is no want of readers in India, and . . . books are in abundant demand. But what books are they? With exception of some professional works. . . , the literature in request, consists, almost exclusively, of Reviews, Magazines, and Novels."[46] Periodical works, which always held a prominent place in newspaper advertisements, would let readers be as *au courant* with metropolitan life as the sea voyages would allow. And the way periodicals satisfied nostalgia and kept the exiled consumer up to date was by reproducing substantial excerpts from other books, connecting the displaced reader in Little London to the broader mass reading public fashioned in the pages and prose stylings of the reviewing industry, as Jon Klancher has described it.[47] The structure of the periodical reminds us that the market for print involved a continuum between and among texts as objects of consumption, from the stark columns of invoices exhibited for sale in newspapers to the organization of the literary reviews to the epigraphs and other intertextual citations in pamphlets, tracts, and books. Across great distances these objects spoke to, and asserted their value in relation to, one another.

For the Calvinistic Baptists, books, reading, and seeing could and often did function otherwise. Within the "missionary culture of print," Ogborn writes, "printing and printed objects could mean something quite different than for the Calcutta commercial press."[48] Like the gift of grace itself, their printed objects were freely given, not offered in exchange. And their theological and evangelical engagements with books as *non*commodified materials were profoundly related to their encounters with that other class of signifying, circulating objects of sight, which they consistently depicted as inhibiting the communication of grace from God through the mediation of Christ and the work of the Holy Spirit to the individual heart of the aspirant.

Like idols, books to be distributed for free held a special place in evangelical rhetoric. "A bible is the great thing that is wanted by us" (*PA* 1:144), wrote Carey in March 1795. By 1800 they had a Bible in the form of the Bengali translation of the New Testament, of which they printed and distributed two thousand copies, along with five hundred copies of the Gospel of Matthew and "large editions" of two tracts written by the mission's *munshi*, Ram Basu.[49] In *Vindication of the Hindoos* (1808), Charles Stuart joined the chorus of opposition to the mission that grew steadily between the Vellore mutiny of 1806 and the renewal of the East India Company's charter in 1813. Calling for a "complete suppression" of the Baptists' activities, Stuart argued that while the missionaries "remain . . . in any part of Bengal; UNDER THE EXERCISE OF THEIR OWN DISCRETION, they will find no difficulty in circulating their admonitory tracts among our subjects. Many thousands of these tracts have already been dispersed, in every direction, throughout the country."[50] As Anindita Ghosh points out, according to the tally of Bengali works distributed from the Serampore Press provided by *Brief View of the Baptist Missions and Translations* (1815), 24,398 tracts were given away between 1812 and 1814, far outnumbering other print formats.[51]

The results of their circulation are difficult to ascertain with confidence, but the rhetoric of the following missionary account from 1806 offers a graphic illustration of the moment of distribution within the evangelical circuit of communication. Carey writes,

> We have had opportunities of circulating tracts, pretty extensively. Two of us with some native brethren, have been at a large assembly of natives at Sooksanger, met for the purpose of worshipping Gunga. Great numbers received the tracts with apparent eagerness, and many swam after the boat for them, when they came away. We have also distributed a considerable number at the annual resort of the people, to the idol Zuggunath, near Serampore. Some of the Brahmans, and others who are influenced by them, tear the tracts which they have received, to pieces, and throw them about the road; but we rejoice in the hope, that many of them are carried away by those who may perhaps read them, and pray that the blessing of God Almighty may attend them.[52]

The observed fact of biblioclasm stands in stark contrast to the hope that many tracts may be carried away and perhaps read, and anecdotes abound of tracts being burned and paper being used "for domestic or sale purposes."[53] Claudius Buchanan similarly reports passing through "a crowd of people listening to their preaching" and seeing "several persons having the printed papers of the Missionaries in their hands. Some of them were reading them very gravely; others were laughing with each other at the contents, and saying, 'What do these words mean?' "[54] In spite of destruction and laughter, both of which reduce signs to unmeaning matter, the missionaries persisted in their faith in the efficacy of print and the pricelessness of the gift freely given: "We have put into the hands of many heathens a treasure greater than that of diamonds" (*PA* 1:203). In the language of the *Periodical Accounts*, the distribution of print, ostensibly the means, often seems to outweigh the end of conversion itself: "No powerful families, no whole villages have yet been conquered; no one god has been trampled upon, and no single idolatrous poojah stopped. . . . Yet we may say on the whole, that God has done much toward the salvation of Bengal. Near 1500 Bengalee new testaments have been distributed; many, many thousands of gospel tracts have been dispersed" (*PA* 3:23–24).

Among the most popular works distributed were tracts composed in Bengali verse by the missionaries' "native brethren": Ram Basu's *The Gospel Messenger* and Petumber Singh's *Good Advice, The Enlightener,* and *Sure Refuge.*[55] According to the *Biblical Magazine* for 1802, which printed Marshman's translation of Ram Basu's poem in English couplets, "Several thousands of the original have been printed by the missionaries, and distributed among the natives of Bengal, who read it with great avidity."[56] Possession of print should ensure regular, direct, and individual access to the legible word. Yet nowhere in either the original Bengali, published as *Dharmma pustakera duta* (The messenger of the book of religion), or the English translation itself (ninety-six lines) does the verb "read" appear.[57] By the early nineteenth century in and around Calcutta there was a "a sizeable population that could read and write" in Bengali, primarily for commercial purposes, as Sanskrit and Persian were the more prestigious languages of religion and poetry. "But the written word was not available only to literate audiences," writes Ghosh. "It was accessible to even wider illiterate groups through communitarian ceremonial reading sessions and local performance traditions," especially the "*Kathakatas,* or collective narrative sessions, where religious works based on Hindu religious epics and mythology were read out by professional Brahmin narrators."[58]

What was unusual, then, was not reading or hearing others read but seeing the forms of print. When Carey relates hearing parts of the recently printed book of Matthew read aloud in a nearby village in November 1800, what strikes him is that "neither the reader nor hearers had seen a book till about two days before."[59] The use of Bengali verse for evangelical tracts represents a collision between two popular cultures of writing, one in which manuscripts or wooden tablets in the vernacular facilitate communication by the spoken word and one in which printed books "are carried away by those who may perhaps read them."[60] *The Gospel Messenger* was originally written in the vernacular and targeted readers as listeners. Even in its English translation, published to promote the mission's methods to readers in England, the poem crystallizes the tension within the evangelical project of distributing print in early nineteenth-century Bengal.

Instead of exhorting prospective converts to read the saving word of God, the messenger begins, "Hear, O ye people! with attentive mind—/ From Hell tremendous, how deliv'rance find," repeating the exhortation to "hear" throughout: "Hear, hear, ye people! hear with greatest care: / You who desire it, come—we'll it declare / . . . / Hear with your mind, would you escape from hell / . . . / Hear, men, this news; with strict attention hear!"[61] But if the spiritual message of the gospel is to be heard, not read, the physical book of the gospel, curiously, is not to be read either. When the physical book appears in the poem in the form of "the *great shaster*," it is to be held and seen, as the poem ends:

> Whoe'er by the *great shaster* have been blest,
> Embracing this, have thrown away the rest.
> Now, O Bengalees, in your tongue 'tis given;
> When printed off, you'll see this gift of heaven.
> If then you feel indeed a wish to hear,
> Come, and with earnest mind, we'll it to you declare.[62]

In order to be seen, the gift of heaven must first be "printed off," but the book never serves as the thing whose materiality is subservient to its legibility. Instead of replacing either the idol or the always absent false "shasters we have formerly possest"[63] with print that, like the body of Christ to the Calvinist and Trinitarian mind, should allow the elected individual to read the signs of freely given grace within his or her own heart, the act of seeing the book merely directs the viewer back to another sense, hearing, and to other human beings, the missionaries themselves, who will declare the gospel message. The book does not play the doctrinal role that it should within the evangelical circuit of communication. Juxtaposed with the idol, the freely distributed book should become the evangelical sign par excellence, the thing that manifests value not in its material and social relations to other things, whether through "strange worship" or exchange, but rather in its legible reference to spirit and the longing of the fallen heart to receive grace through it. No thing could live up to such a calling.

The evangelical circuit of communication also repeatedly breaks down or at least becomes uncertain at the point of distribution, where the missionaries proposed that the spiritual worship communicated by the legible texts they distributed should replace the idolatry commanded by Hindu scriptures, or "shasters." Possession of scripture as knowledge to be read and then held in the mind and heart assumes the prior possession of scripture as a thing to be seen. But while distributing tracts and attempting to engage Hindus in debates, the Baptists repeatedly ran up against the fact that few of their interlocutors would have accepted this initial premise or, indeed, have ever seen the sacred texts of Hinduism. Ogborn reminds us that "unlike the Europeans, and contrary to the assumed importance of the *śāstras*, many Brahmins saw writing as an inferior mode of preserving sacred knowledge, valuing instead particular forms of spoken repetition and memory work."[64] And Lata Mani writes that "the absence of opponents able to engage in the debates initiated by the missionaries did not prompt them to reconsider their assumptions regarding the dominance of scripture in people's lives. Far from it: to the missionaries, ignorance of scripture merely confirmed native degradation."[65]

But the gap in translation between "scripture" and *sastras*—the former thoroughly enmeshed in print culture by the early nineteenth century, the latter not—did more than confirm native degradation in the *Periodical Accounts* and other missionary writings; it also reinscribed the materiality of the freely given, legible book. Carey's journal describes his *"first . . . interview with the Hindoos,"* on 9 November 1793, as follows: "Two boats came to sell us fish; and Mr. THOMAS asked the man in one of them whether they had any shasters? The answer was, 'We are poor men—those who have many cowries (*i.e.* who are rich) read the shasters; but we do not know them'" (*PA* 1:161). Describing the Vedas, Carey complains that "not one in a thousand has ever seen . . . them. Nay I have found many Brahmins so ignorant that they have never seen their *own shasters*" (*PA* 1:130). Similarly, in 1796 Thomas records that after he preached, a Brahmin praised his discourse because it was "just like the *Hindoo Shasters*." Thomas asks him the name of the text to which he is comparing the gospel, and the *Periodical Accounts* reproduce the following dialogue:

A. It is the *Oggour Shaster.*

Q. Have you got it with you?—A. No.

Q. Have you got it in your possession at home?

A. No.

Q. No! Believe in it without possessing it! What would you think of my faith in the Bible, when I tell you that I believe it to be the *Word of God*, if I had not got one? (*PA* 1:283)

The word of God as book should be the paradigm of an evangelical perspective upon materiality according to which every object is a sign of spirit, of the presence or absence of grace. The reason the treasure is greater than diamonds should be that it is freely given and legible rather than merely fungible and visible. But when the missionary attempts to substitute the present, true book for the absent, false shaster, it is the very physicality of the book as something to be owned and seen that usurps its legibility and thus its truth. In this substitution, the nature of reading as the work of an abstract sense becomes absorbed in the rhetoric of possession and visuality.

For all these reasons, the Baptists' zeal for the printed word became suspect to their critics in both England and India, and incidents such as the following would have fed the suspicion. When the first New Testament in Bengali was printed and bound on 7 February 1801, "it was placed on the communion-table in the chapel, and a meeting was held of the whole of the mission family and the newly baptized heathen."[66] The book literally takes the place of the body of Christ, a pattern that raised accusations of "Evangelical Idolatry," in the title of a sermon preached by "a Clergyman of the Established Church" in 1829: "The Bible is not the Saviour. . . . The Bible, with all its glorious doctrines, is not our resting place, is not our soul's home. It describes our resting place . . . but the rest itself, the haven where the tempest-tossed bark would be, is the God of the Bible."[67] Ogborn is absolutely right in saying that "for the missionaries, printing was a sacramental act,"[68] but the circulation of print opens the sacramental nature of the act itself, as well as the objects of its production, to uses and interpretations beyond the scope or control of doctrine. For example, and a vivid one at that, when the press first arrived in Mudnabatty, according to J. C. Marshman the "crowds of natives who flocked to see it, hearing Mr. Carey's description of its wonderful power, pronounced it to be a European idol."[69]

According to the foundational logic of conversion, the idol and the book, *darshan* and reading, have nothing in common. Hindus, the missionaries believed, needed both to see differently and to see different things. To convert subjects, in other words, they found that they also had to convert objects. When Fountain announced that he intended to send a box to Bristol in 1798, his enthusiasm spilled over into an "ideal excursion" in which he imagined the triumph of Christianity over Hinduism and Islam:

> I see Hindoo pagoda's [sic], and Mahomedan mosques all destroyed! Where they stood, christian temples are erected, in which Jehovah is worshipped in the beauty of holiness. The horrid music is heard no more! The frantic dance has ceased! Instead thereof the sanctified heart bounds with sacred pleasure, and the tongue is filled with the high praises of god. The dreadful exploits of devils deified are no longer the burden of the song; but the unparalleled exploits of grace divine! (*PA* 1:423)

He then concludes, "All the idols of the heathen are famished! The Lord and his Name are One in all the earth" (*PA* 1:423). The reference to Zephaniah 2:11 ("The

Lord will be terrible unto them: for he will famish all the gods of the earth") at the conclusion of this iconoclastic reverie is telling. The daily ritual cycle of popular temple worship involves the recitation of mantras, dressing and bathing (*abhisheka*) of the deity, and the reciprocal offering and receiving of food (*prasada*).[70] In order for idols to vanish, to see and be seen no more—in order for *darshan* to give way to reading and the idol to give way to the book in which "The Lord and his Name are one"—they must be famished, starved of the food that they reciprocally consume and return. But Fountain's excursion is truly ideal, and idols neither would nor could simply starve and vanish. Instead, they could be transported and converted. As we will see next, Baptists repeatedly depict the transportation of *murtis* from Bengal over the ocean and into the museum of the Bristol Baptist College as a kind of reverse *pranapratistha*, desacralizing matter and turning idols into blind artifacts, transforming objects of *darshan* into objects of curiosity and iconoclastic zeal.[71] Their circulation thus made room for reading in India while generating evangelical energy and support for the mission in England. Freely distributed print in Bengal, in other words, needed a museum in Bristol.

The Museum of the Bristol Baptist College and the Service of Idols

The attempt to Christianize, domesticate, and desacralize Indian religious objects by transporting them to a museum reveals the contours of a distinct form of early nineteenth-century cultural exposition.[72] Following Theodor Adorno's influential and controversial claim that museums "testify to the neutralization of culture,"[73] theorists of later nineteenth- and twentieth-century art museums have evoked dynamics of "decontextualization"[74] or "detached mastery,"[75] often as Foucauldian strategies of power within what Tony Bennett has called an "exhibitionary complex."[76] But the exposition found in the missionary discourse concerning idolatry was anything but dispassionate or neutralizing. Highly charged and fraught, evangelical recontextualizations of Hindu devotional materials explicitly and openly associated the transportation and transformation of objects with the conversion of subjects. Neither the heterogeneous cabinet of the Enlightenment antiquarian nor the public space of the cultivated bourgeois individual, this form of display insisted that the conversion of people from idolatry to Christianity depended on the conversion of things from idols to artifacts.[77]

The nature of the conversion depended once again on vision: the evangelical museum displays its spoils as evidence that if objects of Indian religious belief and practice could be transformed into English artifacts, then it will also be possible to bring Indian subjects to see things with English eyes.[78] At the same time, however, expositions of transported materials demonstrate the difficult nature of the translation. If English and Indian eyes could only be brought to see the same dead things, English and Indian hearts would also come to feel the same living faith.[79] But just as the missionary accounts contain numerous instances of supposed converts returning to their native religion—"bowing down to idols again" (*PA* 1:64–65)—it repeatedly seems that gods exposed as "primitial spoils" refused to subside into mere objects of antiquarian curiosity, aesthetic representation, or ethnographic knowledge.[80] Instead, in England they came back to life in new forms, either in the museum or on itinerant fundraising tours, where, like distributed books in Bengal, they played a necessary but fraught role in the evangelical project.

In London one could easily see objects of Hindu devotion at the British Museum at Montagu House, the India Museum of the East India Company at Leadenhall Street, the London Missionary Museum at Austin Friars, near Moorgate, or the India Museum at Pall Mall.[81] Although much of the British Museum's collection was not on display in the period and the Company's India Museum focused mainly on items of trade (especially textiles) and natural history,[82] the main attraction at the London Missionary Museum was its exhibition of idols "supplied chiefly by the Missionaries employed by the London Missionary Society" (fig. 9):

> The most valuable and impressive objects in this Collection are the numerous, and (in some instances) *horrible*, IDOLS, which have been imported from the South Sea Islands, from India, China, and Africa; and among these, those especially which were actually given up by their former worshippers, from *a full conviction of the folly and sin of idolatry*—a conviction derived from the ministry of the Gospel by the Missionaries. It is hoped that a view of these "trophies of Christianity" will inspire the spectators with gratitude to God for his great goodness to our native land, in favouring us so abundantly with the means of grace, and the knowledge of his salvation.[83]

Military men and Company administrators such as Edward Moor and Charles "Hindoo" Stuart had been bringing or sending back religious artifacts for some time (fig. 10),[84] but the transportation of idols became a serious part of the nonconformist missionary endeavor. In this respect, London followed where Bristol led. Soon after Carey and Thomas arrived in Bengal in 1793, John Ryland shared letters he had received from the two with the Independent minister David Bogue.[85] Two years later, Bogue became a founding member of the Lon-

Fig. 9. The Museum of the London Missionary Society, on Bloomfield Street. Lithograph published in the *Illustrated London News*, 25 June 1859. © Look and Learn, Peter Jackson Collection, The Bridgeman Art Library.

don Missionary Society, formed in emulation of the Baptist Society. Because of the leading role of Bristol's Dissenters in the early evangelical movement, the library and museum of the Bristol Baptist College became a central site for Indian material culture outside the capital.

Founded by the 1679 trust deed of Edward Terrill, which provided support for the Baptist minister of Broadmead Church to "devote three half-days a week to the instruction" of students, not exceeding twelve, who would be recommended by the churches,[86] the Baptist College was reorganized in 1770 with the formation of the Bristol Education Society. Administered by the society thereafter, the college moved to North Street, where it remained until 1811, at which point it moved to Stokes Croft. The origin of the college museum lies in the bequest of Andrew Gifford (1700–1784), whose father and grandfather were both Baptist ministers in Bristol.[87] Having served briefly as assistant minister at Broadmead in 1728–29, Gifford left Bristol to become pastor at Little Wild Street in London. A devoted book collector, numismatist, natural historian, and antiquarian whose second wife brought him a fortune of £6,000, Gifford was appointed as-

Fig. 10. Eighteenth-century bronze cast of Ganesa (*left*), currently at the British Museum, from the collection of Edward Moor and used by Moor for the frontispiece of *The Hindu Pantheon* (1810) (*right*), one of Southey's sources for *The Curse of Kehama.* © The Trustees of the British Museum. All rights reserved.

sistant librarian at the British Museum in 1757. In 1780 he donated £100 to the college toward the building of a room to house his collection, and upon his death he bequeathed "to the Society of Baptists at Bristol for the education of young men for the ministry . . . my books, library, pictures. . . . Also my curiosities, natural history and the rest of my museum I hereby give to the aforesaid Baptist Academy or Museum at Bristol."[88] The college accounts estimated the value of the bequest at £1,000.[89]

In no small part due to the shipments of Indian materials from Bengal in the first decades of the mission, guidebooks throughout the nineteenth century included the museum on the itinerary of any Bristol visit (fig. 11). *A Chronological Outline of the History of Bristol and the Stranger's Guide through the Streets and Neighbourhood* (1824) begins with a series of "Walks and Rides" for each of eight days. The "Fifth Evening's Walk" takes the pedestrians along Stokes Croft to "The Baptist Academy."[90] There, they would view the museum's prize posses-

Fig. 11. Postcard showing the Bristol Baptist College museum ca. 1960, when it would have looked much as it did after the college moved from Stokes Croft to Woodland Road in 1916. I am grateful to Roger Hayden for this postcard.

sions, including a miniature portrait of Oliver Cromwell, claimed to be "one of the few authentic likenesses in existence . . . [for which] exquisite . . . portrait the Empress Catherine of Russia offered 500 guineas";[91] an original letter signed by George Washington; and the Tyndale Bible of 1526, a rare edition of the first New Testament to be printed in English (purchased by the British Library in 1994 for over a million pounds). Items of considerably less worth ranged from the curious to the gross to the downright implausible: "A Cat found dead, and dried up in a wall with a Rat at her feet"; "A Ball of Hair form'd in a Cow's Stomach"; "A Piece of an Apple Tree, planted by Sir Isaac Newton's father . . . from which an apple falling on Sir Isaac's head, gave him the first idea of the doctrine of Gravitation"; and "A Specimen of Bitumen from the Lake of Sodom."[92]

These artifacts were displayed alongside another class of curiosities, bearing a qualitatively different kind of value. Enough of them had arrived by 1803 to warrant some expense for their accommodation and display: in the annual *Account* of the Bristol Education Society for that year, under disbursements is listed, "Case for the Hindoo Idols," at a cost of £7 17s. 6d.[93] The collection continued to grow. For 28 September 1805 Ward noted, "This evening I proposed to the Brethren to send a set of . . . ornaments . . . belonging to the Hindoo superstition . . . to the Bristol Academy, . . . to which they agreed," and on 30 January 1807 he wrote, "Yesterday a box was sent to England containing Shanscrit Grammars, Ramayun's, &c. I have sent some things for the Bristol Museum."[94] The value of these materials in the museum was the work they did to publicize the mission, earning the college the following entry in John Evans's popular guide *The Picture of Bristol* (1814): "In Stoke's Croft a spacious building has been lately erected by the Bristol Education Society, as an academy for preparing young men for the exercise of the Christian ministry among the Baptists. . . . In the museum are several objects of curiosity and interest, particularly a collection of Hindoo idols . . . which have been sent hither at different times by the Baptist Missionaries in India."[95]

The point of this publicity was to affirm that just as the living word of God was bringing heathens to the truth in Bengal, idols were achieving their true state as dead objects to be viewed in a cabinet in Bristol. The correspondence surrounding the transportation and display of idols, however, reveals a rhetorical slippage by which things retain agency and missionaries figuratively affirm what they seek to deny. Nigel Leask has pointed out the recurrence of prosopopoeia in Fanny Parks's discussions of her collection of idols,[96] and something similar is at work in the missionary writings (and, as we will see, in Southey's *Curse of Kehama*). According to Ward, describing the *pranapratistha* ceremony, which makes the *darshan* of the god possible, "The consecration of an image is accompanied with a number of ceremonies, the most singular of which is that of conveying sight and life to the image, for which there are appropriate formulas, with prayers, inviting the deity to come and dwell in it. After this ceremony, the image becomes sacred."[97] The transportation of idols from India to the Bristol museum should reverse this process, but when Bristol appears at the end of one fascinating entry in Ward's journal for October 1805, the materializing, domesticating, and desacralizing impulse of the entire description is abruptly undermined.

As we saw above, on 28 September 1805 Ward proposed that the brethren send a set of "utensils belonging to the Hindoo superstition, & other curiosities; to the Bristol Academy"; on 20 October he still had idols and Bristol on the brain:

> Our brother Jaggernaut [Dass] before his baptism had hung up in durance vile his image of Jaggernaut in a tree joining his house. One day they ran short of wood to cook with. What was to be done? One of them (either the husband or wife) advised to cut up the god & teach him to boil the pot. The other objected & advised to get rid of him in a more honourable way, viz. by throwing him into the river. The other argued that they really were short of fuel; that Jaggernaut was good dry wood & would burn well, & therefore it was best to turn him to some useful account. This

argument prevailed, & Jaggernaut (the Lord of the world) was cut in two, & half of him was used in boiling the rice of his once devoted worshippers. To this very image these two had prostrated themselves, & they had performed his worship, & regarded him as a god. I hope to preach in this brother's house on Lord's-Day, & if I can lay hold of the other half of Jaggernaut I will send him in triumph to Bristol.[98]

There is a distinct form of exposition and desire at work in the discursive world of the early nonconformist evangelical movement. Recall that according to the catalog of the London Missionary Museum, the "most valuable and impressive" idols in its collection were "those especially which were actually given up by their former worshippers, from *a full conviction of the folly and sin of idolatry*—a conviction derived from the ministry of the Gospel by the Missionaries." Sending Jaggernaut "in triumph to Bristol" is of course a figure of speech, but the passage brings to mind Mitchell's observation that "the best evidence for the life of images is the passion with which we seek to destroy or kill them. Iconophilia and iconophobia only make sense to people who think images are alive."[99] There is a persistent tension, in short, between domesticating assertions that one half of the god is "useful" as nothing more than fuel fit for boiling rice and an implicit knowledge that the other half of "this very image" to which "these two had prostrated themselves" will continue to have a value in the Bristol museum beyond its place in a merely aesthetic or antiquarian economy.

The nature of that value in England emerges in the story of one shipment that probably did not end up in the museum itself but did travel along the evangelical circuit of communication in a revealing way. In a letter of 25 December 1815 Joshua Rowe, missionary in Bihar and Bengal from 1804 to 1825, wrote from Digha to John Saffery, Baptist minister in Salisbury and the Wiltshire agent for the Bristol Education Society:

> Balak Dass . . . has professedly renounced heathenism, but we fear he has not yet fled to Christ. He gave me his *household* gods, which are very small, and made of brass. I have delivered them to a Mr. Boilet, one of the brethren in the 14th regiment, who . . . is returning to England, and has promised to leave them with Mr. Burls, for you. I must refer you to brother Ward's work on the Hindoos for a particular account of them, and only add a few remarks by which you may know them. They are five in number, and you may put them all in your waistcoat pocket. The largest, on one knee, with a tail, is *Hunooman* (monkey); that upon all fours, is *Gopal*; that with full breasts and a flat crown, is *Seeta*, a female; that with a sugar-loaf-cap, is *Ram*; the other has three united together. As you look at them, facing you, that on your right hand, is *Juggunnath*; that on the left, is *Buluram*; and that

in the middle, *Soobhudra*, Juggunnath's sister. These gods have been in the possession of this poor man about forty years. He has taken them [on] two pilgrimages
to Juggunnath's temple, in Orissa. He used to bathe and worship them regularly
every morning and evening; and when he sat down to eat, these gods were placed
along in a row before his food: ere he partook of it, he would put his hands together,
and prostrate himself before them, addressing them in such language as the following: Ram Khao (eat), Hunooman Khao, Juggunnath Khao, Seeb Khao (all eat);
after this ceremony, he would eat his meal.[100]

This letter provides an opportunity to consider the persistence of the "social life
of things," to borrow Appadurai's phrase, in spite of the missionaries' endeavors to reduce objects to lifeless materiality by transporting them, in this case,
from a world of ritual devotion to a minister's waistcoat pocket. It also initiates
a trajectory that can be followed: Balak Dass's gods travel from his house to England, where their new social life generates funds and evangelical energies that
travel back to Bengal, to the mission, and to the Baptist Mission Press, completing their part of the circuit.

If Saffery did take Rowe's advice and consult Ward's *A View of the History, Literature, and Mythology, of the Hindoos* (1815), he would have found the following:
"The Hindoo is taught, that the image is really God. . . . In the apprehensions of
the people in general, therefore, the idols are real deities; they occupy the place
of God, and receive all the homage, all the fear, all the service, and all the hon-
ors which HE so justly claims."[101] Thus Carey, having witnessed a scene of devotion in 1793, reported that although the "general opinion of the learned is, that
the idols are only images," nonetheless "the Brahman . . . who attended this ceremony, told me plainly that *this image was God*" (*PA* 1:131). What Rowe and Ward,
and Carey before them, object to is the life of the object within the devotional
economy of *saguna brahman*, or the personal worship of and interaction with
material forms of God with attributes. (Balak Dass's domestic devotions here
take the specific forms of *abhisheka* and *prasada*.) But the attempt to remove the
objects from this economy and transfer them to an antiquarian one in which
things are matter devoid of spirit founders when the objects seem to revive in
their new context. For these particular idols sent to Saffery in fact embarked on
a new existence not as dead "trophies of Christianity" to be mounted and displayed in the enclosed space of a museum cabinet but as circulating, animated,
and animating pieces of fund-raising propaganda. "These idol gods are arrived,
and in the possession of Mr. Saffery," mentioned the *Baptist Magazine* after reproducing Rowe's letter.[102] They would have arrived in Salisbury in mid-1816,

and on 22 May 1817 John Dyer wrote to Saffery, "I go to Newbury . . . on Saturday, & stay two or three days with them to make their annual Missionary Collection. They have never seen your little Idols, & if they are with you now, & you could trust them by coach, I think they might do service at Newbury."[103]

The service they will do at Newbury suggests that they bear a unique form of value. This value, I think, has everything to do with the peculiar place of idols within the economy of a commercial empire as circulating objects that, like distributed books, are not commodities. Mitchell remarks that "bad objects are not, at least to start with, commodities. . . . Instead, these are objects generally seen as worthless or disgusting from the imperial perspective, but which are understood to be of great and no doubt excessive value to the colonial Other."[104] Recall that one half of Juggernaut was converted from idol to use value—"Jaggernaut was good dry wood & would burn well, & therefore it was best to turn him to some useful account"—while the other half, if laid hold of, would be sent "in triumph to Bristol." Removed from the context of *saguna brahman*, in which they have devotional value, these "bad objects" circulate without accruing exchange value (at least in their initial acquisition), yet their circulation, mutability, and service suggest that they do accrue some new kind of value nonetheless, as if the excessive fetish value disdained by the Baptists as the product of superstition reappears in a different guise as the ambiguous evangelical value of desacralized artifacts whose very actions and sights will produce enthusiastic thoughts and sentiments in, and raise money from, the subjects who behold them.[105]

The use of idols to this end provided an opening for opponents of the missionary movement, one of whom described their service in telling terms. By 1820 the Baptists' techniques had been adopted by the predominantly Congregationalist London Missionary Society and the largely Anglican Church Missionary Society. At a meeting of the latter at Bridgewater on 5 July 1821, "some pointed allusions were made to a person returned from India, and then living in the neighbourhood, whose sentiments were said to be hostile to the object of the meeting."[106] That person, John Bowen, responded in the form of a pamphlet, *Missionary Incitement, and Hindoo Demoralization* (1821), in which he quoted extensively from the *Periodical Accounts* and described the Baptists' "mode of 'bombarding the strong fortress of Bengal'" as follows: "These gentlemen not unfrequently visit a village where they had never been heard of; and perhaps after preaching or reading for an hour or two, distribute a few tracts, and leave the neighbourhood, before an individual resident could thoroughly comprehend the purport of their visit" (36). The pamphlet, however, objects just as strenuously to missionary incitement in England as to that in Bengal, complaining of the "theatrical" nature of evangelical fund-raising: "Images of brass, said to be Indian Deities, are frequently displayed by the Missionary Collectors to their congregations. The dancing of these puppets up and down, coupled with a few rhetorical flourishes and violent gesticulations, is now become a fashionable mode of procuring an honest livelihood" (6).

To Bowen, the Baptists abroad and at home are every bit as bad as their prospective converts: in Bengal, they distribute tracts encouraging the gloomy superstitions of Calvinism; in England, their "experienced agents . . . rove about the country with pictures and puppets, which are distributed to the crowd, and sometimes exhibited from the pulpit, to delude the simple, and inflame the violent" (6–7). Like tracts, idols are not commodities, yet Bowen's anti-evangelical rant conflates spiritual with material goods, implying that they traveled along parallel circuits. "These firms," by which he means the missionary societies, "have all the paraphernalia of the counting house," he writes; "their well-drilled riders are dispatched with commercial punctuality to lay unsuspecting credulity under contribution, when its sympathy has been excited by exaggerated descriptions and theatrical display" (6). To the believer, on the other hand, it is the difference between what flows along the parallel trajectories that affirms the missionary project. In this light, Rowe's labors bring Balak Dass to renounce heathenism and give up his gods, which then set sail for England, where, refusing to play dead, they do service. To complete the circuit, the sympathy their service excites summons the faithful to missionary work and funds the further production and distribution of print, which produces the new convert, who renounces heathenism and gives his household gods to the missionary. The distance between Little London and Serampore, in other words, was the difference between goods and gods, both engaged in the unequal, recursive transactions of empire. And movement between Bengal and Bristol involved a violent historical process of renaming, displacement, and revaluation with respect to both things and the people who used them.

"Amenable to wooden gods": Evangelicalism, Idolatry, and *The Curse of Kehama*

While in Lisbon Southey was planning *The Curse of Kehama*, part of his "plan to render every mythology, which had ever extended itself widely, and powerfully influenced the human mind, the basis of a narrative poem," in Serampore the missionaries were beginning "to talk of baptism."[107] Krishna Pal (1764–1822), a carpenter and former adherent of the monotheistic Kharta Bhoja *bhakti* sect, which included both Hindus and Muslims, had agreed and been deemed ready to put on Christ.[108] The Baptist *Periodical Accounts* in general and the story of the first Hindu to be baptized by the Serampore missionaries in particular should join Southey's favorite early reading, Bernard Picart's *Ceremonies and Religious Customs of the Various Nations of the Known World* (1733–39), as the inspiration for his mythological poem.[109] On 11 December 1800 Ward recorded, "We yesterday fixed on the spot before our gate [*ghat*] in the river. . . . A difficulty has been started that if we baptize in the river the natives will think we suppose there is something sacred in the Ganga. . . . The word Christ is pronounced in Bengalee Kreest. Some mistook at first & thought we said Kreeshnoo."[110] Baptism on the banks of the Hugli could be slippery. On the one hand, in a moment reminiscent of the "boum" effect in E. M. Forster's Malabar Cave, the missionaries are concerned at the ease of mistranslation between antithetical things (water as God / water as symbol) as well as words ("Christ" slides through "Kreest" into "Kreeshnoo").[111] On the other hand, they attempt to counter the effect with a now familiar rhetoric of conquest that, in spite of itself, leaves the reader with an uneasy sense of equivalence in difference:

> We began with singing in Bengallee, "Jesus & shall it ever be," &c. Brother C. then in Bengallee . . . particularly told them that we did not think the river a Dhake, or goddess, but only water, & that the person about to be baptized from among themselves professed by this act to put on Xt. and put off all the debtahs; & all sin. . . . Creeshnoo went down, & was baptized, the words in Bengallee. . . . Ye gods of stone & clay did ye not tremble, when, in the name of the Father, Son, and Holy Ghost, one individual shook you as the dust from his foot?[112]

This baptism took place on 28 December.[113] "Yesterday was a day of great joy," Carey reports, "I had the happiness to desecrate the Gunga, by baptizing the first Hindu."[114] As with the transportation of idols, "gods of stone & clay," the consecration of the soul and the desecration of the thing are reciprocal acts. We have seen how the two were related within the evangelical circuit of communication. Southey's writings on the missionary movement and *The Curse of Kehama* also depicted conversion as a battle, but one in which bad objects suffered a different, less iconoclastic and more instrumental fate.

The warfare of Southey's Hindu epic echoes but revises the mythological, military language in which the Baptists express the victories of Christianity over Hinduism, their "singular phraseology," as Bowen called it,[115] according to which the missionaries' own actions and agency are displaced onto Christ. In the October following his baptism, Krishna Pal accompanied Ward "to see Kallee, at Kalleeghaut," just below Calcutta, where Ward told a group of Brahmins that the

Baptist missionaries "were come to this country to make known the true way of salvation. I then attempted to describe the fall, & consequent universal depravity of man. Then the free mercy of God in salvation, & the fruits of faith in Xt's holiness & heaven. . . . I am glad I have had an opportunity of preaching the gospel here, before the Great Goddess of the Hindoos. Our Saviour will certainly make her fall before the ark."[116] Quoting passages similar to these, Bowen complains that the missionaries see themselves as "'the soldiers of Christ,' who has by their means 'begun to bombard the strong fortress of Bengal, and will assuredly carry it.' And they assert that it is their business, 'now Christ has invaded Bengal, to allure Satan's soldiers to desert their General.'" For Bowen this displacement constitutes a form of idolatry in its anthropomorphism of God: "Unable to invest their ministry with any attributes bespeaking a supernatural origin, they have endeavoured to array the Deity in qualities which would tend to bring him nearer the standard of humanity."[117] His complaint about their methods recalls Raphael's struggle in book 5 of *Paradise Lost* with the "sad task and hard" of relating "To human sense the invisible exploits / Of warring Spirits." Raphael's risky solution, like Milton's own, is to delineate "what surmounts the reach / Of human sense . . . / By likening spiritual to corporal forms." Had the angel left the matter there, Adam might have mistakenly understood the delineation to be purely allegorical, so Raphael tentatively suggests a monistic understanding of the cosmos beyond either myth or allegory by closing his speech with an open and unanswered question: "though what if Earth / Be but a shadow of Heaven, and things therein / Each to other like, more than on earth is thought?"[118] The insistent dualism of the Baptists' phraseology collapses Christian allegory into Hindu myth, equating Christ and Kali by placing them on a battlefield neither sufficiently above earth nor sufficiently below heaven to justify the grace of the former or the dead materiality of the latter.

In the *Edinburgh Review* (April 1808) attack on evangelicalism that provided the occasion for Southey's defense of the missionary movement in the *Quarterly*, Sydney Smith touched a nerve by arguing that although the leaders of the evangelical party might at present make "great professions of toleration, and express the strongest abhorrence of using violence to the natives . . . we have little confidence in such declarations. We believe their fingers itch to be at the stone and clay gods of the Hindoos. . . . We again repeat, that upon such subjects, the best and ablest men, if once tinged by fanaticism, are *not to be trusted for a single moment*."[119] The material and discursive world of trembling "gods of stone & clay," of Jaggernaut sent "in triumph" to Bristol, of "Kallee . . . fall[ing] before the ark," and of fingers itching "to be at the stone and clay gods of the Hindoos" is also the world of *Kehama*, a poem in which Southey would introduce his heroine in a scene combining both idolatry and a figurative baptism, with the latter not necessarily involving the straightforward abandonment of the former.

In late 1799 Southey seemed to know little about Hindu devotion when Ryland showed him "an ugly brass epicene-looking God sitting cross-legged upon a peacock," but by 1804 he had learned much from an extensive course of study. Preparing to submit an essay for a university prize in the fall of that year, Henry Southey appealed to his older brother for help. The theme was to be "On the best Means of civilising the Subjects of the British Empire in India; and of diffusing the Light of the Christian Religion throughout the Eastern World."[120] In reply Robert sent a formidable syllabus, adding, "So long a list will not terrify you, if you have the true Southey pace in reading."[121] Because of the Southey pace in reading, and, as Thomas Love Peacock complained, the Southey penchant for wading "through ponderous volumes of travels and old chronicles," filling his commonplace book with "monstrosities," and then stringing them into epics,[122] his poetry can encourage a sense of the East in general and of India in particular as a patchwork of texts. Assisted by recent editions, criticism of his long poems has investigated the manner in which Southey encountered diverse mythologies, religions, and societies through a bewildering array of sources.[123] But Diego Saglia has rightly suggested that "Southey perceived the East as a reservoir of stories and objects," as "a material-discursive *continuum*."[124] In addition to texts, things played an important role in his works, especially *The Curse of Kehama*, which, along with his writings for the *Annual* and *Quarterly* reviews, was his principal contribution to the evangelical debates leading up to the renewal of the East India Company charter in 1813.

If the tenor of Southey's writings has seemed out of tune with what would become the dominant strain of Romanticism, one reason is that his poetry is not just full of the wrong things but in the wrong way. As Ernest Bernhardt-Kabisch wrote in 1977, Southey was "unable to break through to the new consciousness that we call 'Romantic,'"[125] which is a less interesting way of putting what De Quincey said—that although Southey composed his poems with mechanical regularity and therefore "undubitably they *ought* to have been bad, the world has pronounced them good. In fact they *are* good; and the sole objection to them is, that they are too intensely *objective*—too much reflect the mind, as spreading itself out upon external things—too little exhibit the mind, as introverting itself upon its own thoughts and feelings."[126] Like De Quincey in his "oriental dreams" of "unutterable slimy things" encountered in "Asiatic scenes,"[127] Southey repeatedly and obsessively fills his pages with the same "'bad objects' of empire" that consumed the Baptist missionaries and permeated evangelical discourse. But unlike De Quincey's, his reveries are not necessarily nightmares.

When John Hamilton Reynolds tried (and ostentatiously failed) to turn the corner from urbane rambling to an actual plot in "The Fields of Tothill" (1820), his imitation of Byron's *Beppo*, he instead took yet another comic detour to consider how his predecessors had set about the task of inventing incidents for their characters. After Scott, Hogg, and Moore, Reynolds arrives at the Laureate:

> Southey would put them into India quickly,
>   Make them amenable to wooden gods;
> But I, who do not wish to act so strictly,
>   Would not expose them to such solemn rods:
> They can't be foreign, but they might be sickly,
>   Though snug at home as peas are in their pods;
> There's something grand tho' in Hindoo mythology,
> Yet what to them or me is dusk Theology.[128]

Reynolds's phrasing vividly captures the widespread dissatisfaction with the mechanical nature of Southey's epics, especially when set against the Byronic pose of effortless spontaneity—"the fact is that I have nothing plann'd."[129] It seems that Southey molds his characters out of whatever is at hand and then rushes them into Asiatic scenes, where the first thing to be done is to "Make them amenable to wooden gods." But there is more to Southey's depiction of India, and specifically to his representation of the "dusk Theology" and devotional practices of Hinduism in the context of his poem about conversion. As necessary points of transfer within the evangelical circuit of communication and as highly charged sites of subject-object relations in Romantic-era imperial and religious discourses, idols call for a reassessment of Southey's response to the missionary movement and his critical and creative negotiations between the mind and "external things."

Writing in the *Eclectic Review* for 1811, essayist and former Bristol Baptist College student John Foster described his experience of reading *The Curse of Kehama* as involving a

> strong perception of the ludicrous, as we should feel in seeing a fine British fleet, in full equipment and appointment, sent out to India just for the purpose of bringing back, each ship, a basket of the gods of crockery, or some portions of that

material with which the Lama of Tibet is reported to enrich the craving hands of his devotees, and at length coming into the channel with flags flying, and their cannon thundering, in celebration of their cargo.[130]

For Lynda Pratt, "Foster presents Southey as a failed literary East Indiaman,"[131] and Tim Fulford has described how, according to Foster's simile, "in bringing the Lama's shit to Britain, . . . *Kehama* . . . was an importer of foreign bodies which undermined the oppositions (British/foreign, self/body, body/world) on which national and personal identity was dependent."[132] But we can also follow the other materials imported by Foster's actual and figurative East Indiamen. Like the ships transporting idols from Bengal to Bristol, Southey's poem becomes a vessel bearing "gods of crockery" from India to English ports, bad objects that are characteristically equated by Foster with excrement, pure waste, the residue of value.[133] Southey's imagination has crossed from England to India only to return with worthless things to be displayed before the eyes of the reading public. For Foster, their only value should reside in their ability to be exhibited as mere stuff (crockery or shit) to the Christian viewer. Southey's poem thus not only brings back the wrong things—idols instead of commodities—but then celebrates them for possessing a form of value that Foster and most others would deny.

Southey never went to India, but his poem did: in the *Calcutta Gazette* for 5 December 1811, Tulloh and Co. advertises "Southey's Keharna [*sic*]" among its books for sale.[134] The reception of *Kehama* reveals a strange recurrence of a trope according to which the poem was either a ship that (unlike Southey) had been there and back or a kind of telescope through which one could actually see the landscapes and people of Bengal. The perspective, however, seemed to shift radically for different viewers. Michael Franklin writes that *Kehama* "portrayed Hinduism as a cess of monstrous gods and demonic devotees,"[135] and for many in the early nineteenth century this description of the poem as a vision of Hindu horrors would have seemed perfectly accurate. For instance, Bishop Reginald Heber, anchored off Saugor Island upon arriving at the mouth of the Hugli River in October 1823, witnessed a sheet-lightning storm, which he described in a letter as follows: "When coupled with the unhealthy and dangerous character of the place, and the superstitions connected with it as the favourite abode of Kali, it was impossible to watch the broad, red, ominous light . . . and not to think of Southey's Padalon; and it luckily happened that 'Kehama' was on board, and that many of the party, at my recommendation, had become familiar with it during the voyage."[136] In an 1819 sermon, *On the Character of Idolatry*, E. W.

Stillingfleet laments the "self-immolated victim" who throws himself under the chariot of Jagannath, the "Moloch of the East," citing six lines from *The Curse of Kehama* (14.67–72) in support of his delineation of events six thousand miles away.[137] And when Ward turns to the same festival of *"Jugunnath'hu"* in Orissa, where the car of the god "has crushed to death hundreds of victims, perhaps thousands, and immolates a number every year," he adds, "Southey's description, in his [C]urse of Kehama, though not literally correct, conveys to the mind much of the horror which a christian spectator of the procession of the car cannot but feel."[138] In these instances, *Kehama* is a medium in which the English reader can see the "broad, red, ominous light" of a Bengali storm or experience the "horror which a christian spectator . . . cannot but feel" when viewing the Rath Yatra in Puri.

But there are other instances when Christian spectators view the spectacle and see a very different sight, one apparently far more amenable to the author. For Foster, the problem with Southey's poem was precisely that it conveyed not horror but rather sympathetic identification: "There are Marriataly, Pollear, Yama, Indra, Veeshnoo, Seeva, Padalon, the Swerga, &c.&c. celebrated in the most Christianized country of Europe, by a native poet."[139] Similarly, the anonymous reviewer for the *Monthly Mirror* went so far as to suggest "that Mr. Southey will never acquire all the fame, which his poem is capable of conferring, until he obtain readers who reverence and adore his deities; and that time can never come until *The Curse of Kehama* be translated into *Hindoostanee*."[140]

These responses demonstrate a confusion over the nature of the image, as if the poem, unlike the London Missionary Museum, failed to announce its perspective upon the true value of the *"horrible,* IDOLS" displayed in its verses. And the confusion persisted even though the poem did advertise itself clearly: the first sentence of the Preface reads, "In the religion of the Hindoos, which of all false religions is the most monstrous in its fables, and the most fatal in its effects, there is one remarkable peculiarity. Prayers, penances, and sacrifices, are supposed to possess an inherent and actual value, in no degree depending upon the disposition or motive of the person who performs them."[141] Nonetheless, as horrified as Southey is by what he understands to be the externality of caste, the severing of *punya* (merit) from moral value,[142] and the superstitious rites that reinforce the power of a Brahminical elite, when he turns to popular worship his intense objectivism produces a representation of idolatrous devotion as disconcertingly compatible with the feelings and language of the true faith to which Hinduism should be opposed.

Southey had a lifelong fear of and fascination with what he called "epidem-

ics of the mind,"[143] by which he meant various forms of fanaticism, irrational-
ism, and enthusiasm. The contagion could as easily issue from Jacobinism (the
original context of the phrase) as from Hinduism, Islam, Catholicism, Methodism, Calvinism, or popular superstition and folklore, precisely the subjects in
which Southey immersed himself as reviewer and as poet of *The Fall of Robespierre, Joan of Arc, Wat Tyler, Thalaba, Madoc, Kehama, Roderick,* and *A Tale
of Paraguay.*[144] As we have seen, in the first decade of the nineteenth century
Calvinist evangelicalism and Hindu idolatry collided in early British India, and
Southey could not look away. Over the course of this same decade, Southey became a true believer in the British Empire. Although never without anxiety over
the costs of colonialism, as Tim Fulford and Alan Bewell have shown, he could
still reply to his friend John Rickman's assertion that Indians benefited from
the British presence by simply agreeing that he too was "ardent for making the
world English."[145] On a personal level, he also became a true believer in the Protestant establishment, having abandoned Socinianism for a fairly comfortable
low Arian and Arminian home within the Church of England.[146] But although
he supported conversion, he was no proselytizer: unlike that of the Baptists, his
dedication to the propagation of Christianity, along with his defense of the confessional state, was fundamentally *instrumental* rather than doctrinal or even
salvific.[147] The Baptists' anxieties about idolatry were accompanied by an insistence that the end of all religion, regardless of specific eschatologies or myths of
temporality and transmigration, must be a single and singular Calvinistic form
of conversion leading to repentance, regeneration, and salvation. As Carey wrote
in late 1795 and repeatedly stressed, "Though the land is full of idols, yet I do not
know that the bulk of the people ever worship them with an expectation of obtaining any thing for *the soul*" (*PA* 1:227).

Southey, on the other hand, justifies evangelism in very different terms,
stressing virtue rather than salvation: "The moral institutes of Christianity are
calculated to produce the greatest possible good" (*AR* 1:207), he wrote in the *Annual Review* in 1802. "Why should we convert them?," he asked in the *Quarterly*
seven years later, answering, because "all the institutions of Christianity operate to produce the greatest possible quantity of virtue and of happiness" (*QR*
1:216). Instead of "dwell[ing] upon the great and obvious temporal advantages of
Christianity," however, the Baptists, according to Southey, demonstrate an "ab-
ject prostration of intellect to the dogmas of a miserable and mischievous superstition" (*AR* 1:216–17).[148] Consider his response in the *Annual Review* to one of
the many over-the-top episodes from the missionary journals. On 18 November
1800 Thomas recorded and translated "some of the expressions used in prayer"

by a sick student at Joshua and Hannah Marshman's school in Serampore: "Oh hell! Gnashing, and beating, and beating! One hour weeping, another gnashing! We shall stay there for ever! I am going to hell: I am going to hell! Oh Lord, give me a new heart, . . . and wash away all my sins!" (*PA* 2:162). His delirium ends on a lighter note—"They that will go to heaven: what a happy thing it is!"—and Thomas comments with a straight face, "Many other sweet and hopeful expressions were uttered by this lad" (*PA* 2:163). Having quoted the prayer, Southey writes, "Poor child! sick in bed, and to be encouraged in this dreadful delirium! This is, indeed, a religion for which bedlams, as well as meeting-houses, should be erected. If the mission to Hindostan were connected with nothing but the propagation of such a faith, we should hope the natives would continue to worship Veeshnoo and Seeva, rather than the demon whom Calvin has set up!" (*AR* 1:216–17).

Unlike Thomas, Southey would have been horrified by the idea that unconverted Hindus were condemned to an eternity of gnashing, and beating, and beating: "None but Catholics or Calvinists will now maintain the desperate doctrine, that salvation is exclusively attached to one system of faith, and that they who have never heard of Christ must be damned," he wrote in the *Quarterly Review*, concluding, "It were better to worship the Lingam than to believe this, if this belief were all" (*QR* 1:216). But this belief was not all, and Southey remained a strong and consistent supporter of evangelism: "There are but two methods of extending civilisation," he claimed in 1810, "conquest and conversion,—the latter the only certain one."[149] "It is only by christianizing the natives," he argued, "that we can strengthen and secure ourselves. . . . The interest and existence of the native Christians would be identified with those of the British government, and the church of India be truly the bulwark of the state" (*QR* 1:211). "Christianizing the natives" thus produces the greatest possible quantum of virtue and happiness for Indians and secures British interests. How to Christianize the natives becomes the utilitarian question that motivates Southey first in the reviews and then in *The Curse of Kehama*. To answer the question, Southey turns to mythology in part because in myths things are invested with spirit, with social agency allied to human virtue or vice within shared systems of belief and practice.[150]

One aspect of the Hindu and, specifically, Brahminical "epidemic of the mind," as Southey saw it, gripped his intensely objective imagination strongly. Referring to the loss of caste through accidents having nothing to do with conscience, he called it "an absurdity unparalleled in any other system": "the religion of a Hindoo does not depend upon himself; it is something independent of his thoughts, words, actions, understanding, and volition, and he may be deprived of it by violence, as easily as of his . . . wallet" (*QR* 1:208). The emphasis on externality in the maintenance of caste seemed to provide an easy opportunity, as Southey wrote in ugly terms, to "wash out" their old religion. Scott Waring had told a story of a Hindu who lost caste "by having been compelled . . . to swallow a drop of cow broth," which moved Southey to claim that "a new religion may not immediately be . . . sprinkled into them, but an old one could be washed out. It is but to boil a cow, and supply a fire engine with the broth, and you might baptize a whole Hindoo city out of the Braminical faith" (*QR* 1:210). These lines would seem to suggest that Southey agreed with the Baptists that ritual needed to be replaced by faith and should be retained only with the repeated insistence that ceremonies are purely symbolic. Recall that before Carey baptized Krishna Pal, he preached a sermon in Bengali in which he "declar[ed] that we did not think the river sacred—it was water only" (*PA* 2:127). But Southey in fact held a different view, at once more instrumental and more intense, of the interaction between the mind and nature within rituals and the mythological systems by which they are informed. "Carnality," in fact, has an important role to play, in keeping with Southey's repeated assertions that syncretistic relations between "gross" Hindu mythology and "higher" Christian spirituality can serve rather than impede the cause of evangelism. "If, from their gross notions of incarnations, and obscure fancies of a Trinity, their minds can be . . . dextrously led into the higher . . . doctrines of the Gospel, no teacher should decline it," he wrote in the *Quarterly*. Here, missionaries "have the *Trimourtee* and the *Avatar* ready, and the people are prepared to receive the Bible as the Shaster of the new cast" (*QR* 1:215).

In the reviews, Southey castigates the Baptists for heaping too many "thorns and brambles in the way to the strait gait." "It is not enough," he writes, "that a Hindoo is convinced of the falsehood of his own shasters, and the divine truths of Christianity, he must show that he has had *grace*, that he has experienced the *call*, the *new birth*" (*AR* 1:217). The baptism of Carey's own son was delayed "on account of what one of the Brethren thought a deficiency in his knowledge of his own depravity."[151] And the *Periodical Accounts* report that when a blind Brahmin approached Thomas to say "that he prays to Jesus Christ night and day," claiming "I am the servant of Jesus Christ, in my heart!," Thomas replied with a stern reminder that caste and Christianity were incompatible. "If Jesus Christ were to come and touch your dinner, you would . . . refuse to eat a morsel," he told the Brahmin, who "went away dejected" (*PA* 1:307). For Southey, this is more than just bad strategy, because the seeds of faith do not necessarily sprout solely from the heart. There is an interaction between the heart, the body, and the material

world that is distinct to Southey's objectivism and that invests ritual and ceremony with mythological meanings separate from either the Baptists' transportation and transformation of idols, on the one hand, or the carnality of Brahminical priestcraft as Southey understood it, on the other.

Unlike Thomas, who heaps thorns and brambles in the way of the blind Brahmin, "a catholic," Southey writes (of the mission in Tahiti), "would have gone
through fire and water to have sprinkled an infant in the name of Jesus Christ.
Let us not be suspected of attributing any mysterious importance to a symbolical ceremony; what we assert is, that the way to reclaim idolaters is by changing
their ceremonies: whatever they believe, so long as they are ignorant, they must
believe superstitiously; while they are ignorant, therefore, too much stress cannot be laid upon the ritual of religion" (*AR* 2:198). This was a consistent position for Southey, articulated in similar terms some twenty years later in *A Tale
of Paraguay*, in which "thou may'st [blame] the Papist's erring creed, / But not
their salutary rite."[152] He agrees with the evangelical insistence that there is no
"mysterious importance to a symbolical ceremony"—that rivers are not sacred,
they are "water only"—but whereas the Baptists see the symbolic ceremony as
an opportunity to desecrate the river and open the individual heart to the inner
call, Southey is much more interested in the habituation to specific feelings and
virtues (especially ones associated with domesticity and benevolence) caused by
ritual interactions between the heart or mind, the senses, and the world, idols
and rivers included. This habituation finds its clearest expression in his attempt
to handle idolatry with dexterity in *The Curse of Kehama*. While in the reviews
he asserts that "the way to reclaim idolaters is by changing their ceremonies," in
Kehama even idolatrous rituals, if performed with sincere feelings of piety, can
habituate an instrumental and salutary shift in perspective. There really are no
bad things, only different kinds of social agency.

Southey's goal in the poem, above all, is twofold: he seeks not just to depict
Brahminical religion as the essence of priestcraft and superstition but also to
show that popular forms of Hinduism contain implicitly Christian virtues and
beliefs, and that the majority of Hindus are therefore suited to evangelism.[153] As
he had suggested to his younger brother in 1804, "Superstition . . . even among
the Hindoos, will yield to interest; but it is the interest of all the oppressed castes
to become Christians, and the oppressors are everywhere the few. As for the
Brahmins, let them alone; convert those who pay the Brahmins, and who support them, and the business is done."[154] The poem thus involves a double movement. On the one hand, its numerous scenes of priestly ritual, especially in book
14 ("Jaga-Naut"), offer a negative and straightforward challenge to Brahminism

as naked deception for the sake of power and pleasure, and this gothic part of the work was most memorable for readers such as Heber, Ward, and others. On the other hand, ambiguities emerge in Southey's positive syncretistic attempts to display the popular Hindu religion "of all the oppressed castes," including even the worship of idols, as an implicit form of Protestant Christianity ripe for conversion. As Fulford points out, "Because following its action depended on suspending disbelief in the myths that provided its plot, *Kehama* placed its readers in a similar position to Indians believing stories about their gods and goddesses."[155] In particular, readers found themselves in the position of believing that austerities and sacrifices could grant power (*tapas*), that curses could act upon people and things, that rituals could be more than symbolic, and that idols might actually be able to see.[156] The poem is structured around two key scenes of idolatry. The first, Kailyal's escape in book 2, sets the plot in motion, and the second, Ereenia's voyage to Seeva's home on "Mount Calasay," initiates the conclusion, the final triumph of divine providence over the carnal fanaticism of tyranny, priestcraft, and wealth as combined in the figure of Kehama.

When we initially encounter Kailyal, Kehama is about to punish her and her father for the death of Arvalan: "It chanced that near her on the river-brink, / The sculptur'd form of Marriataly stood; / It was an idol roughly hewn of wood" (2.83–85). As Kehama's soldiers try to tear her away, Kailyal clings to this wooden idol of Marriataly, Sonnerat's version of Mariamman, or Sitala Devi, and Southey quotes Sonnerat's description of her as "the great goddess of the Parias," to whom was given "power to cure the small-pox" (200). The poet then asks, "Didst thou, O Marriataly, see their strife? / In pity didst thou see the suffering maid? / . . . for behold / The holy image shakes! / . . . / And now the rooted idol to their sway / Bends, . . . yields, . . . and now it falls. / But then they scream, / For lo! they feel the crumbling bank give way, / And all are plung'd into the stream" (2.103–14).[157] The outlines of the scene could have come straight from the pages of the *Evangelical Magazine*: soldiers assault an innocent maid who escapes when the wooden idol she clings to falls into a river! The interpretation would be that the things (wood and river) are fundamentally lifeless and that God has used them as the legible signs of his providence. But the poem at least raises the question of the idol's sight and agency in the causal relation between the two: "Didst thou, O Marriataly, see their strife? / . . . for behold / The holy image shakes!" Kailyal floats upon the idol until she is rescued by Ladurlad, and the poet again apostrophizes, "Yea, Marriataly, thou hast deign'd to save! / Yea, Goddess! It is she, / Kailyal, . . . / . . . / Upborne amid the wave / By that preserving power" (3.49–54). In a note to the early "Curse of Keradou" fragment we find that Southey first intended to have a crocodile rescue her from the stream (another scene that might have come right out of the *Evangelical Magazine*).[158] But the substitution of idol for crocodile raises the question anew. If the reader wondered before whether the wooden idol could see, is the reader now to believe the poet, who claims in his own voice that Marriataly has saved Kailyal, or is the "preserving power" an attribute not of the personal goddess but rather of dead wood, which providentially floats?

The point of the ambiguity here is not to suggest that idols might be gods, or that a miracle has taken place. Rather, in their interactions with people, and especially in their participation in the social interactions among people, objects for Southey can possess mythological meanings and agency that exceed their pure materiality: Kailyal speaks "with streaming eyes, / Where pious love and ardent feeling beam. / And turning to the Image, threw / Her grateful arms around it, . . . It was thou / Who saved'st me from the stream! / My Marriataly, it was thou!" (4.87–92). There is no denying the condescension, but "pious love and ardent feeling" beaming from the eyes, not the rescuing agency of the goddess, is Southey's keynote. In Kailyal's visual worship of the idol, the dread carnal idolatry of evangelical discourse here facilitates rather than interferes with the expression of Christian virtues: worship of the material form of Marriataly may be founded upon an "erring creed," but it is a blameless and salutary rite that habituates pious feelings, especially those of domestic affection between daughter and father. "Set up her image here, / And bless her for her aid with tongue and soul sincere" (4.100–101), says Kailyal, and then addresses the goddess, reminding her of past devotions, while "My father sate the evening rites to view, / And blest thy name, and blest / His daughter too" (4.123–25). If Hindus have "gross notions . . . of the *Trimourtee* and the *Avatar* ready" at hand for the missionary or Christianizing poet, they also have "gross notions" of idolatry ready.[159]

Two readers drew different conclusions from similar interpretations. John Foster decided that Southey had gone native: "The Christian poet (unless the appellation is really meant to be disclaimed) formally and seriously puts himself in the attitude of a devout pagan, and in his own person apostrophizes this member of the Indian pantheon, in language of reverence and kindness."[160] James Montgomery also noticed the sympathetic treatment of idolatry but resolved, not that Southey was a devout pagan, but rather that "Kailyal *is* a Christian," as Southey reports his response in 1812.[161] If this is closer to the case, then her own idolatrous devotion—not baptism or any form of evangelism—has been the means of clearing the thorns and brambles from her way to the strait gate. Although Southey begins the process of Kailyal's Christianization by immersing her in a river, the scene is not simply or even primarily a figurative baptism. No sermon is required here to remind the reader that the river is only water and that the idol is only wood.

Furthermore, Marriataly does not just channel the social affections of father and daughter: out of the entire Hindu pantheon Southey has chosen the goddess of smallpox to protect Kailyal from the contagious carnal fanaticism of Kehama and the Brahminical power that supports him.[162] Hindu idolatry, if practiced "with tongue and soul sincere," in fact serves as a vaccine against the epidemic of Hindu carnality and fanaticism embodied in Kehama and Arvalan, and in the Brahmins who abet their tyranny and lust.[163] Just as Kehama's curse upon Ladurlad rebounds upon the tyrant and thus "comes home to roost" (in the words of the mock Greek epigraph to the poem), when he infects Kailyal "with leprosy, / Which . . . / O'er all her frame with quick contagion spread" (19.8–10), the disease effectively inoculates her against Kehama's own desire: "Nor when she saw her plague, did her good heart, / True to itself, even for a moment fail. / Ha, Rajah! with disdainful smile she cries, / . . . / Shall not I thank thee for this scurf and scale / Of dire deformity, whose loathsomeness, / Surer than panoply of strongest mail, / Arms me against all foes?" (19.20–28). In *Kehama*, performing and viewing the "evening rites" of idolatry can be an instrumental practice in which pious affection, not infection, circulates and is strengthened, and even the "remarkable peculiarity" that Kehama's penances lend his words the power to infect Kailyal's body results in the protection of that body from violation and contamination. If Hinduism is an epidemic of the mind, then in the disease lies the immunity.[164]

While Kailyal's popular devotion represents one way to the strait gate, a path along which the social lives of idols in particular serve as signposts toward spiritualization and Christianization, Ereenia's encounter with the idol of Seeva on Mount Calasay in book 19 depicts a second way. This is the road to be taken by "higher" Hinduism, as indicated by syncretistic relations between the two religions. From the deistic perspective, that of John David Paterson and other members of the Asiatic Society, beneath layers of Hindu superstition lies a core of originary truth, a truth shared by (and usually better preserved in) reformed Christianity.[165] In "Of the Origin of the Hindu Religion" (1805) Paterson writes, "The first founders of the *Hindu* religion" confined their descriptions of the deity "to those attributes which the wonders of the creation so loudly attest: his almighty power to create; his providence to preserve; and his power to annihilate or change what he has created." Paterson then comments, "In fact, no idea of the deity can be formed beyond this: it is simple, but it forces conviction upon the mind. This simplicity however was destroyed, when they attempted to describe these attributes to the eye, by hieroglyphics."[166] These hieroglyphics are the pantheon of anthropomorphized gods and goddesses, as well as the material objects in which they are commonly believed to be immanent. But as I've mentioned above and as Paterson here affirms, over and against popular Hindu devotion the *Asiatick Researches* consistently acknowledged a more "pure," Vedantic form of Hindu theology asserting the unity and invisibility of God.

Ereenia articulates this "higher" Hinduism. When he ascends to the top of the mountain, he beholds a series of Saivite devotional materials—a silver bell, a broad table, and a celestial rose—as well as the idol of Seeva himself, the phallic *linga*, or "Emblem which no tongue may tell" (19.135–48), about which Ward could not restrain his "indignation at the shocking violation of every thing decent in this image." "Nor can it be ground of wonder," he added, "that a chaste woman, faithful to her husband, is scarcely to be found among all the millions of Hindoos, when their very temples are polluted with filthy images, and their acts of worship tend to inflame the mind with licentious ideas."[167] Southey's pious Ereenia, however, upon beholding the objects and the idol, first denies their immanence, addressing Seeva, "Thou art not here, . . for how should these contain thee?" (19.173). Next, in an intensely objective scene the poem literally makes the objects disappear. Ereenia

> struck the Bell, which self-suspended hung
> Before the mystic Rose.
> From side to side the silver tongue
> Melodious swung, and far and wide
> Soul-thrilling tones of heavenly music rung.
>
> . . . .
>
> [And] when that Bell had sounded,
> The Rose, with all the mysteries it surrounded,
> The Bell, the Table, and Mount Calasay,
> The holy Hill itself, with all thereon,
> Even as a morning dream before the day
> Dissolves away, they faded and were gone. (19.187–200)

The scene gives way to a "Primal, essential, all-pervading Light" (19.203), and a note in the "Curse of Keradou" fragment reads, "Show him x mythological form first—& let it pass away like a dream, leaving him in the Light."[168] By processes of sight and sound, of interaction with the mythological forms of rose and bell, Hinduism dissolves away even as the morning dream before the day of Christianity.

There is no evangelical iconoclasm here: the material objects seem to summon their own disappearance, freely tolling their readiness to give way to unmediated communion with a spirit that they have never contained, and never could contain. This scene functions as an "ideal excursion" very different from the one envisioned by Fountain, whose fingers itched to be at stone and clay gods. Pagodas are not destroyed, and idols are not famished, but the heart does bound "with sacred pleasure." Whereas the evangelical excursion would replace idolatrous communion with material signs of spirit, for Southey "mythological form" is a necessary part of a providential progression toward the ultimate spiritualization of materiality itself. As Shelley explained after his visit to Southey in 1811, "He *looks forward* to a state when all shall be perfected, and matter become subjected to the omnipotence of mind."[169] In the meantime, external things lead social lives not as idols in which divinity is immanent, nor as signs of grace, nor as fund-raising propaganda, nor as commodities, but rather as mythological forms whose agency constitutes and is constituted by our own social feelings and attachments.

Idolatry is thus a powerful context for Southey and his intensely objective form of Romanticism. *Kehama* is not an "internalized quest romance";[170] the mind of the poet does insistently spread itself out upon external things and does not introvert upon itself. But the external things are different from the dead, desacralized objects on which an evangelical God writes the signs of his grace. As Foster complained, in *Kehama* Southey "formally and seriously puts himself in the attitude of a devout pagan." Foster would have liked to be able to read the idol Marriataly's fall into the stream as a reverse *pranapratistha*, as a simple baptism into sheer desacralized wooden materiality to be displayed in the poem as in a museum case. I don't think, as Foster did, that the sole alternative to Marriataly's materiality is an idolatrous endorsement of her agency as a goddess, or a superstitious acceptance of miracles; rather, divine providence works through and in human perceptions of and social interactions with objects, which are therefore not purely symbolic, for our affections, relations, and stories flow through them. For Southey, between the extremes of Hindu carnality and evangelical spirituality, of things and signs, idols and books, we might say there are myths, the shared systems of belief and experience that set human societies on the path to civilization.

CHAPTER THREE

"I would not have the day return"

Henry Derozio and Rammohun Roy
in Cosmopolitan Calcutta

I am an East Indian, and therefore I ought to be here; I am interested
in the welfare of my countrymen, and therefore I ought to be here; I am
anxious to know what measures have been adopted to promote that welfare,
and therefore I ought to be here; I love my country, and therefore I ought to
be here; I love justice, and therefore I ought to be here.

—*H. L. V. Derozio*

Each week in the spring and summer of 1809 Krishna Pal would make his way
to the Lower Circular Road, well to the east of the fashionable houses on the Esplanade and Chowringhee (see fig. 1), to preach to the Hindu servants of a successful "Portugese [sic] Merchant and Agent."[1] His name was Michael Derozio (1742–1809), and for the preceding four years there had been an intimate
connection between Serampore and the family of this "Native Protestant," as
he was described in the St. John's baptismal register of 1789.[2] On the first of
January, 1805, Ward reports that this "person formerly a catholic, but from inquiry become a Protestant" contributed 1,000 rupees toward the building of
the Lall Bazar Baptist Church in Calcutta, twice as much as any other individual subscriber.[3] In early May 1807 Michael, his wife, Bridget, and two of their
four daughters were baptized by Ward in Serampore, and two months later the
younger of the two daughters, Maria, accompanied him in a one-horse chair to
Serampore to begin giving piano lessons to the missionaries' children. That August, Ward came to the Derozios' house to perform the first adult baptism in
Calcutta itself, of one John Axell, "a soldier in the Artillery in the fort."[4] The following March, Michael wrote to Ward to thank him for sending a Bengali translation of Job, the Psalms and Proverbs, Ecclesiastes, the Song of Solomon, and
the book of Esther, expressing the hope that the book would assist in the conversion of his *sircar*, or household steward. Michael lived just long enough to see
the birth of a grandson to his second son, Francis, and his English wife, Sophia

(née Johnson). Born on 18 April 1809, the child was Henry Louis Vivian Derozio (1809–1831), in whose poetry, according to Herbert Stark and E. Walter Madge, the late nineteenth-century chroniclers of the mixed-race East Indian community, "you will mark the melody of Moore, the mellifluence of Keats, the idealism of Shelley, and the tenderness of L.E.L."[5]

The description of Michael Derozio as a "Portugese Merchant and Agent" in the *Bengal Directory* of 1795 has caused some confusion about his grandson's ancestry. The twin facts that Henry's mother was English and that he identified with the East Indian community suggest that "Portuguese" in the case of his grandfather did not simply mean "from Portugal."[6] Instead, it indicated that Michael was the son of a European father and an Indian mother who had converted to Catholicism, and thanks to the work of Sakti Sadhan Mukhopadhyay, we can now for the first time give them names: Andre and Rita Derozio. Rita Derozio was listed in the burial register of St. John's Church as "a native Christian."[7] In *Letters from the Island of Teneriffe, Brazil, the Cape of Good Hope, and the East Indies* (1777) Jemima Kindersley works through the terminology while explaining the phrase "country-born": "Country-born women are the descendants of an European father, and what is called a Portuguese mother (which people I have before given you some account of)."[8] The earlier passage giving some account of these "black Portuguese" reads as follows:

> The Portuguese priests, of which there are many in India, receive all, baptize, and give them absolution: as soon as they are made christians they call themselves, and are called, Portuguese; the women change their dress, and wear something like a jacket and petticoat; and the men mostly affect to dress like Europeans. . . .
>
> The black Portuguese are a numerous people in all those parts of the country which have been long frequented by Europeans.
>
> They are mostly in mean situations, and are looked upon with great contempt by all the other Indians. . . .
>
> The reason of these black christians being called Portuguese, is from a custom which obtained at the time when the Portuguese were the only Europeans known in India; therefore all the proselytes became of their nation.[9]

And writing in Bengal, William Carey records that the children "of English, French, Dutch and Danes, by native women, are all called Portuguese" (*PA* 2:189). Andre Derozio may have been of European Portuguese descent—other than the name, there is no evidence for or against this supposition, and many Indians and Eurasians came to bear Portuguese names through intermarriage and/or conversion, voluntary or forced[10]—but the recent identification of Rita

Derozio as "a native Christian," Henry Derozio's own self-identification with the East Indian community, and the numerous racialized descriptions of him suggest that his "Native Protestant" grandfather Michael was "class[ed] . . . amongst the Portuguese" in the sense indicated by Kindersley.[11]

In Henry Derozio's brief but prodigious life of twenty-two years and eight months he would become an influential teacher, journalist, activist, philosopher, and poet.[12] Raised in Calcutta, he was educated from the age of six at the academy of the Scottish radical David Drummond on Dhurrumtollah Street. As Derozio's biographer Thomas Edwards writes, "Amongst many of the orthodox inhabitants of Calcutta the Scotch Schoolmaster was looked on as, if not an open disciple of David Hume, nevertheless, a very doubtful person in whose hands to place their children."[13] In 1823 Derozio left school and became a clerk in the firm of J. Scot and Company, where Derozio's father served as chief accountant. In the following year, however, the younger Derozio left Calcutta for Bhagalpur, on the Ganges between Calcutta and Patna in the district of Bihar. There he worked on an indigo plantation run by his uncle Arthur Johnson.[14] Having previously published two poems in the *India Gazette* under the apt pen name Juvenis while in Calcutta in 1822–23, in Bhagalpur he resumed the practice in earnest, and approximately twenty poems by Derozio would appear under that name in the *India Gazette* in 1825.[15] One of these was called *Don Juanics*, which, in four installments starting in late 1825, followed Juan to contemporary Calcutta. By April 1826 Juvenis had become sufficiently well known for an advertisement to appear in the *India Gazette* for the fashionable shop Mortimer and Co. quoting a note from the poem in which Juvenis writes, "The Beaux tell me that frills to shirts 'are not the go' now"; Mortimer and Co. heartily agree, "TO BE SURE THEY ARE NOT," recommending instead "our beautiful SILK NECK-KERCHIEFS."[16]

Back in Calcutta by November 1826, Derozio accepted an appointment as fourth teacher at the Hindu College, which had been founded in 1817 by a group of upper-caste Hindus "to bring Western science, liberal thought, and English language and literature to their sons, but they were at the same time firmly resistant to all threat from cultures alien to their own."[17] As a teacher at the college until his forced resignation in April 1831, Derozio educated a group of Indian students—the "Derozians"—who would drive the protonationalist reform movement later known as "Young Bengal."[18] In 1827 appeared *Poems, by H. L. V. Derozio*, printed at the Baptist Mission Press, which included some of Derozio's poetry from the *India Gazette*, along with much new work. In the following year he published his second volume, *The Fakeer of Jungheera, a Metrical Tale; and Other Poems*. He also wrote "Objections to the Philosophy of Emanuel Kant," which is not extant, along with brief translations from Pierre Louis de Maupertuis's writings on moral philosophy (published posthumously in the *Calcutta Quarterly Magazine*).

As we saw in chapter 1, in this period Derozio and the community that coalesced around him—through the Hindu College and the Academic Association, a debating club founded in 1828—came to play a significant role in the expansion of the periodical press in early nineteenth-century Calcutta. During and after his association with the college, he was involved in several newspaper enterprises, including the *East Indian*, written and run largely by Derozio himself.[19] In August 1831 he spoke publicly and passionately in support of the second East Indians' Petition advocating the redress of legal disadvantages suffered by the East Indian community, and in December of that year he announced his plan to deliver a course of lectures on law and political economy. They were never delivered, however, for the story comes to an abrupt end: throughout the preceding month a cholera epidemic had been claiming approximately fifty lives each day in Calcutta, and on the twenty-sixth of December Derozio would be included in this toll.

As the comparison of Derozio to Moore, Keats, Shelley, and Landon indicates, the reception of his poetry was dominated by a critique of imitation. "The brilliant hues of the Byronic sunset flung their glow over Derozio's sky," melodramatically wrote Stark and Madge,[20] and Derozio has been variously described as "a pigmented Keats"[21] and the "Keats of Anglo-Indian literature,"[22] while Kipling referred to him simply as "the man who imitated Byron."[23] Here is an account of Derozio's teaching from a piece called "Reminiscences of the Hindu College," printed in the *Calcutta Literary Gazette* in 1834:

> Sometimes he would read a canto of Byron . . . , and descant on the beauties of that celebrated poet; more frequently however would he analyze a stanza of his favourite Shelley, on whose metaphysical musings he was too wont to dwell. So great indeed was his partiality for the character of Shelley, that he adopted many of his sentiments, and transfused them also into the minds of his pupils; they who will take the trouble to read the brief memoir prefixed to Shelley's poems, will easily recognize, if they were at all acquainted with Derozio, his imitation of that unfortunate and wildly imaginative genius.[24]

According to a review in the *New Statesman* in 1924, "This Eurasian lad—disinherited, like all his fellows in India, of two worlds—was singularly gifted, and in his brief span of life he did an astonishing amount of work. But . . . [h]is verse . . . is all echoes—of Scott and Byron, Moore and Shelley. One is surprised, indeed, to find that the work of a sensitive youth of mixed race does not contain a single poem directly expressive of himself and his people."[25]

When placed in the context of the religious, social, and political movements of the late 1820s and early 1830s in Bengal, the imitative or, as I will call them, "citational" qualities of Derozio's poetry can be read as part of a significant and largely unacknowledged contribution to Romantic culture. For the most part, attention to Derozio's life and writings has focused on his role in the rise of Indian nationalism and the fraught matter of the advent of "modernity" in India.[26] Although the latter is an understandably resisted term for Indian historiography, it is an important one for any consideration of Romantic conceptions of time and history, of the relation of the present to the past, with the important caveat that, as Kathleen Wilson writes, modernity "is not one moment or age, but a set of relations that are constantly being made and unmade, contested and reconfigured, that nonetheless produce among their contemporaneous witnesses the conviction of historical *difference.*"[27] In this sense Derozio's imitations and echoes were in fact part of the newness of his writings, and were, I argue, "expressive of himself and his people" in terms of his and their specific convictions of their own historical difference and differences. For, as I hope to show, the citations of Romantic poetry that permeate his verse, like his evocations of India's past, enact a form of memory particular to the disinherited condition of Derozio and his heterogeneous community in early nineteenth-century cosmopolitan Calcutta.

Literary dismissals of Derozio's poetry as derivative and imitative correspond to historical assessments of the Hindu College and Young Bengal as Westernized and secularized. Although necessary, these terms need to be complicated. David Kopf sees Derozio as part of "a highly articulate intellectual tradition of extreme Westernization and accompanying cultural alienation,"[28] and it is commonly taken for granted that Derozio and his students were characterized by "their love of the West and intoxication with the English"; in other words, "Denationalizing emasculation was the prevailing characteristic."[29] Goutam Chattopadhyay has provided a spirited defense, and more recently Partha Chatterjee has described the Derozians as participating in "a distinct public sphere of anti-absolutist campaign . . . through associations of mixed racial composition."[30] This chapter provides an extended reflection on the overlapping questions of imitation, secularity, and Westernization in Derozio's writing, on the nature, in other words, of the modernity he and his students imagined for India in the early nineteenth century. That modernity, I propose, is manifested in his poetry by a distinct form of personal, social, and national memory. I will juxtapose the work of memory in Derozio's writings with another return to the past and a different temporality for the sake of reform, the modernizing religious and political program of the influential thinker Rammohun Roy.

For E. P. Thompson and J. G. A. Pocock as for Benedict Anderson, the homogeneous and secular time of capitalism is constitutive of modern nationalism.[31] Building on yet revising this insight, a wide range of theorists of temporality and the nation now understand modernity as inherently a "culture of incomplete modernization"[32] in which plural temporalities coexist in varied, shifting, unequal, and uneasy relations, a "dialectic of various temporalities."[33] In their self-consciously "imitative" modernity, Derozio's writings and community present the secular alternative to the spiritual reformist agenda of Rammohun, which would become associated with the Brahmo Samaj. Whereas Rammohun's "Hindu Unitarianism" employs a negative critique of Christian as well as Hindu forms of polytheism and a positive, syncretistic assertion of universal theism in the service of one modernizing program, citation in Derozio's writing fashions a different "singularity of the heterogeneous Indian modern."[34]

If imitation is the language of Little London—of a binary perspective upon metropole as body and colony as its reflection, with "influence" conceived as a unilinear transfer from the former to the latter—a more cosmopolitan model of circulation finds its literary analogue in a theory of "citation." The heterogeneous position produced by this recursive movement manifests the Anglophone liberal spirit associated with Byron and Shelley as well as expressions of local conflicts experienced by a diverse community of journalists, activists, and poets with the established authorities, both Christian and Hindu, in contemporary Calcutta.[35] Following the "cultural" approach outlined by Charles Taylor, we can consider Rammohun's and Derozio's (distinct) experiences of Calcutta as engaging with a modernity that is simultaneously imported and local. In other words, their alternative modernities are not constituted by a fundamentally (because implicitly) European "set of transformations that any and every culture can go through and that all will probably be forced to undergo."[36] Both Rammohun and Derozio, then, embrace new cosmopolitan worldviews and new local forms of sociability and publicity, driven in particular by the newspaper medium. Their different attitudes toward personal, cultural, and religious memory can open up a frame for reading alternative modernities not as modular imports from Europe but as a complex set of negotiations between tradition and progress, imitation and novelty, the past and the present. These distinct visions of Indian modernity, syncretistic and citational, constitute spiritual and secular responses to the cultural and religious encounters, and the forms of alienation accompanying them, which characterized life in "British India" of the early nineteenth century, especially with the entrenchment of nonconformist and Anglican evangelical-ism and the rise of English-language education after 1813.

As discussed in chapter 1, in newspapers and annuals a body of writing ap-peared that for the first time made it clear to both Britons and Indians that such things as an "Indian literature" in English and an "Indian public" could exist, and these possibilities came with real and clear political consequences in both Calcutta and London. The cultural work of Derozio and Rammohun participated in the development of these two categories, in ways unanticipated by and often unwelcome to metropolitan imaginings of India. At the same time, however, it is essential to see the cultural programs to which their heterogeneous commu-nities contributed as more than a reaction on the part of marginal groups on the periphery of empire to the metropolitan center of power and culture, a binary model that does not do justice to the conditions of early nineteenth-century Ben-gal. The creation of an Anglophone Indian literature and an Indian public, in other words, was both part of and distinct from metropolitan representations of India in particular and the East in general. Contemporaneity through references to fashion, on the one hand, and the syncretization of diverse religious truths, on the other, were more than just stylistic or spiritual responses of the East Indian and liberal Hindu communities within an empire that would relegate Indian-ness to a timeless past and an exoticized alterity; they also served to define and divide groups within Calcutta who were modeling themselves as modern both in concert and in conflict with one another.

East Indians and "Modern Hindoo Sects"

While Derozio's sonnet "My country! in thy days of glory past" (often referred to as "To India—My Native Land," a title assigned by a later editor) is almost too familiar in India today because of its status as a recitation piece for school-children, until recently his work as a whole has been neglected, and many Brit-ish and North American readers will be completely unfamiliar with it. Rosinka Chaudhuri's excellent edition (2008) should help remedy this situation, but be-fore turning to the argument of this chapter, which contextualizes and concep-tualizes the characteristic contemporaneity of Derozio's verse in order to read it against the grain of its reception, I would like to point out that there is an aston-ishing range to his writing in spite of his limited years. Standing in stark con-trast to the charge that his verse "is all echoes," his experiments with short lyrics that observe a limit of one sentence, for instance, are strikingly original. Five of these were published in D. L. Richardson's *Bengal Annual* for 1831. Included by Chaudhuri, these poems, along with all but one of the other pieces in the 1831

Annual, have not been collected in any prior editions, and most considerations of Derozio's work to date have therefore omitted his most mature and original writing. Chaudhuri insightfully suggests that the short lyrics approximate "the ideals of what would, a century later, be celebrated as Imagist verse," recalling "the Japanese Haiku, popularised by Ezra Pound at the height of the Modernist thrust towards concreteness in language."[37] She cites as an example the poem "Beauty," which reads in its entirety:

> Her eyes
> Swam in the light of her own intellect,
> And caught their lustre from her sinless thoughts. (314)

And then there are two short lyrics, "An Intelligent Countenance" and "Fears," both of which experiment with a condensed description of a moment or state of mind, on the one hand, and an informal conversational address to an implicit auditor or interlocutor in the second person, on the other. Thus the whole of "An Intelligent Countenance":

> ———— And as he passed from mood to mood,
> Each change was visible upon his face
> That varied like a dream incessantly,
> Yet spake that language which th' unlettered savage
> Has learned from Nature's teaching; and you saw
> His radiant mind illumining his eye,
> Like the light streaming through a lamp. (317)

The first word immediately opens the poem to implied speech that precedes the utterance, making the poem itself a slice of language and time taken from a larger conversation. And the shift of address in the third-to-last line then places the consciousness of the reader in this past that precedes the poem, giving the closing image the quality of a memory, one of those "points of existence," as Derozio writes in the exordium to "Moods of Mind," another poem that appeared in the 1831 *Annual*, "on which thought and feeling / Have left impressions of themselves, so deep, / That Memory in her backward journey meets / Them, and them ever, on her way" (312).[38]

Blindness to Derozio's originality is the obverse of the inability to look away from his work's "frequent resemblances to the other fashionable poetry of the day, to which his reading seems to have been unfortunately almost exclusively confined," as James Silk Buckingham wrote in his sympathetic review of *Poems* (1827) and *The Fakeer of Jungheera* (1828) in the *Oriental Herald*.[39] The *New*

Monthly Magazine similarly observed in its review of the 1827 volume, "The reading of the youthful writer, if we may judge from his work, has been hitherto principally confined to the poets of our own time."[40] From a different perspective, however, imitation as an insistence on fashion and contemporaneity can be understood as more than confinement—as, in fact, a self-fashioned modernity unique to Derozio's moment and milieu.

There is a revealing analogy to be drawn between the ways early nineteenth-century Protestant Britons viewed Indian religions through the lens of a Judeo-Christian understanding of the category of religion itself and the ways British readers attempted to assimilate English writing by Indians and East Indians. If evangelicals in particular tended to comprehend Indian religions and religious practices in terms of familiar assumptions about the nature of doctrine, scripture, devotion, and sectarian division, it is similarly the case that most British writers, readers, and reviewers could only see Indian Anglophone literature and literary culture in terms of the form, and forms, of European literature and literary culture. Protestant understandings of the relations between the individual, scripture, community, nature, and God, as we saw in chapter 2, shaped the evangelical response to Hinduism. European understandings of national literature, literary forms, and the reading public, we will now see, informed the ways Romantic culture responded to Indian literature in English. The questions that dominated the early nineteenth-century reception of Derozio and other Indians writing in English concerned equivalence and difference, and, understandably, it proved very difficult to consider the cultural work that this so-called imitative writing could and did perform.

If Derozio's writings were "expressive of himself and his people" in ways invisible to nineteenth-century readers, it first bears considering who "his people" were. He consistently referred to himself as an "East Indian," using the phrase as his pen name in the *India Gazette* after outgrowing Juvenis in 1826.[41] Although the term "East Indian" was imprecise and itself a subject of dispute—the two other most common expressions were "Eurasian" and "Indo-Briton," followed by "Anglo-Asian," "Anglo-Indian," and "Asiatick Briton"[42]—it usually indicated mixed-race Christians "descended in most instances," in the language of the first East Indians' Petition to the House of Commons (1830), "on the father's side, from the European subjects of the Crown of Great Britain, and on the mother's side from Natives of India; and . . . in other instances, they are the children of intermarriages between the offspring of such connections."[43] In their second petition (1831) they expanded on this language:

Your petitioners consist:—first, of those, or of the descendants of those, who have been born out of wedlock of native mothers, and who, although of Christian fathers, and united with Christians in faith, in language, in habits, in manners, in feelings, and in opinions, are yet regarded in the eye of the law as without the pale of Christianity. Secondly, that your Petitioners consist of those, or of the descendants of those, who though of native descent (some entirely and some partially) and born in wedlock, profess the Christian religion, and are assimilated to Christians by education, feelings, manners, and opinions, but are, in like manner, regarded by the law as aliens to the Christian faith.[44]

In the early nineteenth century this community held a peculiar position in social, economic, political, and legal terms. "Disinherited . . . of two worlds," as the *New Statesman* put it, they protested that "although . . . closely allied to the European and Native races, they are excluded from almost all those advantages which each respectively enjoys, and are subject to particular grievances from which both are exempt."[45] Along with "native" subjects they shared the disadvantage of exclusion from advancement within the military and civil services of the East India Company, while they did not share the advantage of eligibility for subordinate employment in the judicial, revenue, and police departments. And along with British subjects they shared the disadvantage of being prohibited from purchasing or owning land and from accepting employment with any of those Indian states "which still preserve a shadow of independence."[46] Their main grievance, however, concerned their status, or lack thereof, under the law. All residents, European and Indian, within the presidency were subject to English law administered by the Supreme Court, established by the Parliamentary Regulating Act of 1773. But outside the presidency (in the interior, or *mofussil*) after 1793, although all residents were subject to district Company courts administering Muslim criminal law and either Muslim or Hindu civil law, Europeans had the right of direct appeal to the Supreme Court.[47] Regardless of their Christianity, East Indians outside the presidencies accordingly found themselves subject to Muslim criminal law and either Muslim or Hindu civil law. Thus the petition complained that the East Indian community was effectively "without any written law, binding upon them in the most important relations of life."[48]

Derozio's emergence as a poet and public intellectual coincided with the coalescence of "our *East Indian Community*," as he described it in an essay titled "Education in India," published in the *India Gazette* in August 1826 (88). Because they were associated with both the European and Indian communities yet were neither identified with nor embraced by either, the stage preceding their formal petition for legal and civil rights necessarily involved a difficult discourse of self-definition. "They are a body, and yet they are *not* a body," wrote Derozio, explaining that "this involves a paradox. But it is cleared up when we remark that they are a body, inasmuch as their numbers are great and are becoming greater daily; and they are *not* a body, inasmuch as they do not seem to belong to each other" (88). In the late 1820s and early 1830s they came "to belong to each other." This process, in which Derozio's varied writings and activities played no small part, involved educational, political, journalistic, and literary connections between East Indians, Orientalist and radical Europeans, and the new groupings of elite "Hindu liberals," who were divided between the Derozians and the followers of Rammohun.[49]

The Indian and East Indian community associated with the Hindu College came to be known as "Derozians." Composed primarily of Derozio and his students—especially Krishna Mohun Banerjea, Mahesh Chandra Deb, Peary Chand Mittra, Tarachand Chakrabarti, Prasanna Kumar Tagore, Dakshinaranjan Mukherjee, Hara Chandra Ghose, Radhanath Sikdar, Rasik Krishna Mallik, and Ramtanu Lahiri—they were part of an extensive intellectual, political, and educational culture comprising Rammohun, Drummond, John Grant, David Hare, Buckingham, Dwarkanath Tagore, Henry Meredith Parker, H. H. Wilson, D. L. Richardson, J. W. Ricketts, Charles Pote, William Kirkpatrick, Emma Roberts, Kasiprasad Ghosh, and others. An important part of the Derozians' religious and ideological self-definition involved the attempt to draw clear lines among the "Modern Hindoo Sects," a phrase that served as the title of an 1831 article in Derozio's paper, the *East Indian*. According to this piece, "The Hindoos of Calcutta" were divided into three parties: "the orthodox," the "half-liberal" followers of Rammohun, and the liberal "young gentlemen educated at the Hindoo College."[50] The view of Derozio's poetry as merely responsive to European fashion fails to take into account the actual ways in which his professedly secular community understood and defined itself as part of a religious culture in ferment. Both the so-called half-liberals and the Derozians engaged in religious and cultural warfare against orthodox Christianity (Baptist and Anglican), on the one hand, and orthodox Hinduism (Sakta, primarily, and Vaishnava), on the other. Calling Derozio the "master-spirit of this new era" and "the oracle of Young Bengal," a retrospective "Review of Public Instruction in the Bengal Presidency" (1852) offers an account of the college and remarks that the students' "dislike of Christianity was second only to their dislike of Hinduism."[51] The followers of Rammohun and the Derozians therefore shared the same antagonists and similarly triangulated their polemics between themselves and both the Christian and Hindu orthodox parties of Bengal, with Rammohun allying himself with Unitarians.

Despite these two groups' common ground, however, the differences between them were significant. Of Rammohun the *East Indian* writes, "It is easier to say what [his opinions] are *not* than what they are. . . . Rammohun, it is well known, appeals to the *Veds*, the *Koran*, and the *Bible*, holding them all probably in equal estimation, extracting the good from each, and rejecting from all whatever he considers apocryphal. He has been known to attend and join in prayer both among Christian and Hindoo Unitarians."[52] The *East Indian* concurs with the assessment of the editor of the *Enquirer*, Derozio's student Krishna Mohun Banerjea, who describes Rammohun's followers as *"half-liberals"*: "Sheltering themselves under the shadow of his name, they indulge to licentiousness in every thing forbidden in the shastras, as meat and drink; while at the same [time] they fee the Brahmins, profess to disbelieve Hindooism, and never neglect to have poojahs at home."[53] In contrast, the *East Indian* describes the group of Hindus whom Derozio himself had educated and influenced as follows:

> The last party which we shall name is the smallest, but, in our opinion, the best and most talented. It is composed of several young gentlemen educated at the Hindoo College, bent upon removing from their countrymen the weight of superstition and ignorance under which they have long groaned, and honest enough to avow their sentiments whenever occasion requires. The Editor of the *Enquirer* is of this number, and Baboo Madhub Chunder Mullick is also of the same class.[54]

A later article called "Hindoo Liberals," which appeared in the *Asiatic Journal* in 1836, fills out the description:

> In matters of politics, they are all radicals, and are followers of Benthamitic principles. The very word *Tory* is a sort of ignominy among them. . . . With respect to the questions relative to Political Economy, they all belong to the school of Adam Smith. . . . The science of mind is also their favourite study. The philosophy of Dr. Reid, Dugald Steward, and Thomas Brown, being perfectly of a Baconian nature, comes home "to their business and bosom."[55]

While Rammohun's engagement with Christianity was rooted in comparative scriptural analysis and translation as well as both European and Indian discourses of religious syncretism (the subject of the next section), the Derozians were steeped in the Scottish Enlightenment and the European skeptical tradition: "Their notions of the religion of Jesus were drawn chiefly from Paine's *Age of Reason*, and the pages of Gibbon and Hume." And while Rammohun

sought to reform both Christianity and Hinduism in order to reveal the originary truths hidden beneath the corruptions of each, the Derozians "looked upon
Christianity as but a more refined system of superstition, and upon the Missionaries as cunning impostors, or ignorant fanatics—the Brahmans in short of the
Europeans."[56]

But the Derozians' irreligion requires contextualization in the same sense
as the "Romantic atheism" of the freethinkers described by Martin Priestman,
who warns that unorthodoxy can "be too easily taken for granted—either as a
guarantee of congenial writers' general up-to-dateness or as part of a conspec-
tus so broad as to merge them harmlessly into a 'philosophical' narrative removed from the hurly-burly of the religious and political pressures they actually lived through."[57] What this hurly-burly reveals is that Little London was not
surrounded by either "a sea of pagans" or Anglicized babus. In White Town and
Black Town alike, as we have seen, it intersected with and was undermined by
expressions of public opinion and power in newspapers and religious festivals,
and up the river in Serampore by an entirely different understanding of the circuits of empire, in terms of both what flows along them and to what ends. It also
encountered challenges in Rammohun and Derozio, both of whom it sought to
defuse by labeling them imitators, a charge whose acceptance or denial inaugu-
rated a limited range of perspectives on them as either Westernized imperial
toadies or countercolonial, protonationalist heroes. For most Britons themselves
in Little London, it bears pointing out, imitation was empowering, connecting
them and their microcosm to the world that implicitly emanated from and returned to England. For others, however, the adoption and adaptation of European fashions, ideas, and beliefs required different kinds of negotiations. As
with Rammohun's writings and other activities in Calcutta and England, we
can now understand Derozio's irreligion and "imitative" poetry as more than a
mere nationalist echo of British Romantic poetry and European skeptical, radical (utilitarian), and rationalist politico-philosophical thought. Both Rammohun's Hindu Unitarianism and Derozian memory, therefore, were part of the
simultaneously global and local transformations of early nineteenth-century imperialism, emerging from the circulation of people and ideas as well as from the
alliances and distinctions within and among Calcutta's radical European, East
Indian, and liberal Hindu communities.

Rammohun Roy and Hindu Unitarianism

Born in 1772 in the Bengali village of Radhanagar, Rammohun was the son
of devout Brahminical parents, Ramkanta Roy, a Vaishnava, and Tarini Devi,

daughter of a priestly Sakta family who converted for the sake of the marriage and would spend the last year of her life as a menial servant at the Vaishnava temple of Jagannath in Puri. Educated first at Patna, a Mughal center of culture, and then at Benares (Varanasi), Rammohun acquired Persian, Arabic, and Sanskrit. By the late 1790s he had settled in Calcutta and begun studying English, and between 1803 and 1815 he was associated with the East India Company in both official and unofficial capacities, as *munshi* (language instructor) to Thomas Woodforde, a collector, in Murshidabad in 1803 and 1804 and as *dewan* (manager) to John Digby, a Company writer. In 1803 Rammohun published *Tuhfatu'l Muwâhidîn* (A gift to monotheists), a Persian tract (with an Arabic introduction) critical of popular Bengali religions, but his writing began in earnest after 1815. Between 1815 and 1830 he translated the Upanishads into Bengali and English, initiated and oversaw several newspapers, literary societies, and educational institutions, engaged in public debates with both Christian and Hindu antagonists in defense of the inherent monotheism of both the New Testament and classical (Upanishadic) Hinduism, emerged as the prominent Bengali against the practice of sati, and was the motivating force behind first the Unitarian Mission of Calcutta and then, when that failed, the Brahma Sabha, or Society of Brahma, which in 1842 became the Brahmo Samaj, the Society for the Worshippers of the One True God. In 1830 he sailed for England as emissary of the Mughal emperor to the court of Great Britain, a visit discussed at some length in chapter 4. The "Luther of Brahmanism," as Coleridge had heralded Rammohun in an 1819 letter to Southey,[58] ultimately died in 1833 in Bristol, where he had worshipped at Lewin's Mead Chapel, the Unitarian meeting-house presided over from the 1770s to 1817 by Coleridge's friend and adviser John Prior Estlin.

In 1824 Rammohun complained in "A Letter on the Prospects of Christianity and the Means of Promoting its Reception in India," addressed to Henry Ware, a Unitarian minister in Cambridge, Massachusetts, that his "time and attention" had been "so much engrossed by constant controversies with polytheists both of the West and East."[59] Rammohun equates Trinitarian Christianity, especially in its Particular Baptist and Anglican forms, with corrupt Hinduism as polytheistic, by implication embracing a monotheistic combination of Unitarian Christianity and a purified form of Hinduism (based on scriptural interpretation of the monistic Advaita Vedanta school). But it is too easy to see Rammohun's English writings as presenting a synthesis of Christianity and Hinduism and comfortably corresponding to familiar kinds of European theism. As David Kopf writes, "It may be argued that Bengali Unitarianism was a movement parallel to the Unitarian movements in the West, but some caution must be exercised in this judgment for the reason that the conditions which gave rise to it in Bengal were not akin historically to those of England and America."[60]

In Rammohun's writings and activities we find a distinct form of syncretism emerging from the specific circumstances of Bengal in the years 1815–30. A brief taxonomical survey of syncretisms and the issues involved in the term's history will be helpful. Any attempt to apply the term is immediately complicated by the different disciplinary approaches to it taken by twentieth-century scholars. These approaches can be divided into two broad categories, the anthropological and the historiographical. Social scientists—sociologists, ethnographers, and especially social anthropologists—write about syncretism by examining specific syncretistic *situations*, whereas cultural historians tend to write about syncretism by studying specific syncretistic *methods*. For the former, syncretism is thus a kind of experience, a way of living, usually unexamined by the syncretistic believer, whereas for the latter syncretism is a kind of understanding or knowledge, a way of seeing, generally a conscious practice on the part of the syncretist. Thus, in order to understand the phenomenon, the social anthropologist might study Hindu-Muslim shrines in the Carnatic or Shinto and Buddhist elements of particular Japanese religious festivals, whereas the cultural historian turns to textual debates between Christian apologists, such as Prideaux and Warburton, and deists, such as Toland and Middleton, in the English context or to the Continental mythographical traditions of Banier and Dupuis, Herder and Schlegel.

The anthropological discussion depends on a basic definition. As Helmer Ringgren wrote in 1969, "Roughly speaking, . . . the term syncretism is used to denote any mixture of two or more religions, . . . where elements from several religions are merged and influence each other mutually."[61] After this, however, defining "syncretism" becomes increasingly "tricky," as André Droogers suggests: "Its main difficulty is that it is used with both an objective and a subjective meaning. The . . . objective meaning refers neutrally . . . to the mixing of religions. The subjective meaning includes an evaluation of such intermingling from the point of view of one of the religions involved. As a rule, the mixing of religions is condemned . . . as violating the essence of the belief system."[62] For most of its history the word has thus been a theological term of reproach, *ein theologisches Scheltwort*, in the phrase from the title of an influential 1979 article by Kurt Rudolph.[63] Following Rudolph, syncretism has come to "presuppose encounter and confrontation," and thus Droogers suggests that the "objective and subjective options are not the only alternatives. Syncretism is in the first place *contested* religious interpenetration."[64] Finally, and in accord with the emphasis on contestation, Michael Pye has proposed that syncretism is neither a "mere mixture," what theologians have tended to despise, nor a simple "synthesis," implying that "a new conclusion has been reached." Rather, "in a syncretistic situation . . . the potential claims of the constitutive elements are still alive."[65] But as Tony Stewart and Carl Ernst have indicated, there is a problem with the notion of "constitutive elements," which reveals an "underlying essentialist bias" in its presupposition of "original, essential, and axiomatic categories of cultural and religious experience." For this reason, syncretism is "beginning to lose favor as an explanatory model in critical scholarship. On examination every 'pure' tradition turns out to contain mixed elements; if everything is syncretistic, nothing is syncretistic."[66]

Over syncretistic situations and their constitutive elements the historiographical approach tends to favor syncre*tists* and their methods. In keeping with the landmark studies by Edward Hungerford, Frank Manuel, Elinor Shaffer, Robert Ackerman, and others, Albert Kuhn begins his treatment by writing that "syncretists . . . sought . . . to demonstrate the grand unity of all myths, to show that beneath the seemingly disparate and heterogeneous elements of ancient universal mythico-religious and historical traditions there lay a harmonious tradition."[67] By the early nineteenth century two distinct strands of historiographical syncretism had emerged. We can follow Kuhn in calling the first "sacred syncretism," which began with the seventeenth- and eighteenth-century English tradition of Christian apologetics in the works of Stillingfleet and Gale, Prideaux and Warburton, and culminated in the Romantic syncretists, such as Bryant and Faber, and the new biblical scholarship inspired by Lowth and the German "higher criticism" of Lessing, Herder, and Eichorn. From this perspective, all myths and religious systems could be traced back to one universal source, and that origin was firmly Judeo-Christian in character and deduced according to scriptural authority. The originary religion was thus providentially preserved in the revelation of the Old and New Testaments, whereas all other religions represented corruption, falsehood, and superstition. The other strand was the deistic or infidel "skeptical syncretism," which began with Herbert, Toland, and Bayle and continued through the Encyclopédistes, Volney, and Dupuis, returning to Britain in the works of Drummond and Higgins. From the skeptical perspective too, all myths and religious systems could be traced back to one universal source, but that source was not a proto-Judeo-Christianity but generally some form of universal theism. By this logic, Christianity would then be reduced "to the level of one among many pagan mythologies."[68]

In order to understand Rammohun's contribution to this tradition, we will need to keep both disciplinary approaches in play. To a far greater extent than any of his British contemporaries who were deeply influenced by the ideas of historiographical syncretism, such as Coleridge, Southey, Shelley, Bryant, or Faber, Rammohun lived the phenomenon in both of its senses. During the period, then, a syncretism emerged that was specific to the imperial conditions of cosmopolitan Calcutta in the years 1815–30 and most clearly articulated and lived in the writings and activities of Rammohun and his circle. This form, which needs to be thought of both as a syncretistic situation in the anthropological sense and as a (skeptical) syncretistic method in the historiographical sense, can be called "Hindu Unitarianism."

In anthropological terms, this position emerged from the encounter between the religions that the Calcutta Hindu elite (the *bhadralok*) as well as the less insulated and more "Orientalist" Britons of Bengal experienced as a fundamental aspect of their daily lives. Detailed analysis of this encounter has been performed by David Kopf, Bruce Robertson, and A. F. Salahuddin Ahmed,[69] involving discussion of the discourses, practices, and groupings associated with the Atmiya Sabha, or Friendly Society, debating club, the Hindu College, Rammohun's newspaper ventures, the Calcutta Unitarian Committee and the Unitarian Press, the Vedanta College, the project to translate the Bible into Bengali undertaken by Rammohun and the Serampore missionaries William Yates and William Adam (who, after his conversion to Unitarianism, became the "second fallen Adam"), and finally the well-documented Brahmo Samaj. Because of Rammohun's universalizing approach, Stewart and Ernst's cautionary note need not apply: he did not see "reform" as a synthesis between essential, autonomous elements but rather as a return to eternally recurring truths. What I suggest here is that Rammohun's Hindu Unitarianism was a distinct form of skeptical syncretism that developed a "tropicopolitan" incorporation of Hindu, Muslim, and Christian theologies into, on the one hand, a negative, historicized critique of polytheism, superstition, sectarianism, and priestcraft and, on the other, a positive, transhistorical theism.[70] And in this incorporation we find a model of personal and national progress that, while working against superstition and tradition, does not simply seek to convert premodern India into a mirror or microcosm of modern Europe but rather invests India with a spiritual modernity conceived in universal terms.

Hindu Unitarianism is a typical form of skeptical syncretism in that it depends on a universal primary religion and proposes that all contemporary religions have elements of truth that, if divested from superstition and error, could restore contemporary religions to the purity that is elemental to each and common to all. But whereas European skeptical syncretists tended to write from an unambiguous position of authority and to see themselves as facing pressure from one direction, that of established orthodoxy (*l'infâme*, singular), Rammohun was living and writing in the "tropicopolitan" world of early nineteenth-century Bengal. In other words, to apply Srinivas Aravamudan's terms, he was writing simultaneously from a position defined by the colonizer, a "fictive construct of colonial tropology" or "object of representation," and from the position of "an actual resident of tropical space,"[71] specifically that of a prominent Bengali authorized by education, linguistic abilities, caste, affluence, and influence. Furthermore, if we look beyond the Christian "sectarian" debates with Marshman set off by Rammohun's *Precepts of Jesus* (1820), we find that his Hindu Unitarianism applies syncretistic techniques to a plurality of contemporary religious beliefs and practices. Rammohun presents his religion in negative terms through an equivalence of heterogeneous religious errors. If Rammohun was fending off the Christian orthodoxies of Calvinistic Baptist missionaries as well as Trinitarian Anglicans, he was doing so by likening their beliefs to those of his other opponents, the Krishna-worshipping Caitanya-sect Vaishnavas, who, as mentioned above, made up one of the two principal orthodox Hindu communities of Calcutta. Chief among the religious truths syncretized in a positive manner by Rammohun's writings were the monotheistic and rationalist tenets of classical Hinduism and Unitarian Christianity, but his faith retained the claims of other constitutive elements as well: Robertson has described Rammohun's universal theism as "a latitudinarian composite of popular belief systems available to everyone in the . . . culture of his day," including "Christian, sufi, Sunni Islam, bhakti cult, and Vaisnava doctrines," along with "the teachings of such medieval north Indian saints as Guru Nanak, Dadu and Kabir."[72]

While Rammohun could happily skewer the arrogance of the evangelical premise and approach by equating Trinitarian Christianity with polytheism and idolatry, his support for some missionary activity, especially in the field of education, suggests a distinct understanding of conversion. In "A Letter on the Prospects of Christianity and the Means of Promoting its Reception in India," Rammohun responds to Ware's question regarding the success of Christian missions by quoting the Abbé Dubois, "who, after a mission of thirty years in India," reported that "it is not uncommon on the coast to see natives who successively pass from one religion to another, according to their actual interest. In my last journey to Madras, I became acquainted with native converts, who regularly changed their religion twice a year, and who, for a long while, were in the habit of being six months Catholic and six months Protestant." But Rammohun does not intend for Ware to conclude from this that Unitarians should refrain from embarking on missions to India. In response to Ware's question "Would it be useful to establish Unitarian Missionary Schools for the instruction of the children of natives in the rudiments of a European education, in the English language, in Christian morality, mingling with it very little instruction relative to the doctrines of Christianity . . . ?" Rammohun answers emphatically, "This would be certainly of great use, and this is the only way of improving their understandings, and ultimately ameliorating their hearts."[73]

But it becomes clear that Ware's Anglo-American Unitarianism and Rammohun's Hindu Unitarianism involve different understandings of conversion, and the difference, I think, rests on the more cosmopolitan perspective of Rammohun's syncretism: in Ware's view, Unitarians are best equipped to evangelize India, to transform Hindus into Unitarian Christians, whereas Rammohun believes that Unitarians would add to the enlightenment produced by the free exchange of modern ideas and the knowledge of different traditions. Religious doctrine and morality are universal, transcending national and racial distinctions; therefore, different faiths and communities can reform and refashion themselves in dialogue with one another. As Dermot Killingley writes, in Rammohun's mind travel and "knowledge of their own and other countries" would lead Indians to see the "absurdity of much current Hinduism."[74] And of all places suited to such enlightened exchange, Calcutta, writes Rammohun, is foremost: "Calcutta, the Capital of the British Empire in India, where the natives are more conversant with English, and frequently associate with European gentlemen, is, in my humble opinion, preferable as a field for such efforts to the rest of Hindoostan."[75]

The debates with Marshman over *The Precepts of Jesus* have been discussed many times, but an even more illuminating case, in which different forms of syncretism shape public religious encounter and conflict, is Rammohun's 1823 skirmish with Robert Tytler, a medical doctor in the East India Company's service and a professor at the Hindu College, who is usually described as some combination of "erratic," "eccentric," and "fiery." Conveniently for our purposes, six years earlier, in 1817, Tytler had appeared in print as a sacred syncretistic historiographer in *An Inquiry into the Origin . . . of Budaic Sabism . . . Comprising Observations Serving to Identify the Worship of Buddha with that of Siva.*

Tytler begins his *Inquiry* by distinguishing the implicitly French skeptical tradition from the English sacred one: "The labours . . . of learned men in other countries, from the . . . information derived from eastern sources, . . . tended to . . . sully the lustre of Christianity,—natives of Britain, on the contrary, have employed their oriental acquirements, for the purpose of . . . confirming the authenticity of Scripture."[76] As we would expect, Tytler aligns himself with the Asiatic Society, Bryant, Maurice, and Faber (2). The key to all mythologies, for Tytler, was the Flood: "Every idolatrous form of worship . . . refers for its origin to the . . . dreadful catastrophe of the Deluge" (24). Afterwards, during 367 years of "uniformity" between Noah and Abraham (3), natural religion took the form of worship paid to the "Divine principle . . . of *Regeneration*, that is *creation, destruction,* and *reproduction* . . . by which the Globe, emerging from the abyss of waters, ascended to the mansions of . . . Divine favour" (24). This originary religion divided into two main streams. First, in the West it "ascended" to the revealed truth of Judeo-Christianity. But "in the fertile regions of the East, . . . congenial to the first evolutions of the mind, but little conducive to superior mental improvement" (16), Providence "restrained the illumination of the Gospel from being generally diffused" (20). There the second stream flowed into what Tytler calls "Budaic Sabism," the ancient and natural worship of Siva, and from there both to contemporary Hinduism, which, according to Tytler, is so corrupt that it "hardly admit[s] of being recognised" as a portion "of the grand stream, flowing from the common source" (3), and to contemporary Buddhism, which is a far less corrupt though still "idolatrous . . . and degraded" (106) preservation of the originary and natural religion. Tytler, a fairly typical if stylistically eccentric sacred syncretist, was thus an ideal target for Rammohun's Hindu Unitarian assault, for the two in fact spoke different dialects of the same language. But while Tytler does react against modernity in a fairly straightforward way, Rammohun's tropicopolitan response does not.

Rammohun and Tytler's controversy unfolded between 3 and 23 May 1823, for the most part in the pages of a Calcutta daily, the *Bengal Hurkaru*. In his *Final Appeal to the Christian Public* (1823) Rammohun had invited responses from "any . . . of the missionary gentlemen,"[77] and Tytler accepted the challenge, offering to debate Rammohun either in public or in private. (During this period, Tytler was giving public lectures in justification of the Trinity at several houses in the White Town, just off the northeast corner of the Esplanade and a short distance from Rammohun's house, in the affluent Chowringhee section.) Rammohun declined, pointing out that he had solicited literary discussion with the missionaries, not debate with a layman, but condescendingly offered to publish anything Tytler should choose to send *if* it was accompanied by the signature of a missionary. Tytler, who had no fondness for the Baptists, took exception and wrote that his belief in the divinity of Christ in and of itself qualified him to take up the cause on his own. Rammohun then enraged Tytler by replying, "Whether you be a faithful believer in the Divinity of . . . JESUS CHRIST; or of any other mortal man; or whether a Hindu declares himself a faithful believer in the Divinity of his Holy *Thakoor Trata* RAM, . . . I feel equally indifferent."[78] Rammohun's patronizing tone clearly crossed the line of authority separating Christian and Hindu, agent and object of representation, authority, as well as education, and Tytler thus exploded, as Rammohun's biographer Sophia Collet puts it, in a "frenzy of italics."[79]

Thereafter, Rammohun turns to a satirical technique that could be thought of as a tropicalizing "revision of discourses of colonial domination":[80] he stops writing under his own name and assumes the persona of "Ram Doss" (servant of Rama), an orthodox Vaishnava Hindu onlooker who, supposedly, has decided to leap into the fray and join forces with Tytler *against* the heretical Hindu Unitarian Rammohun Roy. Ram Doss writes to Tytler,

> I am . . . astonished that a man of your reputed learning . . . should be offended at the mention of the resemblance of your belief in the Divinity of Jesus Christ with a Hindoo's belief in this Thakoor, because you ought to know that our religious faith and yours are founded on the same sacred basis, . . . the MANIFESTATION OF GOD IN THE FLESH. . . . You cannot surely be ignorant that . . . RAM was the King of the Rughoos and of Foreigners, while in like manner JESUS was King of the Jews and Gentiles. Both are stated in the respective sacred books . . . to have performed very wonderful miracles and . . . both have been worshiped by millions up to the present day.[81]

Failing to see through the disguise, Tytler was furious, not least because Ram Doss had set the New Testament on the same level as the *Ramayana*, which Tytler had previously disparaged as "childish" in *Budaic Sabism*.[82] Ram Doss, then, equates Christian and Hindu beliefs in divine incarnation, specifically the orthodox Christian faith in the mystery of the Trinity and the Vaishnava doctrine that Brahman is identical with Rama and Krishna, the seventh and eighth avatars of Vishnu.[83]

Later, in *Answer of a Hindoo to the Question, "Why do you Frequent a Unitarian Place of Worship . . . ?"* (1827), Rammohun would drop the satirical veil and include among his answers, "Because I feel already weary of the doctrine of 'Man-God' or 'God-Man' frequently inculcated by the Brahmans, in pursuance of their corrupt traditions: the same doctrine of Man-God, though preached by another body of priests better dressed . . . and eminently elevated by virtue of conquest cannot . . . excite my anxiety or curiosity."[84] Ram Doss's satirical sacred syncretism presents the obverse. The originary religion is idolatry, the "doctrine of

'Man-God,'" and thus Tytler's Christian orthodoxy and Ram Doss's own Hindu orthodoxy are equally pure revelations of natural truth, their common "root." Ram Doss continues, making matters worse:

> The . . . narrow-minded believers in *one* INVISIBLE GOD accuse the followers of the Trinity as well as us the sincere worshippers of Ram and other Divine Incarnations, of being Idolaters, and policy therefore might have suggested to you the propriety of maintaining a . . . brotherhood among all who have correct notions of the manifestation of God in the flesh, that we may cordially join and go hand in hand, in opposing, and, if possible, extirpating the abominable notion of a SINGLE GOD, which strikes equally at the root of Hindooism and Christianity. (893)

In a final satirical thrust, Ram Doss suggests that Tytler has broken with his polytheistic brethren and become a "schismatic," according to the title of the pamphlet Rammohun would eventually publish, maintaining the disguise while collecting the articles in which the debate unfolded. In *A Vindication of the Incarnation of the Deity, as the Common Basis of Hindooism and Christianity, against the Schismatic Attacks of R. Tytler, Esq., M.D. . . . By Ram Doss* (1823) the author magnanimously invites Tytler to return to the fold and join him in stamping out their "common enemies, the Unitarians," and especially "Rammohun Roy, . . . this stubborn Heretic," whom "we Hindoos regard . . . in the same light as Christians do Hume, Voltaire, Gibbon and other sceptics."[85]

Rammohun as Ram Doss thus "provincializes" Tytler's sacred syncretism, to borrow Dipesh Chakrabarty's term, finding in it a premodern superstitious acceptance of polytheism and idolatry. In contrast, the tropicopolitan satire projects an image of universal and transhistorical monotheism as well as a contemporary Indian culture informed by a cosmopolitan embrace of European skeptical thought, Indian scriptural interpretation, and the truths underlying diverse, contested, and interpenetrating systems of belief. The rejection of the "doctrine of 'Man-God'" allows for a spiritual modernity, which is only superficially a contradiction in terms: unlike Tytler and his ilk, who are trapped in sacred or mythological time—there is really no difference, in the end, between the primal error of idolatry and contemporary Trinitarian Christianity—India for Rammohun has entered the time of historical process and development. The modern in and of itself is therefore not defined as intrinsically European, and the modern universal history revealed by Rammohun's skeptical syncretistic critique and composite faith does not proceed in purely secular time, for eternal truths recur. Both Europe and India share premodern histories in which truth was obscured by error, and in both cases parochial superstition endures and coexists

with modernity, though in progressive states of reformation. From the syncretistic perspective of Hindu Unitarianism, Europe is thus a scene, but not *the*
scene, of "the birth of the modern,"[86] just as India is a scene, but not *the* scene,
of premodern tradition.

Derozio, Memory, Modernity

When syncretism is understood as "borrowing" or "influence," as Stewart and
Ernst have written, examples of syncretistic situations "nearly always define the
'source' as dominant over the passive recipient, which is also therefore 'derivative' and less authentic."[87] If Coleridge suffered from a common European blindness about the complexities of Rammohun's reformist writings in simultaneously exalting him as and reducing him to the "Luther of Brahmanism," the
reception of Derozio's fashionable verse as imitative similarly provided a partial
view. Just as a revised vocabulary of syncretism is required to understand Rammohun's program in the context of cosmopolitan Calcutta, "imitation" can be
replaced with another term, "citation," in order to reveal the power of Derozio's
poetry within an imperial culture often experienced by its contemporaries as
circulating and fluid rather than static and oppositional. Neither allusion, reflection, nor imitation, citation is a deliberate reference to a shared and mobile
literary experience.[88] Viewed in isolation, which is to say purely through the lens
of an imperial ideology that replaces cultural complexity with binary relational
identities, Derozio can be elevated and dismissed as "the Keats of Anglo-Indian
Literature." But read in the context of the East Indian community, the radical
European and liberal Hindu cultures to which it was connected, and the new
Indian public—which is to say in the context of the local and global conditions of
cosmopolitan Calcutta—his writing can reveal radically different aspects.

Reading Derozio can at times feel like entering an echo chamber in which
the Romantic canon reverberates. A quick catalog includes "A Dramatic Sketch"
(1830), discussed below, which is full of Wordsworthian, Coleridgean, and Shelleyan notes; "Dust" (1827), in which "Julian and I walked forth, and soon we
came / Unto the tomb of a high son of fame; / The marble told his deeds, his
years, and name" (153); the title poem of *The Fakeer of Jungheera* (1828), an Eastern
tale in the style of Byron and Moore that also echoes Shelley's lyricism and gives
a nod to Southey's *Thalaba* ("How beautiful is moonlight" [213]); the distinctly
Shelleyan sonnets "To the Moon" (1828) and "To the Rising Moon" (1828);[89] "The
Golden Vase" (1828), which is indebted to Keats's *Isabella*, and "Song: 'As waits a
watcher of the skies . . .'" (1830), an adaptation of Keats's famous sonnet; "Love's
First Feelings" (1827), which is inspired by L.E.L.; and "Here's a Health to thee,

Lassie!" (1827), in the spirit of Burns. I have already mentioned Derozio's explicit adaptation of Byron in *Don Juanics*, a poem to which we will return in the next chapter. In "Poetry," printed in the *India Gazette* in February 1824, two months shy of his fifteenth birthday, he takes aim at one of Byron's favorite targets, satirizing "pension'd Southey" for "his dear-bought laurel":

> Dear bought, if bought with prostitution's pay;
>> Dear bought, if talents, such as might aspire,
> To snatch with fearless hand a sun bright ray,
>> Flashing from inspiration's hallow'd fire,
> Grope, like the purblind mole, their darkling way,
>> In Bathos sunk, and grovelling in the mire—
> Inditing Epics, Odes, and such like things,
> Abusing freedom, and bepraising Kings. (276)

In that same month a sparkling prose piece by Derozio, "On Drunkenness," appeared in the *Helter-Skelter* under the pseudonym Leporello. Its thesis was that "the whole moral beauty, the very pith and marrow of what Philosopher Square would call 'the eternal fitness of things' in conviviality, consists in simultaneous and contemporaneous intoxication" (73).[90] In the course of proving his argument, the fourteen-year-old author proclaims his sophistication and erudition—"I might, if I chose, (for my classical learning is prodigious,) deluge the Magazine with quotations; but I have, I trust, said enough" (78)—through a furious yet casual (i.e., drunken) interweaving of direct or oblique allusions to Byron, Beaumont and Fletcher, Quintilian, Pope, de Staël, Samuel Johnson, Godwin, Addison and Steele, Fielding, Ovid, Horace, Scott, Lesage, the Old Testament (2 Samuel and Esther), Homer, Cervantes, Campbell, Plato, Xenophon, Dryden, Tacitus, Blackstone, Shakespeare, Moore, and Newton. Presenting his mastery of classical and fashionable literature, Derozio here, as in his later verse, self-consciously patterns himself through citations as an educated wit and man of the day.

In keeping with Buckingham's own agenda for Indian self-definition in the *Calcutta Journal* (discussed in chapter 1), his review published back in London in the *Oriental Herald* (July 1829) critiques Derozio's two volumes of poetry as if they were journals merely "echoed from the Prints of Europe to those of India":

> His style and manner, though borrowed in a great degree from Byron, are characterised also by frequent resemblances to the other fashionable poetry of the day. . . . Thus, we are continually reminded of Moore's "Lallah Rookh," and Miss

Saunders's "Troubadour," . . . The "Fakeer of Jungheera," is a personage lineally descended from "The Corsair," and near of kin to the "Veiled Prophet of Korassan;" and his lady-love, Nuleeni, is as "warm and wild," and woe-begone, as one of L. E. L's. extatic damsels, whose only occupation is to kiss—and die.[91]

Derozio should "turn to better models and better subjects," advises Buckingham, suggesting that he "lay Moore and Byron on the shelf, burn the 'Troubadour' and the 'Improvisatrice;' read Shakespeare, Milton, Spencer, the old dramatists, and Robert Burns" (117). Buckingham then takes an interesting tack in proposing that the way for Derozio to "stick to TRUTH and NATURE in word and thought" (117) is both by forsaking fashionable literature for the British classical canon and by embracing his *"native"* identity: "The page of Indian history, of his *native* India, in all its 'glory and its gloom,' lies spread before him. The present condition and future prospects of India, are also themes of deep and inspiring interest. Let him turn to these" (117). As I hope to show in the readings that follow, the present condition and future prospects of India were at the very core of Derozio's poetry, though that condition and that future were different from those that even Buckingham, let alone mainstream metropolitan media and culture, could imagine.

The synthesis of imitation and novelty in Derozio's poetry can be read, though with an important qualification, as a self-fashioned reversal of the kind of masquerade performed by British Romantic writers who followed de Staël's poetical policy and stuck to the East. Nigel Leask has provided a helpful way of thinking about the "costume poetry" of Jones, Southey, Byron, and Moore: "Whilst Jones's *Hymns* enriched English poetry with a new, Hindu 'costume' and imagery, they stopped short of imitating Oriental poetic form. . . , thereby establishing an acceptable, because adequately generalized paradigm for future exotic poetry. . . . The cultural particularism of Hindu 'costume' was mediated by the poetic vehicle of the Pindaric or Miltonic Ode."[92] Derozio reverses the direction, but with a distinction: he effortlessly assumes each and every fashionable metropolitan poetic guise, yet unlike his British counterparts, he pays little or no deference to the kind of difference or distance that would demand mediation between metropole and empire, as well as their attendant forms. Because it both is and isn't his inheritance, British Romantic poetry for Derozio can become a kind of transnational masque in which the rules of the game are not the same as those of nationalism underpinned by racial, religious, economic, and even temporal distinctions. For Leask, part of the foundation of costume poetry is the division between the modernity of the culture that represents and the eternal stasis of the culture represented: "Safely located within the timelessness of a classical ideal, Jones's vision of Indian culture (particularly attractive to us in the light of subsequent British denigration), nonetheless, exemplifies the ethnocentric strategy described by Fabian as 'the denial of coevalness' to non-European cultures."[93] Derozio's reversal of the costume is an assertion of coevalness, an insistence that his present is emphatically a now-time (*Jetztzeit*).

In the famous passage explaining that "history is the subject of a structure whose site is not homogeneous, empty time, but time filled by the presence of the now," Benjamin writes, "Thus, to Robespierre ancient Rome was a past charged with the time of the now which he blasted out of the continuum of history. The French Revolution viewed itself as Rome incarnate. It evoked ancient Rome the way fashion evokes costumes of the past."[94] "Evokes" in the translation, however, does not capture the full resonance, for what fashion does is "cites" (*zitiert*). When citation replaces imitation as our interpretive frame, I am proposing, we can read Derozio's fashionable poetry as negotiating between the present and a past that, far from simply being a lost national origin, is "charged with the time of the now."[95]

The reception of Derozio's poetry, in this respect, bears contrast with that of Kasiprasad Ghosh, the graduate of the Hindu College who refuted Mill's *History* in a series of remarks printed in the *Government Gazette* in 1828, published a volume of English poetry titled *The Sháïr* (Persian for "Minstrel") in 1830, and wrote various other works of poetry and prose for newspapers, journals, and annuals.[96] In the preface to *The Sháïr*, Kasiprasad announced himself as "the first Hindu who has ventured to publish a volume of English Poems."[97] *The Sháïr* is connected to Derozio's 1827 and 1828 volumes in a number of ways. Marked throughout by association with the community of the Hindu College, it opens with "To Horace Hayman Wilson, Esq.," addressed to Derozio's friend and Visitor to the college.[98] This poem takes its first line—"Harp of my country! Pride of yore!"[99]—directly from the last line of Derozio's famous sonnet "The Harp of India"—"Harp of my country, let me strike the strain!" (97)—a piece that Kasiprasad then explicitly adapts in "The Viná; or the Indian Lute." Kasiprasad's title poem is indebted to Derozio's "Fakeer of Jungheera," and through that poem to Moore. And as Derozio did in his 1828 volume, Kasiprasad includes two sonnets to the moon, as well as a poem addressed to Henry Meredith Parker, a Company official and poet who became an important magnet for interracial sociability in the late 1820s and was a friend of both writers, as well as of their mutual friend Emma Roberts, author of *Oriental Scenes* (1830), which Derozio saw through the press.[100]

Kasiprasad's work, however, met with a very different reception from Dero-zio's. In addition to the important factors of religion and race, a chief distinction lay in Kasiprasad's more frequent recurrence to Indian themes. In spite of Buck-ingham's implication that Derozio ignored "his *native* India," Derozio did pro-vide verses in his two volumes that could have satisfied the metropolitan appetite for authentic poetry capturing the exoticism of the Orient, including "Song of the Indian Girl," "The Enchantress of the Cave," "The Song of Antar the Arab," "Song of the Hindoostanee Minstrel," and "The Fakeer of Jungheera." But these are vastly outweighed by poems such as those on the cause of liberty in Greece, or "Italy," or "To My Brother in Scotland," or "Tasso," or "Yorick's Skull." Kasip-rasad, on the other hand, in poems such as "The Sháïr," "The Hero's Reward," "Song of the Boatmen to Ganga," and especially his series "The Hindu Festi-vals," foregrounded an Indianness that gratified rather than threatened expecta-tions of what "the first Hindu who has ventured to publish a volume of English Poems" should write.

"But a few years back," claimed the *Asiatic Journal*, "such a prodigy in liter-ature, as a volume of English poems, written by a Hindu, printed at an Indian press, clothed not merely in the English language but in its genuine idiom . . . would have excited at least as much astonishment and interest as a camelopard, a pair of united twins, or even a Malay mermaid." The reviewer then expressed his "pleasure in finding that the Hindu mind is apt to receive the seeds of European learning, and that . . . English literature is likely to take permanent root amongst the natives of Hindustan."[101] The *Englishman's Magazine* (1831) declared that "he is most at home in the Hindu Festivals, and his local and amatory verses,"[102] and when L.E.L. included "Song of the Boatmen to Ganga" in *Fisher's Drawing Room Scrap Book* (1835), she introduced the poem by praising Kasiprasad's talent, add-ing, "His native literature is full of subjects for poetry of the highest order; sub-jects, however, requiring much fine taste and much judgment, which could only be acquired by a knowledge of European literature."[103]

But the way in which he was "most at home" in writing about Indian themes in English reveals an interesting subset of costume poetry. For Kasiprasad was open about the extent to which he was versifying Indian subjects that had al-ready been translated into European idioms. Thus he describes the genesis of "The Hindu Festivals" as follows: "Being one day in conversation with a friend on the subject of publishing his poems, he [Kasiprasad] was suggested the im-portance and utility of writing something by way of national poetry; and hav-ing then no other Indian subject at hand which he could make a choice of, but the Hindu Festivals. . . , he versified them into small pieces of poetry."[104] The friend was most likely H. H. Wilson,[105] whose suggestion that Kasiprasad write "national poetry" would seem to have led him to provide just the kind of authenticity and detail that Orientalist writers had strived to achieve, from Jones in *Sacontalá* (1789) to Wilson in his *Mégha Dúta* (1814). But in fact Kasiprasad's immediate source lay not in Sanskrit or local experience or personal belief but in a series of articles on the "Hindu Kalendar" printed in the *Government Gazette* in the spring of 1827. Thus Kasiprasad introduces the "Akshayá Tritiyá" as "the anniversary of Creation and the commencement of the *Satya Yuga* or golden age," while the *Government Gazette* had described the festival as "the anniversary of creation, or the first day of the Satya Yug, or age of purity."[106] Similarly, "The Hero's Reward," based on Kalidasa's drama *The Vikramorvasiyam*, would seem to be precisely the kind of work in which his "native literature" provided the subject for national poetry, yet the poem, Kasiprasad writes, "was written after having perused Dr. Wilson's translation of the 'VIKRAM URVASI, or the Hero and Nymph.'"[107] Welcomed as a translator of Indian literature, nature, and religion into the "genuine idiom" of English language and literature, Kasiprasad was in fact warmly received for translating from translations, for masquerading as an Orientalist masquerading as an Indian.[108]

Derozio, on the other hand, reversed the direction of the disguise. Recall the *New Statesman's* surprise "that the work of a sensitive youth of mixed race does not contain a single poem directly expressive of himself and his people." Derozio did write poems expressive of himself and his people, but not *directly* so, precisely because direct expression was and is a powerful imperialist fantasy. Derozio, on the other hand, presented Indianness in general and Hindu liberalism in particular not as an authentic exoticism or preserved antiquity to be exported for metropolitan consumption but rather as one performance among many in a cosmopolitan and global world driven by fluid and shifting styles, voices, desires, and forms. And it was a performance staged by memory, of Romantic poetry as well as of the lost glories of Indian history, that dissolved easy borders between European and Indian, the present and the past, originality and imitation, experience and imagination, authenticity and mimicry. While the syncretistic approach of Rammohun's Hindu Unitarianism mined the present for preserved originary universal truths with which to modernize religious and cultural identities, memory in Derozio's writings represents a different relation of the present to the past, and thus an alternative vision of the modern self that inhabits that present.

Buckingham's review in the *Oriental Herald* quotes a letter he has received that condescendingly marvels at Derozio's poetic facility. The East Indians, "with whom the poet must have associated," the correspondent writes, speak a "language, which can hardly be called English. . . . It is . . . as if a Briton, of the time of Severus, had suddenly written a poem in good Latin."[109] Projecting Derozio back into the antique past so as to bring him forward to the present as an anomaly, the image suggests how much of a charge his East Indian mastery of contemporary European idioms carried. Whereas Buckingham could attempt to invent a new Indian publicity by rejecting a model of journalism containing "no more of original disquisition than has been first echoed from the Prints of Europe to those of India" and proposing in its place one that would at least open up the possibility of "omitting altogether the information coming to us from Europe,"[110] echoes for Derozio necessarily played a very different role.

Especially in Derozio's most mature poems, those published in the *Bengal Annual* in 1830 and 1831, a central theme concerns the construction of the present, both personal and political, through memory. The present is one in which the English language, Romantic poetry, skeptical European philosophy, and contemporary forms of print, publicity, sociability, and religious life combine to enable a particular relation to the remembered past. His status as a "nationalist" poet has depended on the claim that, as Chaudhuri summarizes, he "habitually mourned, and desired the resurrection of, the lost glories of ancient India."[111] The claim rests primarily on the two works with which his name has remained associated over the course of the last century, the sonnets "The Harp of India" and "My country! in thy days of glory past." In the latter Derozio writes, "Well—let me dive into the depths of time, / And bring from out the ages that have rolled / A few small fragments of those wrecks sublime, / Which human eye may never more behold" (173). I will focus on three important longer poems that deserve to be widely read by students of early nineteenth-century verse in English—"The Ruins of Rajmahal," from *Poems* (1827); the newly reprinted "Philosophical Utopia: A Fragment," from the *Bengal Annual* for 1831; and "A Dramatic Sketch," from the *Bengal Annual* for 1830—but taken as a whole, his work simply does not "dive into the depths of time" in order to resurrect lost glories or summon the return of an originary, timeless spirit.

In "The Ruins of Rajmahal" the poet reflects upon the site of a decaying mosque, the Sona Masjid, in Gaur, the late medieval capital of Bengal, near Malda. Contrasting the silence and stillness of the desolate present with the sacred activity of the proud past, the "vesper hymn" and "morning prayer," the verses read by priests "from hallowed Al Koran" (139), the poet hears the ruins "sadly speak of what is gone" in tones "To which . . . / The memory is rivetted!" (140). Unlike Wordsworth's tree and field in the Intimations Ode, which "speak of something that is gone," the ruins provoke feelings of personal as well as historical loss. But as in Wordsworth's Ode, although memory produces longing, that longing is ultimately not for restoration, and Derozio's speaker asserts, "I would not have the day return / That saw these wrecks in all their pride— / As he who weeps o'er Beauty's urn / Feels what he felt not by her side" (140). The poet here expresses a strange but completely characteristic consciousness that the work of memory is at once delusive and creative: instead of preserving and representing the experiential past ("what he felt"), memory invests the past with meaning in order to invent the present, and thus the risk of viewing the ruin is that the viewer will become like the lover who "Feels what he felt not." The lines do evoke a sense of loss, but the poet would not return to the earlier state; rather, he needs to come to terms with a present paradoxically structured by emotions that he never actually felt but that have nonetheless been produced by memory. (Recall "Moods of Mind," in which "Memory in her backward journey" does not encounter past "Points of existence" but instead meets the "impressions" left *on* those points by "thought and feeling.")

The analogy between the historical memory of the poet viewing ruins and the personal memory of the lover weeping "o'er Beauty's urn" is then extended to his perception of his "native land" itself. "Her spirit is not wholly fled," he writes:

Some trace shall be of what has been,—
Its image, though in darkness cast,
A holy relic of the past;
A dazzling meteor fleeting by,
An Iris in a cloudy sky;
A vesper breeze in summer shade,
A sunbeam in the gloomy glade—
A tone than music nothing less,
A rose-bud in the wilderness! (141–42)[112]

Echoing Shelley's string of similes in "To a Skylark," Derozio's metaphors seem to describe the trace as a thing that makes present its lost origin. But the rejection of nostalgia—"I would not have the day return"—belies the elegiac tone of the poet's reflection upon the "spirit" of his "native land." If, like the Sona Masjid itself, these metaphors are each a kind of ruin, they do not serve as temporal telescopes allowing the poet or reader to see the lost origin of nationhood, or the endurance and continuity of national identity, in a dehistoricized synthesis of culture and nature. Unlike the strain of English nationalist ruin poetry explored by Anne Janowitz,[113] "The Ruins of Rajmahal" insists that the past is an invention of the present as much as, if not more than, the present is an invention of the past.

Believed by Derozio to have been built by Shah Shuja, son of the emperor Shah Jehan and Mumtaz Mahal, the Sona Masjid represents the lost glories of Indian history, but the reason why the poem resists resurrecting Mughal grandeur involves more than the pervasive British and Hindu ideology of Muslim tyranny.[114] For Derozio, the past itself is never something simply to be resurrected, and memory is never simply a mirror. Thus a note to "The Ruins of Rajmahal" associates the long history that transformed the mosque into a ruin—"And ruthless hands have reft away / The marble that might mock decay"—with contemporary imperialist plunder, both in India and abroad. "Lord Elgin robbed Greece of her ruins," reads the note, adding, "and none but those of 'gentle blood' have had opportunities of following his example; 'But every carle can lord it o'er' *this* 'land'" (171). The adaptation of Byron's line from *Childe Harold's Pilgrimage*[115] directs the reader to resist accepting an easy narrative of glory and decay driven by a simple division between conqueror and conquered, and the poem makes clear that the ruins bear traces of a long process of depredation: "The stranger, though no child of fame, / Upon thy walls hath writ his name," and Derozio comments, "The walls of the Mosque . . . are covered with the names of European and native travellers" (140). For that matter, the poem also directs the reader to resist any easy narrative relating the present and the past as discrete moments either divorced from historical process or existing in a coherent and clearly ordered continuum. The note quoting Byron concludes, "The Sona Musjid has been plundered of its marble slabs . . . but to say how the spoiler has spoiled this 'abode of kings,' would require more time and paper than I can bestow at present" (171).[116]

As indicated by "The Ruins of Rajmahal," his evocations of fashionable poetry, and the history of his work's reception, the fragments of sublimity that Derozio sought to excavate were anything but timeless. Like many of his longer poems—"The Enchantress of the Cave," "Ada," "The Fakeer of Jungheera," "The New Atlantis," "Moods of Mind," and others—"Philosophical Utopia: A Fragment" opens with an exordium set off typographically from the rest of the verses,[117] and these lines begin a complicated process of investing the past with now-time in order to reinvent the present. The exordium frames the poem as a kind of dream vision in which "Memory" transports the speaker to Epicurus's garden in ancient Athens, where a group of philosophical young men enact a doctrine of benevolent and imaginative friendship:

And whither do ye bear me, shadowy dreams?—
I now am wandering with the mighty dead;
And as I pace through vistas dark, my tread
Startles sweet sleeping echoes; then the gleams
Of days, whose light devoted Memory
Has made perpetual, break upon my way,
Till I am not a being of to-day,
But seem a portion of the past to be.
Now with the patriot-poet's fire I burn,
Now to the garden of the Sage I turn,
And Epicurus! chief to thine and thee. (315)

Memory at first appears to initiate a straightforward kind of time travel, bearing the poet back until he "seem[s]" to become "a portion of the past," but the triple emphasis on "now" introduces a play on time that this poem, among others, will perform. "Now" is spoken in the present tense by the poet after memory has done its work, and it is unclear whether memory has altered the poet's consciousness in the present so that he now burns "with the patriot-poet's fire" and turns to the garden in the act of composing the poem itself, or whether memory has actively transported him to the past, in which case he would be speaking in the past and invoking it as the present. Immediately after the exordium the poem switches to the past tense—"They sat them on the ground" (315)—and the evocation of Apollo signals the antique setting, but the description of the youths that follows suggests that the ambiguity of the exordium is significant and that memory has acted more like a dream, in which time is always plural, than like a time machine.

After all, if the garden of the sage is taken at face value, then the poet is remembering things he has never experienced, and this is a preliminary way to think about Derozio's evocations of lost glory to the end of nationalist sentiment. Memory does startle "sweet sleeping echoes," but not just of classical antiquity. For the youths themselves form a community of sociability that simultaneously evokes Epicurean friendship, a Shelleyan "spirit of Love" (317), and an idealism unmistakably identified with the Derozians and the Hindu College: "many a plan / For spreading wide the ties that fasten man / Even to his slighted brotherhood they formed" (316). Citing *Laon and Cythna*, in which Laon calls his communion with "deathless minds" a "glorious intercourse,"[118] the speaker of "Philosophical Utopia" presents the youths of the garden as earthly exiles from the heavens: "Above them hung the sky, to which sometimes / They looked like exiles towards their native clime, / . . . / . . . The pure scene / Was fitted to the minds that on it gazed: / I often fancied, as their eyes were raised, / That there might be between them and the sky / Mysterious intercourse" (316). Exile becomes a metaphor that distances both youths and poet from homes—the sky in the case of the youths, the past in the case of the poet—that they never knew, and never could have known.

The metaphor thus develops a play on both space and time: while the youths are exiled from the sky, the "native climes" from which the speaker is exiled would seem to be the garden itself and the past in which the garden is only "made perpetual" by memory. A "generation without fathers and children," Susobhan Sarkar influentially described the Derozians,[119] obscuring as much as he revealed by the implicit comparison to the Decembrists of 1825, for the poem is indeed about the strains of being perceived, and perceiving oneself, as such. Unconnected to and thus unmoored from the past and the future, the poet is an exile in time, and his journey homeward through memory becomes a daring and transgressive voyage, like the conversation of the youths, which is a form of "Mysterious intercourse" between them and their lost home: "And O! how daring is the love of those / Who, suffering what the idle world deem woes, / Send out their minds on dark untraversed seas / In search of happiness, although the breeze / That swells their sail is death" (316). Chaudhuri rightly identifies "a certain homo-erotic strain" in these lines,[120] and the transgression works on several levels. Like the youths, the poet too sends out his mind on the "dark untraversed seas" of imagination. The contemporary resonances are all too audible, and travel across the dark seas, or *kala pani*, which in a literal sense was polluting and could place elite "twice-born" Hindus outside of caste, serves as an encompassing image for Derozio's Hindu students' rejection of orthodox beliefs and devotional practices along with the prohibitions on the consumption of alcohol and beef. At the meeting on 23 April 1831 that led to Derozio's resignation, the nine managers of the Hindu College considered a memorandum of nineteen proposals, the first of which was that "Mr. Derozio being the root of all evils and cause of public alarm should be discharged from the college and all communication, between him and the pupils be cut off," and the third of which was that "all those students who are publicly hostile to Hindooism and the established custom of the country and who have proved themselves as such by their conduct should be turned out."[121]

Crossing the seas as a physical and mental act produces forms of social death, then, but this death, the poem proclaims, is also a new life. To strangers it seems that the youths have suffered the woes of exclusion and exile, and thus barred themselves from "All joy on earth":

> But there were dreams of bliss
> Which crowded o'er their vision at the call
> Of strong Imagination, lord of all
> The future and unseen.—It is a power
> Which gives existence to the unborn hour;
> And at its summons bids events attend,
> Events which are too beautiful to bend
> To stern Reality's unyielding mould.—(316)

Evoking *Prometheus Unbound, Hellas,* and "Ode to the West Wind," Derozio's "strong Imagination" both destroys and creates, but the shift of tense and the verb "attend" distinguish its creative power as more than an echo. For the movement of creation between past and present is reciprocal: the poet has imagined the youths of the garden into being, just as their daring dreams gave birth to the present hour, and thus the past ("were dreams") and present ("is a power") coexist in one dense or heterogeneous tense. And in this double tense, imagination "bids events attend, / Events which are too beautiful to bend / To stern Reality's unyielding mould." Events, actual lived happenings, intransitively attend in the sense that they stretch outward toward something awaited, unborn, and unnamed, but simultaneously these events are also ideal in that as they stretch into the future they will not "bend" to the mold of reality.

As in Byron's *Don Juan,* a countermodernity or at least a resistance to the empty time of commodity culture is inseparable from and in fact part of the fashionable expression of the divided and alienated modern self, and my preliminary formulation of memory in the cause of nationalist sentiment—the poet is remembering things he has never experienced—can now be expanded: he can remember things he never experienced because disinherited memory is the borderland between the lived and the dreamed, the present and the past, the real and the imagined, as well as the imitated and the invented. In remembering the classical past of Greece or India as in citing Shelley and Byron, Derozio is fashioning a newness in which the old distinctions do not apply, for that is exactly what fashion does, blasting the past out of the continuum of history. Citation thus repeats (imitates) and performs, creating a "Philosophical Utopia" that, in the old punning sense, is both an ideal place and no place, where events attend to the mind's power without bending to the constraints of the real. The vision

accordingly ends with a synthesis of loss and recompense, absence and presence, completing the lyric form of imaginative voyage and return that leaves the
speaker's consciousness, and by extension his world, transformed: "Gone / Are
those who here lay talking," yet contemporary local nature—"That rill, the grass,
the flowers, the stars above"—retains the music of their remembered conversation and, like the poem itself, has "caught from those young men the spirit of
Love" (317).

"A Dramatic Sketch" also pursues this complicated negotiation between the
authority of the past and the present culture of the East Indian and liberal Hindu
community associated with Derozio. Recalling the dialectics of imagery in Shelley's dialogues, especially "The Two Spirits: An Allegory," and clearly influenced
by Hume's *Dialogues Concerning Natural Religion*, the dramatic form of the piece
is important, for it is a discussion of belief and doubt held by a "Devotee" and his
"Follower." Rather than following Hume and projecting his Philo and Cleanthes
into a generic classical Grecian setting, as he did in "Philosophical Utopia," however, Derozio chooses a classical Hindu scene and tradition for this poem. Set
"Among the Western Himalayas" near a "small cave," the discussion unfolds between a Devotee, or *guru*, and his young Follower, his *shishya* or *chela*. The tradition invoked is that of *parampara*, or the "succession" of knowledge from teacher
to disciple. The relationship thus enables conservation and continuity of knowledge and faith from one generation to the next. But unlike the questions and
answers of a catechism, the structure of *guru parampara* is uniquely conservative and progressive at the same time, for, as in the paradigm of Krishna and Ar-
juna in the *Bhagavad Gita*, the process of succession involves the antidogmatic
posing of difficult problems by the disciple as the means by which he comes to
accept the inherited wisdom of established authority. In "A Dramatic Sketch,"
however, the Follower speaks respectfully and lovingly to the Devotee but strives
unsuccessfully "to reconcile my soul, / To those great lessons, which from you I
learn."[122] This moving poem struggles with the alienation necessarily produced
by cultural encounter, internal exile, and religious disinheritance, in this case
the alienation of pupil from teacher, child from parent, new from old, present
from past, and ultimately self from self: "I turn me to your fixed light," says the
Follower, "But all my meditation ends in grief, / Because it tells me that I strive
to break / The link that binds me to my race" (270–71).

Published a year before Derozio's resignation from the Hindu College, the
poem synthesizes the challenges that the Derozians were posing, in the form of
Hindu liberalism, to themselves and their families. In 1828 he and his students
formed the Academic Association, the first predominantly Hindu debating so-

ciety conducted in English, which met fortnightly and garnered significant attention in the press. Topics discussed included "free-will, fore-ordination, fate, faith, . . . the attributes of God, and the arguments for and against the existence of deity . . . ; the hollowness of idolatry, and the shams of the priesthood."[123] A firestorm followed, ignited not just by the subjects of discussion and the philosophical rejection of established beliefs and practices but by the social environment in which the discussions took place, involving intercommunal dining as well as the consumption of alcohol and beef. As the *Oriental Magazine* derisively put it, they were "actually *cutting* their way through ham and beef, and wading to liberalism through tumblers of beer."[124] The "Native Managers" of the college responded by ordering all teachers to "abstain from any communications on the subject of the Hindu religion with the boys or to suffer any practices inconsistent with the Hindu notions of propriety."[125] It had already been made clear that no communications on the subject of Christianity were to be made either, and when the missionaries Alexander Duff (Church of Scotland) and James Hill (a Congregationalist) announced a course of lectures on natural and revealed religion, the managers forbade attendance at "societies at which political or religious discussions are held."[126]

The supposed secularism of the institution was thus in fact a defensive *response* on the part of the orthodox Hindu managers against the perceived threats of evangelicalism and irreligion. On the one hand, then, the college was not secular at all. As Anita Coomer has argued, "The way [the managers] emphasise the 'Hindoo' character of the institution takes away much lustre from their image as projectors of 'secular education.'"[127] On the other hand, as a reading of "A Dramatic Sketch" in this context demonstrates, the threat posed by Derozio was not secularity in any straightforward manner either. After he sent his strongly worded letter of resignation to the managers of the college, he received a reply from Wilson, who wrote that he "should like to have the power of speaking confidently" on the charges brought against him. The first two of these charges were, "Do you believe in a God?" and "Do you think respect and obedience to parents no part of moral duty?"[128] In response to the first charge, Derozio affirmed that he had taught Hume's "celebrated dialogue" but said that he had also furnished his students with Reid's and Stewart's "more acute replies to Hume" and therefore

if I am to be condemned for the Atheism of some, let me receive credit for the *Theism* of others. Believe me, my dear Sir, I am too thoroughly imbued with a deep sense of human ignorance, and of the perpetual vicissitudes of opinion, to speak with confidence even of the most unimportant matters. Doubt and uncertainty besiege us too closely to admit the boldness of dogmatism to enter an enquiring mind. (323)

In response to the second charge, he wrote, "I have indeed condemned that feigned respect which some children evince, as being hypocritical and injurious to the moral character; but I have always endeavoured to cherish the sentient feelings of the heart, and to direct them into proper channels" (324). Wilson had described Derozio's letter of resignation as "severe," and both to the managers and to Wilson Derozio wrote with restrained but audible indignation. The severity of his candor, however, stands in contrast to the tone of "A Dramatic Sketch," which can and should be read as the poetic companion piece to this letter and as the artistic expression of the circumstances surrounding Derozio's resignation.

Before its turn to blank-verse dialogue, the poem begins with a hymn to God, "king of the lotus-throne" who "bid Himávat rise":[129]

> Is there no voice in this solitude,
> Which tells the soul in its calmer mood
> Of a world of bliss, untinged with care,
> Beyond the interstellar air;
> > And bids it raise
> > Its hymn of praise
> And love, to the One Eternal Good?
> There is a voice in the wandering breeze,
> > Which says—it is by divine command
> That the tempest rides over troubled seas,
> > Or raves, like a maniac, through the land.
> > > And ever is seen
> > > In the vernal green
> > Which clothes the mountain trees,
> > > An omnific hand,
> > > And a mind that planned
> > Whatever the vision sees . . . (266)

The hymn, behind which can be heard "A Summer Evening's Meditation," "Tintern Abbey," Coleridge's "Hymn Before Sunrise," and Shelley's response (imitation?), "Mont Blanc," needs to be placed in the context of the dialogue that follows. Taken on its own, the "voice in this solitude" could suit the Coleridgean "abstruser musings" of "Frost at Midnight" and lead to the apperception of "that eternal language, which thy God / Utters."[130] But the utterance of this "hymn of praise / And love, to the One Eternal Good" proves to be precisely the kind of orthodox worship endorsed by the Devotee but *resisted* as sufficient by the Follower, and by the poem itself. Eschewing doubt and uncertainty, the hymn answers its own question ("Is there no voice?") with bold assurance ("There is a voice"), and upon the conclusion of the hymn the Devotee asks rhetorically, "Is not this wholesome occupation, boy, / Good for the spirit's health?" (267). At the heart of his teaching is a life of ascetic devotion and rural seclusion: "This is the home of peace! / The peopled city, and the crowded street / Dim and extinguish that celestial flame / Which consecrates the eremite's still cave" (268). "Your pardon, Sir," respectfully answers the boy (268), who proceeds to unfold his struggle with the asceticism and retirement that is to be his inheritance: "my rebellious feelings, running wild, / Dash, in the face of reason, all the chains, / With which I fain would shackle them for aye" (269).

Unlike the mental voyage-and-return structure of "Philosophical Utopia," the dialogue works against the odic form of the hymn in particular and the greater Romantic lyric in general. Nothing is resolved, and instead the dialogue articulates the egalitarian and urban ethos of Hindu liberalism without losing sight for a moment of the personal, social, and temporal alienation with which it was necessarily infused. The Follower replies that a "gloom" has settled on his mind, "And I, condemned to darkness and despair, / Scarce reck the genial influence of joy" (268):

> there is something in me, which forbids,
> My mind to taste the blest delights you know.
> There is a sympathy which bids me turn,
> To those whom I have loved and left behind,
>
> . . . .
>
> Our passions may be checked, but not destroyed;
> It is not more in our power to change,
> Internal than external form; but we may bend,
> And shape to our own purposes the mind,
> By the omnipotence of use. I know,
> How much has been, and how much may be done:
> But would you root out sympathy, and tear
> A generous passion from the human breast?
> O Sir! forgive my youth—: but I do think,
> That man must be man's brother and his friend. (269)

Those whom the Follower has "loved and left behind" dwell in the "sacred city" (271) of Benares, where the Follower passed the first fourteen years of his life. Far from dimming and extinguishing holy feelings, the "peopled city, and the crowded street" are sites of sociability and sympathy. The poem thus implicitly juxtaposes the idealized classical Hindu setting with contemporary Benares or, by extension, the Derozians' crowded Calcutta. For an Orientalist, the small cave in the western Himalayas would signal "a Time other than the present of the producer of anthropological discourse,"[131] and that producer would be the metropolitan and imperial European agents of culture and knowledge, agents who participate in an ideology of difference and distance between subjects and objects as well as between the present and the past, with all their attendant geographical, religious, and racial associations. But it is telling that Derozio has chosen the sacred city of Benares as the home from which the Follower has been exiled.

For in the poem the western Himalayas and the city do not reject each other any more than do the Devotee and the Follower. Like odic hymn and skeptical dialogue, the two instead coexist in uneasy, disjunctive, and often, but not always, uncomprehending interchange, just as asceticism coexists with sympathy, parents with children, age with youth, orthodoxy with liberalism, premodernity with modernity, religion with secularity. The young Follower's internal form makes him a representative of the new, but he realizes that the task before him is to shape that form to his own purposes through the choices he will have to make, and is in the process of making. There is no simple mutual exclusion here between the Devotee's religion and the Follower's nascent secularity, let alone any negation of the former to allow the latter, supposed to have been always present, to emerge. I am evoking Charles Taylor's critique of "subtraction stories," according to which "the essential character was always there, but previously it was impeded by factors that have since been removed."[132] "A Dramatic Sketch" does not portray a "subtraction story"; that is, Westernization triggers the removal of superstition, priestcraft, and idolatry, allowing secularity to emerge. Rather, the poem stages a difficult choice that is both a loss and a remaking.[133]

And the Follower's closing words—"man must be man's brother and his friend"—capture the cosmopolitan alienation produced by these conflicts, for they reveal that the small cave in the Himalayas holds a copy of Robert Burns, or at least that lines from Burns inhabit the Follower's memory. He cites, in fact, the verses that served as a kind of password, or "manifesto,"[134] among the Derozians. Describing a meeting of the Academic Association, Alexander Duff reports,

More than once were my ears greeted with the sound of Scotch rhymes from the poems of Robert Burns. . . . One of the sons of Brahma . . . suddenly gave utterance, in an apparent ecstacy of delight, to these characteristic lines:—

> "For a' that, and a' that,
>   Its comin yet, for a' that,
> That man to man, the world o'er
>   Shall brothers be, for a' that."[135]

And among Derozio's last published writings was an article in the *East Indian* on an examination held at his old school, David Drummond's academy, in which he expressed delight at witnessing "the exertions of Hindoo and Christian youth, sitting together in the same classes for academical honours," and asked,

> when the Hindoo and the Christian have learned from moral intercourse how much there is to be admired in the human character, with no reference to difference of opinion in religious matters, shall we not be brought nearer than we now are to that happy condition
>
> > When man to man the world o'er,
> > Shall brothers be, and a' that. (359)

Projected onto the classical scene and into the foundational relationship of succession, of religious and cultural conservation and continuity, the citation infuses the past with the present as it turns the Follower's idealized struggle and alienation into an expression of the contemporary egalitarianism of Burns's lines as well as of the actual conflicts between the Derozians and both Christian and Hindu authorities.

"Thou ravest, boy," responds the Devotee, counseling "prayer and meditation" (270), but in his next speech he returns to the theme of the hymn, asking,

> Hast thou e'er held communion with the stars
> In midnight's silence deep, and never felt
> A wild uprising of the soul, as 'twould
> Have sprung to bring those wonders from their sphere,
> Or mixed itself with their celestial rays?
> Are they not eloquent of things which make
> Man's nature half divine, and to his soul,
> Speak the high language of another world;
> Waking from out the wilderness of thought,

Those mighty workings which exalt the mind,

Then leave it in a darker earthlier hour,

To wonder at its own omnipotence? (272)

Having cited Burns, the dialogue here subtly echoes and revises the opening hymn itself, in which the "voice in this solitude" spoke of "a world of bliss . . . / Beyond the interstellar air." Here too the stars "Speak the high language of another world," but the difference is that now this other world is also emphatically this world: "These feelings are not strangers to my breast," responds the Follower, "And oft have wild desires possessed my brain, / Wild as imagination could create; / . . . / But wherefore should I draw a circle round / The joys I long to know?" (272). Communion in silence now provokes for the Devotee a "wild uprising" not incompatible with the Follower's "wild desires," and in their eloquence the stars articulate not a future communion between the soul and God but rather the presence of divinity within nature and the human mind. The exquisitely reciprocal fit between the two, the "high argument" of Wordsworth's *The Excursion*,[136] is here expressed in the language of *rasa*, the aesthetic experience of ecstatic union with God.

So the relationship between the spiritual Devotee and the secularizing Follower is more complex than the straightforward narrative of Westernization would allow. In *Translation of an Abridgment of the Vedant* (1817), Rammohun had expressed "no ordinary feeling of satisfaction" at seeing "many respectable persons of my countrymen, to the great disappointment of their interested spiritual guides, rise superior to their original prejudices, and inquire into the truths of religion."[137] In "A Dramatic Sketch" the "secular" Derozio is more open to a mutually honest and disinterested, if difficult, relationship between "spiritual guides" and their followers, both of whom sincerely "inquire into the truths of religion" even as the latter feel obliged to depart from the former. Although the Follower is alienated from the faith of the Devotee, his liberal enthusiasm is not a simple rejection or displacement of that faith, a natural supernaturalism, for the poem's highest and most enthusiastic expression of sympathetic benevolence is produced by and in the dialogue's citation of the orthodox hymn. Faith was to be his inheritance, but through no fault of his teacher he has inherited something else instead, just as the speakers of "The Ruins of Rajmahal" and "Philosophical Utopia" remember what they never experienced and actively feel what they felt not. To be divided from one's inheritance is to be divided from oneself, as the poem is divided formally between orthodox ode and skeptical dialogue. The poem concludes with a Shelleyan discussion of the youth's love for a woman—"I love! / Why should there be a secrecy in love, / When there is nought of shame? Shall I conceal / A passion that has purified the soul[?]" (273). The disinherited and divided self has discovered in its alienation the power to feel, to create, and to renew.

This power, of course, comes at a price: the relinquishing of one inheritance for another. From one mid-nineteenth-century perspective on Young Bengal, the Follower is like "Those who have received a liberal English Education . . . [and] have only learnt to condemn their own language, observances and religion, and to extol every thing relating to the white-skinned denizens of England."[138] Based on an idea of the authentic India as fundamentally closed off, this interpretation extends forward both to Victorian racial imperialism and to twentieth-century communalism. Without denying the wounds of colonialism, another perspective on the second and third decades of the nineteenth century can portray the new inheritance as part of a different history, that of Amartya Sen's argumentative India,[139] where traditions of pluralism, heterodoxy, and rational debate could be open to the cosmopolitan cross-pressures of the Hindu College, an English-language school managed by the orthodox establishment where an East Indian mixed-race teacher and his Hindu students read Hume along with Byron and Shelley and, to encode their liberalism, cite the poet of the Scottish peasantry.

In Rammohun and Derozio spiritual syncretism and secular memory, respectively, constitute divergent perspectives on the past that produce different visions of Indian modernity. Cosmopolitan Calcutta, therefore, is where Derozio ought to be, and to forget the particular conditions of the European, East Indian, and Indian communities with which his life and writings intersected and to see him as a naïve imitator of Romantic poetry who sought to invent an Indian nation in its image is to recapitulate the literary history that has dismissed him as either an imitator or a curiosity. He is both of these, but if we theorize imitation and invention as more than mutually exclusive alternatives, close reading of the curious forms of memory and imagination to be found in his citational verse reveals a body of Romantic poetry in English that deserves to be considered as part of the global culture of Romanticism. Which is not to say that Derozio's poetry does not also deserve to be considered as part of a distinct Indian literary and cultural history. What I have tried to imply in this chapter is the extent to which these two approaches can overlap. Derozio is not "a pigmented Keats," but neither can he be read apart from either pigmentation or Keats, or from the other Romantic poets whose language provided so much of the matrix of his thought and expression. In a lecture delivered in 1926, Birendra Binode Roy rightly protested that "full justice has not been done to him":

> To refer to him as "the Keats of Anglo-Indian Literature" is, to my way of thinking,
> an entirely wrong way of looking at him. English literature is one and indivisible;
> the bisection of it on a racial basis is unfortunate in the extreme and should not
> be tolerated. The best that has been written in the English language is worthy of
> a place even in the most exclusive histories of English literature, no matter what
> colour the skin of the writer may have. Towards pure artists like Derozio, there
> should be a more liberal attitude than has been displayed by European writers on
> Anglo-Indian literature.[140]

I would not say that "English literature is one and indivisible," and the opposite extreme of "World Literatures in English," conversely, is nebulous and anodyne. Romanticism, however, was a cultural movement defined by the perpetual creation of the new through repeated acts of imaginative return—to the past, to romance, to nature, to childhood. As such, it was not confined by national or geographical boundaries, and its desires and modes of expression were as mobile as its proponents and its texts, none of which could circulate throughout the empire and its various cultures without being echoed, adapted, transformed, and challenged, that is, without being cited.

CHAPTER FOUR

"Little Bengal"
Returned Exiles, Rammohun Roy, and Imperial Sociability

On our return home from Vauxhall a few evenings since, where
we had been wondering at the unaccustomed presence of a learned
Brahmin, Ram Mohun Roy, we were somewhat startled to find on our
table a sufficiently neat volume called "The Sháïr," printed at Calcutta—
sold at No. 3, Durrumtollah—and addressed "To the Editor of the
Athenaeum, with the compliments of the author, Kasiprasad Ghosh."

—The Athenaeum, *18 June 1831*

Printed in Calcutta, David Lester Richardson's *Bengal Annual* for 1833 opened
with a curious prose piece by Derozio's friend Henry Meredith Parker called
simply "An Oriental Tale." But this was no ordinary Oriental tale. In it, for instance, Tamerlane and Lord Clive are contemporaries, and a Brahmin is a Muslim. And a confused one at that, for although apparently a Shiʻa himself, he
hates Shiʻas and hopes they all burn their beards and catch cold: " 'La illa Allah!'
cried the brahmin, 'let us praise Mohommud and Ali the son of Fatima. May
the beards of the Sheahs become as burnt pye-crust, and their noses as curds
and whey—Allah il Allah—Mohommud Russool e Allah,' thus cried the devout
brahmin from the high minar."[1] Parker wrote the tale as a sly screed against
the London reviewers, who had complained that earlier issues of the *Bengal Annual* were insufficiently Oriental. As epigraphs he takes the following two passages, parenthetically venting his frustration with their less than firm grasp of
geography:

"To us at this side of the Ganges" (which side?) "subjects entirely Indian, or at
least Asiatic, would be in general much more acceptable than those, which we can
easily obtain in our northern climate."   *Monthly Review.*

"[']The Bengal Annual' comes from about our antipodes," (really!) "from the
Calcutta Press, and is printed upon India paper. It would be well if the Eastern
character had entered a little more into its contents."   *Morning Herald.* (1)

Parker struck back by writing a tale so Oriental that practically no one who hadn't lived in India could possibly have understood the vocabulary or grasped just how ludicrous, not to mention how full of historical, religious, and cultural solecisms, the entire tale was—"an Oriental tale with a vengeance," a later reader called it.[2] With the London reviewers and both London and Calcutta readers in mind, the narrator mocks the "English critics" who "complain that we are not Oriental enough" (1) and then calls to his servant:

> Joseph—a duwaut, filled with the blackest ink of Agra, and forty thousand new Persian cullums—good!—a fresh chillum—saturate the tattees with goolaub—scatter little mountains of roses, chumpah, and baubul blossoms about the room—bring me a vast serai of iced sherbet, pure juice of the pomegranate, you understand, and now here goes.

———————

> It was a magnificent morning in the month of May, 17—, the thermometer stood precisely at 138° Farenheit in the sun, but was some degrees lower in the shade. It was a magnificent morning. (2)

The *jeu d'esprit* then opens with a bang, literally, a "crash" that turns out to be a sound ostensibly heard every day in India: "Let us see what is the matter—oh! as I supposed," it is a boa constrictor crushing the ribs of a tiger and a buffalo at the same time (2–3). The tale concentrates the alienation that metropolitan readers and Anglo-Indians, as longtime British residents of India were called, both abroad and at home would experience in each other's languages and lives.

At the end of "An Oriental Tale" the hero, the English Major Mimms, and the heroine, the Brahmin's daughter, Nealini, are married and set sail for London, where they settle in Marylebone: "As for the hero and heroine of our tale," the narrator asks, "who does not recollect the parties of the accomplished Lady Mimms at her mansion in Portland Place, her golden pawn-box, her diamond hookah, the emerald in her nose, and her crimson silk trowsers?" (16).[3] Their choice of settlement is no accident, for Portland Place lay at the geographical heart of the Anglo-Indian community in London. By the mid-1830s the *Quarterly Review* could designate "that European Elysium of Asiatics—the streets north of Cavendish and Portman Squares" as "Little Bengal" (fig. 12).[4] It was there that many returned East India Company functionaries chose to live along with their wives, children, and servants, giving rise to the first Indian restaurant, Dean Mahomet's Hindostanee Coffee House, on George Street (Portman Square) in 1810, the Royal Asiatic Society of Great Britain and Ireland on Grafton Street in 1823, and the Oriental Club in Hanover Square in 1824.[5]

Fig. 12. "Little Bengal" (Marylebone and Mayfair), from Greenwood's Map of London (1827). Copyright © The British Library Board.

If Little London in Bengal was both a reality and a microcosmic fantasy surrounded and intersected by a semiautonomous world that was at once expansive and new, Little Bengal in London similarly presented more than one face
to itself, the nation, and the empire of which it was a part. As we will see, Little Bengal was every bit as much and as little Indianized as Little London was
Anglicized, and at work in each was a struggle between communities, tastes,
ideologies, and ways of life. The fictional Major Mimms "with his side curls
and his pig-tail, his no-shirt collar and . . . orange-tawney visage" (16) and Ne-
alini/Lady Mimms may have returned to throw grand parties at their mansion
in Portland Place, but the real-life Oriental tale of their predecessors, the Savo-
yard mercenary General Benoît de Boigne and his elite Muslim wife, Halima/
Hélène Bennett, also known as Noor Begum, ended less happily.[6] Arriving in
London with their daughter, Banu, and their son, Ali Baksh, in April 1797, they
settled in a house on Great Portland Street.[7] Within a year, however, de Boigne
had left Hélène for Adèle d'Osmond, the seventeen-year-old daughter of an impoverished French aristocratic family. When Abu Talib Khan "had the good fortune to form an acquaintance with two or three Hindoostany ladies" during
his residence in London in 1801–2, one of them was "Noor *Begum*, who accompanied General de Boigne from India. She was dressed in the English fashion,
and looked extremely well. She was much pleased by my visit, and requested me
to take charge of a letter for her mother, who resides at Lucknow."[8] At the time
of this visit, far from wearing crimson silk trowsers at a mansion in Portland
Place or even in a house around the corner on Great Portland Street, Hélène was
dressed in the English fashion and living in Enfield, from where she would move
to a cottage, Rangers' Lodge, in St. Leonard's Forest, near Horsham, Sussex, in
1804. There she resided until her death in 1853, a Catholic convert remembered
locally as "the Black woman" who attended Mass every Sunday, smoked "long
pipes," wore "magnificent rings," and gave generously to the poor.[9]

In all of these figures we see a range of positions characterized by dislocation.
"Exile," "immigrant," "expatriate," "colonialist," "traveler"—these are the shifting terms produced by imperial circulation. Abdul JanMohamed has helpfully
distinguished among these and other categories,[10] and his distinctions will come
into play below, but in the period "exile" was the term most commonly used to
describe the condition of British colonialists in India, who were then called "returned exiles" upon their retirement or while on furlough in London. I will accordingly apply the word as an umbrella term capable of covering a range of cultural, social, and ideological situations, while remaining alert to the disparities
and overlaps between them. In this chapter my interest in exiled communities

in Calcutta and London emerges from the ongoing efforts of the "new imperial history" to move beyond a binary model of metropolitan center and imperial periphery. The attempt to think instead about circulation and mobility results from the critiques in the 1990s of what John Mackenzie had called the established pattern of "centrifugal" analysis, which addressed "the radiation of influences from Britain into its wider hinterland."[11] "Centripetal" approaches to British imperial historiography, on the other hand, associated with the pioneering work of Gauri Viswanathan, Sara Suleri, Simon Gikandi, and others, have focused on "the imprint of empire on 'national' British culture at home."[12] But if, as discussed in the preceding chapters, we have come to reject the pregivenness of metropole and colony as separately constituted autonomous spheres along with the unilinear transfer of "influence" from one to the other, be it centrifugal or centripetal, we require new models to help us see beyond the terms of modular nationalism in the definition of national cultures under conditions of early globalization.[13] This has been the focus, in very different ways, of Viswanathan's more recent work along with that of Srinivas Aravamudan, Dipesh Chakrabarty, Maya Jasanoff, Kathleen Wilson, Daniel O'Quinn, Lynn Festa, and Sudipta Sen.[14]

Defining exile as "the unhealable rift forced between a human being and a native place, between the self and its true home," Edward Said writes that "most people are principally aware of one culture, one setting, one home; exiles are aware of at least two, and this plurality of vision gives rise to an awareness of simultaneous dimensions, an awareness that . . . is contrapuntal."[15] In Said's reflections, contrapuntalism characterizes both a way of reading and the exilic consciousness that informs and enables such reading. It is a practice and a perspective, each emerging from, if not exactly rooted in, a position of dislocation. And it is this contrapuntalism that, for Said, at least partially answers the question, "If . . . exile is a condition of terminal loss, why has it been transformed . . . into a potent, even enriching, motif of modern culture?"[16] For JanMohamed, however, different forms of border crossing produce different kinds of exiles, and the position of the "specular border intellectual" emerges to describe the location of Said himself, the subject who, "while perhaps equally familiar with two cultures, finds himself or herself unable or unwilling to be 'at home' in these societies" and who "subjects the cultures to analytic scrutiny rather than combining them," using his or her "interstitial cultural space as a vantage point from which to define, implicitly or explicitly, other, utopian possibilities of group formation."[17]

This range of positions forced upon exiles in the present is distinctly postcolonial. The "old Indians" discussed in this chapter did not have exile forced upon them; they were colonialists.[18] But they were called exiles and thought of themselves as such, so their lives, and the representations of their lives, need to be considered as part of a historical continuum. The Charter Act of 1813, as we saw in chapter 2, represents one critical turning point in the history of the early empire in India. Another was Lord Bentinck's governor-generalship (1828–35), which witnessed transformations in major aspects of administrative policy and self-definition in the dismantling of the eighteenth-century Orientalist legacy begun by Mill's *History of British India* in 1817 and culminating in Macaulay's "Minute" of 1835.[19] An uncritical acceptance of this progression, like a Whiggish interpretation of the path from Mill to Macaulay, can obscure how the Bentinck years, by virtue of their transitional nature, produced experiments with cultural forms that cannot be adequately explained as Orientalist, Anglicist, or Westernizing. An element of this transitional moment, the narrative of exile was extremely malleable, as capable of generating new combinations of people, language, and power as of ossifying individual identities and hardening social relations of domination and control.

Romantic exile takes various forms as a productive topos, be it the urban exile from rural community tied to land that leads Wordsworth to idealize nature as a lost birthplace or the Continental exile from a home nation that lets Byron and Shelley imagine the global liberalism of the cosmopolite. In all cases, the exile holds two worlds in mind and exercises a "plurality of vision" upon them. Exile thus joins other social impulses of the Romantic imagination's awareness of simultaneous dimensions, from autobiographical reflection on childhood and communion with nature to political radicalism and religious enthusiasm. In each instance of exile—in England, on the Continent, in India—there are "spaces," in de Certeau's sense, that allow the charting of new paths through recursive relations among terms that are themselves mobile and embodied and therefore in process, as opposed to the relations that constitute a "place," which is taken as fixed and pregiven, like a point on a map. By "pregiven" I mean understood to be known in advance of one's own experience of it. And like a point on a map, a place stands in established relations with other places. Space, in de Certeau's well-worn phrase, is "practiced place,"[20] a point on a lived itinerary rather than on a map, to borrow Sandra Pannell's helpful analogy, a putting into practice or an embodying of place through a range of uses, from the everyday to the uncommon, and through stories.[21]

The difference between an emblematic instance of the voyage out and a later account of the return home highlights how experience of one telling space hinges on practices of exile. William Jones's famous "Discourse" on the institution of the Asiatic Society (1784) begins, "When I was at sea, last August, on my voyage to this country, . . . I found, one evening, on inspecting the observations of the day, that *India* lay before us, and *Persia* on our left, whilst a breeze from *Arabia* blew nearly on our stern." He describes this intermediary state as a "situation so pleasing in itself" and goes on to suggest that members of the new society will use the scant moments of leisure afforded by their exile to inquire "into the history and antiquities, the natural productions, arts, sciences, and literature of *Asia*."[22] Couched in the language of disinterested knowledge, their leisure, like their business, will contribute to the administration of empire: their exile will be productive. D. L. Richardson's "On Going Home," on the other hand, captures the different structure and emotional dynamic of the same space for the returning Anglo-Indian, describing the heightened state of expectation of "home-seeking exile[s]" as they sail from Calcutta to London: "Each new occurrence in their progress . . . make[s] their hearts bound within them," and one such occurrence is "the discovery of a ship, like a speck of cloud on the far horizon—a dinner or a dance with the strangers, when the two little oaken worlds in the vast space of waters, arrive in contact." While alone on the waters, the returning exile may be able to show where he is on the map, but he feels himself to be nowhere. Then for the brief moment when "the two little oaken worlds . . . arrive in contact," he is somewhere, at a dinner or a dance. When the ships part, somewhere becomes nowhere again, the implication being that the ephemeral moment of contact was a foretaste of the permanent repatriation that will follow at the end of the itinerary, upon arrival home. But for Richardson's returning exile as for many residents of Little Bengal, this repatriation never happens: "his own birth-place is like a scene in a foreign land."[23]

As I've suggested in the preceding chapters, and as Mary Ellis Gibson has recently brought to life in great detail in *Indian Angles*, exile did operate as a generative language in India not just for the well-documented Asiatic Society in the late eighteenth century but for a dynamic cohort of Britons, mixed-race East Indians, and ethnic Indians alike in the early nineteenth century, including Richardson, Parker, Roberts, Derozio (recall "Philosophical Utopia"), the radical journalist James Silk Buckingham, Kasiprasad Ghosh, and others who contributed to the so-called Bengal Renaissance. This chapter will juxtapose two other manifestations of displaced, imperial sociability that could not have been more different from one another. Both were part of the recursive presence of Indian people, commodities, and social practices in London. On the one hand, there were the "returned exiles" of Little Bengal, which was both a geographical space and, like all spaces in de Certeau's sense of the word, a set of practices and therefore an idea. On the other hand, there was Rammohun Roy, who landed in Liverpool on 8 April 1831 with his three servants, Ramratna Mukherji, Ramhari Das, and Shaikh Baxoo; his adopted son, Rajaram; and his friend James Sutherland, former assistant editor of Buckingham's *Calcutta Journal* and subsequently editor of the *Bengal Hurkaru*.[24] A traveler who never returned home, Rammohun would die in Bristol on 27 September 1833. He spent the intervening two and a half years mostly in London, where he energetically entered into the social life of the capital, and the periodical press covered his every move. These two tales of imperial sociability, both Oriental in their own way, and the spaces particular to them allow us to reconsider the Romantic story of exile and dislocation in the imperial context by adding to it the figures of the returned colonialist in Little Bengal and the elite Indian traveler.[25]

Oriental Tales and Orient Pearls

If Parker's target in "An Oriental Tale" was the London reviews, his intended readership was more complex. The satire draws attention to the distance between two Anglo-Indian reading publics, one returned to and located in England and the other circulating between the three Indian presidencies—Calcutta, Madras, and Bombay—and London, a circuit that also included Cape Town and St. Helena as regular ports of call. These readerships would have experienced the satire in different ways depending on their location and movement. In London, the tale would have been something of an inside joke among returned expatriates, reminding them of their shibboleths and gently mocking their state as strangers in a familiar land. Turning from the pages of the *Athenaeum* or, depending on their politics, the *Oriental Herald* or the *Asiatic Journal*—both were available in the Reading Room of the Oriental Club[26]—they would laugh at themselves and their lingo while shaking their heads at English readers with little or no knowledge of India, the very land on which their empire, and thus their metropolitan ways of life, depended. In an 1828 essay in the *New Monthly Magazine* titled "Society in India" the author complained, "It is quite provoking to remark, how ignorant every body is about India. . . . Many country gentlemen, perhaps, would not have found out to this day, that such a country existed, had they not heard of it as being a convenient lumber-room for stowing away supernumerary children."[27]

In India, where exile and trade marked Britons as an innately mobile readership, however, the potential buyers and readers of the *Bengal Annual* also would have understood the tale as an inside joke, but inside a different kind of circle. In Little London the double-edged nature of the tale would have been to demonstrate simultaneously that Britons in India could master that most metropolitan of tropes, the depiction of extreme alterity in a way that transparently and fluently evokes the most familiar features of national fiction, and that Britons in India were participating in what Johnson, Maxwell, and Trumpener have called a "cosmopolitan literary sphere"[28] through vocabulary, imagery, and events inaccessible to a provincial audience back home. Circulation, in other words, was not just the lifeblood of a trading empire but also the master note of its literature. Just as commodities, religious materials, paintings, and people are transformed in and by movement, the facts of mobility and exchange necessarily inflect imperial poetry and prose.

So if Nealini sails from Little London to become Lady Mimms wearing crimson silk trousers in Little Bengal, the opposite trajectory was possible as well, and a compelling example is Derozio's *Don Juanics* (1825–26), which picks up where Byron left off and brings Byron's hero to contemporary Calcutta. Upon disembarking, "Juan cried 'Coach!' but an uncouth machine / On four men's shoulders borne, was brought—a litter / That Momus in his mirth, called '*Palankeen*', / Though the Bengallee thinks '*Palkee*' much fitter" (37–38). In typically Derozian style, the process of imitating Romantic writing both relocates and dislocates, leaving Juan out of place but willing, cosmopolite that he is, to learn how to navigate a new world of fashion: "Go in—but how? legs foremost, or a straddle? / Both on one side, they'd surely dangle down: / Then sit across—it was too wide a saddle: / Not on the top, for then he might get *brown*; / Nor on the poles, for there he'd roll and waddle.— / They show him how,—he points towards the town" (38). But still more suggestive than Juan's struggles to get into a palanquin, or his shopping spree to outfit his house in Chowringhee, or his purchase of a Stanhope carriage is the Byronic digressive insertion of authorial identity, in this case the pseudonymous "Juvenis," into the drama: "Forgive me, Reader! mine's a wandering Muse, / And I am very young—not seventeen" (36).[29] This imitative, itinerant Muse, however, wanders and digresses in an unexpected and revealing manner. Moored but yet to leave the ship, Juan stood on deck and "thought (for think we will / When the blank soul has nothing else to do) / On fleeted days . . . / . . . / Such thoughts will come, wherever we may roam, / And one will always point to *Home, sweet Home!*" (34). The poem was published in four installments in the *India Gazette*. In that context, these lines speak directly to the community of readers and writers who were consuming and producing poem after poem about exile in the pages of the Calcutta papers, the same community that would soon constitute the market and authors of the Indian annuals, starting with David Lester Richardson's *Bengal Annual* in 1830.[30]

So when the Indian-born Juvenis digresses as follows by identifying with Juan's and the implicitly European reader's thoughts of *"Home, sweet Home!"*—"But I am wandering.—We left Juan thinking;—/ His thoughts were somewhat similar to mine" (35)—a strong claim is made for mobility as a generative element not just of imperial life but of the imagination, including that of a young native of India:

> Even I (though India is my native land)
>> Can picture to my mind a parting scene;
> The lonely maiden weeping on the strand
>> For all that is and all that once had been,
> Then gently waving her up-lifted hand,
>> As glides the ship o'er waters vast and [sheen;]
> One last, long, lingering look she takes—and then
> "Heaven guard thee, love! and may we meet again!" (34)

Although India is the author's "native land," his citational command of the ottava rima and his fashionable tag from Gray's "Elegy" code the virtuosic Juvenis, and his land, as in transit, as part of a cosmopolitan culture and space in the process of being pictured and invented. In circulation, neither Derozio nor his native land becomes English. And although *Don Juanics*, like "An Oriental Tale," does provincialize the European or Indian reader who isn't in on the joke—the European reader who doesn't know, in this case, that "the Bengallee thinks '*Palkee*' much fitter" and the Indian reader who does not know English or Byron—that is not the main thrust of the poem. Rather, Derozio, Byron, and potentially the European and Indian readers in Calcutta or elsewhere simultaneously identify with native lands and, through imaginative acts of wandering, experience the generative melancholy and blithe sophistication of the Romantic global exile's "nautical existence."[31]

In following Parker's Lady Mimms/Nealini to London and Derozio's Juan to Calcutta we have begun to trace the contours of a powerful liberal ideology informed by the recursive rhythms and possibilities of imperial space. Most Europeans in Calcutta surely did look home in an uncomplicated manner, subscribing to a raw civilizational hierarchy, and most Britons in London viewed Calcutta (if they viewed it at all) as essentially a British province in a savage land. But the alternative in the early nineteenth century was not the previous Orientalist premise "that India and Europe were part of a common civilization whose roots stretched to the furthest reaches of antiquity," as Siraj Ahmed describes it,[32] and the concomitant hope for an Oriental renaissance that would reinvigorate Europe, but rather a cosmopolitan assertion of a new global sphere of culture, exchange, free trade, and competition.

When in 1834 Richardson launched, or rather relaunched, his second Indian annual, the *Orient Pearl*, he decided to open the silk-covered volume with an "Introductory Sonnet" by Parker:

> "Showers on her kings barbaric, pearl and gold."
>   Thus sang the Master-spirit, strong and sage,
>   Of this far land, when his mind's pilgrimage
> Led him where Ganges' sunny waters rolled.
> How had that glorious being felt consoled
>   To have read upon the future's mystic page
>   That "gorgeous Ind" would, in a better age,
> Dearer than those, improvement's jewels hold.
> Are there *not* signs, prophetic as the breeze
>   Is in its light gusts of the full Monsoon;
> Though scarce it rustles the green Pepul trees,
>   Or floats the pale cloud o'er the silver Moon?
> Yes! And with such to cheer us, we unfurl
> Once more our silken sail, and launch the ORIENT PEARL.[33]

The "Master-spirit" is Milton, who depicts Satan seated "High on a throne of royal state, which far / Outshone the wealth of Ormus and of Ind, / Or where the gorgeous east with richest hand / Show'rs on her kings barbaric pearl and gold."[34] By imagining Milton's pilgrimage of the mind to India and then the consolation he would have taken could he have read the page of futurity, the sonnet stages two parallel and ultimately unified prophetic transmutations. First, the real pearl and gold of the barbaric past become the dearer jewels of improvement in the poem's present and future. Second, the signs of this transformation of material wealth into abstract value are compared to the present breeze that prophesies the coming monsoon. Because ships must wait for the monsoon before they can sail from "this far land" for England, the present breeze encourages the collective authors as sailors ("us") of the annual as ship to "unfurl / Once more our silken sail, and launch the ORIENT PEARL." The "pearl" thus prophesies not just "improvement's jewels" but, what is the same thing, the "PEARL," the annual itself; the jewels showered as gifts by a self-contained East on its own kings become the commodities of an open imperial trade, set in motion by the wind, and the silken-sailed ship to be launched for England is the silk-covered book, its freight poetry.

The annual thus begins by imagining an empire in which the vehicles of un-
fettered trade are books and the commodities that circulate are poems, suggesting that the improvement of modernity is a commerce, driven by wind, of words.
Implicit in Parker's sonnet, which only unfurls its sail, but explicit in "An Oriental Tale," which actually arrives, is the question not just of production and authorship but of consumption and readership: when the PEARL lands on English
shores, what markets will it find for its freight? Full of exilic longing for home
as the Indian annuals are, they were also competitive. Priced high in London, at
sixteen shillings to a guinea, the *Bengal Annual* and the *Orient Pearl* were pit-
ted against their more elegant leather-bound or silk-covered, gilt-edged domestic
counterparts, such as Rudolf Ackermann's *Forget Me Not* and Letitia Landon's
Fisher's Drawing Room Scrap Book.[35] The annuals thus challenged a metropolitan audience to consume imperial culture and thereby keep up with the global-
izing progress of history.

And sometimes it did just that, as in the epigraph to this chapter: on a summer evening in 1831, a few weeks after Burford's Panorama of Calcutta closed
in Leicester Square, Cockney School veteran and newly appointed editor of the
Athenaeum Charles Wentworth Dilke returned home from Vauxhall, which had
been abuzz with wonder at "the unaccustomed presence of a learned Brahmin,
Ram Mohun Roy," to find waiting for him at his house in Lower Grosvenor Place
"a sufficiently neat volume called 'The Sháïr,' printed at Calcutta—sold at No. 3,
Durrumtollah—and addressed 'To the Editor of the *Athenaeum*, with the compliments of the author, Kasiprasad Ghosh.'" The *Athenaeum* had been started
by Buckingham in 1828, and Kasiprasad, as we have seen, was a contributor to
both the *Orient Pearl* and the *Bengal Annual*, a copy of the latter of which (for
1830) found its way into the library of the Oriental Club, where it remains today.[36]
And a Calcutta reviewer of the *Bengal Annual* for 1832 assumed that the book
would be purchased in India as a gift to link the exile abroad to the recipient at
home, complaining, "It is a pity that there is no embellished fly leaf on which a
donor of the volume to a friend beyond the great Ocean that rolls between India
and Albion, might give a value to the gift by inscribing his name on it."[37] In the
early 1830s it must have seemed that fashionable London truly had become Little
Bengal, an impression that the purveyors of print to a market hungry for Indian
cultural imports and news of Indian events would have been keen to encourage. The presence of Rammohun Roy at Vauxhall and the sight of *The Sháïr* on
Dilke's table suggest that the East had arrived and made itself at home in emblematic sites of metropolitan sociability and domesticity, and not just as Orientalist fantasy but on its own terms, at least to a greater extent than ever before.

Jaut Bhaees in Hanover Square:
Returned Exiles and the Oriental Club

Still, we should not overstate the case, or lose sight of the sense of startled wonderment with which Dilke relates the twin appearances as unaccustomed and unexpected. For Little Bengal was a complex social formation, in some ways tied to the larger life of the capital and in other ways completely closed off, just as in some ways it was part of a global sphere of social circulation and in others an airless world unto itself. The alienation and new forms of community experienced in London by expatriates returned from India suggest that exile and travel could just as easily be suffocating as generative conditions, producing a metropolitan audience at once eminently ready for the East's arrival and profoundly unprepared. Before turning to Rammohun's romantic, even erotic encounter with London sociability in order to witness the ways an elite, multilingual religious and political reformer from Bengal used and was used by metropolitan society, then, I want to give a detailed account of one London scene in which Indian cultural products, such as curries and the Indian annuals, were consumed and in which "Indianized" social practices took place.[38]

The foundation and source of the Anglo-Indian community in London were primarily the late eighteenth- and early nineteenth-century civil and military services in India. Holders of the more prestigious positions in the civil service and the upper officers of the military service, writes P. J. Marshall, were "likely to be drawn from lesser landed gentry, commercial and professional families," mostly from "London and the south of England and from Scotland."[39] According to Patrick Colquhoun's *Treatise on the Wealth, Power, and Resources of the British Empire* (1814), out of the 201,477 men in the service of the East India Company's civil and military departments, approximately 6,000 received annual salaries of between £200 and £10,000.[40] These figures comprise servants both abroad and in England, including the army of upper clerks at Leadenhall Street (the Company's headquarters, where Charles Lamb was earning £480 in 1815). And a very small but influential group within the domestic Anglo-Indian community was made up of the staffs of the Company's two colleges—Haileybury, for the education of civil servants, and Addiscombe, for military cadets—where junior faculty earned an annual salary of £200 and senior faculty up to £500.[41] The moneyed community of returned Anglo-Indians also incorporated some portion of the approximately 4,000 British free merchants in the East. Including military officers and civil servants with "liberal incomes" from the Company and some free merchants, then, these men involved in the trade and administration of the empire abroad, who passed substantial portions of their lives in India, provided the pool of Anglo-Indian cultural consumers in London possessing the prestige required for clubbability and the discretionary funds to buy luxury books like the Indian annuals.

By the second decade of the nineteenth century the first two generations of these Anglo-Indians who had passed the better part (if not all) of their adulthood in India were retiring and returning to London. The earlier "nabobs" of the mid- to late eighteenth century had spent less time in India, made as much as they could, and returned to lives of conspicuous consumption, combining rural retirement with the London seasons.[42] The new generations in the early nineteenth century were primarily men who had left Britain in their teens and returned in their forties or even fifties, often aged beyond their years. Henry Barkley Henderson's *The Bengalee: or, Sketches of Society and Manners in the East* (1829) describes a homecoming after a "sad absence . . . of more than the third part of a century."[43] In a piece published in the *Asiatic Journal* in 1837 titled "Reflections of a Returned Exile," which we'll revisit below, the author "sit[s] down to make some memoranda of my feelings, on returning to Europe, after a residence in India of twenty-two unbroken years," from about 1813 to 1835. He writes that his experiences are typical of "an absentee of twenty-five or thirty years."[44] "Reflections of a Returned Exile" juxtaposes two classes of "Europeans proceeding to revisit their native country": those whose "fortune is made, and who [return] to India no more," and those "who are merely taking a three or five years' trip to Europe . . . and are, after that, to resume duties in Bengal."[45] Over the first third of the century, the former class of so-called old Indians predominated, but by 1844 the *Calcutta Review* could comment on the now numerous young officers back in London on furlough—after every ten years abroad servants received a three-year furlough, including the voyages out and back—and compare the present with the preceding two decades:

> The race of genuine old Indians is nearly extinct. Few men now pass thirty or forty years in the country without a visit to Great Britain. There may be a few of the ancient flock still to be found looking into the Oriental Club. . . . But, ere long, a regular, liver-diseased, parchment-faced, shivering, querulous, rich old Indian, who feels himself when at home as in a foreign land, so strange and distasteful to him are its manners and customs, will soon become as rare as a mummy.[46]

In the heyday of this ancient flock, from roughly 1810 to 1835, when these men returned to London they found themselves not just perpetually cold but also in unique occupational and social predicaments, each of which I will treat in turn.

Occupationally, such men were expected to use their newfound leisure to bring their experiences of the East to bear on the production of knowledge that would inform the administration of the empire. This could happen in various ways, as demonstrated by the examples of Nathaniel Brassey Halhed, who became a civil secretary; Charles Wilkins, who served as East India Company librarian and visitor and examiner at the Company college at Haileybury; Alexander Hamilton, professor of Sanskrit at Haileybury; and, above all, Henry Thomas Colebrooke, president of the Asiatic Society of Bengal from 1806 to his departure for England in 1815, in whose career the continuities between Anglo-Indian scholarship in England and in India were strongest.[47] "Since his return to Britain," write Rosane and Ludo Rocher, "Colebrooke's primary concern had been to integrate data on India into the purview of a vast range of scientific societies."[48] In London he accordingly joined or became a fellow of the Geological, Linnean, and Royal Societies, the Athenaeum, the Royal Institution of Great Britain, and the Astronomical, Zoological, and Medico-Botanical Societies. Through his participation and publications, Sanskrit literature and philosophy and Eastern mathematics—Indian "science" broadly conceived—became part of a modern, international sphere of scholarly and intellectual exchange, not records of the "pre-historical origins of and connections between families of nations" and languages,[49] as the Rochers write, in the earlier, dominant mode (not the only one) of Jones and the Asiatic Society of Bengal.

Such occupational dispositions of returned exiles led to the creation of the Royal Asiatic Society of Great Britain and Ireland in 1823, which was connected to the Asiatic Society of Bengal in several ways beyond the involvement of Colebrooke and Wilkins. As of 1829, a member of either society was entitled to use the libraries of both societies, to attend meetings of both, and to join the other without the requirement of a formal nomination.[50] But in Colebrooke's "Discourse" delivered at the first general meeting of the society, on 15 March 1823 at the Thatched House Tavern, St. James, the main emphasis is on the distinct role that returned exiles in London should play within the ongoing imperial mission. He implicitly announces the connections between the societies in London and Calcutta by echoing Jones's own 1784 "Discourse," proposing, "It is the history of the human mind which is most diligently to be investigated: the discoveries of the wise, the inventions of the ingenious, and the contrivances of the skilful." But he only explicitly refers to his predecessor by reminding his audience that in London they have one thing that those who remain in Calcutta do not: "One requisite is wanting, as long since remarked by the venerable founder of the Asiatic Society of Bengal: it is leisure; but that is enjoyed on their return to their native country. Here may be arranged the treasured knowledge which they bring with them; the written or remembered information which they have gathered." Just as the Orientalist program of the Asiatic Society, and indeed of the Warren Hastings regime, contributed to the administration of British India, the agenda of the new society is part of the different imperial mission in the 1820s. Colebrooke describes the society's goals in telling terms in the very years when Britain was expanding the market for British goods in India. Explaining what is to be done with "the treasured knowledge which they bring with them," he could be talking instead about imported raw cotton: the goal of the society will be to "[return] in an improved state that which was received in a ruder form."[51]

Socially, however, returned exiles found themselves in a different situation. As we have seen, most of them were officers in the Company's military service. Normally, such men would have joined one of the gentlemen's clubs of the capital, probably the Guards or the United Service Clubs, but unlike officers of the Royal Army and the Royal Navy serving abroad, Company officers relinquished their rank upon returning home, therefore enjoying less prestige and encountering barriers to membership at the very clubs for which their status, experience, and wealth should have fitted them.[52] But a further attribute unfitted them too, namely, their tastes and habits. "From our political and commercial relations with India," opened an 1831 guide, "Indian Cookery, as Practised and Described by Natives of the East," "it is well known that a very considerable number of individuals and families in this country have, from a long residence in the East, acquired a strong predilection for Indian modes of life."[53] Of the newly established Oriental Club the *Age* reported, "The large room is to be opened two nights in the week for the exhibition of nautches, *à la mode Indienne*."[54] It is easy to exaggerate the "Indianized" nature of these returned expatriates, and one of my goals is to distinguish between the *representations* of this community as Indianized and what I propose to be its actual significance, its place within the language and history of exile and especially its contribution to our understanding of the spaces of exile.

But if phrases like "Indian modes of life" or "*la mode Indienne*" will need to be qualified, the fact remains that when these individuals and families returned to England, the mode of life they had acquired abroad found no correspondent sociable places in metropolitan London. A well-known fictional example is Thackeray's shivering collector of Boggley Wollah Jos Sedley, who upon his first return home in 1813 "dined at the fashionable taverns (for the Oriental Club was not as yet invented)," while upon his second, in 1827, "his very first point, of course, was to become a member of the Oriental Club: where he spent his mornings in the company of his brother Indians, where he dined, or whence he brought home men to dine."[55] For in February 1824 an elite group had met at the house of the newly formed Royal Asiatic Society, on Grafton Street, just south of Hanover Square, where they struck a committee and resolved "that it appears . . . to be desirable to form a Society . . . to be called the ORIENTAL CLUB."[56] According to the prospectus drawn up at this meeting, "The British Empire in the East is now so extensive, and the persons connected with it so numerous, that the establishment of an institution where they may meet on a footing of social intercourse, seems particularly desirable. It is the chief object of the Oriental Club to promote that intercourse" (1–2). The qualifications for membership were as follows: "having been resident or employed in the public service of His Majesty, or the East India Company, in any part of the East—belonging to the Royal Asiatic Society—being officially connected with the administration of our Eastern Government abroad or at home" (1). And the stated objects of the establishment were:

> *First*: to give to persons who have been long resident abroad the means of entering, on their return, into a society where they will not only associate daily with those they have known before, but have an opportunity of forming acquaintance and connections in their own country. *Secondly*, to give to those who have resided or served abroad the easy means of meeting old friends, and of keeping up their knowledge of the actual state of our Eastern Empire, by personal intercourse and friendship with those recently returned from scenes in which they have once acted. (1)

Temporarily located on Lower Grosvenor Street, the Club in 1826 purchased the freehold to 18 Hanover Square, where the existing townhouse was torn down and the new clubhouse built at a cost of £17,000, to be finished in 1828.[57]

The colonialists who returned in the 1820s and 1830s added a new dimension to London's elite social world, its "clubland." This coincided with the great era of club expansion: the old aristocratic clubs of St. James—White's (1693), Boodle's (1762), and Brooks' (1764)—were joined between 1819 and 1836 by the new clubs of St. James—Arthur's, the Oxford and Cambridge, and the Carlton—and by the predominantly bourgeois clubs of Pall Mall—the Traveller's, the Athenaeum, and the Reform Club. As the Asiatic Society of Bengal in Calcutta, founded in 1784, gave rise to the Royal Asiatic Society in London in 1823, and the Royal Asiatic Society led to the Oriental Club around the corner in the following year, so did the Oriental Club in London inspire the founding of the Bengal Club in Calcutta in 1827, followed by the Madras Club in 1832 and the Byculla Club in Bombay in 1833. The new dimension, therefore, was a unique space of circulation, a kind of itinerant sociability, which has been evocatively described by Mrinalini Sinha as "colonial clubland."[58] Here, in order to pose a question about colonial clubland, I'd like to return to de Certeau's distinction between place and space. Whereas place is stable, space is produced by the intersections of mobile, relational elements, and while a place is one thing defined against others, space is variable in direction and time. So my question is, what kind of space was colonial clubland, and how does the instantiation of that space in Hanover Square participate in the language and history of Romantic exile?

One of the repeated themes in all the sources pertaining to Little Bengal in general and the Oriental Club in particular is just how unproductive and sealed off they were. Although the Oriental Club was founded by the very same members of the Royal Asiatic Society who were actively giving weekly papers and publishing the society's *Transactions* and then its *Journal*, contributing, in other words, as was expected of them, to the body of information on the basis of which the Company's Board of Directors and Board of Control would receive and respond to communications from its governments abroad, the popular responses to the society and the club could not have been more different. Under the aegis of the Asiatic Society these men were seen as an active and useful, if overly specialized, cadre; as members of the Oriental Club these same men became an enervated race apart. As the *Calcutta Review* puts it, "The old Indians, who frequent the Oriental Club, complain of many disorders, and are doubtless afflicted with some—*ennui* not being the least. . . . There is something in British air, which seems prematurely to rust the minds of returned Indians, who often from active energetic men, possessing first-rate abilities and eager to turn them to good account, sink suddenly into indolent listless drones."[59] In *The Bengalee*, Henderson reports that "at home . . . the canker of inactivity and want of employment begins to eat it's [sic] way into our spirits . . . ; then it is that the dull and changeless prospect before us, and the seeming weary, tasteless, unprofitable retirement we have chosen, become involuntarily and gloomily contrasted with the many heart-stirring events we were formerly participators in."[60] But the best line goes to Macaulay, in whose words the ex–civil servant would have been "a man of consequence in the East. In Europe he knows he will be considered as an old, yellow-faced bore. . . . He was powerful. He was eminent. He was comfortable. He is utterly insignificant."[61]

P. J. Marshall has admirably risen to the challenge of making something significant out of this insignificance in an incisive analysis of why the Oriental renaissance described by Raymond Schwab took hold in France and Germany, while having "only an ephemeral career" in England[62] despite the fact that the pioneering late eighteenth-century works of Orientalism were produced by Britons with the assistance of *pandits* in Bengal. Schwab's case is surely overstated, as Nigel Leask suggests and as I hope the beginning of this chapter has shown, but it needs to be taken seriously with respect to the elite ranks of civil servants and military men who were expected to return home and write in ways that would feed the empire of information and knowledge as described by C. A. Bayly.[63] For Marshall, as the services grew, the communities in India and England became increasingly inward-looking, specialized, and self-contained, "[speaking] to one another about their own particular concerns rather than about universal concerns to a curious British public, as an earlier generation had been able to do."[64]

Like most writers about the culture of the early British Empire in India, especially in the wake of Said, Marshall treats Orientalism primarily as a discursive body of knowledge. But when we think instead about embodied social practices and their representations, about the Oriental Club instead of the Asiatic Society, the self-contained nature of this community can lead us to a different though complementary set of questions and conclusions. If Marshall has asked why the Oriental renaissance lost steam in England in the early nineteenth century, my version of the question is as follows: if the contrapuntal consciousness of exile made it "a potent, even enriching, motif of modern culture" for the Asiatic Society of Bengal; for the community of men and women, Britons, mixed-race East Indians, and Indians brought together by journalism, educational institutions, and the Indian annuals; and for the Royal Asiatic Society of Great Britain and Ireland, why, then, did the returned exile's Indianized sociability at the Oriental Club not also involve a plurality of vision that functioned similarly?

To answer this question, we need to think about the great gap between the way returned exiles were thought of and represented as Indianized and the actuality of their sociability and tastes, which were neither British nor Indian but rather part of the unified "imperial social formation"[65] we've been following Sinha in calling colonial clubland. For starters, the fact is that most of the fare served by the kitchen of the Oriental Club was English: chops, steaks, game, fish, and oysters.[66] And although Dean Mahomet sought to attract the first generation of returned "Indian gentlemen" to his Hindostanee Coffee House by advertising in the *Times* that there "they may enjoy the Hoakha, with real Chilm tobacco, and Indian dishes, in the highest perfection,"[67] it is another fact that he went bankrupt after two years.[68] On the other hand, nautches were held and curries were served at the Club: on 18 January 1830 the Club committee reported, "Sample of Curry powder sent to the Club order'd to be tried & reported on by the Cook." And on 24 January 1831, the kitchen having switched from curry powders to the more expensive curry paste, the committee realized that it would have to raise its price in the coffee room: "The Committee directed the charge for a curry made of curry-paste to be increased it being ascertained that the charge heretofore made caused a loss to the club."[69] Partaken along with standard English fare, then, *chilam* and curry no more Indianized the "Indian gentlemen" who consumed them than so-called ethnic food transforms the being of Western diners today, and in fact the two phenomena inhabit opposite ends of the same imperial continuum.

But to read the press coverage of the Club and other accounts, you'd think not just that the members subsisted solely on curries but that they had in fact come to constitute a separate race through exposure to a foreign climate, the consumption of foreign foods, and the adoption of foreign social practices: "Climate, indulgences incident to climate, provincial habitudes, distances from home; not one of which but has had its share in getting up that strange complex being, that bundle of whims and oddities, whom upon his arrival in England we 'clepe an 'old Indian.' For old Indians, plant them where you will, are a distinct race; on Choultry-plain, or at the Oriental Club; in Choringa, or Portman-square."[70] Over and over, Anglo-Indians are described as racially distinct in representations that bring together the color of curry and the color of their complexions. Echoing and expanding on the *John Bull*, which went so far as to describe the clubhouse itself as "of a curry colour," *Freeman's Journal* remarked, "It is seldom that the colour of a house bespeaks the character of its inmates; but the Oriental Club-house has this peculiarity, that its out[er] walls have the true sallow Bengal complexion."[71] In 1834 the *New Monthly Magazine* gave a rich account of

> the Oriental—or, as the hackney-coachmen call it, the Horizontal Club—in Hanover-square, . . . its little windows, looking upon nothing, give the idea of mingled dulness and inconvenience. From the outside it looks like a prison;— enter it, it looks like an hospital, in which a smell of curry pervades the "wards,"— wards filled with venerable patients, dressed in nankeen shorts, yellow stockings and gaiters, and faces to match. . . . It is the region of calico shirts, returned writers, and guinea-pigs grown into bores.[72]

I am less concerned with the truth or falseness than with the fact of these representations, which work on two levels. On the one hand, old Indians become a distinct race, but that race is also understood here as a quality that is the same in Calcutta and London, "on Choultry-plain, or at the Oriental Club; in Choringa, or Portman-square." According to these accounts, Britons lost their racial markers in India, became something else while there, and then brought it back with them to London, where they seek to re-create the world they've left behind. Race is fixed, and space is place. But the realities of imperial circulation and descriptions of the language of old Indians suggest something else.

As I've mentioned, Dean Mahomet, proprietor of the Hindostanee Coffee House, went bankrupt in 1812. Although the Hindostanee seems to have limped on under new ownership—Bryant Lillywhite has it open until 1833[73]—I can find no connections between the Oriental Club and the Hindostanee, but its main competitor, the Jerusalem Coffeehouse, which was "frequented by gentlemen who are, or have been in the service of the honourable East India Company" and where "the earliest accounts of the departure, arrival, and loss of ships in the company's service" could be had,[74] was still going strong in the City. I was intrigued by the connections we can document between the Oriental Club and the Jerusalem, which catered to men either recently arrived or preparing to depart: the Oriental Club's early members books provide places of residence, which reveal that most members resided either in Little Bengal or in India, but several, such as Captains Adams and Beadle on the very first pages for 1824–25, list their address as "Jerusalem Coffeehouse."[75] What this realization brought home to me was the extent to which the Oriental *was* an interstitial space between two worlds, call them Chowringhee and Portman Square, but one that did not function in the same generative way as other itinerant spaces of exile. The Oriental Club was not simply a place of retirement: its members were active in the Royal Asiatic Society and circulating between England and India, as a liminal address such as Jerusalem Coffeehouse suggests.

And recall that one of the objects of "meeting old friends" at the Club was to allow returned exiles to "[keep] up their knowledge of the actual state of our Eastern Empire." Yet when Anglo-Indians and their critics in the popular press alike describe the Club, it does not function in the same manner as other spaces of exile or participate in other imperial stories. One way that the empire took its revenge in the early nineteenth century was by turning its agents, not into nabobs happy to bring their foreign tastes, wealth, families, and servants back to England, but into strange complex beings, oddities whose characteristics neither corresponded nor spoke to other characters in the plot. Exile abroad, in other words, offered individuals and communities roles to play and a language in which to express the alienation and estrangement that post-Enlightenment culture was coming to define as constitutive conditions of modern life. "You feel yourself an exile in the East," wrote Thomas Carlyle to D. L. Richardson, "but in the West too it is exile. I know not where under the sun it is not exile."[76] In spite of Carlyle's attempt to universalize, however, the unique exile-at-home of the returned colonialist produced an alienation without an other or others to give it meaning.

In keeping with the disparate structures of exile abroad and at home, the distinct language of old Indians operated differently depending on the location of its utterance. In India they longed for home with characteristic nostalgia, and talked and wrote of London. But as in "An Oriental Tale" and numerous other contributions to the literature of the Indian press, their exilic language was capable of polyphonic qualities that resonated as part of a transnational literary commerce. In London, as James Grant describes the conversation at the Oriental Club in *The Great Metropolis* (1836), "India and Indian matters form the everlasting topics of their conversation. I have often thought it would be worth the while of some curious person to count the number of times the words Calcutta, Bombay and Madras are pronounced by the members in the course of a day."[77] The specialized nature of their talk about Indian matters supports Marshall's hypothesis, but there is more to it. While accounts of consumption at the Oriental Club regularly racialize the inhabitants of Little Bengal, Anglo-Indians themselves responded in a surprising fashion, consistently describing themselves not as a separate race but as speakers of a distinct language, the language Parker wields so ably in "An Oriental Tale" and that *Hobson-Jobson* would gloss at the end of the century.

Europeans in the East and back home, wrote the "Returned Exile," "think themselves Jaut Bhaees," literally brothers of the same *jati*, or occupational subcaste, a phrase "used metaphorically by Anglo-Indians to express intimate friends."[78] It is both the register—not of race but of caste—and the meaning of the slang phrase, depending on the location of its use, that interest me. For the "Returned Exile" provides a great account not just of this oft-repeated theme, the "sort of slang language" of Anglo-Indians, but of the unique form of alienation it produced in London: "One of the difficulties which an Indian finds, on returning home, is that of making himself understood" (70). The author then takes the implicitly metropolitan reader through the vocabulary required to understand the following sentence: "I have a *shouq* for . . . machines, but I don't understand the *hickmut* of this watch; I think it is rather a *bunao*, for there's no *thikauna* in its going, and I know that my *Sirkaur* and the *Ghurree Waula* . . . are *jaut bhaees*" (72).[79] In India this slang expressed particular social relations of power, defining and consolidating the *"jaut"* by signaling its forms of friendship, command, inclusion, and exclusion.[80] There it was a marker of loss and alienation that thereby could and did signify a plurality of vision and language that, as in "An Oriental Tale," *Don Juanics*, and "Reflections of a Returned Exile" itself, partic-

ipated for better and worse in the heterogeneous, polyglot, and polyphonic culture of the Bengal Renaissance. In London it becomes something else entirely,
still a marker of loss but one that now emblematizes the peculiar plight of old
Indians: their slang at home may incorporate Indian words, but it is no longer
polyphonic, for no one else understands it. They are thus doubly circumscribed,
jaut bhaees both without a *jati* and in the absence of any other *jatis*. Brothers without an occupation, they have nothing to do in their leisure and no one else with
whom to communicate, speaking a hybrid language whose counterpoint was
inaudible, incomprehensible, or discordant in the new location of its utterance.

So Little Bengal *was* achieved through recursive relationships to two places,
Calcutta and London, abroad and home. But as JanMohamed reminds us, it is
not sufficient to say that the generative nature of exile depends on plurality of
vision, for we also need to take into account what he calls the "intentionality"
of the intellectual orientation of the exile.[81] In other words, contrapuntal consciousness has different intentions vis-à-vis the two (or more) cultures it places
in counterpoint, one of which is defined as *home*. In India, the exile's colonial
itinerary was clear: exile provided defined roles, hegemonic or critical, in an epic
story of empire. And so long as one's occupations in London were seen as part
of the ongoing imperial project, this story could be lived at home by sustaining
Colebrooke's "primary mission," as Rosane and Ludo Rocher write, "to raise
his compatriots' awareness of the commercial and intellectual opportunities of
their colonial situation and to make England a country open to the world, a free
trader in goods and in knowledge."[82] But in England there remains the risk that
the returned exile will have no home, and no story but that of a *jaut bhaee* in
Hanover Square.

"The Rajah was there": Rammohun Roy
and the Romance of Conversation

But the Oriental Club and colonial clubland were only one part of a larger imperial social formation, and when Rammohun landed in Liverpool in 1831 and pro-
ceeded to dive into a number of different social scenes, he found himself both
contesting and contested by competing forms of sociability. And partly but by
no means entirely as a result of his very presence, these forms of community,
display, interaction, and communication were now more than ever tied to, and
aware of their ties to, the wider conversable world beyond the walls of the salons,
taverns, theaters, chapels, and churches in which they transpired.[83] "Rammohun Roy attracted more attention in London," wrote Emma Roberts, "than Lord
Wm. Bentinck, or any preceding governor-general, did in Calcutta."[84] As Lynn

Zastoupil has recently documented in remarkable detail and depth, through correspondence, friendship, and print Rammohun played an integral role, both before and after his arrival, in a newly globalized Unitarian culture spanning public and private spaces in Calcutta, London, Bristol, and Boston, along with other strongholds of religious nonconformity.[85] If the collective authorship and readership of the Indian annuals in Calcutta, on the one hand, and the elite sociability of colonial clubland in London, on the other, juxtapose two intimately conjoined but clearly differentiated experiences of alienation and dislocation, the introduction of Rammohun into metropolitan society in general and Unitarian circles in particular represents a dramatic assertion of an alternative set of tastes, values, and social practices.

In Calcutta, Rammohun found himself engaged in a highly polemical world in which the chief camps included Orientalist and Anglicist supporters of Company rule; Buckingham and the radical opposition; the Serampore Baptists; Unitarians; Anglican Trinitarians; Scottish Presbyterians, who would be joined by Alexander Duff shortly before Rammohun's departure; the partially secularized Derozians, influenced by Derozio and David Hare; the orthodox Hindu establishment, including members of the committees of the Hindu and Sanskrit Colleges and *pandits* of the College of Fort William; as well as the reformed Hindu liberals, of whom Rammohun was the leader. In London, the occasionally overlapping divisions through which Rammohun moved were fewer but no less charged or complex, involving primarily Unitarians, Utilitarians, Anglican evangelicals, the East India Company, and its opponents. And especially among the critics and supporters of the Company in London were to be found individuals who had extensive personal experience of alliances and enmities on both sides of the ocean, from Rammohun's old friend Buckingham to founding member of the Royal Asiatic Society and the Oriental Club Sir John Malcolm, who was among the eighty present at the dinner "given at the City of London Tavern, by the Honourable the East India Company, to the celebrated Bramin, Rammohun Roy" on 6 July 1831.[86]

But it was mainly, though not exclusively, with the Unitarians that Rammohun found himself at home. Above all, as has been so well described by Zastoupil, Dermot Killingley, Amit Ray, Subrata Dasgupta, and others, Rammohun's fierce devotion to the single, simple tenet of monotheism, a unified, impersonal, and indivisible Godhead, against the polytheistic corruptions of an originary and universal faith within both Christian and Hindu traditions, made him and the Unitarians natural allies.[87] So too did their common, unwavering support of the Reform Bill, which upon its passage, and thus before his eventual bitter disenchantment with the Grey administration and the reformed Parliament, Rammohun heralded as "the salvation of the nation, nay of the whole world."[88] But beyond theology and politics, though divorced from neither, there remains to be considered another aspect of this alliance, involving a romance, of sorts, a manipulation of signs through conversation, flirtation, displays of sensibility, and exchanges of gifts.

Unitarian society and the "Hindu Reformer" Rammohun were prepared to embrace and make use of each other in England because of a common set of cultural codes suturing sensibility and theology. By the 1830s, Unitarianism was no longer the "rational Dissent" it had been in the decades following its semi-official founding as a denomination in the 1770s, especially with the establishment of Theophilus Lindsey's Essex Street congregation in 1774.[89] The lineage from Essex Street to Rammohun's visit is easily drawn: attending Lindsey's first sermon was his close friend Joseph Priestley, who in 1791 became minister of the Gravel Pit Meeting in Hackney, where he was succeeded in 1794 by Thomas Belsham, who, upon his own acceptance of the ministry of the Essex Street congregation in 1805, was succeeded at Gravel Pit by Robert Aspland, whose sermons there Rammohun attended and who founded the *Monthly Repository*, one of the main avenues through which Rammohun's writings were made known to the English public.

This continuity, however, could easily obscure the extreme transformation undergone by Unitarianism over the course of these fifty-odd years. For one of the ways that Unitarianism established its polite respectability in the period was through an internal debate, to which Anna Barbauld and the Aikin family circle were central, over the roles of feeling, enthusiasm, and public worship within rational religion. In the late eighteenth-century culture of sensibility, Hartleian associationism and belief in the human Christ as a man of feeling allowed Unitarians as diverse as the Presbyterian Barbauld and the lapsed Anglican Coleridge to present Unitarianism as an escape from superstition and established power not into cold, radical "Socinian" abstraction but rather into a simultaneously rational and familial faith.[90] "Socinianism Moonlight—Methodism &c A Stove!" Coleridge jotted in his notebook in 1799.[91] At the same time, as Jon Mee has shown, the modernizing impulse of rational Dissenting conversation as a form of knowledge production, often at the expense of politeness, associated with Priestley and the Lunar Society was giving way to a warmer but still progressive form of sociability linking domestic life and civic virtue.[92] By raising the temperature of Unitarian devotion and conversation, of course, and especially by humanizing Christ, Unitarians risked running from one extreme to the other, enthusiasm. Most considerations of enthusiasm focus on the rise of Methodism in the eighteenth century and millenarian movements associated with Richard Brothers and Joanna Southcott. But the transformation of Unitarianism was part of the same history, as Unitarians themselves were deeply and uncomfortably aware.

Unitarian society, furthermore, was not just conditioned by its own internal developments with respect to its theological positions and devotional practices and by its external relations to other nonconformist denominations and the Established Church. In the early nineteenth century, its self-presentation to a broad English public as a uniquely universalizable form of Christianity and its networked relations among individuals, publishers, and congregations connecting London, provincial cities and towns, Bengal, and New England brought it into competition in a global market of ideas. In Belfast in 1833 J. Scott Porter preached a Unitarian sermon "Occasioned by the Lamented Death of the Rajah Rammohun Roy," in which Rammohun's life served as evidence that Unitarian Christianity "is on the advance. . . . And we see enough to convince us, that the hope of its becoming, at last, a universal faith, is no chimerical project. This is the end at which Christianity aims. With no other triumph, short of this, will it be satisfied . . . a faith embraced by all, and purifying every soul."[93] The dynamic encounter with Rammohun was fostered by this side of Unitarian publicity, its new role as part of an imperial social formation in which, according to its own self-idealizations, Rammohun served as the incarnation of a reasonable and feeling faith that circulated freely in the form of letters, people, and print.

Rammohun, the rational reformer who denied the Trinity, divested the precepts of Jesus of all mystery, and opposed Hindu superstition and idolatry, became the figurative and literal embodiment of sensibility. And, as I'd like to show in a brief interlude on Orientalist fictions of the period, by the time of his visit sensibility had also been thoroughly encoded in Hinduism itself. It is more than coincidence that a number of novelistic depictions seemed to have come to life in the person of Rammohun. I will briefly touch upon three, the first and third now fairly familiar and the second all but unknown (all as it should be).

Among the more startling pronouncements by a Romantic heroine must be the following: "Henceforth, Arabella," writes Sophia Goldborne from Calcutta, "you are to consider me in a new point of view.—Ashamed of the manners of modern Christianity, . . . I am become a convert to the Gentoo faith, and have my Bramin to instruct me *per diem*."[94] Set in 1784–86, during the final days of Warren Hastings's government, and published in 1789, during the second year of Hastings's trial before the House of Lords, Phebe Gibbes's *Hartly House, Cal-*

cutta maps this moment of colonial history onto the personal crisis that results from its heroine's initial vow "never to marry in Indostan" (6).[95] The vow would not be upheld, and the novel ends with a series of marriages, including Sophia's own to a young "beau," Edmund Doyly, whose "dignity . . . proved him to be of European birth and education—of taste and sentiment" (88). There is another youth of sentiment, however, whose attentions she actively solicits and gladly admits, a prepossessing Hindu, or "Gentoo," referred to by Sophia throughout her letters simply as "my Bramin." While Doyly has returned to England during the middle section of the novel, Sophia's Brahmin instructs her in his faith and eventually inspires her flighty and brief conversion, which comes to a sudden end, not coincidentally, along with his own life.

For Sophia, Hinduism (like India) is saturated with European literary conventions. Her frequent quotations impose a quixotic vision upon all she beholds; of her favorite, Thomson, she writes, "To taste the beauties of this poet's pencil, Arabella, you must visit Bengal, where, I am more than ever convinced, he penned his glowing descriptions" (28). Even when she is not quoting, the lens of her reading remains firmly in place. Describing the Durga Puja, Sophia portrays the procession: "A certain number of Bramins . . . with countenances such as Guido would have bestowed on a heavenly saint, led the way" (80). Unwittingly, her language filters Sterne's *Sentimental Journey*, in which Yorick describes the head of a Franciscan monk as follows: "It was one of those heads, which Guido has often painted. . . . It would have suited a Bramin, and had I met it upon the plains of Indostan, I had reverenced it."[96] Like Sophia's visual perceptions of India itself, her reverence for her Brahmin is thus suffused by sentiment, and her experience of Hinduism comes pre-aestheticized. But as Michael Franklin suggests, her openness to Indian culture and her determination to learn everything she can of her Brahmin's religious beliefs are also "predicated upon the pluralism and enlightened tolerance of this brief Jonesian period of sympathetic and syncretic admiration for India,"[97] and in this he supports A. L. Basham, who writes, "One feels that the author had . . . come under the influence of eighteenth century rationalism and deism."[98] I agree with the broad association of the novel's perspective upon Hinduism with syncretistic admiration for India; further, when we look at the work's brief engagement with Hinduism as an actual belief system, we find something more intriguing than a young heroine who articulates her author's Enlightenment rationalism.

Sophia sees Hinduism as essentially compatible with the Judeo-Christian dispensation: it is a monotheistic faith based on the belief in a Supreme Being and in the immortality of the soul. But what moves Sophia, aside from the physical attractions of her Brahmin, eventually to claim that she has converted is precisely the one aspect of Hindu belief that the novel presents as distinct, the cycle of reincarnation, "metempsychosis," or "transmigration into different bodies, according to the lives they had led in their pre-existent state" (75), within the system of *samsara*.[99] And the reason why this aspect of Hinduism leads to her conversion has nothing to do with the usual deistic premise of skeptical syncretism, namely, that truths in each individual religion are to be discovered by following them back to unitary origins, themselves the sources of modern religious plurality and diversity. Whereas skeptical syncretists such as Jones and Francis Wilford would reconcile the Hindu doctrine of metempsychosis with Christianity by tracing Gnostic doctrines of the preexistence of the soul from the Upanishads back to Jewish mysticism, the Platonic One, the Orphic mysteries, and Pythagoras, and then further back to the Egyptians and Chaldeans, Sophia elevates Hinduism over Christianity because "the Gentoos . . . live, Arabella, . . . the most inoffensively and happily of all created beings—their Pythagorean tenets teaching them, from their earliest infancy, the lesson of kindness and benevolence" (50). "The doctrine of the metempsychosis," she writes, "is to me the religion of humanity," a conclusion she finds "apparent from the marking effect it has on the conduct of the Gentoos," for by it "their hearts are softened into a tender concern for the kind treatment of every creature living" (76). Sophia's religion is neither evangelical nor skeptical; instead, hers is the cult of sensibility, a cult, it turns out, to which the doctrine of metempsychosis is particularly well suited. Transmigration, according to Sophia's understanding of karma, makes benevolence not just duty but self-interest, effectively turning love of self into love of others, for love, her Brahmin affirms, "softens the sensibility, expands our natural virtues, extinguishes every idea of . . . competitorship, and unites all created beings in one great chain of affection and friendship" (104).[100]

Another fiction that briefly flirts with Hinduism in general and reincarnation in particular before retreating to the safe ground of sentiment is the anonymous *I'll Consider of It* (1812), the epigraph-cum-caveat on whose title page reads, "*Consider* it not too *deeply*."[101] In it, twenty-three-year-old Henry Denbigh and his sickly father return from India and establish themselves in Little Bengal, in "a magnificent house in Portman-square, which was adorned with all the grandeur and luxury of oriental splendour" (1:115–16).[102] Unusually young and eligible for a returned Anglo-Indian, after his father's death Henry passes his time at the "Hindostan coffee-house," where he enjoys "a high seasoned dish of curry" and smokes his hookah (1:119–20). Like Sophia's, his conversion offers an opportunity for both sentiment and satire: "Whether he had received his creed from some of the Indian Bramins, or whether [from] the kind humanity of his nature, which assured him that all animals can feel pain, yet he firmly believed in that part of Hindoo doctrine, Transmigration" (1:121–22). This belief sets up a subplot in which a mixed-race servant, Thomas Jenkins, disguises himself as a Brahmin, Nahred, who had been known to Denbigh in India. Although Nahred had been "torn in pieces by a tyger" (3:14) four years earlier, Jenkins plays on Denbigh's belief in a caricatured version of reincarnation in order to persuade him, through a kind of "it narrative" of the soul, that Nahred's had migrated into the tiger that devoured him, and that the tiger had then been captured and brought to England only to die in the menagerie at Exeter Change, from where the soul progressed (ascended, with a nod to Swift?) through a monkey, a pig, a puppy, a beggar, a "link-boy at the play-houses," an attendant at the Lord Mayor's feasts, a horse, and finally "into the body you now behold, exactly similar, in form, feature, colour, and proportion to that which, about four years before, was left mangled and lifeless amongst my Hindoo brethren" (3:89–91). The deception accomplished and Denbigh's trust earned, Jenkins promptly relieves him of his pocket book and fine gold watch. Although this incident turns Denbigh "against his favourite study" and leads him to break "his pythagorean vow" (3:144)—that is, vegetarianism—neither the Orient nor its wealth has corrupted the "handsome gay East Indian" in any meaningful or lasting way. For his belief in transmigration, once removed, only reveals the core of sensibility, the "kind humanity of his nature," which made him susceptible to belief in the doctrine in the first place: he remains "all heart, all generosity, . . . possessed of true nobleness of soul and sentiment" (3:215), and accordingly wins the heart of the beautiful and virtuous Charlotte Clarkson.

If *Hartly House, Calcutta* and *I'll Consider of It* offer fairly straightforward flirtations with Hinduism as a religion of feeling, Sydney Owenson's *The Missionary: An Indian Tale* (1811) is less lighthearted and more complex in its depiction. As a sentimental novel, it trades in the common trope of gendered opposition between East and West, Hindu and Christian.[103] Thus the encounter between Owenson's heroine, the Hindu priestess Luxima, and hero, the Portuguese missionary Hilarion:

Silently gazing, in wonder, upon each other, they stood finely opposed, the noblest specimens of the human species, as it appears in the most opposite regions of the earth; she, like the East, lovely and luxuriant; he, like the West, lofty and commanding: the one, radiant in all the lustre, attractive in all the softness which distinguishes her native regions; the other, towering in all the energy, imposing in all the vigour, which marks his ruder latitudes: she, looking like a creature formed to feel and to submit; he, like a being created to resist and to command.[104]

The novel later complicates these terms, however, when Luxima, "a creature formed to feel and to submit," actively saves Hilarion, "a being created to resist and to command," from death by auto-da-fé, the bloodthirsty sentence of the Inquisition to which he has passively submitted with "holy resignation."[105] A similar degree of nuance marks the novel's ambiguous conclusion. The erotic contact between European evangelicalism and its feminized object of conversion ends with devastating consequences for both Luxima and Hilarion, leaving the former dead and the latter "a wild and melancholy man," a shattered recluse "whose religion was unknown, but who prayed at the confluence of rivers, at the rising and the setting of the sun."[106] Rather than paternalist protection and conversion, under contemporary circumstances evangelical communion results in physical death and an empty and sterile spiritual syncretization. But Owenson also maps the optimistic pluralism of William Jones onto numerous points of spiritual contact, valorizing the synthesis of metaphysical, Platonic, Vedantic, Sufistic, and deistic ideas associated with the court of the Mughal emperor Akbar and captured in the novel by the brief appearance of Akbar's great-grandson Dara Shikuh as a *preux chevalier*. Owenson thus hovers between despair that intercultural romance only leads to death in the novel's present and hope that acts of mixing might take root in more congenial soil.

Because of fictions like these, to which below we will add Elizabeth Hamilton's *Translation of the Letters of a Hindoo Rajah* (1796) and Jones's translation of Kalidasa's *Sakuntala* (1789), when Rammohun arrived in England the spaces he entered presented itineraries to be followed as much as to be scripted. The challenge, and the opportunity, is captured by his biographer Sophia Dobson Collet's retrospective summation of his visit: "India became incarnate in him, and dwelt among us . . . Rammohun Roy stood forth the visible and personal embodiment of our Eastern empire."[107] All the accounts of his social interactions from the period of his visit, however, paint a very different picture, for if anything he embodied not "our Eastern empire," with all the resonance of opposition and possession the phrase implies, but rather an energetic cosmopolitanism and a mastery of "localization" (an important term to which we'll return), both of which participated in the imperial social sphere we have been considering.

Certainly the press coverage did call attention to his appearance, seldom failing to mention his turban and "rich Eastern dress,"[108] but in fact his embodiment of India in this simple sense, brilliantly satirized by Harriet Martineau as "lionism," was something that various accounts described as *contrary* to his real successes in English society. Thus Sutherland, writing in Buckingham's *Parliamentary Review*, doesn't celebrate but rather laments the fact that "there were too many who sought to *lionize* him, and turn him to account as an attraction to fill their rooms at their routes or *soirées*. The old Dowager Countess of Cork, who assembles the literary, the scientific, the religious, and all sorts of characters of distinction, by turns, was among the earliest of his pressing inviters."[109] Martineau describes a "singular trial" at an "evening party" hosted by "Lady S.," possibly Lady Mary Shepherd, who, "having two drawing-rooms open, had provided a 'lion' for each. Rammohun Roy was stationed in the very middle of one, meek and perspiring; and I was intended for the same place in the other."[110] Unlike Rammohun, Martineau escaped her doom by hiding "with two or three acquaintances behind the folding-doors," where she remained "till the carriage was announced."[111] In a later article, "Literary Lionism" (1839), Martineau's experience that evening returned in the form of a cautionary tale to any "woman who has written a successful play or novel" in the event that she be so unfortunate as to attend "the soirée of a 'lionising' lady": "She sees a 'lion' placed in the centre of each of the two first rooms she passes through,—a navigator from the North Pole in the one, a dusky Egyptian bey or Hindoo rajah in another; and it flashes upon her that she is to be the centre of attraction in a third apartment."[112] Far from the meek, perspiring image in the former account or that of generic, Oriental placeholder in the latter, in the period itself Rammohun was lauded in the popular press not for being set apart or put on display but for a different kind of performance, friendship.

In his *Parliamentary Review*, Buckingham chose to introduce Sutherland's "Sketch of Rammohun Roy" (1834) as a print medium in which, instead of encountering an exotic other, English readers would experience "all that familiar intercourse which none but a friend could enjoy: they will, in short, become the companions of the Indian philosopher, in the vast solitude of the ocean, and in the busy haunts of populous cities—in the solemnity of the place of worship, and in the gaiety of the evening party."[113] In Buckingham's own "Sketch," published in the *Parliamentary Review* the year before, he described the "many occasions" in Calcutta when the two would drive in Rammohun's carriage "around the Circular Road, and in the outer suburbs of the city, from an hour after sunset till past midnight": "never, perhaps, was 'the feast of reason and the flow of soul' more completely participated in than by us, who unbosomed ourselves to each other without the least reserve, and drank deeply of the fountain of mutual and reciprocal communication of every thought and sentiment that occupied the inmost recesses of our hearts." Buckingham records that Rammohun would regularly join a "select party" of Buckingham's friends for breakfast, when "the conversations were conducted with the greatest decorum and fairness, an accomplishment in which the Orientals far excel the Europeans, whose conversational powers are much inferior to those of the people of Asia, and who are greatly deficient (the English, perhaps, more than any other nation) in that deference to the opinions of others, and that willingness to learn as well as to teach, which gives the greatest charm to a mixed society."[114]

The most important work on Rammohun, as I have indicated, has been written from the perspective of the history of ideas. By addressing his religious and political publications in Calcutta, and now, thanks to Zastoupil, his participation in a transatlantic and especially Unitarian public sphere, such scholarship has shown how Rammohun Indianized the progressive narrative of liberal imperialism[115] and saw "the growth of freedom in India as an essential part of a wider trans-national quest of humanity for self-realization."[116] And for the most part, examinations of Rammohun's life and work have approached his time in England as a continuation and evolution of his beliefs and agendas. Attention to the structure and spaces of conversation, both intimate and public, suggests two new directions. First, although the "decorum and fairness" of Buckingham's idealized and sentimentalized communication is "an accomplishment in which the Orientals far excel the Europeans," it is not in and of itself Oriental, and although "the English, perhaps, more than any other nation," are therein deficient, their deficiency is not in and of itself English. Rather, for Buckingham this kind of conversation is a cosmopolitan virtue that at present has found fertile soil in the mixed society of Calcutta, from where it will reform and liberalize the provincial and self-contained character of English society through the media of Rammohun himself, of print in general, and of the *Parliamentary Review* in particular. And second, to read about the evolution of Rammohun's thought in England, you would think that he spent his time there primarily in the company of James Mill, Jeremy Bentham, Charles Grant Jr., and King William IV.[117] In fact, some of his closest friends were named Janet Hare, Ann Kiddell, and Catherine Castle. By turning to his performances of friendship, especially friendship with women, I hope to add a new layer to the story of his ideas and enrich our understanding of imperial sociability within a transnational print culture.

Upon his arrival in London, Rammohun first settled in Little Bengal, at 125 Regent Street, where he lived from late April to about July 1831. From there, possibly due to "advice that was any thing but disinterested," presumably Sandford Arnot's, he moved to a "magnificent abode"[118] at 5 Cumberland Terrace, where he remained for roughly three months, until about October 1831. He then took up residence at 48 Bedford Square, with the family of John and Joseph Hare, the brothers of Rammohun's and Derozio's friend David Hare, until September 1833, while passing from August or September 1832 to January 1833 on a trip to France.[119] In September 1833 he left London to pay a visit to Stapleton Grove, an estate a few miles northeast of Bristol, the home of Lant Carpenter's ward, Catherine Castle, where Rammohun's son, Rajaram, had been studying under the tutelage of Castle's aunt Ann Kiddell. Rammohun died there at the end of the month and was buried on the grounds of the estate.[120] From the moment he set foot in London, he was called upon by "visitors of all ranks and classes," receiving "two or three invitations to parties for every day in the week."[121] While at Bedford Square, he "kept a plain chariot with a coachman and footman in neat liveries" and "adopted and adhered to the style of a private gentleman, of moderate fortune; though still courted by the first men in the kingdom."[122] As the *Asiatic Journal* put it in 1833, "His inclination, nay his object in coming to Europe, led him into every kind of assemblage, religious, political, literary, social; in Churches, at the Court, at the Senate, in private parties and conversaziones."[123]

A brief look at Rammohun's letters from the first three weeks of June 1833 gives a sense not just of his social activities but of his manner of communication, especially with women. On the first of the month he wrote to an unknown addressee, probably Kiddell in light of the remembrance to Castle and Caroline Rutt (almost certainly one of the daughters of John Towill Rutt),

> My dear Madam, I beg to know to what Chapel you & Miss Castle intend to go on Sunday morning, that I may make previous arrangements & do myself the pleasure of accompanying you. The Revd. Mr. Fox preaches at South Place Finsbury; Mr. Tagart at Portland Street; Mr. Aspland at Hackney. My carriage contains four or five persons; another conveyance therefore would be superfluous. Be good enough to favour me with a reply tomorrow and remember me to Miss Castle & Miss Rutt.[124]

Like Castle's guardian, Carpenter, and Rutt's (presumed) father, all three preachers were prominent Unitarians. William Johnson Fox, one of whose sermons we will consider below, and Aspland had been coeditors of the *Monthly Repository*, which Fox took over in 1831, and Edward Tagart succeeded John Bowring as foreign secretary of the British and Foreign Unitarian Association in 1832. Attendance at sermons placed Rammohun at the center of Unitarian society, and the outings themselves provided opportunities for free and easy conversation. Eleven days later he wrote in a similar vein to Kiddell, "Dear Madam, As Astley's

Theatre commences at a quarter past six o'clock p.m., I propose doing myself the pleasure of calling upon you and your friends to the Theatre" (2:783). And then on the twenty-second he wrote to Castle, "Ma chere Demoiselle, I hope you will excuse the boldness when I take upon myself to remind you of your promise to read the publication of a certain learned Brahmin which I have brought to your notice. You may begin with page 4 and afterwards read the preceding part" (2:783). Biswas notes, "The book cannot be identified. The possibility of its being one of the publications of Rammohun himself . . . cannot however be ruled out" (2:784), a supposition that Rammohun's writerly reticence about imposing on his reader ("You may begin with page 4 . . .") strongly supports. In carriages, chapels, and theaters, on the one hand, and through the exchange of letters and gifts of print, on the other, Rammohun successfully reconciles the roles of learned Brahmin, Unitarian, and polite gentleman of fashion and sentiment.[125]

Almost in passing, Dermot Killingley expresses the remarkable insight that in London, as opposed to in Calcutta, Rammohun's "views were expressed in polite conversation rather than in print."[126] This is a half-truth, however, with respect to his expressions on both sides of the ocean. In Calcutta his political and religious interventions involved not just pamphlets, tracts, and newspapers but also meetings, societies, and public dinners. And in London he continued writing and publishing. But Killingley's insight is a real one in another sense, for in London polite conversation and print culture interpenetrated in ways we are still only coming to understand.[127] It was not just that, as we will see and as Rammohun was acutely aware, his social engagements would be covered by the press—this is part of the reason why he was so careful about maintaining dietary and other laws of purity[128]—but that print itself entered into social exchanges both materially and symbolically. And this integration and intertwining constituted his performance of politeness. The Bristol Baptist critic John Foster, predisposed to dislike Rammohun, nonetheless came away impressed, describing his character as "unaffected, friendly, and, in the best sense of the word, polite."[129] Anyone who has lived in a foreign language or even just spent time abroad or traveled will know how difficult it is to be "unaffected" when one doesn't feel at home, and the numerous descriptions such as Foster's remind us that Rammohun's performance of unaffected politeness, or "suavity,"[130] was always also an act of localization, for affect and politeness are thoroughly local and contingent.

No performance is possible, of course, without an intuitive grasp of the audience's expectations and of the codes and calibrations appropriate to the venue. And Rammohun was peculiarly prepared to play the role. His own experiences of writing in English, Arabic, Persian, Sanskrit, and Bengali for different readerships in India and abroad had made him a master of localization, defined by Zastoupil as the ability to situate "a text within the linguistic and cultural horizons of the target audience."[131] The argument originates with Killingley, who demonstrated that Rammohun was "keenly aware of the importance of public opinion" and therefore "careful about the way he presented himself and his personal history" in different languages and to their correspondent publics.[132] As Zastoupil summarizes, "Rammohun engaged Muslim, Hindu, and Christian audiences by appealing to their own scriptures and employing their respective rationalist traditions."[133] Debates over Rammohun's true beliefs, and especially over the question of his conversion to Christianity, thus give way to analysis of a figure who accepted that while truth is universal in and of itself, our understanding of it is shaped by the language and location in which it is expressed. (Recall his adoption of personae, from that of the orthodox Ram Doss to that of the *pandit* Sivaprasad Sarma.) Integral to the history of Rammohun's ideas, then, localization can also provide a way of understanding his modes of social interaction.

Brought to bear on the wide range of sources documenting Rammohun's social life in England, localization in this sense reveals another side of the dislocated forms of sociability we have been considering. In particular, as Dipesh Chakrabarty's discussion of the gap in translation between European "sympathy" and the Bengali "understanding of a person's inborn capacity for *shahanubhuti* (*shaha* = equal, *anubhuti* = feelings)"[134] suggests, friendship and conversation were grounds for transcultural negotiation and localization every bit as much as theology and law. Not an exile but a polyglot traveler, Rammohun engaged in acts of social localization that, when successful (and they weren't always), were profoundly contrapuntal, bringing Indian and European identities and codes into relations that undermined the autonomy of each and asserted the interplay of the two within a cosmopolitan social organization. This is not to suggest a simple or transparent translatability between cultural idioms but instead to describe Rammohun's acts of translation as performances that depended upon the constant awareness of local obstacles to and opportunities for communication.

One such obstacle and opportunity, apparently, was his physical appearance. "At a party at a friend of ours" hosted by "Captain Mauleverer, who had known the Rajah in India and was very much attached to him," records Lucy Aikin, "we . . . overheard one of the guests, an Indian officer of rank, say angrily 'What is that *black fellow* doing here?' "[135] But while racial prejudice was real in the period, also (and apparently more) powerful was the association between the elite male Hindu body and sensibility prefigured in Sophia's Brahmin and realized in Rammohun as the famed opponent of sati. Within a month of his arrival, a "Sketch of the Great Hindoo Philosopher Rajah Ram-Mohun-Roy" in *Alexander's East India Magazine* (May 1831) set the pattern by describing him as "of a robust and manly figure; the features of his countenance are deeply expressive," with "a smile of soft and peculiar fascination; the forehead towering, expansive, and commanding; the eye dark, restless, full of brightness and animation, yet liquid and benevolent, and frequently glistening with a tear when affected by the deeper sensibility of the heart."[136] The sketch went on to notice that "his manners are characterized by suavity blended with dignity, verging towards either point according to the company in which he might be placed, whether that of friends or strangers; to ladies his politeness is marked in the most delicate manner, and his felicitous mode of paying them a well-timed compliment, has gained him very many admirers among the fair sex."[137] Similarly, the *Asiatic Journal* highlighted that "amongst the female sex, he was an especial favorite; his fine person, and soft, expressive features, the air of deferential respect with which he treated them, so repugnant to the ideas ordinarily entertained in Europe of Asiatic manners, and the delicate incense of his compliment, perfumed occasionally with the fragrance of Oriental poetry, in which he was well versed, made a strong impression in his favour."[138]

His closest female friendships, as I've suggested, were with three fairly obscure women: Janet Hare (illegitimate daughter of Alexander Hare, brother of David Hare), who lived in the same household with Rammohun at the home of her uncles John and Joseph in Bedford Square; Catherine Castle; and her aunt Ann Kiddell.[139] Records of these friendships beyond sources like the letters I've mentioned above are fleeting, but his interactions with three higher-profile women, Lucy Aikin, Harriet Martineau, and Frances Kemble, have left vivid traces.

Probably because Lucy Aikin more than anyone else embraced Rammohun's reputation as the opponent of sati and therefore an advocate for women, the press responded with intimations of a love affair between the two and went so far as to suggest that they were engaged. In June 1832 the *Court Journal* reported, "The Rajah Ramohun Roy is said to have obtained the affections of the accomplished daughter of an eminent medical practitioner, who is likely to become Mistress RAMMOHUN ROY."[140] The other papers quickly picked up the story, which made its way literally around the world, to Tasmania, where it was reprinted in the *Hobart Town Courier* in December 1832, and which probably led to the rumor after his death that the two had been privately married.[141] Writing in September 1831 from the suburban village of Hampstead to William Ellery Channing in Boston, Aikin announced, "He is indeed a glorious being, . . . with more fervour, more sensibility, a more engaging tenderness of heart than any *class* of character can justly claim."[142] He had come to Aikin's home in Hampstead to meet Joanna Baillie, and, apparently, to discuss with her "the Arian tenets" of her *View of the General Tenour of the New Testament Regarding the Nature and Dignity of Jesus Christ* (1831). But fortunately for Aikin, "We then got him upon subjects more interesting to me—Hindoo laws, especially those affecting women. . . . His feeling for women in general, still more than the admiration he expressed of the mental accomplishments of English ladies, won our hearts."[143]

In a pattern we will see repeated, Rammohun's presence fulfilled the cosmopolitan aspirations of Unitarian society: "Just now my feelings are more cosmopolite than usual," Aikin announced, "I take a personal concern in a *third* quarter of the globe, since I have seen the excellent RAMMOHUN ROY."[144] Through its now personal concerns, mediated by religious conversation and the language of sensibility, a salon in the village of Hampstead already linked to North America becomes a point on a global circuit. Unlike Mary Carpenter, as Zastoupil points out, Aikin was moved by her meetings with Rammohun not to follow "the fashion of benevolence" among women and promote projects of interventionist philanthropy but rather to become "interested in social history to understand what hindered or assisted the development of women's faculties and talents" worldwide.[145] This outcome, I think, was in keeping with the space in which her account of Rammohun unfolds, a Unitarian salon where polite conversation permits the circulation of ideas and feelings among individuals within a coterie of published intellectuals. But other spaces, like the Unitarian Chapel in South Place, off Finsbury Circus, involved different itineraries and alternative relations among speakers and listeners, spectators and spectacle.

At the time of Rammohun's visit, Harriet Martineau was inheriting from Anna Barbauld, Lucy Aikin's aunt and the teacher of Martineau's own father, the mantle of prominent female Unitarian intellectual, which she would wear until her departure from the Unitarian fold in the late 1840s following her trip to Egypt, Palestine, and Syria.[146] By 1831 she was also already an authority on India, and, I am all but convinced, had read Derozio's "A Dramatic Sketch."[147] In keeping with its ongoing ideology of noncoercive universalization, in advance of its annual meeting in May 1831 the Unitarian Association had advertised three prizes "for the best essays whose purpose should be the introduction and promotion of our faith among Catholics, Jews, and Mahometans."[148] Martineau had been told of the results in advance, but at the meeting they were announced as follows: "After the strictest and most impartial investigation the premiums are all awarded to the same individual. It cannot but be thought most honourable to the successful competitor, Miss Harriet Martineau of Norwich, that her compositions have united all suffrages" (3:49). Whether or not her later attempts to distance herself from Unitarianism colored her retrospective account, even in her letters written on the day the spectacle of Rammohun figures more prominently than any other aspect of the occasion. At the morning service before the meeting, "The Rajah was there. Little as I had reckoned on the mere sight of him, I shall never forget it. Never did I see anything so touching" (3:47). On the voyage to England, Rammohun had severely injured his knee disembarking from the ship at the Cape, and in London his injury seems to have multiplied the impression he made upon Martineau and others:

> He looks spirit-broken and wasted by illness. . . . So melting an expression of meek suffering was never seen. I could not have pressed upon him for an introduction, as a hundred [l]adies did. . . . The people actually stood on the benches to catch a glimpse of him. What a moment it was to me, when the most beautiful of the hymn-tunes was being sung, when the Rajah was bending his head on his breast, and my old friend Dr. Carpenter was sitting next to him! (3:47–48)

Descriptions of Rammohun in public repeatedly emphasize the crowds that gathered around him wherever he went. Outside London he had served as a mere marvel of the exotic East for ignorant provincial mobs—he's the "King of Ingee!" crowds in Manchester and on the road to the capital were reported to have exclaimed, or, even though Tipu had died more than thirty years earlier, "*Tippoo Sabe* . . . come to England for to visit King William."[149] In Manchester "many of the 'great unwashed' insisted upon shaking hands with him; some of the *ladies*, who had not stayed to make their toilets very carefully, wished to embrace him, and he with difficulty escaped an honour which he by no means desiderated."[150]

Accounts of the metropolitan crowd at the Finsbury Unitarian Chapel, however, evoke another set of codes for a different audience. At the Unitarian Association meeting held on 25 May 1831 and chaired by Aspland, Martineau was welcomed by the minister William Johnson Fox, who directed her to a quiet pew: "In a very few minutes the whole place . . . was filled to overflowing. The windows, even, were crowded."[151] Suddenly "a buzz announced that the Rajah was coming" (3:49). In a letter to her mother written that evening, Martineau reflects on the day and paints a remarkable set piece: "There is something about

Rammohun Roy that melts one irresistibly, and the more, the more one looks at him. . . . The meek expression of his countenance, his majestic bending figure, and the peculiarities of complexion and costume, made it such a picture as I shall never again behold. The enthusiasm was beautiful" (3:49). Everything about Martineau's description signals a successful localization produced by an encounter between Rammohun and Unitarian society in which both parties are determined to see themselves and each other in recursive terms: Rammohun retains his "peculiarities of complexion and costume," while assuming a posture of devotion consonant with Unitarian hymns, and the overall effect of the Rajah's presence at the symbolic core of Unitarian society is "enthusiasm." Rammohun's meekness in Martineau's telling, it bears adding, should not be confused with passivity; rather, reminiscent of Buckingham's admiration for the Oriental accomplishment of "deference to the opinions of others" in conversation, it signals a willingness and ability to forgo egotism and actively open the self to the ideas, feelings, and expectations of others within a culture of sentiment. "He always leads the conversation, and expects others to follow," she explains, "and he talks to people in their own way or what he thinks such, with exquisite politeness, and a knowledge which appears almost miraculous. With all this cultivation, the most remarkable thing about him, his finest characteristic, is his intensity of feeling" (3:50). As we will see in his friendship with Frances Kemble and their exchanges of gifts, the intense enthusiasm with which viewers responded to and described Rammohun's melting expressions is a sign of "the politics of translating difference"[152] as opposed to an inscription of European taste and sentiment onto a latter-day Sophia's Brahmin.

To reach the very different site of his flirtation with Kemble, the premiere actress of the day, all Rammohun had to do was walk across Bedford Square to the house of Basil and Anne Montagu, at number 25. Unlike the salon in Hampstead, where he won hearts by discussing the preexistence of Christ and Hindu laws regulating widowhood, the location of London's foremost literary soirée summoned an urbane and genteel performance. In *Records of a Girlhood* (1878) Kemble recalls, "Among the remarkable people I met at their [the Montagus'] house was the Indian rajah, Ramohun Roy, philosopher, scholar, reformer, Quaker, theist, I know not what and what not, who was introduced to me, and was kind enough to take some notice of me."[153] Her blithe and no doubt liberating disregard for Rammohun's sectarian or theological allegiances—"I know not what and what not"—must have set the tone in late 1831, and Rammohun initiated the ensuing conversation on subjects suited to the interlocutor and the space:

He talked to me of the literature of his own country, especially its drama, and, finding that I was already acquainted with the Hindoo theatre through the medium
of my friend Mr. Horace Wilson's translations of its finest compositions, but that
I had never read "Sakuntala," the most remarkable of them all, which Mr. Wilson
had not included in his collection (I suppose because of its translation by Sir William Jones), Ramohun Roy sent me a copy of it. (1:290)

An acquaintance if not really a friend of Rammohun's, Wilson already connects
the two in advance of their meeting, but it is the heavily coded gift of Jones's
translation of *Sakuntala* that Kemble later "values as a memento" of their conversations (1:290). Also valuable in this same currency was Rammohun's emotional response to theater in general and Kemble's acting in particular. In an
entry in her diary for 22 December 1831, while she was performing the lead
role in Thomas Southerne's *Isabella, or The Fatal Marriage*, Kemble remarks, "I
played very well. The Rajah Rammohun Roy was in the Duke of Devonshire's
box, and went into fits of crying, poor man!" (3:144).

Rammohun's "fits of crying" recall Dipesh Chakrabarty's discussion of Rammohun's successor as a reformer of Hindu widowhood, Iswarchandra Vidyasa-
gar (1820–1901), celebrated in his Bengali biography of 1895 for his "propensity
to cry in public."[154] By the time of Rammohun's arrival, he was firmly associated with the abolition of sati in 1829, but his renowned sympathy for the suf-
ferings of others had a different valence in England than in Bengal. In England,
Rammohun joined Clarkson, Wilberforce, and other heroes of the movement to
abolish the slave trade as a man of feeling according to a natural theory of sentiments inherited from Adam Smith and David Hume.[155] In this light, Rammohun indicated that Indians were as capable as Europeans of a universal response
to suffering through imaginative acts of sympathy characteristic of the modern,
enlightened subject. But in Bengal, Rammohun's fame rested on his inborn, not
universal, character "as *shahriday* (with *hriday* or heart), and therefore marked
by the capacity for *shahanubhuti*," the exceptional intensity of feeling that is possessed by the *rasika* according to the *rasa shastra*.[156] Rammohun was thus the
great soul, according to the title of Nagendranath Chattopadhyay's 1881–82 biography, *Mahatma Raja Rammohun rayer jibancharit* (The life of Mahatma Raja
Rammohun Roy). The gift of Jones's *Sakuntala* perfectly captures the localization of Rammohun's fame in Bedford Square, a translation of established celebrity as opposed to mere adoption or mimicry of fashionable European sentiment. For to a greater extent than Owenson's syncretistic treatment of Hilarion
and Luxima, Jones's translation of *Sakuntala* prepared the ground for Rammo-

hun's contrapuntal performances in English as both a European man of feeling and an exceptional *rasika* like the play's protagonist Dushmanta.[157]

A few months after he sent this gift, at another "pleasant party" at the Montagus', on the evening of 6 March 1832, he again left an impression: "His appearance is very striking," Kemble writes, "His picturesque dress and colour make him, of course, a remarkable object in a London ballroom. His countenance, besides being very intellectual, has an expression of great sweetness and benignity." By then Rammohun was apparently sufficiently at ease with Kemble to talk with her in her own way: "We presently began a delightful nonsense conversation, which lasted a considerable time, and amused me extremely."[158] Viciously satirized by Thackeray in *The Newcomes* (1853–55) in the chattering figure of Rummun Loll aping sentiment in the drawing room of Oriental Club member Colonel Newcome—"The heathen gentleman . . . was seated by one of the handsomest young women in the room, whose fair face was turned towards him, whose blond ringlets touched his shoulder, and who was listening to him as eagerly as Desdemona listened to Othello"[159]—this kind of nonsense conversation is far more compelling in the context of 1832.

The localized nature of their flirtation involves a consciousness on Rammohun's part of his own charisma as conditioned not by assimilation or "uncritical gregariousness"[160] but by his religious authority, which he was just as willing to display in Unitarian Hampstead and Finsbury as to send up in Bedford Square. "I was turning away from him for a few moments, to speak to Mr. Montague," Kemble recounts,

> when the Rajah recalled my attention to himself by saying, "I am going to quote the Bible to you: you remember that passage, 'The poor ye have always with you, but Me ye have not always.' Now, Mr. Montague you have always with you, but me you have not always." So we resumed our conversation together, and kept up a brief interchange of persiflage which made us both laugh very much, and in which he showed a very ready use of English language for a stranger.[161]

In his religious debates in Calcutta as in his polite conversations in London, Rammohun's ability to quote the Bible did more than authorize him to discuss Christianity. It also summoned aesthetic responses to himself and his speech: "It was *beautiful* to hear him quote Scripture," wrote an anonymous reporter of a conversation with Rammohun at another London soirée two weeks later, describing him further as "remarkably attentive to listening."[162] If, as JanMohamed proposes, the intentionality of the exile is directed to the home culture, while that of the immigrant is directed to the host culture,[163] the elite traveler's persiflage with Kemble reveals a more recursive structure. At home in Bedford Square in two distinct registers—biblical quotation and gallantry—fused by wit, Rammohun conducts the "interchange" not in order to demonstrate his own ease but rather to redirect *Kemble's* intentions toward him. Every intention, every look and word, therefore, is also a summons, the initiation of a return. And the exchange of signs through polite conversation then spills into an exchange of print. The gift of *Sakuntala* had already been given and received. The day after the soirée at the Montagus', Kemble noted in her journal, "I sent 'The Merchant of Venice' to Ramohun Roy, who, in our conversation last night, expressed a great desire to read it." And two days later, on 9 March, "Rehearsed 'Francis I.' When I came home found a charming letter and some Indian books, from that most amiable of all the wise men of the East, Ramohun Roy."[164]

Rammohun's "ready use" of the English language takes multiple forms—in speech, writing, and gifts of print—and circulates through various social spaces, both public and private. This open mode of itinerant sociability in Bedford Square and elsewhere makes him the cosmopolitan antithesis of a *jaut bhaee* in Hanover Square. Although in June 1831 Rammohun was elected an honorary member of the Royal Asiatic Society, which from its inception had been open to honorary members, be they "foreigners, European or Asiatic," who would be "admitted to the meetings of the Society when in England, and invited to correspond with it when abroad,"[165] he never visited the Oriental Club. Nor would he have been welcome there, especially after his alliance with Charles Grant Jr., president of the Board of Control, resulted in the passage in August 1832 of the Jury Act, granting the eligibility of Indians to serve on juries and to officiate as justices of the peace. Grant's defenses of the bill, which relied on Rammohun's "Remarks in Answer to the Objections Raised by the Court of Directors against the Introduction of the Jury Bill," had been unsuccessfully opposed by a petition to the House of Lords drawn up at the Oriental Club, a fact Rammohun did not fail to mention in his account of this victory to Prasanna Kumar Tagore, editor of the *Reformer*, back home in Calcutta.[166]

But if Rammohun's interactions took place for the most part outside Little Bengal and came with a radically different set of communicative prospects, they also brought their own unique risks, in the constant possibility that localization might fail and that his personae might escape his control. Recall Martineau's remark that he "talks to people in their own way *or what he thinks such.*"[167] An eerie but I don't think accidental instance of the cross-hatched relationship between print culture and Rammohun's performances presents itself in the correspondence between an incident in Elizabeth Hamilton's *Translation of the Letters of a*

Hindoo Rajah (1796) and events of 1831–32. In Hamilton's satirical novel the Anglophilic Rajah Zaarmilla has come to England only to have many of his naïve assumptions about British and especially Christian virtue overturned. Believing that newspapers exist to communicate true and unbiased information, he is horrified to find "a paragraph inserted in a newspaper . . . which, after mentioning my name, and describing my person, falsely and wickedly insinuated, 'that I had come there on behalf of the Hindoo inhabitants of Bengal, to complain of the horrid cruelties, and unexampled oppression, under which, through the mal-administration of the British governor of India, we were made to groan.' "[168] A mere eight days after his arrival in England, the *York Herald* described Rammohun as "formerly a Hindoo Brahmin" who "embraced Christianity" and now "professes Unitarianism," adding: "It was reported at Liverpool, on Friday, that he is at the head of a deputation of Brahmins, who intend to intercede with the British Government and the India Company, to permit the continuance of burning widows with the remains of their husbands. Such a rumour is improbable. But if it be true, the Christianity of Rammohun Roy is the mere cloak of his cunning."[169] Within two months Rammohun felt the need to intervene. On 16 June 1831 a letter appeared in the *Times* and was reprinted a day later in the *Morning Chronicle*. "One of my objects in visiting this country," Rammohun wrote,

> has been to lay before the British public a statement, however brief, of my views regarding the past condition and future prospects of India. . . . Perceiving that different parties—friends or strangers to me, I know not—have been making contradictory statements regarding my supposed opinions respecting the Indian question, &c., I beg to say, that as soon as my health, now convalescent, permits, I shall hasten to publish, in a printed form, my opinions.[170]

And then he requested, "I beg you will oblige me by refraining from indulging any correspondents who may feel disposed to use my name, either in support or in opposition to their particular sentiments."[171]

But the use of his name continued to haunt him. Not only did he, like Zaarmilla, find his positions and beliefs misrepresented but he also found himself transformed *into* Zaarmilla. A year (to the day) after he issued his request in the *Times*, the *Royal Cornwall Gazette* published a satirical piece written in the assumed voice of Rammohun to a friend, "Hafid." But the voice assumed made a use of the English language that had far more to do with Elizabeth Hamilton than with Rammohun: "My Dear Friend," he is purported to have written, "I promised you when I sailed from the regions of the East to visit the Island, which is the native soil of that wonderful people, who have become our Lords and Masters, that I would send you an account of the chief matters which might engage my attention."[172] If "lionism" risked reducing recursive sociability to embodiment, reifying conversation and "stationing" Rammohun as a meek, perspiring, and immobile "centre of attraction" instead of its agent and object, this print satire carried out a parallel hypostatization of his language itself. "Oh! Hafid! The veil has been lifted up," he is made to exclaim, before concluding, "The British nation are very wonderful, but they are very unhappy.—I am longing to bathe in the Ganges, and to walk in my gardens, and to enjoy the sun-beams, and to be free from sad thoughts. From thy friend, RAMMOHUN ROY."[173]

After his death the contest continued. Aware that Rammohun's presence and words had transformed the Finsbury Chapel into an itinerant, cosmopolitan space, William Johnson Fox preached at the very same site an obituary sermon, "A Discourse on Occasion of the Death of Rajah Rammohun Roy," for which he chose the following two texts: "Now the Lord had said unto Abram, Get thee out of thy country, and from thy kindred, and from thy father's house, unto a land that I will show thee" (Gen. 12:1); "And he went out, not knowing whither he went" (Heb. 11:8). The occasion and the texts allowed Fox to assert that "Abraham was an Oriental; and whatever the nation of the individual, I apprehend that an Orientalism of nature and mental character belongs to this class of reformers. I mean by Orientalism, a tendency towards the spiritual, the remote, the vast, the undefined."[174] Associated with reform, religious and political, Rammohun Orientalizes Unitarianism in a sense we need to acknowledge as part of the culture of exile within nineteenth-century liberal imperialism: "Another mark of this type is the departing, always figuratively, and often in a literal sense, from the paternal home, and the shrines in which worship the family or the countrymen of him to whom, in his youth, God speaks, that he may benefit mankind."[175] It was his embodiment and performance of this Oriental, exilic spirit that made the traveler Rammohun into "a citizen of the world."[176] A very different memorialization appeared in the *Asiatic Journal*, the East India Company mouthpiece, which opened its obituary as follows: "Betwixt Asiatics and the nations which belong to our system of civilization, there is a line of separation so broadly marked, that they seem superficially, in respect to moral as well as physical properties, almost to be of distinct species."[177] This was the contest, between those who saw Rammohun crossing a "line of separation" and those who would transform that line into a different, connective space: "He had long wished to observe society under the influence of liberal institutions," Fox preached, concluding, "He wished the sea to become the same broad highway for his countrymen that it is for the merchants, the travellers, and the literati of free and civilised nations."[178]

Epilogue

In 1834 Horace Hayman Wilson, chair of Sanskrit at Oxford University and director of the Royal Asiatic Society, sent a series of letters to his old colleague on the Hindu College Board of Managers, Ramkamal Sen, clerk to the Asiatic Society of Bengal and superintendent of the Sanskrit College.[1] Wilson lamented that "the people here care . . . little about anything literary, and not much about anything scientific. Eating, ostentation and politics are the total of English existence. I have a very mean opinion of my countrymen" (15). Complaining of the "morbid vanity about Englishmen that disposes them to undervalue everything that is not of their own country and in it also" (16), he then wrote, "England is divided into many little Englands—there is an England of fashion, of classical learning, of antiquities, of science, of profession, of commerce, of speculation, of politics—all dabble in the last; but in each of the former, it is a mere accident if one set knows anything of what is going on in another" (17). For this returned Anglo-Indian, experience of imperial life had provincialized England, dividing it into "local and disconnected" fields of interest (17). Into this segmented and provincial world, as we saw in chapter 4, came a cosmopolitan traveler, Rammohun Roy, who had challenged Little London throughout the 1820s and did the same, in different ways, for Little Bengal during his two years in England and even after his death in 1833.

What makes a space little? On the one hand, a little space is an enclave, separate from and alien to the larger space that surrounds its borders. When Wilson nostalgically compares Calcutta to "little Englands," he implies a relation of scale and integration at work even at the heart of colonial authority: although England is surrounded by the seas, it remains little and detached. Expansiveness is a matter of connectedness and communication, within and beyond borders; one set knows nothing of what is going on in another, and while England's ships may rule the seas, its people seldom look beyond them. But provincial as Englishmen seemed to Wilson, in his letter their morbid vanity is just that, a metropolitan bigotry that leads them to undervalue national, international, and what we might call interdisciplinary progress in literature and science, and this is the sense in which they are local and disconnected. But displaced, colonial little spaces, like Little London and Little Bengal, are local and disconnected in a second sense as well: they are not only cut off from the surrounding, host space but also at least partially alienated from the source culture, both by distance and by imitation. Even as they replicate, they do so without the historical rootedness or authenticity of the source and in ways uneasily adapted to and disaggregated from the host.

When people, ideas, and things cross borders between colonial spaces defined as either little or large, different sets of values and meanings accompany them. Consider the characteristically little-colonial logic of comparison, a process involving the movement of definitions in one direction, from the source of authenticity to the locus of imitation. We saw that Derozio has been called "a pigmented Keats" and Rammohun the "Luther of Brahmanism," and what follows is merely the start of a much longer list that could be assembled of such comparisons: Vyasa, of course, was the "Indian Homer," and Kalidasa the "Indian Shakespeare";[2] the *Asiatic Journal* named Emma Roberts the "L.E.L. of the city of palaces";[3] Buckingham was the "Indian Cobbett";[4] Rammohun has been compared to Erasmus, Derozio to Pico de la Mirandole, and Duff to Ignatius Loyola;[5] the self-made Ramkamal Sen was "like Benjamin Franklin";[6] Charles Wilkins was the "Caxton of India";[7] Ramgopal Ghosh, the "Demosthenes of Bengal";[8] and Ramtanu Lahiri, the "Arnold of Bengal";[9] while the nautch singer Nikhee was the "Billington of the East."[10] The logic is persistent, even among contemporary Anglo–North American cultural and literary historians of empire: so long as we know the real Keats, Luther, Homer, Shakespeare, Letitia Landon, and so on, we don't really need to know much about the imitations, and it often seems a mere accident if we do.

To return to Scott's suggestive metaphor at the end of *The Surgeon's Daughter*, with which I opened chapter 1, without the cross-stitch the shawl is of considerably less value. In spaces where scale is determined by unidirectional or recursive perspectives, the inimitable cross-stitch is everything or nothing. There are no inimitable cross-stitches that imbue material—wool, wood, bronze, paint on canvas, ink on paper—with spirit, yet it is precisely by projecting spirits—of labor, creativity, or God—into matter that we see and experience ourselves as individuals and, especially, as groups. For instance, as imitative as they were,

I do not think that Derozio and his students were "like the imitative operatives at Paisley" at all, but not because they complemented their imitations with any cross-stitch, British or Indian. Instead, their historical circumstances made them aware that their modernity was being denied and devalued by the very distinction between authenticity and imitation that their activities in the 1820s and the "angry 'thirties of the nineteenth century," as Goutam Chattopadhyay shrewdly put it,[11] were undermining if not surpassing. And this was the case regardless of the fact that with the subsequent consolidation of the Raj, the potential of this cultural configuration to exceed the logic of comparison would never be realized.

After all, Scott's "merciless old lady" concludes her argument not with an assertion that one out of ten thousand knows the true spirit that imbues the authentic article but rather with the claim "that there is some way of knowing a thing that cost fifty guineas from an article that is sold for five." Hers is an argument about the value of a commodity. But there are other values, of people and of things, as in Wilson's charge that Englishmen "undervalue everything that is not of their own country and in it also." His reduction of England to little Englands, local and disconnected, with its implicit comparison to a more capacious Calcutta, abandons authenticity for integration, for the correspondence among different areas of knowledge and spheres of life. In the alternatives to Little London in Bengal and Little Bengal in London such encounters were by no means always benign or even harmonious, but they did present a different model of, and perspective on, value not as authenticity but as the meeting of spirits, from Buckingham's "SPIRIT OF THE INDIAN JOURNALS," Kalikrishna Deb's expectation that Lord Bentinck and his suite would see Durga, and the protest of the "native" who observed Brunsdon "packing up a number of idols for the Bristol Museum" and told him that "it was a very great sin to box them in that way" to Southey's intensely objective imagination, Derozio's citations, and Rammohun's conversational exchanges in London.

In October 1844 another box set sail, this time from Bristol to Leicester, Massachusetts. "In a box of *wonderful contents* (which have been exhibited at my house previously to their transmission to Boston)," wrote the Unitarian John B. Estlin, son of John Prior Estlin, to Samuel May Jr., Unitarian abolitionist, "I have put 12 little papers, each containing a portion, (6 of them a *lock*,) of the hair of the late *Rammohan Roy*."[12] This too was a sin, a violation of "Gentoo customs" in reality if not in *Hartly House, Calcutta*, which once again prefigured in fiction what would follow in fact. After Sophia's Brahmin dies, she writes to Arabella that she has "begged the Sekar to procure, if that indulgence is not incompatible with the

Gentoo customs, a lock of his hair, for the purpose, my dear girl, of making it a mental talisman."[13] The locket will be "set with pearls" and given as a gift to Arabella, "for its virtues will be abundant" (135). "They refused me not," Sophia reports a few pages later, "a lock of this saint's hair, and I have had it elegantly set for his sake" (137). But of course it really wasn't for his sake, and that is the real sin, though a forgivable one in the context of the sentimental fiction. "Should time and chance restore me to my country," writes Sophia with pitch-perfect egotism, "I will erect a pagoda in Britain, to perpetuate the remembrance" not of the man himself but of the triumph "that so exemplary a character was on the list of my Bengal acquaintance" (135–36). With the brief, submerged, and dim flame of sexual attraction extinguished by his death, Sophia meets no one but herself in the lock of hair, a mental talisman of her own mind, its abundant virtues encompassing only her own copious self-regard.

If no spirits meet in the lock of this saint's hair, the twelve little papers that traveled from Bristol to Boston might tell a different story. In late December 1844 the packets were exhibited for sale at the eleventh annual antislavery fair, held in Amory Hall, Boston. There Samuel May reported seeing "very many pretty & beautiful things from Bristol," among them the samples of Rammohun's hair. "I was in Boston last week, and visited the Anti Slavery Fair or Bazaar. . . ," he wrote to Estlin, adding that he was "much pleased with the very neat manner in which the packets of hair were done up."[14] Earlier, Estlin had told May, "We shall be much interested, and *you* may be much benefitted on another occasion, by our knowing how the articles we send, sell, & what are the most valuable."[15] Worlded from Bengal to Bristol to Boston, shorn from a corpse in violation of custom and converted, these articles could have been purchased for their exoticism or their link to celebrity, or for the personal self-satisfaction and self-identification of the abolitionist buyer, or because gathered in each lock were strands of worldwide liberty, sympathy, and principled opposition. Or for a combination of these reasons. "The little packets of the hair of Rammohun Roy, I cannot doubt, will find ready purchasers," replied May, surmising, "Some there are, I know, and doubtless many whom I do not know, who would rejoice to possess one of these undoubted relics of a most extraordinary man."[16] Why some would or did rejoice, with what feelings of possession and connectedness, and with what consequences are open questions.

Introduction

1. Marshman, *Life and Times*, 2:20.

2. A recent survey has been provided by D. Ghosh, "Another Set of Imperial Turns?" See also Ballantyne, *Orientalism and Race* and *Between Colonialism and Diaspora*; Burton, *After the Imperial Turn*; Hall and Rose, "Introduction"; Howe, *New Imperial Histories Reader*; Stoler and Cooper, "Between Metropole and Colony"; and K. Wilson, *New Imperial History*. An early critique of center-periphery models that has influenced my thinking is Arjun Appadurai's "Disjuncture and Difference in the Global Cultural Economy."

3. Stoler and Cooper, "Between Metropole and Colony," 1.

4. Cohn, *Colonialism*, 4.

5. Important literary studies that focus primarily on British writings about India include Joseph, *Reading the East India Company*; Krishnan, *Reading the Global*; Leask, *British Romantic Writers and the East* and *Curiosity*; Majeed, *Ungoverned Imaginings*; Makdisi, *Romantic Imperialism*; O'Quinn, *Staging Governance*; Suleri, *Rhetoric of English India*; Teltscher, *India Inscribed*; Trumpener, *Bardic Nationalism*; and Wright, *Ireland, India, and Nationalism*. Exceptional cultural studies that range between writings by Britons and by Indians include Aravamudan, *Tropicopolitans* and *Guru English*; R. Chaudhuri, *Gentlemen Poets in Colonial Bengal*; Gibson, *Indian Angles*; Jasanoff, *Edge of Empire*; and Viswanathan, *Masks of Conquest* and *Outside the Fold*.

6. I use "East Indian" throughout in its early nineteenth-century sense to mean mixed-race Christian Eurasians; see chapter 3 for a discussion of the term and the community. Although there is a significant amount of ambiguity in the period, many East Indians considered themselves to be "Indians," especially by the early 1830s, following their two petitions to Parliament for redress of legal disadvantages. When I separate East Indians and Indians rhetorically—in lists, for example—I do not mean to imply that the former community was not part of the latter. See R. Chaudhuri, "Politics of Naming."

7. *AJ*, n.s., 8 (August 1832): 331.

8. Hereafter cited as *Bengal Annual*, followed by the year (in Arabic numerals) for which the annual appeared.

9. Quoted in Derozio, *Derozio, Poet of India*, 9. The piece continues: "Yea, this is truly the *Augustan* age in Calcutta. In walking the streets 'tis ten to one but the observer stumbles against a Poet every ten yards. In Wellington square, . . . Poets do so abound, that

straw ought to be scattered along the pathways . . . so as to prevent the rattling of chariots and buggies . . . from disturbing the heavenly meditations of the inspired inhabitants, and the accouchment of ideas" (10).

10. I discuss these terms further in chapter 4. See also D. Carey, "Reading Contrapuntally."

11. Although I focus on circulation between Calcutta and London, there are many other ports that could be added to the account, especially Cape Town and St. Helena, or, on the overland route, Basra and Bandar-e Abbas (formerly Gombroon), on the Strait of Hormuz.

12. Hall and Rose, "Introduction," 1.

13. In referring to Rammohun by his first name (Roy was an inherited honorific), I follow standard convention.

14. See Nechtman, *Nabobs*.

15. P. Chatterjee, *Black Hole of Empire*, 55–62. See also Marshall, *Impeachment of Warren Hastings*. For an excellent recent treatment of the Hastings trial in general and Sheridan's role in particular, see D. Taylor, *Theatres of Opposition*, 67–118.

16. Byron, *Lord Byron's Letters and Journals*, 3:101 (28 August 1813).

17. Ibid.

18. The major South Asian presence in London in the early nineteenth century was the transient community of lascars (Indian sailors hired in groups as opposed to individually) centered around the Company's contracted depots in Shoreditch and Shadwell, though impoverished lascars circulated throughout England and Ireland. See Fisher, *Counterflows to Colonialism*, 137–79; and Visram, *Ayahs, Lascars and Princes*, 34–54.

19. As printed in the *Calcutta Morning Post*, the clauses (resolution 13) read as follows: "That it is the duty of this country, to promote the interest and happiness of the native inhabitants of the British dominions in India, and that such measures ought to be adopted, as may tend to the introduction among them, of useful knowledge, and of religious and moral improvement. That in the furtherance of the above objects, sufficient facilities shall be afforded by law, to persons desirous of going to, and remaining in India for the purpose of accomplishing those benevolent designs." *CMP*, 26 November 1813, 5D. See also Carson, *East India Company and Religion*, 130–50. I regret that I did not become aware of Carson's new work until the present book was in an advanced stage of completion.

20. The *diwani*, granted by the Mughal emperor Shah Alam II in the Treaty of Allahabad after the Battle of Buxar, symbolically authorized the Company to collect revenue and administer civil law.

21. Published by order of the House of Commons in 1813, C. Grant's "Observations On the State of Society among the Asiatic Subjects of Great Britain" was written "chiefly" in 1792.

22. "Sketch of the Origin, Rise, and Progress of the Hindoo College," 72.

23. Aravamudan, *Guru English*, 27.

24. Killingley, *Rammohun Roy*, 84.

25. Kopf, *British Orientalism*, 192. Killingley has complicated this understanding of Rammohun's firm division between Vedantic purity and post-Vedantic corruption, arguing that while its general outlines are accurate, Rammohun held that not only the Upanishads but also the Puranas and Tantras "contained both pure monotheism and teachings

related to figured gods," with the purity of the former Vedantic teachings "intended to supersede the latter in the minds of those capable of understanding them" (*Rammohun Roy*, 83). Many Western writers have been confused by Rammohun's references to Veda, the Vedas, and *sruti*. By all of these terms, he does not mean the four collections we commonly refer to as the Vedas today—the Rig, Yajur, Sama, and Atharva Vedas; instead, he means the Upanishads, also known as Vedanta ("the end of the Veda"). Killingley clarifies: Rammohun "probably knew nothing of the Veda beyond the Upanisads. . . . In Rammohun's time there were few printed texts in Sanskrit and no concordances; Vedic texts were hardly accessible directly, except to those who had been through the traditional Vedic discipline of memorizing them" (87).

26. Kopf, *British Orientalism*, 192.

27. Mittra, *Life of Dewan Ramcomul Sen*, 46–47.

28. Kopf, *British Orientalism*, 192–96.

29. Pennington, *Was Hinduism Invented?*, 171.

30. Majumdar and Dhar, *Presidency College Register*, 2.

31. Macaulay, "Minute on Indian Education," 237–38.

32. Warner, VanAntwerpen, and Calhoun, "Editors' Introduction," 25.

33. E. W. Stillingfleet, *On the Character of Idolatry*, 48.

34. Ibid.

35. I regret that I have had to limit my study to encounters between Protestant Christianity and Hinduism instead of, as originally intended, considering Bengali Islam and other faiths in the region as well. For the most part, my use of the terms "Hindu" and "Hinduism" corresponds to the early nineteenth-century colonial European and Indian understanding of Indian religions as a single, unified faith incorporating various sects. For a discussion of the criteria that define Hinduism as "a collective term for certain religions, religious communities, and socioreligious systems" (20), see Michaels, *Hinduism*. For important treatments of Hinduism as a construct, see Lorenzen, "Who Invented Hinduism?"; Nicholson, *Unifying Hinduism*; Pennington, *Was Hinduism Invented?*; Stietencron, "Hinduism"; and Viswanathan, "Colonialism."

36. I use the term *murti* or its most literal translation, "image," whereas my frequent references to "god(s)" and "idols" should be taken in the context of and in keeping with early nineteenth-century usage.

37. Anderson, *Imagined Communities*.

38. P. Chatterjee, *Nation and Its Fragments*, 5.

39. On the relations between the White Town and the Black Town and the internal divisions within each, see Banerjee, *Parlour and the Streets*, 19–78; and S. Chattopadhyay, *Representing Calcutta*, 76–135.

40. R. Chaudhuri, *Gentlemen Poets*; Gibson, *Indian Angles*.

41. Derozio, *Derozio, Poet of India*; Derozio, *Song of the Stormy Petrel*; S. Mukhopadhyay, *Derozio*. Selections of Derozio's poetry and prose appear in Macdonald and McWhir, *Broadview Anthology of Literature of the Revolutionary Period, 1770–1832*; and Keirn and Schürer, *British Encounters with India*.

42. Bhabha, *Location of Culture*, 126.

43. Ibid., 208.

44. R. Chaudhuri, introduction, lxxx–lxxxi.

45. S. T. Coleridge, *Collected Letters*, 4:917.

46. Robbins, "Introduction Part 1." In my use of "cosmopolitan" the term still signifies "allegiance . . . to the worldwide community of human beings" rather than to the nation. M. Nussbaum, "Patriotism and Cosmopolitanism," 4. But at the same time it need not "offer a clear-cut alternative to nationalism" and in fact can "[work] together with nationalism rather than in opposition to it" (Robbins, "Introduction Part 1," 2). In other words, cosmopolitanism is often a constitutive element of nationalism, as in the case of the Indian nationalisms of early nineteenth-century Calcutta. The nineteenth-century cosmopolitanisms that I treat are among those gestured to by Tony Ballantyne, who argues that even as "the power of the nation state was consolidated" and the Enlightenment culture of cosmopolitanism gave way to nationalism, "new, self-consciously 'modern' forms of cosmopolitanism were emerging." Ballantyne, "Empire, Knowledge and Culture," 134.

Chapter 1 • *"Little London"*

Epigraph: Fhlathúin, *Poetry of British India*, 1:55.

1. Scott, *Chronicles of the Canongate*, 287.
2. Ibid.
3. Atkinson, *City of Palaces*, 15.
4. Freitag, introduction, 2.
5. Ibid.
6. Bayly, "Rammohan Roy," 37.
7. Freitag, introduction, 7.
8. Cohn, *Colonialism*, 4.
9. Partha Chatterjee's critique, in *Nationalist Thought and the Colonial World* and *Nation and Its Fragments*, of Benedict Anderson's model of nationalism as a Western "modular" form has influenced scholarship associated with the Subaltern Studies Group.
10. Sudipta Sen, *Distant Sovereignty*, xvii.
11. Buckingham, *Letter to Sir Charles Forbes*, 4. "Doubly-delegated" because divided between the Board of Directors and the Board of Control.
12. See the introduction for a discussion of the term "orthodox."
13. Barns, *Indian Press*, 74.
14. A. F. S. Ahmed, *Social Ideas and Social Change*, 56.
15. Townsend, *Annals of Indian Administration*, 272.
16. These were preceded by two periodicals in Bengali published by the Serampore mission with extensive assistance from Hindu *pandits*, the monthly *Dig Darshan* (1818) and the daily *Samachar Darpan* (1818). On 14 May 1818, a little over a week before the first issue of the *Samachar Darpan* appeared, on 23 May, the *Government Gazette* printed an advertisement in which one Harachandra Roy announced a new Bengali newspaper to be called the *Bengal Gazette*; no copies survive, and the paper does not seem to have lasted long. The *Samachar Darpan* and the *Bengal Gazette* were thus the first Indian-language newspapers to be published in India. See A. F. S. Ahmed, *Social Ideas and Social Change*, 84–85; and S. B. Singh, "Growth of Public Opinion," 9–10.
17. In 1831 also appeared the *Reformer*, which became the mouthpiece of the Brahmoist followers of Rammohun, edited by Prasanna Kumar Tagore, a manager of the Hindu College.
18. Buckingham, *Letter to Sir Charles Forbes*, 15.
19. Ibid., 15–16.

20. Ibid., 16.

21. Townsend, *Annals of Indian Administration*, 272–73.

22. Habermas, *Structural Transformation*, 24.

23. Townsend, *Annals of Indian Administration*, 272–73.

24. Quoted from Leicester Stanhope's reply to "An Old Indian" in "On a Free Press in India," *AJ* 12 (November 1821): 429–31; the passage appears on 429. The debate between "An Old Indian" and Stanhope played out first in London and then in the dueling *John Bull in the East* and *Calcutta Journal* in late March 1822. Stanhope responded, "In this sentiment I concur, but would in the mean time have it free to produce this result. The *Old Indian* reasons like that fond Granny, who would not allow her son to bathe till he could swim" (429). Stanhope reprinted the debate in *Sketch of the History and Influence of the Press in British India*, which appeared shortly before Stanhope left in September 1823 for Greece as agent of the Greek Committee. Having cut his utilitarian teeth in Calcutta and London, he clashed with Byron over the establishment of a free press in Greece, to which Byron was opposed "in *the present state*" of the country: "Colonel Stanhope and myself had considerable differences of opinion on this subject, and (what will appear laughable enough) to such a degree that he charged me with *despotic* principles, and I *him* with *ultra-radicalism*." Byron, *Lord Byron's Letters and Journals*, 11:139 (19 March 1824).

25. Buckingham, *Second Letter to Sir Charles Forbes*, 44.

26. Ibid., 47–48.

27. Buckingham, *Prospectus of a New Paper*, 1.

28. Anderson, *Imagined Communities*, 7.

29. Buckingham, *Prospectus of a New Paper*, 2.

30. The *Sambad Kaumudi*, a weekly, ran from December 1821 to October 1822. It was started by Tarachand Dutta and Bhabanicharan Bannerji, but Bhabanicharan resigned in March 1822 to start the rival *Samachar Chandrika*. He was succeeded as editor of the *Sambad Kaumudi* by Rammohun, with whom the newspaper came to be firmly associated. Rammohun also edited the *Mirat al-Akhbar* until he resigned in protest over the Press Ordinance of 1823 and the deportation of Buckingham.

31. *CJ*, 20 December 1821, 519.

32. Ibid.

33. G. Chattopadhyay, *Awakening in Bengal*, 1:xiii–xiv.

34. Bayly, *Recovering Liberties*, 50–60; Kopf, *British Orientalism*, 191.

35. *CJ*, 14 February 1823, 618.

36. *AJ* 14 (August 1822): 137.

37. Ibid., 142.

38. Marshman, *Life and Times*, 1:348.

39. Strachey, *India*, 1–2.

40. Ibid., 5.

41. *CJ*, 14 February 1823, 617–18.

42. Buckingham, *Letter to Sir Charles Forbes*, 8–9.

43. Although Rammohun was invested in propagating public discussion in Bengali, when writing in English he did tend to assume that English was the language of public opinion. Thus in *A Defence of Hindu Theism* (1817), his reply to Sankara Sastri, English master at the Madras Government College, who had argued (against Rammohun's *Translation of an Abridgment of the Vedant* [1817]; originally published in Calcutta with the Cena

Upanishad in 1816) in favor of the worship of divine attributes as deities, Rammohun first regretted that Sankara had chosen to conduct a sacred debate in English rather than Sanskrit and then added, "Nor need it be alleged that, by adopting this established channel of controversy [i.e., in Sanskrit], the opportunity of appealing to public opinion on the subject must be lost, as a subsequent translation from the Sanskrit into English may sufficiently serve that purpose." Rammohun Roy, *English Works*, 89.

44. *AJ*, n.s., 7 (April 1832): 281.

45. Ibid., 283.

46. Ibid., 285.

47. Biswas, *Correspondence of Raja Rammohun Roy*, 2:720.

48. See Zastoupil, *Rammohun Roy*, 151–62.

49. Mehta, *Liberalism and Empire*, 20–21.

50. Anderson, *Imagined Communities*, 185.

51. Lynn Hunt, "Experience of Revolution," 674.

52. See A. Ghosh, *Power in Print*; and Gupta and Chakravorty, *Print Areas* and *New Word Order*.

53. Hunt, "Experience of Revolution," 674, 677.

54. Nigel Leask has discussed relationships between panoramic displays and colonial exoticism, and the starting point of my argument here is indebted to his premise that "the shift from a mercantilist to a colonialist phase of imperialist ideology was productive of a new relationship between the metropolitan spectator and the exotic—now, often, in the strict sense, *colonial*—image." Leask, "Wandering through Eblis," 170.

55. On the Barker family—Robert was the father of Henry Aston and Thomas Edward Barker—and the establishment of the panoramas in Leicester Square (1794) and the Strand (1802), see Altick, *Shows of London*, 128–41. For the most comprehensive sources on the history of the panorama, see Comment, *Panorama*; Hyde, *Panoramania!*; Oettermann, *Panorama*; Oleksijczuk, *First Panoramas*; and Wilcox, "Early History of the Panorama." And for a recent extensive treatment of the panorama in relation to the picturesque, see S. Thomas, *Romanticism and Visuality*, 1–19.

56. Galperin, *Return of the Visible*, 50; De Almeida and Gilpin, *Indian Renaissance*, 161.

57. Dibdin, *Reminiscences of a Literary Life*, 1:146–48.

58. Comment, *Panorama*, 19.

59. Charlesworth, "Subverting the Command of Place," 142, 131.

60. Ibid., 134. Compare Comment's claim that "the invention of the panorama was a response to a particularly strong nineteenth-century [*sic*] need—for absolute dominance. It gave individuals the happy feeling that the world was organized around and by them, yet this was a world from which they were also separated and protected, for they were seeing it from a distance. A double dream came true—one of totality and possession." *Panorama*, 19.

61. G. Wood, *Shock of the Real*, 103.

62. Ibid., 109. J. Jennifer Jones has argued against this reading of Wordsworth's response to the panorama in "Absorbing Hesitation."

63. Galperin, *Return of the Visible*, 43.

64. Ibid., 40.

65. Ibid., 55.

66. O'Quinn, *Staging Governance*, 342.

67. C. Taylor, *On Wednesday, October 1, 1806,* . . . , 1, 2.

68. Slade, *Turkey, Greece and Malta,* 1:129–30.

69. W. Jones, *Letters of Sir William Jones,* 2:749.

70. *Athenaeum* 90 (15 July 1829): 445.

71. See "Explanation," in Burford, *Description of a View.* None of the early nineteenth-century panoramas survive, so reconstructions of them are based on the printed "Explanations," which reproduced the panorama either as a circular (anamorphic) image or, as here, in two horizontal frames. See Oleksijczuk, *First Panoramas,* 127–71. For the dates of Burford's Panorama of Calcutta, see *Examiner,* 28 February 1830, 132, and 22 May 1831, 336.

72. *Morning Chronicle,* 8 April 1830, 3B.

73. *Gentleman's Magazine* 100 (March 1830): 251.

74. In the late 1830s, James B. Laidlaw's Panorama of Calcutta was praised for the "fidelity" with which it depicted the city's "extensive and gorgeous public buildings," implying a greater emphasis on architecture, in addition to which a "procession of an Eastern prince, with all its attendant splendour, has been judiciously introduced, and not only serves to enliven the scene, and rivet the attention of the audience, but affords an opportunity for the exhibitor to explain the religious and other customs of the Hindoos, the different castes into which they are divided, the origin of their superstitious creed, and to convey much useful and interesting information." *Bristol Mercury,* 15 June 1839, 3F.

75. The British Library holds a copy of Fiebig's panoramic lithograph, colored, as one long (24 x 210 cm.) single foldout sheet, bound (Calcutta, 1847), shelfmark V 12765.

76. *Examiner,* 28 February 1830, 132.

77. *Gentleman's Magazine* 100 (March 1830): 251.

78. *Athenaeum* 122 (February 1830): 123–24.

79. *Gentleman's Magazine* 100 (March 1830): 251.

80. Ibid.

81. *Lady's Magazine,* n.s., 1 (31 May 1830): 280. This was one among several inaccuracies, he reported: "the festival . . . is kept in April, and not in October, as stated in the description"; "I have seen the festivals . . . of all seasons, . . . and I never saw elephants in the procession"; "The Hindoos bring their idols along the Cheringy-road . . . and send them down the river with lights; but this is done between eight o'clock in the evening and twelve at midnight, whereas the painting represents the scene in broad day-light" (280). The young friend nonetheless concludes, "Still, making allowance for the broad license which the artist has taken, and the consequent excusable exaggerations, those who have been to Calcutta will be struck with its accuracy" (280).

82. Burke, *Writing and Speeches,* 217.

83. *Athenaeum* 122 (February 1830): 123.

84. Ibid., 124.

85. Burford, *Description of a View,* 8.

86. Ibid., 7. Among the first films to be shot in India was the Warwick Trading Company's *Panorama of Calcutta* (1899), which can be viewed at www.colonialfilm.org.uk/node/275 (accessed 21 June 2012). A completely different medium from the circular, painted panorama, the film was shot from a boat as it moved along the river. The individual viewer who gazes through the lens is distanced from the numerous people on the *ghats* by perspective, the barrier of water, and rapidity of movement. Online, however, the

film can now be easily paused, revealing curious looks in response, which break down the separation and create a very different effect from that of the film watched at regular speed. Further undermining the authority of the anthropological gaze is the irony that the film was miscataloged and in fact depicts the *ghats* of Varanasi, not Calcutta.

87. See *CMP*, 24 January 1812, 1B (Dover); 13 March 1812, 1C (Edinburgh); and 29 January 1813, 1A (Ramsgate); and Sandeman, *Selections from Calcutta Gazettes...*, 5:613 (Battle of Waterloo).

88. In the advertisement in *CMP*, 29 January 1813, 1A, the Bengali word for "panorama" is a transliteration. Thanks to Rosinka Chaudhuri and Abir Lal Mitra for their comments.

89. *Putnam's Monthly* 10 (August 1857): 199. Although the source is late, "the Exchange and Public Rooms" were built in the late eighteenth century, as their proprietor advertised them for sale in 1799 under "pressure of debts contracted in the building of them": "The Exchange and public rooms from their centrical [*sic*] situation in Calcutta, may be looked on as the most valuable property in it; they are calculated for various purposes—for Assembly rooms of the first order—for Public Offices—and for the first shops in the world." Seton-Karr, *Selections from Calcutta Gazettes*, 532–33.

90. *CG*, 28 December 1797, 2A. Alternatively, the rotunda might have been a centrally located temporary structure. A third, more tenuous conjecture is that there was formerly a circular structure at the western end of the Writers' Buildings in Tank Square (later rebuilt as the octagonal wing housing the Bengal Legislative Council Chamber). I am grateful to Michael Franklin, Charles Allen, G. M. Kapur, and Ranabir Ray Choudhury for their correspondence on the subject.

91. Roberdeau, "Calcutta in 1805," 45.

92. *CG*, 21 January 1808, 1B.

93. W. Foster, "British Artists in India," 46; *CG*, 28 April 1808, 1B.

94. Oettermann, *Panorama*, 45.

95. Dubbini, *Geography of the Gaze*, 75, 6. "Henceforth, only many partial, multiple, and autonomous viewings would make it possible to grasp the reality of rapid change" (6), and according to Dubbini, these viewings found their correspondent medium in the film montage.

96. Ellis, "Spectacles within doors," 144. Ellis writes, "The locality paradox produced by the panorama made viewers unable to rationalise the relationship between the place they know themselves to be in (Leicester Square) and the locality they now see themselves in (the roof of Albion Mill, the deck of a frigate at Spithead). Sooner or later, however, depending on the viewer's perspicuity, this confused state gave way to a realisation that the delusive prospect is a painting: brush strokes, the edges of the cylindrical perspectival plane, the view's still immobility, all these technical limitations become apparent" (144).

97. Benjamin, *Arcades Project*, 532; see also 17–18 and 527–36.

98. Otto, "Between the Virtual and the Actual," para. 50.

99. *CG*, 20 February 1812, 3D. The Panorama of Edinburgh ran for about six weeks. Perhaps inspired by Williams and Hohler's sale of the Panorama of Dover, in late March Gould and Campbell advertised, "To be Sold by Public Auction . . . on Wednesday next, the 1st April, *Peremptorily to the highest bidder*, the Panorama of the City of Edinburgh, Which has been exhibited for some time past at the Rotunda and highly admired." *CG*, 26 March 1812, 3A.

100. A salt print titled *A Rotunda in a Garden, Calcutta*, was produced by Frederick Fiebig ca. 1850.

101. The other two panoramas exhibited in 1812–13 also resonate as symbolic points of departure: Ramsgate (the port town) and Edinburgh (with so many Scots among the population of Britons in Bengal).

102. *AJ* 2 (1 July 1816): 35.

103. *Orient Pearl* for 1835, 47. As with the issues of the *Bengal Annual*, I cite issues of the *Orient Pearl*, which appeared for 1832, 1834, and 1835, as *Orient Pearl*, followed by the year for which the annual appeared.

104. Freitag, introduction, 7.

105. See Hobsbawm and Ranger, *Invention of Tradition*.

106. *Morning Post*, 27 February 1830, 3D.

107. *CMP*, 31 December 1813, 3C.

108. *AJ* 23 (1 May 1827): 671.

109. G. Chattopadhyay, *Bengal*, 77–78.

110. Ibid., 78. For an excellent discussion of the painting that appears in this volume as figure 8, *Europeans being entertained in Calcutta during Durga Puja*, by William Prinsep, see S. Chattopadhyay, *Representing Calcutta*, 161–63.

111. On these and other forms of entertainment, see Banerjee, *Parlour and the Streets*, 78–146.

112. E. Roberts, *Scenes and Characteristics of Hindostan*, 2:360.

113. Derozio, *Song of the Stormy Petrel*, 398.

114. *AJ* 2 (1 July 1816): 35. In *A Collection of Two Hundred and Fifty Coloured Etchings*, Balthazar Solvyns depicted devotees lining up to make *prasada*, or food offerings, and take *darshan* in the Durga Puja *pandal* of a wealthy family (sec. 12, no. 4). I discuss *darshan* at greater length in chapter 2.

115. Gibbes, *Hartly House, Calcutta*, 80.

116. Bose, *Hindoos As They Are*, 118.

117. *Hindu Holidays*, 3, 16.

118. *AJ* 23 (1 May 1827): 671.

119. Ibid., n.s., 1 (April 1830): 199.

120. *Bengal Hurkaru*, 12 October 1829, 3A.

121. *AJ* 16 (July 1823): 90.

122. *Friend of India*, 24 September 1835, 305.

123. C. Hall, *Civilising Subjects*, 293.

124. Freitag, introduction, 3–4.

125. McDermott, *Revelry, Rivalry, and Longing*, 41.

126. S. Chattopadhyay, *Representing Calcutta*, 88–92, 141–67.

127. Derozio, *Song of the Stormy Petrel*, 396.

128. Ibid., 398–99.

129. *CJ*, 22 September 1819, 183.

130. McDermott, *Revelry, Rivalry, and Longing*, 14.

131. Killingley, *Rammohun Roy*, 28.

132. In this respect, there are parallels between McDermott's reevaluation of Durga Puja and Nicholas Dirks's treatment of caste as an invented tradition. "Caste, as it came to be known under later colonial rule," writes Dirks, "is not in fact some unchanged rem-

nant of ancient India, not some single system, that reflects a core civilizational value, not a basic expression of Indian tradition." *Scandal of Empire*, 295.

133. For a classic statement on (re)invented tradition, see Bernard Cohn's discussion of British adaptations of Mughal durbars before and after the Rebellion of 1857, especially his treatment of British misconstruals in the eighteenth century of gift exchanges—the presentation of *nazr* (tribute money) and *peshkash* (other valuables) to the ruler, and the ruler's granting of titles and presents of *khil'at* (robes and other symbolic, and symbolically ordered, articles of clothing)—as bribery and corruption, in "Representing Authority in Victorian India." See also Eaton, "Between Mimesis and Alterity."

134. *AJ* 23 (1 May 1827): 671.

135. Derozio, *Song of the Stormy Petrel*, 398.

136. Bentham, *Works of Jeremy Bentham*, 10:577. On Bentinck's administration and the utilitarian tradition, see Stokes, *English Utilitarians and India*, 150–68.

137. Derozio, *Song of the Stormy Petrel*, 399.

138. *AJ*, n.s., 1 (April 1830): 199.

139. *Bengal Hurkaru*, 28 September 1830, 2D.

140. Freitag, introduction, 11.

141. Ward, *View of the History*, 1:xxxvii.

142. P. Chatterjee, *Black Hole of Empire*, 124. See also Jasanoff, *Edge of Empire*; and D. Ghosh, *Sex and the Family*. Critics commonly associate the celebratory perspective with the writings of William Dalrymple, especially *White Mughals*.

Chapter 2 • *Secret Sharers and Evangelical Signs*

1. Hall and Rose, "Introduction," 3.

2. Southey, *New Letters*, 1:213.

3. Most of the museum's holdings were sold off over the course of the mid- to late twentieth century, but these sales are difficult to trace, with the exception of the final one. I have acquired a copy of the "Auction Sale Catalogue of the Remaining Contents of Bristol Baptist College, Woodland Road, Bristol" (Tamlyn and Son, Bridgwater Auction Rooms, 30 June 1998), which lists various nineteenth-century Indian paintings, miniatures, and watercolors but no devotional items other than "A 19ᵗʰ century Indian circular stone stele depicting four images of Buddha, 6½ in. high, and two native painted stone figurines, 7½ in. high" (lot 58).

4. In light of Southey's description of the figure as "epicene-looking," it could have been Karttikeya's *sakti*, or female energy, Kaumari or Karttikeyani, though this is less likely. See A. K. Chatterjee, *Cult of Skanda-Kārttikeya*.

5. The *Baptist Magazine* reproduces a letter from Digha that includes the following description: "On the 14th and 15th [of November], the Kartik Puja, as it is called, will take place. Kartik is the son of Shib and Durga, and god of war. He is represented as a handsome young man riding on a peacock." *Baptist Magazine* 29 (July 1837): 321. "Kartik" in the name of the puja refers to the month, and the festival is primarily devoted to Vishnu and Krishna.

6. On the locations of Madnabati and Mahipaldighi, see Sangupta, *West Bengal District Gazeteers*, 51–53. An English factory had been established in Malda since 1771.

7. Hereafter, in both text and notes, I cite the *Periodical Accounts Relative to the Baptist Missionary Society* parenthetically by volume and page. Fountain was obsessed with idol

worship from the moment he landed in Bengal, writing in November 1796, "Here one beholds the high places of idolatry under every green tree, where deluded millions sacrifice to devils" (*PA* 1:322). Immediately before the Durga Puja of 1798 he exclaimed in a letter of 12 October, "Oh! that I could see more of the angels of Christ flying towards Bengal, to call men from the service of dumb idols, to that of the living God. While I am writing, the drums are beating in the villages, preparatory to one of their greatest acts of idolatry" (*PA* 1:478).

8. Although Morris was in Clipstone, the timing suggests that Fountain sent a box to Bristol as well, in keeping with the common practice of communication between the missionaries and the society (or the box may have gone directly to Morris, who could have forwarded some of the curiosities on to the museum). Southey says that "they had just sent over" this idol, which makes Fountain's shipment the most likely means of its arrival.

9. Southey, *Life and Correspondence of Robert Southey*, 2:136.

10. See the introduction, n. 19, for the text of the clause.

11. See Potts, *British Baptist Missionaries in India*. Grant died on 31 October 1799 (shortly after arriving), Fountain in August 1800, Brunsdon in July 1801, and Thomas in October 1801.

12. For valuable overviews of the debate, see Cutts, "Background of Macaulay's Minute"; Fisch, "Pamphlet War"; and Carson, *East India Company and Religion*, 110–29. On Southey's role in particular, see Bolton, *Writing the Empire*; Cutmore, "Plurality of Voices"; and Speck, "Robert Southey's Contribution."

13. W. J. T. Mitchell, *What Do Pictures Want?*, 146, 159.

14. Southey, "Periodical Accounts relative to the Baptist Missionary Society, for propagating the Gospel among the Heathen," *AR* 1 (January 1802): 207–18; "Transactions of the Missionary Society," *AR* 2 (January 1803): 189–201 and *AR* 4 (January 1804): 621–34; "Account of the Baptist Missionary Society," *QR* 1 (February 1809): 193–226; "Transactions of the Missionary Society in the South Sea Islands," *QR* 2 (August 1809): 24–61. Whereas I usually provide bibliographic information for periodical writing in notes, because of the frequency of quotation from these review articles I cite them parenthetically in the text, including volume and page numbers but omitting dates.

15. Ward's journals are in the Angus Library of Regent's Park College, Oxford, MS. BMS IN/17 (A). I cite by date and quote throughout from the transcription (a "draft typescript") made by E. Daniel Potts, *William Ward's Missionary Journal*, thus: Potts, *William Ward's Missionary Journal*, 4 February 1801.

16. Appadurai, "Introduction," 5; W. J. T. Mitchell, *What Do Pictures Want?*, 146. Appadurai observes that "even though from a *theoretical* point of view human actors encode things with significance, from a *methodological* point of view it is the things-in-motion that illuminate their human and social context" (5).

17. For a particularly insightful and energetic rehearsal of the "'notes' of the Evangelical mind," see Stokes, *English Utilitarians and India*, 29–31.

18. Lewis, *Life of John Thomas*, 8.

19. Ibid., 9.

20. Ivimey, *History of the English Baptists*, 4:64.

21. W. Carey, *Enquiry into the Obligations of Christians*, 62.

22. Thomas's wife, Ann, their daughter, Betsy, and "Thomas' 'black boy Andrew'" had departed a few weeks previously and were waiting in Calcutta upon the party's arrival. Lewis, *Life of John Thomas*, 237.

23. Marshman, *Life and Times*, 1:124.

24. Ogborn, *Indian Ink*, 206.

25. Kesavan, *History of Printing and Publishing in India*, 42.

26. E. Carey, *Memoir of William Carey, D.D.*, 444.

27. Potts, *William Ward's Missionary Journal*, 4 February 1801.

28. *ER* 11 (January 1808): 359.

29. Bourdieu, *Distinction*, 101.

30. *ER* 11 (January 1808): 342.

31. On the seventeenth-century context of the interpretation of "wonders," see D. Hall, *Worlds of Wonder*, 71–116. Of the fire, Carey wrote on 25 March 1812 to John Ryland, president of the Baptist Missionary Society, "The Lord has smitten us, he had a right to do so, and we deserve his corrections. I wish to submit to His sovereign will, nay, cordially to acquiesce therein, and to examine myself rigidly to see what in me has contributed to this evil." G. Smith, *Life of William Carey, D.D.*, 268. Jon Mee writes that in their responses to the Baptist Missionary Society writings, "Southey and many of his contemporaries implicitly feared that the enthusiasm of the seventeenth century was alive and well all around them." Mee, *Romanticism, Enthusiasm, and Regulation*, 66.

32. G. Smith, *Life of William Carey, D.D.*, 420. Smith describes Carey's garden at Serampore as "his oratory, the scene of prayer and meditation, the place where he began and ended the day of light—with God" (305).

33. Gaudio, *Engraving the Savage*, 113.

34. Ward's *Account of the Writings, Religion, and Manners of the Hindoos*, published in four volumes in 1811, was abridged and reissued in a two-volume second edition in 1815–18 as *A View of the History, Literature, and Mythology, of the Hindoos: Including a Minute Description of their Manners and Customs, and Translations from their Principal Works*, the title by which it became better known.

35. Halbertal and Margalit, *Idolatry*, 1.

36. Calvin, *Institutes of the Christian Religion*, 1:383–84.

37. Strictly speaking, God then says, "Thou shalt see my back parts; but my face shall not be seen" (Exod. 33:23).

38. On the two senses of the rabbinic expression *avodah zarah* (strange worship), see Halbertal and Margalit, *Idolatry*, 3–4.

39. Eck, *Darśan*, 3; see also C. J. Fuller, *Camphor Flame*, 59–62.

40. Rammohun Roy, *English Works*, 173.

41. Kopf, *British Orientalism*, 207. On Mrtyunjay, see Killingley, "Rammohun Roy's Controversies," 149.

42. Rammohun Roy, *Translation of an Abridgment of the Vedant*, viii. The work was originally published in Calcutta in 1816, omitting the translation of the Cena Upanishad.

43. Howsam, *Cheap Bibles*; A. Ghosh, "Between Text and Reader"; Price, *How to Do Things with Books*. See also Zemka, "Holy Books of Empire."

44. Darnton, "What Is the History of Books?," 11.

45. *Oriental Literary Observer* 21 (22 May 1831): 248. The second Indian annual, the *Orient Pearl* (1832, 1834–35), whose editorship Richardson transferred to the mixed-race East Indian friend and associate of Derozio, William Kirkpatrick, between the issues for 1834 and 1835, was less nostalgic. The two annuals are discussed in chapter 4.

46. *Bengal Annual* for 1830, 5.

47. Klancher, *Making of English Reading Audiences*.

48. Ogborn, *Indian Ink*, 208.

49. Marshman, *Life and Times*, 1:141, 132–35. On Ram Basu, see S. K. Chatterjee, *Ram Ram Basu*.

50. Stuart, *Vindication of the Hindoos*, 170.

51. A. Ghosh, "Between Text and Reader," 164. *Brief View of the Baptist Missions and Translations* includes an appendix listing "Books gratuitously distributed," which provides the following figures for works in Bengali: "Pentateuch," 255; "Historical Books," 283; "Poetical Books," 167; "Testament," 388; "Luke, &c. (a Scripture selection)," 1,086; "Hymns," 8,162; "Tracts," 24,398; and "Life of Christ," 474 (37).

52. Carey, Williams, et al., *Serampore Letters*, 118.

53. A. Ghosh, "Between Text and Reader," 166.

54. Buchanan, *Christian Researches in Asia*, 34.

55. A. Ghosh, "Between Text and Reader," 172. I have not been able to find evidence that Krishna Pal's popular Bengali hymn, translated by Marshman as "O thou, my soul," was published and distributed, but I assume that it was.

56. "Gospel Messenger," 329.

57. I am grateful to Anindita Ghosh and Rosinka Chaudhuri for their correspondence and assistance with *Dharmma pustakera duta*, an eight-page pamphlet (14 x 9 cm), three copies of which are held in the Angus Library, Regent's Park College, Oxford. The tract was later translated into Oriya and Telugu in an influential version titled *The Jewel Mine of Salvation*.

58. A. Ghosh, "Uncertain 'Coming of the Book,'" 32–33. On the *kathakatas*, see Bhadra, "Performer and the Listener."

59. E. Carey, *Memoir of William Carey, D.D.*, 426.

60. "Printed books were strange to the Bengalis then," recorded Thomas's biographer, C. B. Lewis, and Thomas "soon found reason to think that those he gave away would have been received with more favor had they been more thoroughly native in shape and appearance. At Guptipara, a pandit told him that he would have read the gospel to his pupils, if only it had been in a shastra-like form, i.e. with each page consisting of six or eight very long lines." *Life of John Thomas*, 365.

61. "Gospel Messenger," 330–31.

62. Ibid., 331.

63. Ibid., 330.

64. Ogborn, *Indian Ink*, 224.

65. Mani, *Contentious Traditions*, 96.

66. Marshman, *Life and Times*, 1:141.

67. *Evangelical Idolatry*, 8–9.

68. Ogborn, *Indian Ink*, 208.

69. Marshman, *Life and Times*, 1:80.

70. See Flood, *Introduction to Hinduism*, 6–7; and C. J. Fuller, *Camphor Flame*, 4–75. Steven Rosen writes that "the image incarnation of the Lord is a divine 'descent' by which the Lord entrusts himself to human care. The deity is a divine guest and he must be treated as such. Therefore, he is offered incense, flowers, lights, hymns, and food—all of this is pleasing not only to the devotee's senses, but also to the Deity. Moreover, this interaction establishes a loving exchange between devotee and God." Rosen, *Essential Hinduism*, 194.

71. Unlike Bill Brown and other theorists of things (who tend to build upon Heidegger's taxonomy), I do not distinguish between "things" and "objects." Although the process of converting idols into artifacts could have illuminated the thingness of idols, I have not found any such moments in the missionaries' accounts. Brown writes, "We begin to confront the thingness of objects when they stop working for us: when the drill breaks, when the car stalls, when the windows get filthy, when their flow within the circuits of production and distribution, consumption and exhibition, has been arrested, however momentarily." Brown, "Thing Theory," 4. Idols stop working in some ways when they become artifacts, but they immediately begin working in other ways, just as they also begin to flow within different circuits of distribution and exhibition.

72. Mieke Bal considers "the ambiguities involved in gestures of exposing," ambiguities that emerge from the "possible discrepancy between the object that is present and the statement about it." Bal, *Double Exposures*, 2. On domestication, see Bolton, *Writing the Empire*, 236–42.

73. Adorno, *Prisms*, 175.

74. Sherman, "Quatremère/Benjamin/Marx," 123; Stewart, *On Longing*, 165.

75. N. Thomas, "Licensed Curiosity," 116.

76. Bennett, *Birth of the Museum*, 60–61. Susan Stewart describes the Metropolitan Museum of Art as "that most insistent denial of history and context" (*On Longing*, 65). See also Bann, *Clothing of Clio*, 91–92; Gidal, *Poetic Exhibitions*, 32–34; W. Ray, *Logic of Culture*, 120–34; G. Wood, *Shock of the Real*, 131; and Gaskell's polemical review of Crimp, Elsner and Cardinal, and Sherman and Rogoff.

77. On the museum in the Romantic period as a "halfway point between the princely private enthusiasms of the Renaissance wonder cabinet and the public institution of the Victorian museum," see Pascoe, *Hummingbird Cabinet*, 3.

78. See N. Thomas, *Entangled Objects*, 151–62, for a discussion of missionary work in the South Pacific: idols "provided an extremely powerful mechanism through which the fact of conversion could be materially expressed and displayed" (156).

79. As evangelicals anxiously noted, furthermore, East India Company policies and practices suggested that English eyes were not united in their perceptions. On 3 January 1802 Ward recorded that "last week a deputation from the Government went in procession to Kallee Ghat, & made a thank offering to this goddess . . . in the name of the Company, for the victories & successes which the English have lately obtained in this country. Five thousand rupees were offered. Several thousand natives witnessed the English presenting their offering to this idol. We have been much grieved at this act, in which the natives exult over us." Potts, *William Ward's Missionary Journal*, 3 January 1802. And James Peggs would later dedicate a long chapter of *India's Cries to British Humanity* to the "British Connexion with Idolatry," especially the annual grants made by the East India Company to major temples, from whose visitors the Company in turn collected a pilgrim tax.

80. "Almost the same, but not quite" was Homi Bhabha's formulation for the disturbing and distorting acts of colonial imitation on the part of the colonized. *Location of Culture*, 86. For the Baptist missionaries, the conundrum of translating the material life of Indian religion into lifeless artifacts and of replacing those artifacts with the living Word in the material form of the book raises the specter of affinities between evangelical Christianity and Hinduism, along with their respective devotional objects and ways of seeing, supposed antitheses that come to seem almost the opposite, but not quite. This reading

corresponds to Mitchell's interpretation of idols as among the "'bad objects' of empire," but see the previous note: clearly the generalization of idols as "bad objects" cannot be applied uniformly, as consideration of idols and idolatry from the perspectives of Ward, Moor, Stuart, and Jones would also show.

81. The India Museum at Pall Mall was really a salesroom. See Altick, *Shows of London*, 427.

82. Desmond, *India Museum*, 15–31.

83. *Catalogue of the Missionary Museum*, iii–iv.

84. For a discussion of Stuart's collection, see Davis, *Lives of Indian Images*, 163–67.

85. On the origins of the Baptist Missionary Society, see Stanley, *History of the Baptist Missionary Society*, 9–15.

86. Bosworth, *Baptist College, Bristol*, 12.

87. Whelan, "Glance at the 1795 Catalogue," 38.

88. Champion, *Farthing Rushlight*, 65, 89.

89. *Account of the Bristol Education Society . . . 1809*, 35. Hereafter I cite these reports in the form *Account . . . 1809*. Also in 1784, the college received two other substantial legacies: 1,000 guineas from Alderman Frederick Bull, a founding member of the Education Society; and the classical library of Fr. Thomas Llewelyn, valued at more than £1,500, according to the Bristol Education Society accounts. Moon, *Education for Ministry*, 16–17; *Account . . . 1809*, 35. On the library, see Whelan, "Glance at the 1795 Catalogue."

90. *Chronological Outline*, 4:xxv.

91. Bosworth, *Baptist College, Bristol*, 5.

92. *Alphabetical Catalogue*, 129; *Account . . . 1820*, 41; *Curiosities of Bristol and Its Neighbourhood*, v.

93. *Account . . . 1803*, 13.

94. The list of Indian materials could go on. *Account . . . 1813* mentions "Several Curiosities, presented to the Museum by Mr. HONE, of Bristol, and a *variety of Articles* used in the *Pagan worship* of Hindostan, presented by the MISSIONARIES of Serampore" (37); *Account . . . 1816* lists "*Specimens of Hindosthanee Writing Paper*. Presented by JONATHAN SCOTT, Esq. Clifton" and "*An East Indian Fan of Feathers*, saved from the wreck of the Alexandria, by the Rev. DANIEL WAIT, Bristol" (36); and *Account . . . 1817*, "*A Collection of Indian Drawings*. Presented by the Rev. W. WARD, of Serampore" and "*Specimens of Indian Wheat*. Presented by Mr. H. JONES, Student" (37).

95. Evans, *Picture of Bristol*, 61. Between 1814 and 1823 Evans returned to the museum. In the 1814 guide he wrote, "We have visited the museum, though not frequently; but we apprehend that the stranger would experience no difficulty in obtaining access to such objects, as would be generally considered gratifying to a laudable curiosity" (61), while for *The New Guide* (1823) he revised as follows: "We have visited this museum recently with great pleasure, and know that the stranger would experience no difficulty in obtaining access to such objects as are generally considered gratifying to a laudable curiosity" (71).

96. Leask, *Curiosity*, 241.

97. Ward, *View of the History*, 2:xlvi.

98. This anecdote also appears in a letter from Rowe to Saffery, 13 November 1805. Rowe omits the reference to the Bristol museum but adds, "Whenever we send a box to England, I shall endeavour to collect a few little things to send you." Five days later (25 October 1805), Ward records, "Kreeshnoo brings word that the whole village have risen

up against . . . Jaggernaut"; and for 20 December 1805, "Poor Bro. Jaggernaut has been dreadfully beat by his neighbour." Potts, *William Ward's Missionary Journal*, 25 October 1805, 20 December 1805.

99. W. J. T. Mitchell, *What Do Pictures Want?*, 93.

100. *Baptist Magazine* 8 (October 1816): 434. The original letter is in Angus Library, Regent's Park College, Oxford, Reeves R7/37.

101. Ward, *View of the History*, 2:xxxvi–xxxvii.

102. *Baptist Magazine* 8 (October 1816): 434.

103. John Dyer to John Saffery, 22 May 1817, Reeves R16/4. By December 1818 another set of idols was en route to Saffery. See William Hope to John Saffery, 7 December 1818,. Reeves R20/10: "I have received . . . from Calcutta . . . a letter from Mr. Sutton in which he says 'I have presumed to commit to your care 2 boxes which you will probably receive with this. The one directed for Mr. Saffery Salisbury . . . contains some of the Images of the Hindoo Gods & [I wd?] wish you to send it to one of the London Coaches in order to be forwarded to London & the Coach Office in London will forward it to Salisbury.'" The Reeves Collection calendar seems to suggest that these are the same idols as those mentioned above in the letter of 25 December 1815, but if Dyer was requesting those idols from Saffery in his letter of 22 May 1817, then these must be a different set.

104. W. J. T. Mitchell, *What Do Pictures Want?*, 158. The three types of "bad objects" addressed by Mitchell in the context of empire are idols, fetishes, and totems. Mitchell also refers to "bad objects" as "objects of the Other" and adds, "I'm loosely adapting psychoanalyst Melanie Klein's notion of the split 'part-object,' more precisely, 'imagos, which are a phantastically distorted picture of the real objects upon which they are based.' Bad objects . . . are objects of ambivalence and anxiety that can be associated with fascination as easily as with aversion" (158).

105. Under the heading "Contributions received by the Treasurer of the Baptist Missionary Society, from May 14, to June 24, 1821," the *Baptist Magazine* lists £2 from "Rev. John Saffery, (collected by the Exhibition of Idols)." *Baptist Magazine* 13 (July 1821): 327.

106. Bowen, *Missionary Incitement*, iii.

107. Southey, *Life and Correspondence of Robert Southey*, 3:351; G. Smith, *Life of William Carey, D.D.*, 137.

108. See Jackson, "From Krishna Pal to Lal Behari Dey," 187–88. *Bhakti* worship involves loving and generally personal and enthusiastic devotion.

109. Picart, *Ceremonies and Religious Customs*. On the influence of Picart, see Pratt, "'Where . . . success [is] certain'?," 132–33.

110. Potts, *William Ward's Missionary Journal*, 11 December 1800. "The Hindoos, says Mr. Marshman, often confound the names of *Kreeshnoo* and *Christ*, which they pronounce *Creestoo*. After discoursing with them, it is nothing uncommon for them to conclude with this: 'Your *Creestoo* and our *Kreeshnoo* are one'" (*PA* 2:318). Marshman attempted to clear up the confusion by writing a poem titled "*The Difference*: Or, *Kreeshnoo* and *Christ* compared" (*PA* 2:318–19).

111. In the wake of the Vellore mutiny, one of the mission's Bengali publications of concern to the Secret Committee of the Court of Directors in 1807 was a "Distinction" in which the missionaries asked, "O BELOVED Hindoos! . . . Why do you constantly say that Crishn and Christ are the same?" "Distinction."

112. Potts, *William Ward's Missionary Journal*, 28 December 1800.

113. On 27 January 1801 Daniel Brunsdon visited the family of Krishna Pal. In his journal Brunsdon records the response of Krishna Pal's sister-in-law, "Joymooni" [Jeyamuni?], to Brunsdon's farewell remark: "On coming away I told them to remember that one word, Jesus Christ came into the world *to seek and to save that which was lost*. 'O yes, says Joymooni, my mind's book is open, in which I write down every thing that I hear about Jesus Christ'" (*PA* 2:109). Whether or not Jeyamuni actually said this, rhetorically it is a true evangelical triumph of the book over the idol that at the same time affirms Gyan Prakash's claim that "subaltern . . . subjects register their presence by acting upon the dominant discourse, by forcing it into contradictions, by making it speak in tongues." Prakash, "Impossibility of Subaltern History," 293. (The turn of phrase resonates, for by this time John Thomas and Dorothy Carey had each descended into madness: during the baptism, "Mr. Thomas, who was confined to his couch, made the air resound with his blasphemous ravings; and Mrs. Carey, shut up in her own room on the opposite side of the path, poured forth the most painful shrieks." Marshman, *Life and Times*, 1:139.) In Brunsdon's relation of Jeyamuni's reply, the Hindu convert no longer sees God as immanent in things; rather, her mind itself becomes a book, open to record and make legible the living word that we "hear about Jesus Christ." But just as the transportation of idols fails to banish spirit from substance and instead facilitates its expression in different forms, the transformation of the mind into a book and the word that we hear into writing reveals an inescapable anxiety about the nature of conversion through grace. Signs of grace, after all, should indicate that grace is actually present, yet here in the substitution of book for mind we find instead the contrary logic of a supplement. It is as if the book goes too far in its redirection of the material idol's gesture to more material: when the object takes over and the mind becomes the book—when the origin becomes the supplement—the words written on its pages cease to signify the presence of grace itself but instead only gesture to other signs of grace, to the external words that the convert has heard and recorded. On Krishna Pal and Jeyamuni, see Jackson, "From Krishna Pal to Lal Behari Dey."

114. E. Carey, *Memoir of William Carey, D.D.*, 442.

115. Bowen, *Missionary Incitement*, 23.

116. Potts, *William Ward's Missionary Journal*, 28 October 1801.

117. Bowen, *Missionary Incitement*, 23, 24.

118. Milton, *Paradise Lost*, 122 (bk. 5, lines 564–66, 571–73, 574–76).

119. *ER* 12 (April 1808): 173–74.

120. "Advertisement." The contest was initiated by Claudius Buchanan, who donated the funds for a series of prizes on similar subjects at various English, Scottish, and Irish universities and colleges. Fisch, "Pamphlet War," 27.

121. Southey, *Selections from the Letters*, 1:301. "Your prize question seems oddly worded," Southey began, "for, in the common acceptation of civilisation, Hindostan is a highly civilised country" (1:284).

122. Peacock, *Peacock's Four Ages of Poetry*, 15.

123. The sources of Southey's notes to *Thalaba the Destroyer*, *Madoc*, and *The Curse of Kehama* are carefully traced in *Robert Southey: Poetical Works, 1793–1810*. See also Bolton, *Writing the Empire*, 229–36; Simmons, "Useful and Wasteful Both"; Tucker, *Epic*, 89–92; and White, *Early Romanticism*, 152–81.

124. Saglia, "Words and Things," 172.

125. Bernhardt-Kabisch, *Robert Southey*, i.

126. De Quincey, "Lake Reminiscences," 459. Referring to this passage, Daniel Sanjiv Roberts points out that De Quincey's implicit distinction between "Southey's mind . . . and the interiorized nature of (Wordsworthian) romantic poetry is remarkably prescient of new historicism's critique of the romantic ideology." "Beneath High Romanticism," 38.

127. De Quincey, *Confessions of an English Opium-Eater*, 70–71.

128. [Reynolds], *Fancy*, 62.

129. Byron, *Lord Byron*, 520 (canto 4, stanza 5).

130. Madden, *Robert Southey*, 144.

131. Pratt, " 'Where . . . success [is] certain'?," 147.

132. Fulford, "Plants, Pagodas and Penises," 196.

133. See Garcia, "In the Name of the 'Incestuous Mother.' "

134. *CG*, 5 December 1811, 2C.

135. Franklin, "Passion's Empire," 185. Similarly, for Marilyn Butler the poem "illustrates the horrors of Hindu government on lines similar to [Charles] Grant's ["Observations On the State of Society among the Asiatic Subjects of Great Britain"]." Butler, "Byron and the Empire in the East," 72.

136. Heber, *Narrative of a Journey*, 2:285–86. He repeats the scene, as well as the reference to *Kehama*, in his journal: "We were now approaching the side of the river opposite Kedgeree . . . and nothing met the eye but a dismal and unbroken line of thick, black, wood . . . which one might easily imagine to be the habitation of every thing monstrous, disgusting, and dangerous, from the tyger and the cobra di capello down to the scorpion and mosquito—from the thunder-storm to the fever. We had seen the night before, the lightenings [*sic*] flash incessantly . . . and what we now saw was not ill-fitted for a nursery of such storms as Southey describes as prevailing in his Padalon" (1:6). Heber and Southey had met in 1820, before Heber's departure for India as bishop of Calcutta. Speck, *Robert Southey*, 181. See also below, n. 157.

137. I quote from E. W. Stillingfleet, *On the Character of Idolatry*, 16. The sermon then cites the lines from *The Curse of Kehama* on p. 62.

138. Ward, *View of the History*, 2:xxx–xxxi.

139. Madden, *Robert Southey*, 142.

140. Ibid., 134.

141. Southey, *The Curse of Kehama*, ed. Daniel S. Roberts, vol. 4 of *Robert Southey: Poetical Works, 1793–1810*, 3. All subsequent quotations of the poem are from this edition; references are to canto and line numbers.

142. For an insightful discussion of *punya* in relation to *The Curse of Kehama*, see Rangarajan, "Imperial Babel," which argues that Southey's "definition of *punya* turns Hinduism into a system of pure capitalism in which power is wholly disassociated from moral value."

143. Southey, "Lives of the French Revolutionists," *QR* 7 (June 1812): 414.

144. In the *Courier* for 29 September 1814, Coleridge associates Jacobinism with idolatrous religion, arguing that the spirit of Jacobinism first arose among the Germans and that the "germs of contagion" then spread to France through translations and expatriate "confederated enthusiasts": "Here first this religion of iniquity stept forth into open day, a mighty Church, visible and militant! Throughout continental Europe were its Moloch altars erected, and the bones of its countless victims still lie bleaching around their re-

cent ruins." The spirit, he claims, often hides itself in the guise of philosophy, sensibility, and philanthropy, but when it appears openly as Jacobinism itself, the earlier figure
of idolatrous religion leads Coleridge straight to Southey's poem: "Behold it in that, its
next, and boldest metamorphosis, like the Kehama of our laurel-honouring laureat, one
and the same, yet many and multiform and dividuous, assaulting with combined attack
all the gates and portals of law and usage, in all the blazonry of open war!" Coleridge, *Essays on His Times*, 2:383–84.

145. Unpublished letter, 5 January 1811, quoted in Carnall, *Robert Southey and His
Age*, 125. See also Fulford, "Blessed Bane," "Heroic Voyagers and Superstitious Natives,"
"Pagodas and Pregnant Throes," and "Plants, Pagodas and Penises"; and Bewell, "True
story . . . of evils overcome."

146. See the discussion of Southey's early religious development in White, *Early Romanticism*, 154–62.

147. See Craig, *Robert Southey and Romantic Apostasy*, 152–65. In a letter to Henry Nel-
son Coleridge of 8 May 1836, Hartley Coleridge emphasized Southey's instrumentalism
as the connection between his early radicalism and his later conservatism: "*Entre nous*,
I think he has retained, even in his ultra-toryism, and high-churchmanship, the fundamental error which made him, in the heat of youth, somewhat of a revolutionist; he expects a great deal more from positive institutions than God ever intended they should
produce." H. Coleridge, *Letters*, 190. My thanks to Alan Vardy for drawing my attention
to this letter.

148. Southey's disdain for dogma in general and for the doctrine of innate depravity in particular (whether Calvinistic or Catholic) was an enduring theme. In *Joan of Arc*
(1796) his heroine opposes her religion of nature to "the points / Abstruse of nice religion, and the bounds / Subtile and narrow which confine the path / Of orthodox belief"
(bk. 3, lines 385–88): "Ye have told me, Sires, / That Nature only teaches man to sin! / . . . /
. . . No, REVERENDS! no, / It is not Nature that can teach to sin: / Nature is all Benevolence—all Love, / All Beauty! . . . / . . . / . . . Nature teach sin! / O blasphemy against the
Holy One, / Who made us in the image of himself, / Who made us all for Happiness and
Love, / Infinite happiness—infinite love, / Partakers of his own eternity" (3:432–51). *Joan
of Arc*, ed. Lynda Pratt, vol. 1 of *Robert Southey: Poetical Works, 1793–1810*, 52–53.

149. Southey, *Life and Correspondence of Robert Southey*, 3:281.

150. On Southey's endorsement of "systematic myth," see Fulford, "Blessed Bane,"
para. 11.

151. Potts, *William Ward's Missionary Journal*, 16 January 1801.

152. Southey, *Fragments and Romances*, ed. Tim Fulford and Rachel Crawford, vol. 4 of
Robert Southey: Later Poetical Works, 1811–1838, 61 (canto 3, stanza 24).

153. In a published letter dated November 1816, the French Roman Catholic missionary the Abbé Jean Antoine Dubois would draw a different conclusion from the same
premise: "The Hindoos may be divided into two classes—the impostors, and the dupes.
The latter include the bulk of the population of India; and the former is composed of the
whole tribe of Brahmins. Now, in a society composed of such materials, we can entertain
but very faint hopes of improving the interests, or extending the benefits of the Christian
religion." Dubois, *Letters on the State of Christianity in India*, 87–88.

154. Southey, *Selections from the Letters*, 1:301.

155. Fulford, "Plants, Pagodas and Penises," 197.

156. On Southey and *tapas*, see Franklin, "Drafts upon Heaven." Franklin rightly sees greater empathy in Sydney Owenson's depiction of *tapas* than in Southey's, which operates in "crudely monetarist terms." Franklin, "General Introduction and [Meta]historical Background,'" 25.

157. Heber, who often viewed India through the lens of Southey's poem, came across a place on the Hugli, a few miles above Chinsura, where "the banks of the river are precipitous, and Southey might have taken the spot as the scene of his Kailyal, and the image of her guardian goddess falling down the crumbling steep into the river." Heber, *Narrative of a Journey*, 1:88.

158. Southey, *The Curse of Kehama*, includes the draft fragment, in which Southey sketches the scene as follows: "Laderlad on the shore sees Kalyal floating down the stream. her crocodile has saved her, her bitch is swimming beside while she is caressing the beast that preserved her" (274).

159. If Southey's choice of Marriataly for Kailyal's "household" god—as opposed to the proverbially haughty Durga, whose worship was associated with the elites—is sympathetic and apt, so is his choice of Voomdavee (Bhuma Devi or Bhudevi), affiliated with the earth and the virtue of patience, for Ladurlad's, as Michael Franklin points out. Franklin, "Drafts upon Heaven," 269.

160. Madden, *Robert Southey*, 188.

161. Holland and Everett, *Memoirs of the Life and Writings of James Montgomery*, 2:333. Shelley too read Kailyal in this way, writing to Elizabeth Hitchener in 1811, "The Curse of Kehama which you will have is my most favorite poem—yet there is a great error, *faith* in the character of the divine Kailyal." Shelley, *Letters*, 1:101.

162. In "Blessed Bane," Fulford offers a detailed discussion of the dynamics of disease and contagion in the contexts of South American colonialism and Southey's *Tale of Paraguay* (1825).

163. The verbal echo of "materiality" in the name Marriataly must be mere coincidence, yet the logic of vaccination is at work here too: disease and immunity share the same root cause.

164. A similar dynamic appears in Herbert Tucker's insightful suggestion that "Southey's notes to *Thalaba* [express] cognitive superiority to the imaginative content of the poem," thus "inoculating *Thalaba* against itself." Tucker, *Epic*, 90.

165. Jones's hymns to Hindu deities provide the clearest poetic expression of syncretism. And see Leask, *British Romantic Writers*, 98–102, on the "pure deism lying at the Vedic source of Hindu polytheism" (100), a subject that has received an extensive and nuanced treatment in Franklin, "Radically Feminizing India."

166. Patterson [Paterson], "Of the Origin of the Hindu Religion," 44–45.

167. Ward, *View of the History*, 2:xxii.

168. Southey, *The Curse of Kehama*, 280.

169. Shelley, *Letters*, 1:211–12, emphasis added.

170. Bloom, "Internalization of Quest-Romance."

Chapter 3 • *"I would not have the day return"*

Epigraph: From a speech at a public meeting held at the Town Hall, Calcutta, 28 March 1831, commemorating the first East Indians' Petition to Parliament, quoted in

Derozio, *Derozio, Poet of India*, 343. Unless otherwise indicated, all quotations of Derozio's poetry and prose are from this edition, hereafter cited parenthetically in the text.

1. The description of Michael Derozio is from the *Bengal Directory* of 1795, quoted in Madge, *Henry Derozio*, 2. I discuss the term "Portuguese" below; it is a loose term designating Hindu converts to Catholicism and their often mixed-race descendants. Derozio's house was on the east side of the Lower Circular Road just south of Jaun Bazaar Street, currently 155 A. J. C. Bose Road. Derozio, *Song of the Stormy Petrel*, 489.

2. Madge, *Henry Derozio*, 2.

3. The Serampore mission itself also contributed 1,000 rupees. In this paragraph I rely on Derozio, *Song of the Stormy Petrel*, 464–74 (app. 9), which conveniently reproduces transcriptions from Ward's journals and other materials relevant to the connection between the Serampore community and the Derozio family.

4. *Baptist Magazine* 71 (November 1879): 512.

5. Stark and Madge, *East Indian Worthies*, 19.

6. I use the term "East Indian," discussed below, in its contemporary sense to mean mixed-race Christian Eurasians, usually the offspring of a European father and an Indian or mixed-race mother. See R. Chaudhuri, "Politics of Naming."

7. S. Mukhopadhyay, *Derozio*, 62.

8. Kindersley, *Letters*, 272.

9. Ibid., 169–70.

10. I am grateful to Sakti Sadhan Mukhopadhyay, who is of the opinion that Andre Derozio was of European Portuguese descent, for his correspondence on this question.

11. See Carton, *Mixed-Race and Modernity in Colonial India*, 11–27.

12. The main biographical sources on Derozio are Edwards, *Henry Derozio*, and Madge, *Henry Derozio*, and there is useful material in the appendices of Derozio, *Song of the Stormy Petrel*, but the best overview by far is Rosinka Chaudhuri's introduction to Derozio, *Poet of India*, xxi–lxxxi.

13. Edwards, *Henry Derozio*, 5.

14. Edwards describes Johnson as the husband of Derozio's mother's sister (*Henry Derozio*, 3), but as Madge points out, Johnson was in fact Derozio's uncle in two or even three other ways: having first been married to Henry's paternal aunt Maria, after her death in 1810 he married her younger sister Bridget, and it was also said that he was the brother of Henry's mother, Sophia Johnson (Madge, *Henry Derozio*, 5).

15. R. Chaudhuri, introduction, xxvii.

16. Derozio, *Derozio, Poet of India*, 47. The advertisement is reproduced on p. 50.

17. Mukherji, "Hindu College," 42–43.

18. On the Young Bengal movement, see R. Chaudhuri, introduction, lix–lxvii and "Young India"; Kopf, *British Orientalism*, 253–63; and Sumit Sarkar, "Complexities of Young Bengal."

19. See R. Chaudhuri, introduction, xlii–xliii; and Asoka Kumar Sen, "Derozians and Journalism." Derozio was the managing editor of the *Hesperus*, of which no copies survive. Only one issue of the *Parthenon* appeared, on 15 February 1830, "the first native paper in English," according to the *Bengal Spectator*. Quoted in Chanda, *History of the English Press in Bengal*, 126.

20. Stark and Madge, *East Indian Worthies*, 19.

21. Dover, *Half-Caste*, 144.

22. Quoted in Anthony, *Britain's Betrayal in India*, 61.

23. Kipling, *Plain Tales from the Hills*, 59.

24. W. W., "Reminiscences of the Hindu College," 189.

25. *New Statesman*, unsigned capsule review.

26. For a helpful and cogent survey of the extensive bibliography on Indian modernity in colonial and postcolonial studies, see Krishnaswamy, "Postcolonial and Globalization Studies," 5–8; see also R. Chaudhuri, introduction, lxvii–lxxxi.

27. K. Wilson, "Citizenship, Empire, and Modernity," 159. Or as C. A. Bayly writes, "An essential part of being modern is thinking you are modern." *Birth of the Modern World*, 10.

28. Kopf, *British Orientalism*, 253.

29. Quoted in G. Chattopadhyay, *Awakening in Bengal*, xlviii.

30. G. Chattopadhyay, *Awakening in Bengal*, xi–liv; P. Chatterjee, *Black Hole of Empire*, 157.

31. Thompson, "Time, Work-Discipline, and Industrial Capitalism"; Pocock, *Machiavellian Moment*; Anderson, *Imagined Communities*.

32. Jameson, "End of Temporality," 699.

33. Bhabha, *Location of Culture*, 152. Thus Partha Chatterjee argues that to see in modernity a mere "copresence of several times—the time of the modern and the times of the premodern—is only to endorse the utopianism of Western modernity," in place of which Chatterjee proposes a "heterogeneous time of modernity." P. Chatterjee, "Anderson's Utopia," 132. Similarly, Talal Asad writes that "we need to think . . . of heterogeneous time: of embodied practices rooted in multiple traditions, of differences between horizons of expectation and spaces of experience—differences that continually dislocate the present from the past, the world experienced from the world anticipated, and call for their revision and reconnection." Asad, *Formations of the Secular*, 179. See also Sassen, "Spatialities and Temporalities," 223–24.

34. R. Chaudhuri, introduction, lxviii.

35. This memory, far from being simply imitative or, to introduce Homi Bhabha's influential categories, an object of nationalist pedagogy, is also performative, and in the meeting of these two functions—in what I call "citation"—expresses the double or "disjunctive time of the nation's modernity." *Location of Culture*, 142. Bhabha describes the "split between the continuous, accumulative temporality of the pedagogical, and the repetitious, recursive strategy of the performative" as follows: "The nation's people must be thought in double-time; the people are the historical 'objects' of a nationalist pedagogy, giving the discourse an authority that is based on the pre-given or constituted historical origin *in the past*; the people are also the 'subjects' of a process of signification that must erase any prior or originary presence of the nation-people to demonstrate the prodigious, living principles of the people as contemporaneity: as that sign of the *present* through which national life is redeemed and iterated as a reproductive process" (145).

36. Charles Taylor, "Two Theories of Modernity," 172–73.

37. Derozio, *Derozio, Poet of India*, 311.

38. Derozio's poems in the *Bengal Annual* often begin with an exordium printed in a smaller font, set with wider margins, and written in a meter and rhyme scheme different from the ensuing body of the poem. Chaudhuri's edition prints such lines in italics.

I give them in Roman, as they were printed in the *Bengal Annual*. After the blank-verse exordium, "Moods of Mind" becomes a lyrical ballad about the impossibility of express-ing strong emotion: "I cannot speak; for words are weak / To carry feelings forth— / The vestures cold of placid thought, / To passion little worth" (312).

39. Buckingham, "Derozio's Poems," 116.

40. *New Monthly Magazine*, unsigned review, 105.

41. The new name also marks a turn to political and historical subjects in poems such as "Address to the Greeks" and "The Ruins of Rajmahal." See R. Chaudhuri, "Politics of Naming."

42. Hawes, *Poor Relations*, 89.

43. "Petition of the East Indians," 262–63.

44. "East Indian's [*sic*] Meeting," 159.

45. "Petition of the East Indians," 263.

46. "East Indian's [*sic*] Meeting," 159.

47. See Travers, *Ideology and Empire*, 181–206; Sudipta Sen, "Imperial Subjects on Trial"; and Kolsky, "Codification."

48. "East Indian's [*sic*] Meeting," 159.

49. With a high fee of five rupees per month, the Hindu College was primarily ac-cessible to elite students, though Sumit Sarkar points out that "with the exception of Dakshinaranjan Mukherji, none among the prominent Derozians came from particu-larly well-established or rich families." "Complexities of Young Bengal," 511. Tarachand Chakrabarti, Krishna Mohun Banerjea, Ramgopal Ghosh, and Ramtanu Lahiri were all free scholars sent up to the Hindu College from David Hare's school. Ibid., 528.

50. "Modern Hindoo Sects," 174. The article was reprinted from the *East Indian* in the *Asiatic Journal* in April 1832 (from which I quote), meaning that the original piece ap-peared in the *East Indian* in fall or winter 1831 and thus may have been written by Dero-zio, though it could have come from the pen of one of the paper's other leader writers. See R. Chaudhuri, introduction, xlii. Edwards writes, "Kirkpatrick, M. Crowe, R. Fen-wick and other East Indians were the chief leader writers of the old East Indian." *Henry Derozio*, 8.

51. "Review of Public Instruction," 350–51, 354.

52. "Modern Hindoo Sects," 174.

53. Ibid.

54. Ibid.

55. "Hindoo Liberals," 224.

56. "Review of Public Instruction," 354, 360.

57. Priestman, *Romantic Atheism*, 253.

58. S. T. Coleridge, *Collected Letters*, 4:917.

59. Rammohun Roy, *English Works*, 875.

60. Kopf, *Brahmo Samaj*, 9.

61. Ringgren, "Problems of Syncretism," 7.

62. Droogers, "Syncretism," 7.

63. Rudolph, "Synkretismus." A few early instances include: "*Syncretism*, . . . a con-fused jumble of all sorts of Religions" (Maimbourg, *History of Arianism*, 1:156); "The er-rors of Syncretism, . . . [an] attempt . . . to unite the absurdities of the different sects with the purity of the gospel" (Formey, *Concise History*, 215); and "Syncretistical monster . . .

a mixture of the opinions of all sects, highly inimical to . . . christian truth—in consequence of which Arianism, Mahometanism, Popery, bad policy, [and] the scholastic jargon took place" (Triebner, *Answer to the Pamphlet*, 11).

64. Droogers, "Syncretism," 12, 20.

65. Pye, "Syncretism versus Synthesis," 5–6.

66. Stewart and Ernst, "Syncretism," 586.

67. Kuhn, "English Deism," 1094. See also Hungerford, *Shores of Darkness*; Manuel, *Eighteenth Century Confronts the Gods*; Shaffer, *"Kubla Khan"*; and Ackerman, *Myth and Ritual School*.

68. Kuhn, "English Deism," 1108.

69. Kopf, *Brahmo Samaj*; Robertson, *Raja Rammohan Ray*; and A. F. S. Ahmed, "Rammohun Roy and His Contemporaries."

70. See Aravamudan, *Tropicopolitans*.

71. Ibid., 4.

72. Robertson, *Raja Rammohan Ray*, 25–26.

73. Rammohun Roy, *English Works*, 878, 882.

74. Killingley, *Rammohun Roy*, 5.

75. Rammohun Roy, *English Works*, 885.

76. Tytler, *Inquiry*, 2.

77. Quoted in Collet, *Life and Letters of Raja Rammohun Roy*, 138.

78. Rammohun Roy, *English Works*, 891.

79. Collet, *Life and Letters of Raja Rammohun Roy*, 140.

80. Aravamudan, *Tropicopolitans*, 6.

81. Rammohun Roy, *English Works*, 892.

82. Tytler, *Inquiry*, 18.

83. Ram Doss was not the only persona that Rammohun adopted: another invention was the *pandit* Sivaprasad Sarma. Whereas Ram Doss sees Hindu and Christian orthodoxies as compatible, Sivaprasad too "is zealous to defend the brahmanical schools of thought," as Dermot Killingley writes, yet has "attempted to understand Christian doctrine but found it incoherent." *Rammohun Roy*, 149.

84. Rammohun Roy, *English Works*, 201.

85. Rammohun Roy [Ram Doss, pseud.], *Vindication of the Incarnation of the Deity*, 891, 906.

86. Chakrabarty, *Provincializing Europe*, 28.

87. Stewart and Ernst, "Syncretism," 587.

88. As my discussion below clarifies, my use of the term "citation" is shaped by my reading of Walter Benjamin's "Theses on the Philosophy of History" (in Benjamin, *Illuminations*, 255–66) rather than by Judith Butler's "citational politics" or, via Butler, Jacques Derrida's "citationality" partly because, as here, I want to stress the deliberate nature of the technique as a form of historical intervention, assertion, and interpretation. For Butler identity is repeatable and rehearsable because it is deployed through labile, Nietzschean signs that do not have a performer or agent behind them. Butler, *Bodies That Matter*; Derrida, "Signature Event Context."

89. On Derozio and Shelley, see R. Chaudhuri, introduction, xxxvi–xxxix.

90. "Amiable readers of the Helter-Skelter," writes Leporello, "sympathise in my sorrows! I stand alone in the world. Like Godwin's St Leon, there is a gulph fixed between

me and my species; for since Harry Norman married and grew steady, I have not met an individual who can advance, as it were hand in hand with me, from the first glass to the last . . . and from thence progressively upwards, bottle by bottle, until we arrive at that happy stage, where as the Thermometer impressively informs us, 'spirits boil!' " (71–72).

91. Buckingham, "Derozio's Poems," 115–16.

92. Leask, "Wandering through Eblis," 177.

93. Ibid.

94. Benjamin, *Illuminations*, 261.

95. Ibid.

96. In "Autobiography of Kasiprasad Ghose," published in *Hand-Book of Bengal Missions*, Kasiprasad lists his other works as including *The Vision, a tale, On Bengali Poetry, On Bengal Works and Writers*, and *Sketches of Ranajit Singh* and of *The King of Oude*, adding that at the time he was engaged in writing *Memoirs of Native Indian Dynasties* (508). Poems by Kasiprasad also appeared in the *Orient Pearl*: "Storm and Rain" in the *Orient Pearl* for 1834, and "Evening on the River" and "The Native Lover's Song" in the *Orient Pearl* for 1835.

97. K. Ghosh, *The Sháïr*, i.

98. The Visitor was appointed by government to serve on the Hindu College board as the European representative of the supervisory General Committee of Public Instruction. See below, n. 121, for the constitution of the board.

99. K. Ghosh, *The Sháïr*, 1.

100. On Roberts, see Leask, *Curiosity*, 217–27.

101. "English Poetry by a Hindu," 105.

102. *Englishman's Magazine* 1 (June 1831): 379.

103. Landon, *Fisher's Drawing Room Scrap Book*, 18.

104. K. Ghosh, *The Sháïr*, ii.

105. R. Chaudhuri, *Gentlemen Poets*, 74.

106. *Supplement to the Government Gazette*, 24 May 1827, 2.

107. K. Ghosh, *The Sháïr*, 79.

108. I do not mean to suggest that there is not more to Kasiprasad's English writings themselves, but only to emphasize the dynamics of his reception in the English press. On the "complicated Orientalist intertextuality" in Kasiprasad's poetry and annotations, see R. Chaudhuri, *Gentlemen Poets*, 72–77, quotation on 72.

109. Buckingham, "Derozio's Poems," 111.

110. Buckingham, *Prospectus of a New Paper*, 1, 2,

111. R. Chaudhuri, "Ideology of Indianness," 175.

112. The line "A tone than music nothing less" was omitted from the version in *Poems* (1827) but printed in the original version in the *India Gazette*. Derozio, *Derozio, Poet of India*, 141.

113. See Janowitz, *England's Ruins*.

114. See R. Chaudhuri, "Ideology of Indianness."

115. Byron, *Lord Byron*, 75 (canto 2, line 707).

116. In this respect, the poem bears comparison to D. L. Richardson's "Lines Written by Moonlight on a Pillar of the Ruins of Rajmahal, in the East Indies," a conventional meditation on ruins, the "mouldering walls" of which "sadly tell how earthly pride decays, / How human hopes, like human works, depart, / And leave behind—the ruins of

the heart!" Richardson, *Sonnets, and Other Poems*, 64. From the perspective of Derozio's poem, Richardson's—written on a pillar—would itself be one of the inscriptions spoiling "this 'abode of kings.'" And while the note, with its quotation of Byron, takes Lord Elgin as the model plunderer, the most highly publicized precedent in the Indian context of "ruthless hands" reaving away marble would have been those of Charles Grant Sr., who oversaw the removal of marble from the ruins at Gaur in 1784 to provide materials to pave the new St. John's Church in Calcutta.

117. See above, n. 38.

118. Shelley, *Complete Poetry*, 159 (canto 2, stanza 20, lines 172–74).

119. Susobhan Sarkar, *Bengal Renaissance*, 21.

120. R. Chaudhuri, introduction, xl.

121. Derozio, *Song of the Stormy Petrel*, 329. The first proposal was then put to a vote in the form of the following question: "Whether the Managers had any just grounds to conclude that the moral and religious tenets of Mr. Derozio as far as ascertainable from the effects they have produced upon his scholars are such as to render him an improper person to be entrusted with the education of youth" (330). Four of the managers—H. H. Wilson, Prasanna Kumar Tagore, Srikishen Singh, and David Hare—spoke in defense of Derozio, while three—Radhakanta Deb, Radhamadhab Banerjea, and Ramkamal Sen—opposed him and two—Chandra Kumar Tagore and Rasomoy Dutt—remained neutral, stating that they "knew nothing of the ill effects of Mr. Derozio's instructions except from report" (330–31). But when it was then asked "whether it was expedient in the present state of public feeling amongst the Hindoo Community of Calcutta to dismiss Mr. Derozio from the College," the results shifted and six agreed that it was either necessary or expedient to dismiss him; only Srikishen Singh voted that it was unnecessary, and both Wilson and Hare "declined voting on a subject affecting the state of native feeling alone" (331).

122. *Bengal Annual* for 1830, 268. Chaudhuri's edition omits a page (271) of the poem as it was originally printed in the *Bengal Annual* for 1830. I therefore quote the poem from that source, where it appeared on pages 265–75.

123. Edwards, *Henry Derozio*, 32.

124. *Oriental Magazine* 1 (October 1843), reprinted in Madge, *Henry Derozio*, 42. See also R. Chaudhuri, "Young India."

125. Majumdar and Dhar, *Presidency College Register*, 9.

126. Ibid.

127. Coomer, "H. H. Wilson and the Hindu College," 32.

128. Derozio, *Derozio, Poet of India*, 321.

129. God seated on the lotus throne is Vishnu, and Himávat here is the Himalayas.

130. Coleridge, *Complete Poems*, 231–32 (lines 6, 60–61). Echoes could go both ways, and although Keats, Shelley, and Byron died before Derozio's poetry could become known in England and neither Wordsworth nor Coleridge seems to have encountered it either, one young writer who apparently did was Harriet Martineau, whom I discuss in chapter 4.

131. Fabian, *Time and the Other*, 31.

132. Charles Taylor, "Afterword," 301.

133. Ibid., 303.

134. Derozio, *Derozio, Poet of India*, 357.

135. Duff, *India and Indian Missions*, 615. The lines are from "Is There for Honest Poverty" (37–40), in Burns, *Selected Poems*, 182.

136. Wordsworth, *Poetical Works*, 5:5 (lines 63–71).

137. Rammohun Roy, "Translation of the Cena Upanishad," in Rammohun Roy, *Translation of an Abridgment of the Vedant*, iv.

138. *Friend of India*, 1 June 1848, 343.

139. See Amartya Sen, *Argumentative Indian*.

140. Quoted in Anthony, *Britain's Betrayal in India*, 61. Cedric Dover quotes from this same lecture: "[Derozio] must be regarded as a minor but genuine member of the Romantic Movement, and had, says Professor B. B. Roy (in an article published in the *Calcutta Review* some twelve years ago), 'the same freethinking mind, the same challenge to orthodoxy, the same fundamental melancholy, the same love of mythology, and the same command over the resources of the English language.'" *Half-Caste*, 157. Anthony does not provide a source, nor have I been able to locate the lecture in the *Calcutta Review*.

Chapter 4 • *"Little Bengal"*

Epigraph: *Athenaeum* 190 (18 June 1831): 392.

1. *Bengal Annual* for 1833, 5–6; hereafter "An Oriental Tale" is cited parenthetically in the text. In the revised version published in *Bole Ponjis* (1851), to heighten the confusion Parker adds Hindu exclamations to the Muslim Brahmin's cries: "Allah il Allah—Ram Ram—Huree bol—Mohommud Russool e Allah." Parker, *Bole Ponjis*, 2:148.

2. Laurie, *Sketches of Some Distinguished Anglo-Indians*, 513.

3. A joke in the naming of Nealini may have been Parker's attempt to rescue her from Southey: book 1 of *The Curse of Kehama* ends with the sati of the two wives of Arvalan, son of Kehama, one of whom is called Nealliny.

4. *QR* 58 (February 1837): 96. For a treatment of returned colonialists and their patterns of settlement in London and elsewhere (especially Cheltenham Spa, Eastbourne, and Brighton) in the later nineteenth century, see Buettner, *Empire Families*.

5. I give the primary addresses of the institutions. Founded in a series of meetings in January through March 1823, the Asiatic Society moved into its lodgings at 14 Grafton Street in January 1824; and the Oriental Club, founded in early 1824 and initially housed at 16 Lower Grosvenor Street (present-day Grosvenor Street, east of Grosvenor Square), moved to 18 Hanover Square in 1828. Curries had long been available for home consumption, and although they had also been obtainable among other offerings in coffeehouses (such as the Norris Street Coffee House on the Haymarket) since at least the 1770s, the Hindostanee was the first to market itself as specializing in Indian fare. See Lizzie Collingham's chapter "Curry Powder: Bringing India to Britain," in *Curry*, 129–56.

6. On Halima / Hélène Bennett, see Friswell, "Indian Princess"; Young, *Fountain of the Elephants*, passim; Fisher, *Counterflows to Colonialism*, 184–85; and D. Ghosh, *Sex and the Family*, 149–52, 163–69. She was the sister-in-law of General William Palmer. For the story of this family circle, see Dalrymple, *White Mughals*.

7. D. Ghosh, *Sex and the Family*, 165.

8. A. Khan, *Travels*, 149.

9. Young, *Fountain of the Elephants*, 294–95. A responsible speculation, that as a youth growing up at Field Place, near Horsham, Shelley may have seen and subsequently described Hélène, seems to have hardened into a fact. In her 1968 biography, Jean Over-

ton Fuller wrote that Hélène's "name and the poet's are never connected, yet it would be surprising if an observant boy never noticed the new, strange, dusky figure, and it may be that some memory of her underlies the creation of the several Asian maidens who enter into Shelley's poetry." *Shelley*, 20. Subsequently, Rozina Visram mentioned that "Hélène Bennett is said to be the Indian woman the poet Shelley was referring to when he described the lady wandering the Forest of St Leonard." *Ayahs, Lascars and Princes*, 36. Raymond Head then wrote, "Hélène . . . may have been the Indian lady whom the poet Shelley used to see wandering in nearby St Leonard's forest." *Indian Style*, 15. Next, Rosie Llewellyn-Jones claimed, "There is good evidence that Helena was the Indian lady that the poet Shelley mentioned as wandering about in the neighbouring St Leonard's Forest." *Engaging Scoundrels*, 92. And Dalrymple then described the Zoffany portrait of General William Palmer and his family, including Palmer's wife, Fyze, and her sister, Nur Begum, who later "inspired Shelley, who saw the woman known locally as 'the Black Princess' wandering lonely and forlorn around St. Leonard's Forest." *White Mughals*, 380–81. No sources are cited for these claims. After fruitlessly searching for any reference by Shelley to an Indian woman wandering in St. Leonard's Forest, and after consulting with Nora Crook, Neil Fraistat, Tilar Mazzeo, and Jeremy Knight, I have concluded that the game of telephone began with "it would be surprising if," which became "is said to be," followed by "may have been" and "There is good evidence that," finally landing on "Shelley . . . saw." The closest thing to a source involves the almost certainly mistaken attribution to Shelley of an essay called, yes, "A True Story" in the 12 July 1820 *Indicator*, which describes the author's vivid childhood memory of having once seen a "tall slender female . . . looking sorrowfully and steadily in my face. She was dressed in white, from head to foot, in a fashion I had never seen before; her garments were unusually long and flowing, and rustled as she glided through the low shrubs near me as if they were made of the richest silk" (319). Although perhaps Orientalized by her dress, the woman is not described as Indian, and her hair is "pale brown" (319). The piece has been variously attributed to Charles Lamb as early as 1831 (and was included in early twentieth-century editions of Lamb) and to Leigh Hunt by Swinburne (see Lamb and Lamb, *Works*, 7:979); to Shelley by Walter Peck in "An Essay by Shelley" and then in *Shelley: His Life and Work*, 1:5; and to a very young Benjamin Disraeli by J. Logie Robertson in Disraeli, *Tales and Sketches*, 1–3, after which it was included in Disraeli, *Bradenham Edition*, 3:365–67. Although Shelley's authorship has not been disproven, there is no evidence for it, and it seems highly unlikely on stylistic grounds; the case for Disraeli's authorship seems the strongest. It is also frequently mentioned that Shelley's "Fragments of an Unfinished Drama" may have been inspired by Hélène.

10. JanMohamed, "Worldliness-Without-World," 223.

11. Mackenzie, *Propaganda and Empire*, 2.

12. M. Sinha, "Britishness," 496. See also Viswanathan, *Masks of Conquest*; Suleri, *Rhetoric of English India*; and Gikandi, *Maps of Englishness*. As Gikandi writes, "Englishness was itself a product of the colonial culture that it seemed to have created elsewhere" (x).

13. The two richest metaphors for the kind of circulation that involves the multidirectional, fluid, but unequal movements of people, ideas, commodities, and capital between mutually constitutive spaces are contrapuntal and recursive. The former, a musical metaphor, has received considerable attention following its use by Edward Said in *Culture and*

Imperialism and elsewhere. "In the counterpoint of Western classical music," Said writes, "various themes play off one another, with only a provisional privilege being given to any particular one; yet in the resulting polyphony there is concert and order, an organized interplay that derives from the themes, not from a rigorous melodic or formal principle outside the work" (*Culture and Imperialism*, 59–60). Recursiveness, a mathematical idea, expresses the dependence of the outcome of an operation upon a previous output, as in the Fibonacci sequence (0, 1, 1, 2, 3, 5, 8, 13, etc.), in which each term is the sum of the two preceding terms, the equation for which is $F(x) = F(x–1) + F(x–2)$; that is, the fifth term is the sum of the fourth term plus the third term. Movement through the sequence is thus always at once forwards and backwards, so to speak, as the former is generated by the latter.

14. See Aravamudan, *Tropicopolitans* and *Guru English*; Chakrabarty, *Provincializing Europe*; Jasanoff, *Edge of Empire*; K. Wilson, *Island Race*; O'Quinn, *Staging Governance*; Festa, *Sentimental Figures of Empire*; and Sudipta Sen, *Distant Sovereignty*.

15. Said, "Reflections on Exile," 173, 186.

16. Ibid., 173.

17. JanMohamed, "Worldliness-Without-World," 219.

18. Along with displaced Africans, lascars were the real exiles of early nineteenth-century London. See Fisher, *Counterflows to Colonialism*, 137–79; and Visram, *Ayahs, Lascars and Princes*, 34–54.

19. Kopf, *British Orientalism*, 241.

20. de Certeau, *Practice of Everyday Life*, 117.

21. Pannell, "From the Poetics of Place," 163.

22. W. Jones, "Discourse," ix, x.

23. Richardson, "On Going Home," 66, 64–65.

24. Ramratna was an associate of Rammohun's and may not have acted in the capacity of a servant, even though Rammohun posted a servant bond of 1,000 rupees for him, as he did for the other two. Fisher, *Counterflows to Colonialism*, 252.

25. At a late stage of completing this book, I read in manuscript Saree Makdisi's *Making England Western*, which vividly describes how an "internal Orient" is to be found in the nineteenth-century discourse and history of "city Arabs"—working-class "white" Britons depicted as racially, nationally, and civilizationally distinct and as much in need of improvement as Arabs elsewhere—and in the enclaves of London's underworld, especially St. Giles and Seven Dials. Arguing that "the 'distant' had first to be *distanced* from the center," that "the 'Arabs,' in short, had to go, in order for England to become (or even claim to be) 'English,' 'white,' 'Western' in any kind of recognizable way," Makdisi concludes that Orientalism was not just a "Western style for dominating, restructuring, and having authority over the Orient" (Said, *Orientalism*, 3) but also inextricable from an "Occidentalism" that *produced* what we think of as the West. I realize that my account of Little Bengal, an elite community, is part of this larger story about London's struggles to become a Western capital by purging itself of its own internal East, which permeated marginal societies both low and high.

26. At meetings of the Club committee on 15 and 22 August 1825, Major Pringle Taylor complained that the *Oriental Herald* and the *Asiatic Journal* for July were missing, and the committee "ordered that a notice be put up in the Reading Room requesting of any member who have [sic] carried away the said publications to bring them back without delay." Oriental Club Minutes, 1824–28, LMA 4452/01/03/001, 147.

27. "Society in India," 224. Ignorance of India in England was a repeated theme in Calcutta writing. The *Calcutta Government Gazette* (as reprinted in the *Calcutta Magazine*) hoped that the *Bengal Annual* for 1832 would "break in upon this shameful apathy" on the part of the English public, which views "India with a cold askance and stepmother-like regard." *Calcutta Magazine and Monthly Register*, 58.

28. Johnson, Maxwell, and Trumpener, "*Arabian Nights*," 244.

29. One admiring reader wrote a letter to the *India Gazette*, printed on 13 April 1826, doubting the author's claim to be so young: "It is generally believed that he is a *wee bit* older, and I think so too—twice that would most probably give the number of his years, or I have guessed wrong." Quoted in Derozio, *Derozio, Poet of India*, 52.

30. The writings of this community are now in print and easily available. See Gibson, *Anglophone Poetry*; and Fhlathúin, *Poetry of British India*.

31. Byron, *Lord Byron*, 436 (canto 2, stanza 12).

32. S. Ahmed, "Orientalism," 168.

33. *Orient Pearl* for 1834, vii. Technically, Richardson was relaunching the annual, which first appeared as the *Orient Pearl* for 1832. Right before the annual appeared for 1834, Richardson transferred the editorship to the East Indian William Kirkpatrick, who had been a close friend of Derozio's, but the preface to the *Orient Pearl* for 1834 acknowledged, "The change in the Editorship of the present work being of recent date, almost the entire merit of the compilation is due to its former Editors" (iii). Kirkpatrick's name appeared as editor on the title page of the *Orient Pearl* for 1835.

34. Milton, *Paradise Lost*, 26 (bk. 2, lines 1–4). The primary allusions of the phrase "orient pearl" are to *Paradise Lost*, bk. 4, line 238, and bk. 5, line 2, and to *Antony and Cleopatra* 1.5.41.

35. The *Bengal Annual* ran from 1830 to 1836, and the *Orient Pearl* appeared for 1832, 1834, and 1835. The *Bengal Annual* for 1831 and the *Orient Pearl* for 1832 and 1834 tried hardest to compete with the London annuals. The *Bengal Annual* for 1830 was 8vo in 4s (octavo in 4 signatures), 22 x 13.5 cm, not bound in silk or gilt-edged, though at least one purchaser (of BL ST579) saw fit to have the edges cut and gilded and the book bound in three-quarter maroon leather over morocco-grained red cloth with ornamental gilt fillets on the boards, the spine blind tooled and elaborately gilded. The prospectus for the *Bengal Annual* for 1831 announced, "It having been suggested to us, from various quarters, that the binding of the last year's Annual was not sufficiently ornamental, the next will be bound in colored silk and be gilt-edged in the manner of the most elegant of the London Annuals. This improvement could not have been effected without a great additional expense, if we had not resolved on a change in the form of the book, from an octavo to a duodecimo" (405). The annual for 1831 accordingly appeared in a smaller format (12mo [duodecimo] in 6s, 17.5 x 11 cm), covered in purple watered silk (still visible on BL PP.6892) with red endpapers and gilded edges. Thereafter, starting with the third volume, the appearance became less lavish and the format still smaller, approximately 15 x 10 cm, depending on binding. It should be noted that with wove paper, print formats can be difficult to establish with certainty, and physical descriptions in early nineteenth-century reviews can be contradictory and unreliable. Although I'm fairly certain of the formats given above for the annuals for 1830 and 1831, the formats that follow throughout this note are conjectural, based on size and number of leaves per signature: 1832, 16mo in 8s; 1833, 16mo in 8s; 1834, 18mo in 6s; 1835, 18mo in 6s; 1836, 18mo in 6s). For a higher price, the

1834 annual (and possibly those for 1833, 1835, and 1836) could be purchased with higher-grade calf and gilded edges. Illustrations were a problem throughout the annual's run. The first volume included seven plates, significantly in the form not of engravings but of (locally made) etchings. The 1831 annual had no illustrations, and its preface informed the reader, "Should the present volume acquire a larger circulation than its predecessor, an order will be sent home for such pictorial illustrations [i.e., engravings] as will place the work on an equality, in point of elegance and beauty of appearance, with the London publications of the same class" (iii). Neither the 1832 annual nor the 1833 annual included illustrations, but the preface to the annual for 1834 expressed the hope that the "attraction of London Engravings" would gratify the reader, conceding that these were "the *first impressions*, or proofs before the letter, of engravings intended for the embellishment of a London Annual for 1834" (vii). The annuals for 1834 and 1835 could be purchased with or without plates. The publication of the 1836 annual was "delayed in the expectation of embellishments from England. In this the publishers have been disappointed" (v). I have not been able to examine the copy of the *Orient Pearl* for 1832 listed in the catalog of the National Library of India, but it was bound in silk (see Derozio, *Derozio, Poet of India,* 364), as was the *Orient Pearl* for 1834, which appeared in a similar format to the *Bengal Annual* for 1832, 12mo in 6s, 17.25 x 10.5 cm (BL PP.3776 is richly bound in dark blue full leather with a fairly ornamental Orientalist pattern stamped and tooled, gilt-edged). The *Orient Pearl* for 1835 was in the smaller format, approximately 15 x 10 cm (16mo in 8s), also advertised in silk.

36. I am grateful to Laurence Singlehurst, librarian of the Oriental Club, and June Aitken, personal assistant to the Club secretary, for their assistance.

37. *Calcutta Magazine and Monthly Register,* 57. On intimacy and the function of hand-written inscriptions in printed books, see Piper, *Dreaming in Books,* 128–38.

38. See esp. Fisher, *Counterflows to Colonialism;* and Visram, *Ayahs, Lascars and Princes* and *Asians in Britain.*

39. Marshall, "British-Indian Connections," 51.

40. Colquhoun, *Treatise,* app. 45.

41. Fisher, *Counterflows to Colonialism,* 112–15.

42. See Nechtman, *Nabobs.*

43. Henderson, *Bengalee,* 422.

44. "Reflections of a Returned Exile," 65.

45. Ibid., 67.

46. "English in India," 10.

47. Rocher and Rocher, *Making of Western Indology,* 131.

48. Ibid., 163.

49. Ibid., 202.

50. Beckingham, "History of the Royal Asiatic Society," 15.

51. *AJ* 15 (May 1823): 499, 500, 498.

52. Forrest, *Oriental,* 23. I am grateful to Douglas Peers for his correspondence. Many Company officers continued to use and be known by their rank even if it no longer served as more than an honorific.

53. Arnot, "Indian Cookery," iii.

54. *Age* 173 (7 September 1828): 283.

55. Thackeray, *Vanity Fair,* 28, 765. See also Zoli, "Black Holes."

56. The London Metropolitan Archive holds an original copy of the prospectus, from which I quote: Oriental Club Prospectus, LMA 4452/01/03/001, 1. It was reproduced in *Oriental Herald* 2 (May–August 1824): 143–44. The standard sources on the Oriental Club are Baillie, *Oriental Club and Hanover Square*; Forrest, *Oriental*; Innes, *Oriental Club. Library*; and Wheeler, *Annals of the Oriental Club*.

57. The Oriental Club moved to its present location, around the corner in Stratford Place, in 1961–62, and the building in Hanover Square was demolished in 1964.

58. M. Sinha, "Britishness," 504.

59. *Calcutta Review* 14 (July–December 1850): 266–67.

60. Henderson, *Bengalee*, 436.

61. Macaulay, *Letters*, 3:204.

62. Schwab, *Oriental Renaissance*, 43.

63. Leask, *British Romantic Writers*, 10; Bayly, *Empire and Information*.

64. Marshall, "British-Indian Connections," 54.

65. M. Sinha, "Britishness," 491.

66. Forrest, *Oriental*, 53.

67. *Times*, 27 March 1811, 1B.

68. The Victuallers Register for the division of Holborn in 1810, which records Dean Mahomet's license, reveals no other establishments on George Street or the surrounding area catering by name to the Anglo-Indian market (the only other name that evokes the East is the generic Turk's Head on Harley Street). Victuallers Register, 1810, LMA MR/LV/11/132. On the Hindostanee, see Fisher, *Travels of Dean Mahomet*, 149–52; and Collingham, *Curry*, 129–30.

69. Oriental Club Minutes, 1829–32, LMA 4452/01/03/002, 77, 166.

70. "Society in India," 226.

71. *John Bull*, 29 September 1828, 309; *Freeman's Journal and Daily Commercial Advertiser*, 24 September 1830, n.p.

72. *New Monthly Magazine* 40, no. 159 (March 1834): 375.

73. Lillywhite, *London Coffee Houses*, 269.

74. Ibid., 291.

75. Oriental Club List of Members, 1824–25, LMA 4452/04/02/002.

76. Richardson, *Literary Chit-Chat*, 192.

77. J. Grant, *Great Metropolis*, 1:136.

78. "Reflections of a Returned Exile," 67, 70.

79. With the italicized words translated, followed by alternative translations in parentheses, the passage would read, "I have a *passion* (taste, rage, love) for . . . machines, but I don't understand the *working* (philosophy, wisdom) of this watch; I think it is rather a *sham* (made-up affair), for there's no *regularity* (certainty, trustworthiness) in its going, and I know that my *native steward* and the *watch-maker* . . . are *intimate friends*." As with the "nomadic races of England," whose "use of a slang language" Henry Mayhew points out, the vocabulary of Anglo-Indians marks them as non-normative and racially distinct. Mayhew, *London Labour*, 1:2. See Makdisi's forthcoming *Making England Western*.

80. On a different kind of jargon involved in relations of power, see Majeed, "Jargon of Indostan."

81. JanMohamed, "Worldliness-Without-World," 219.

82. Rocher and Rocher, *Making of Western Indology*, 131.

83. The phrase "conversable world," used most influentially by Hume in *Essays, Moral and Political*, 2:1, appears as early as the *Tatler* 153 (30 March–1 April 1810) in Steele, *Lucubrations of Isaac Bickerstaff Esq.*, 3:191, but I primarily have in mind Jon Mee's *Conversable Worlds*.

84. E. Roberts, "Sketches of Indian Society," 115.

85. Zastoupil, *Rammohun Roy*, 41–56. See also Aravamudan, *Guru English*, 37–44.

86. *Standard*, 9 July 1831, 1D.

87. Along with Zastoupil, see Killingley, *Rammohun Roy*, 128–55; A. Ray, *Negotiating the Modern*, 71–74; and Dasgupta, *Bengal Renaissance*, 39–71. As an Arian, Rammohun differed from mainstream Unitarianism with respect to the nature of Christ: the Unitarian Society's London reprint of Rammohun's *Precepts of Jesus* (1824) included a preface by Thomas Rees that offered the following apologia: "The Unitarian Society . . . are aware that, holding, as they do, the strict and proper humanity of Christ as one of their fundamental tenets, they may possibly be charged with a dereliction of principle in their circulating, under their authority, a work which maintains his pre-existence and superangelic rank and dignity." *Precepts of Jesus. . . . To which are Added, the First, Second, and Final Appeal*, xiv.

88. Biswas, *Correspondence of Raja Rammohun Roy*, 2:733.

89. Lindsey preached his inaugural sermon on 17 April 1774 at Essex Street, where a new chapel was built, to be opened in 1778, thus beginning the gradual establishment of Unitarianism as a denomination.

90. White, *Early Romanticism*, 17–86, 119–51.

91. Coleridge, *Notebooks*, 1:467.

92. Mee, *Conversable Worlds*, 37–38, 118–24.

93. J. Porter, *Growth of the Gospel*, 8.

94. Gibbes, *Hartly House, Calcutta*, 111.

95. From its first appearance in 1789 through Monica Clough's 1989 edition, the novel was assumed to be a semiautobiographical memoir written on the basis of firsthand experience. In the *Analytical Review* Mary Wollstonecraft called it an "entertaining account . . . apparently sketched by a person who had been forcibly impressed by the scenes described. Probably the ground-work of the correspondence was actually written on the spot." *Analytical Review* 7 (June 1789): 147. And describing 1780s Calcutta in the introduction to his 1925 edition of Eliza Fay's *Original Letters from India*, E. M. Forster quoted from the correspondence of one "Miss Sophia Goldborne, a contemporary of Mrs. Fay's and sometimes her rival in the narrative style" (21). All we know of Gibbes comes from a series of applications she made between 1799 and 1805 to the Royal Literary Fund, which was founded in 1790 to support indigent writers of talent and industry. Isobel Grundy has plausibly conjectured that the "book very likely reflects her appropriation and radical revision of epistolary texts by her son." Grundy, "The Barbarous Character We Give Them," 79. "I have been years a widdow," Gibbes wrote in her application of 14 October 1804, "& during that period having the distress of Losing an only son at Calcutta, for the advancement of whose flattering prospects, I narrowed my originally Limited widdowed [widdow's?] provision, for he died, [poor creature?] before he was enabled to make me *one* transmittance" (my transcription). Phebe Gibbes to the Literary Fund, BL, MS Loan 96 RLF 1/74/3.

96. Sterne, *A Sentimental Journey*, 5. Elsewhere her plagiarisms are not unwitting, a

fact she admits: "My dear Arabella, I have one caution to give you, which is, not to set me down for a plagiarist, though you should even stumble upon the likeness, verbatim, of my descriptions of the Eastern world in print; or once presume to consider such printed accounts as other than honourable testimonies of my faithful relations." Gibbes, *Hartly House, Calcutta*, 76. Sterne's other contribution to the tradition of the sentimentalized Brahmin, unknown until the mid-nineteenth century, is the exchange between himself and Eliza Draper as "the Bramin and Bramine." Sterne, *A Sentimental Journey*, 107.

97. Gibbes, *Hartly House, Calcutta*, xxiv.

98. Basham, "Sophia and the Brahmin," 28.

99. An example of one of Sophia's plagiarisms, the language of her claim here is lifted directly from William Guthrie's *New Geographical, Historical, and Commercial Grammar*, 546.

100. Another early instance of the type is the "young Bramin" in Starke, *Widow of Malabar*.

101. The reference is to *Macbeth* 2.2.27. The full title of the novel, which capitalized on the popularity of Edward Nares's *Thinks-I-to-Myself. A Serio-Ludicro, Tragico-Comico Tale*, 2 vols. (London, 1811), is *I'll Consider of It! A Tale, in Three Volumes, in which "Thinks I to Myself" is Partially Considered*.

102. Henry Denbigh is apparently named after the friend of the deceased Captain Percy, Henry Denbeigh, in Hamilton, *Translation of the Letters of a Hindoo Rajah* (1796).

103. See Franklin, "Radically Feminizing India."

104. Owenson, *Missionary*, 109.

105. Ibid., 247.

106. Ibid., 260.

107. Collet, *Life and Letters of Raja Rammohun Roy*, 174–75.

108. *Preston Chronicle*, 21 May 1831, 2B.

109. Sutherland, "Sketch of Rammohun Roy," 1068.

110. The conjecture is Linda H. Peterson's in Martineau, *Autobiography*, 173.

111. Martineau, *Harriet Martineau's Autobiography*, 1:243.

112. Ibid., 1:280.

113. Sutherland, "Sketch of Rammohun Roy," 1057.

114. Buckingham, "Sketch of the Life," 115. Rammohun "would never partake of any food (from a determination to preserve his caste)" (115).

115. Koditschek, *Liberalism, Imperialism*, 96.

116. Bayly, "Rammohan Roy," 40. Nigel Leask takes a different approach, offering a conjectural but persuasive argument for the influence of Rammohun's writings in the London periodical press ca. 1817–18 on Shelley (*British Romantic Writers*, 139–54). The "Rammohunian Shelley," for Leask, abandons the Volneyan spirit and utilitarian assimilationism of *The Revolt of Islam* in favor of the polyphony of *Prometheus Unbound*, especially in Demogorgon's "formless embodiment" of power and "sceptical negative" method of dialogue (148).

117. Cf. Fisher, *Counterflows to Colonialism*, 250–59.

118. Sutherland, "Sketch of Rammohun Roy," 1069.

119. There is a blue (commemorative) plaque at what is currently 49 Bedford Square.

120. The coffin was reinterred in Arno's Vale cemetery, Bristol, in 1843.

121. Arnot, "Biographical Sketch," 667.

122. Sutherland, "Sketch of Rammohun Roy," 1070.

123. *AJ*, n.s., 12 (September–December 1833): 206.

124. Biswas, *Correspondence of Raja Rammohun Roy*, 2:781–82.

125. The phrasing "which I have brought to your notice" leaves it slightly uncertain whether Rammohun gave the publication to Castle, but his habit of giving pamphlets and books (see the discussion of his exchanges with Frances Kemble below) makes it likely.

126. Killingley, *Rammohun Roy*, 150.

127. See Mee, *Conversable Worlds*, 17–26, 239–54.

128. Invited to the Unitarian anniversary dinner on 8 February 1832, Rammohun replied, "It is truly mortifying for me to hesitate even for a moment to comply with a request of one whom I so highly esteem and respect. But I have before explained to you how much attending public dinners might be injurious to my interest in India and disagreeable to the feeling of my friends there." In the end he agreed to join the party "after dinner at 9 o'clock . . . at the London Tavern." Collet, *Life and Letters of Raja Rammohun Roy*, 201–2.

129. Carpenter, *Last Days*, 129.

130. Sutherland, "Sketch of Rammohun Roy," 1065; Martin, "Rajah Rammohun Roy."

131. Zastoupil, *Rammohun Roy*, 28.

132. Killingley, *Rammohun Roy*, 148.

133. Zastoupil, *Rammohun Roy*, 170.

134. Chakrabarty, *Provincializing Europe*, 126.

135. Le Breton, *Memories of Seventy Years*, 171. In *The East India Voyager* Emma Roberts singles out "black fellow" as an "invidious epithet" (105). See also Gibson, *Anglophone Poetry*, 122.

136. "Sketch of the Great Hindoo Philosopher," 565. The "Sketch" possibly is by Robert Montgomery Martin or was subsequently lifted by Martin and included without attribution in his obituary, "Rajah Rammohun Roy." Note the echoes of Hilarion in "towering" and "commanding."

137. Ibid.

138. *AJ*, n.s., 12 (September–December 1833): 206.

139. Janet Hare's father's name was Alexander, though Peary Chand Mittra's *Biographical Sketch of David Hare* inadvertently introduced some ambiguity into the historical record by referring to him as both Alexander (iv) and James (3).

140. Reprinted from the *Court Journal* in *Morning Post*, 2 July 1832, 3C.

141. *Hobart Town Courier*, 7 December 1832, 2E. Zastoupil writes, "Lucy Aikin fits perfectly the woman described. Whether she was the woman whom—according to gossip circulating after his death—Rammohun had privately married is a matter of conjecture." *Rammohun Roy*, 90; see also ibid., 205n118.

142. Carpenter, *Last Days*, 105.

143. Ibid., 106.

144. Ibid., 105.

145. Zastoupil, *Rammohun Roy*, 93.

146. See Webb, *Harriet Martineau*, 283–309.

147. Before writing "Sabbath Musings. No. II," published in the *Monthly Repository* in 1831, she seems to have read and internalized "A Dramatic Sketch," which appeared in the *Bengal Annual* of the preceding year. The timing suggests that the echoes of Derozio's poem in the following passages from Martineau's "Musings" (emphasis added) are more

than coincidence. The piece begins by asking, "*Is there not a voice in this solitude which tells* a different tale" (235), followed shortly by a "*wandering breeze*" (235) and "*praise*" (235), after which there is the exclamation, "How full of *bliss* is life and the *world?*" (237), followed by reference to a "*tempest*" (238).

148. Martineau, *Harriet Martineau's Autobiography*, 3:49.

149. Sutherland, "Sketch of Rammohun Roy," 1067–68.

150. Ibid., 1067.

151. Martineau, *Harriet Martineau's Autobiography*, 3:48.

152. Chakrabarty, *Provincializing Europe*, 127.

153. Kemble, *Records of a Girlhood*, 1:290.

154. Chakrabarty, *Provincializing Europe*, 125.

155. Ibid., 127.

156. Ibid., 126.

157. Franklin, *Orientalist Jones*, 265. On the reception of Jones's translation of *Sakuntala* as promoting a natural order based on a sympathetic relationship between humanity and divinity, see Rudd, *Sympathy and India*, 82–85.

158. Collet, *Life and Letters of Raja Rammohun Roy*, 200.

159. Thackeray, *Newcomes*, 78. In the name "Rummun Loll" Rammohun becomes a "rum 'un" (an odd one) who lolls (reclines idly), while "Loll" also evokes "loll shrub" (claret) and bears a striking resemblance to "Doss" in Rammohun's pseudonym Ram Doss, though an intentional reference seems unlikely.

160. The phrase is Edward Said's, from "Mind of Winter," 54.

161. Kemble, *Records of a Girlhood*, 3:203.

162. Biswas, *Correspondence of Raja Rammohun Roy*, 2:1105, 1107, emphasis added.

163. JanMohamed, "Worldliness-Without-World," 227.

164. Kemble, *Records of a Girlhood*, 3:204.

165. *AJ* 15 (March 1823): 265.

166. I. Singh, *Rammohun Roy*, 3:458. According to the London Metropolitan Archives catalog description of the Oriental Club records, "Non-British subjects could be granted honorary member status from 1831," a date that cannot be merely coincidental to Rammohun's visit and his election as an honorary member of the Royal Asiatic Society. It was not until June 1845 that Mohun Lal and Dwarkanath Tagore were admitted during their visits to London as the first honorary non-European members of the Club. Oriental Club Minutes, 1845–48, LMA 4452/01/03/006, 43, 45. Rammohun did mingle socially with members of the Oriental Club at the anniversary dinner of the Royal Asiatic Society on 11 May 1833, held at the Thatched House Tavern on St. James. *Athenaeum* 291 (25 May 1833): 332. In attendance at Rammohun's induction in June 1831 and the dinner in May 1833 was Mountstuart Elphinstone, who was sympathetic to what he saw as Rammohun's contributions to the "strong spirit of reform as applied to the science, religion, and morals" of India. Colebrooke, *Life of the Honourable Mountstuart Elphinstone*, 2:135; see also 2:344–45.

167. Martineau echoes the extensive criticism of Rammohun for saying what he thought people wanted to hear: "The great defect of his . . . character, was a want of firmness to say that which would be unpleasant to individuals or bodies of men . . . a wish to please all parties" (Arnot, "Biographical Sketch," 667); "In fact, no matter what the creed of the parties with whom he conversed. . . , he was sure to impress them with an idea, ei-

ther that he was of their peculiar faith, or that they had converted him to it. A lady once observed to me, that she was rejoiced to find that he was a sincere Trinitarian" (Sutherland, "Sketch of Rammohun Roy," 1065).

168. Hamilton, *Translation of the Letters of a Hindoo Rajah*, 246.

169. *York Herald*, 16 April 1831, 3C.

170. *Morning Chronicle*, 17 June 1831, 4B.

171. Ibid.

172. *Royal Cornwall Gazette*, 16 June 1832, 2E.

173. Ibid., 2E–F.

174. Fox, "Discourse," 126.

175. Ibid., 127.

176. Ibid., 130.

177. *AJ* 12 (September–December 1833): 195.

178. Fox, "Discourse," 139–40.

Epilogue

1. The letters are reproduced in Mittra, *Life of Dewan Ramcomul Sen*, 15–17. For a capsule biography of Ramkamal, see Sastri, *Ramtanu Lahiri*, 180.

2. Richardson, *Selections from the British Poets*, lxxvii.

3. *AJ*, n.s., 8 (May–August 1832): 332.

4. Arnot, *Sketch*.

5. Fallon, "Christianity in Bengal," 454.

6. Mittra, *Life of Dewan Ramcomul Sen*, 48.

7. G. Smith, *Life of William Carey, D.D.*, 242.

8. Derozio, *Song of the Stormy Petrel*, lvii.

9. Sastri, *Ramtanu Lahiri*, 163.

10. Sandeman, *Selections from Calcutta Gazettes*, 4:370.

11. G. Chattopadhyay, *Awakening in Bengal*, lii.

12. Clair Taylor, *British and American Abolitionists*, 230–31. Some of Rammohun's hair remained in Bristol: Zastoupil treats this incident and provides a photograph of two of Rammohun's locks in the Bristol City Museum and Art Gallery in *Rammohun Roy*, 94–95.

13. Gibbes, *Hartly House, Calcutta*, 135.

14. Samuel May to J. B. Estlin, 30 December 1844, in Clair Taylor, *British and American Abolitionists*, 231.

15. Clair Taylor, *British and American Abolitionists*, 230.

16. Ibid., 231.

Primary Sources

An Account of the Bristol Education Society: For the Year [1803, 1809, 1813, 1816, 1817, 1820]. Bristol, 1803–20.

"Advertisement." Appended to An Essay on the Best Means of Civilising the Subjects of the British Empire in India, and of Diffusing the Light of the Christian Religion throughout the Eastern World; to which the University of Glasgow Adjudged Dr Buchanan's Prize, by John Mitchell. Edinburgh, 1805.

An Alphabetical Catalogue of all the Books in the Library, belonging to the Bristol Education Society. Bristol, 1795.

Arnot, Sandford. "Biographical Sketch of Rajah Rammohun Roy." Athenaeum 310 (5 October 1833): 666–68.

———, trans. "Indian Cookery, as Practised and Described by the Natives of the East." In Miscellaneous Translations from Oriental Languages, vol. 1. London, 1831.

———. A Sketch of the History of the Indian Press During the Last Ten Years; with a Disclosure of the True Causes of Its Present Degradation; Proved to Have Been Produced by the Extraordinary, and Hitherto Unheard of Conduct of Mr. James Silk Buckingham. With a Biographical Notice of the Indian Cobbett, Alias "Peter the Hermit." London, 1829.

Atkinson, James. City of Palaces; a Fragment. And Other Poems. Calcutta, 1824.

Banier, Antoine. Histoire générale des cérémonies, moeurs, et coutumes religieuses de tous les peuples du monde. 7 vols. Paris, 1741.

Barbauld, Anna Letitia. Anna Letitia Barbauld: Selected Poetry and Prose. Ed. William McCarthy and Elizabeth Kraft. Peterborough, ON: Broadview, 2002.

Bayle, Pierre. Dictionnaire historique et critique. 2 vols. Amsterdam, 1697.

The Bengal Annual. A Literary Keepsake for [1830–36]. Ed. David Lester Richardson. Calcutta, 1830–36.

Bentham, Jeremy. The Works of Jeremy Bentham. Ed. John Bowring. 11 vols. Edinburgh, 1838–43.

The Bhagavad-Gita: Krishna's Counsel in Time of War. Trans. Barbara Stoler Miller. New York: Bantam, 2004.

Biswas, Dilip Kumar, ed. The Correspondence of Raja Rammohun Roy. 2 vols. Calcutta: Saraswat Library, 1992–97.

Bogue, David, and James Bennett. History of Dissenters, from the Revolution in 1688, to the Year 1808. 4 vols. London, 1808–12.

Bose, Shib Chunder. *The Hindoos As They Are: A Description of the Manners, Customs, and Inner Life of Hindoo Society in Bengal.* 2nd ed. Calcutta, 1883.

Bowen, John. *Missionary Incitement, and Hindoo Demoralization: Including Some Observations on the Political Tendency of the Means Taken to Evangelize Hindoostan.* London, 1821.

Brief View of the Baptist Missions and Translations. London, 1815.

Bryant, Jacob. *A New System, or, an Analysis of Ancient Mythology: Wherein an Attempt is Made to Divest Tradition of Fable; and to Reduce the Truth to its Original Purity.* 3 vols. London, 1774–76.

Buchanan, Claudius. *Christian Researches in Asia: With Notices of the Translation of the Scriptures into the Oriental Languages.* Cambridge, 1811.

Buckingham, James Silk. "Danger of the Native Press." *Calcutta Journal* 1, no. 39 (14 February 1823): 617–19.

——. "Derozio's Poems." *Oriental Herald* 22, no. 67 (July–September 1829): 111–17.

——. *A Letter to Sir Charles Forbes, Bart. M.P. On the Suppression of Public Discussion in India.* London, 1824.

——. *Prospectus of a New Paper, to be entitled The Calcutta Journal, or, Political, Commercial, and Literary Gazette.* Calcutta, 22 September 1818.

——. *A Second Letter to Sir Charles Forbes, Bart. M.P. On the Suppression of Public Discussion in India.* London, 1824.

——. "Sketch of the Life, Writings, and Character of Ram Mohun Roy." *Parliamentary Review,* supplement to vol. 4, no. 32 (1 February 1833): 113–20.

Burford, Robert. *Description of a View of the City of Calcutta; Now Exhibiting at the Panorama, Leicester Square.* London, 1830.

Burke, Edmund. *The Writing and Speeches of Edmund Burke.* Gen. ed. Paul Langford. Vol. 1, ed. T. O. McLoughlin and James T. Boulton. Oxford: Oxford UP, 1997.

Burns, Robert. *Selected Poems.* Ed. Carol McGuirk. London: Penguin, 1993.

Byron, George Gordon. *Lord Byron: The Major Works.* Ed. Jerome J. McGann. Oxford: Oxford UP, 1986.

——. *Lord Byron's Letters and Journals.* Ed. Leslie A. Marchand. 12 vols. Cambridge, MA: Harvard UP, 1973–82.

Calcutta Magazine and Monthly Register. 1832. Original Papers. Calcutta, 1832.

Calvin, John. *Institutes of the Christian Religion.* Ed. John T. McNeill. 2 vols. Philadelphia: Westminster, 1967.

Carey, Eustace. *Memoir of William Carey, D.D.* London, 1836.

Carey, William. *An Enquiry into the Obligations of Christians, to Use Means for the Conversion of the Heathens. In which the Religious State of the Different Nations of the World, the Success of Former Undertakings, and the Practicability of Further Undertakings, are Considered.* Leicester, UK, 1792.

——. *The Journal and Selected Letters of William Carey.* Ed. Terry G. Carter. Macon, GA: Smyth & Helwys, 2000.

Carey, William, John Williams, et al. *Serampore Letters: Being the Unpublished Correspondence of William Carey and Others with John Williams, 1800–1816.* Ed. Leighton Williams and Mornay Williams. New York, 1892.

Catalogue of the Missionary Museum, Austin Friars; including Specimens in Natural History, Various Idols of Heathen Nations, Dresses, Manufactures, Domestic Utensils, Instruments of War, &c.&c.&c. London, 1826.

A Chronological Outline of the History of Bristol and the Stranger's Guide through the Streets and Neighbourhood. 4 vols. London, 1824.

Coleridge, Hartley. *Letters of Hartley Coleridge.* Ed. Grace Evelyn Griggs and Earl Leslie Griggs. London: Oxford UP, 1936.

Coleridge, Samuel Taylor. *The Collected Letters of Samuel Taylor Coleridge.* Ed. Earl Leslie Griggs. 6 vols. Oxford: Clarendon, 1956–71.

———. *Essays on His Times.* Ed. David V. Erdman. 3 vols. *The Collected Works of Samuel Taylor Coleridge.* Princeton, NJ: Princeton UP, 1978.

———. *The Notebooks of Samuel Taylor Coleridge.* Ed. Kathleen Coburn and A. J. Harding. 5 vols. London: Routledge, 1957–2002.

———. *Samuel Taylor Coleridge: The Complete Poems.* Ed. William Keach. London: Penguin, 1997.

Collet, Sophia Dobson. *The Life and Letters of Raja Rammohun Roy.* Ed. Dilip Kumar Biswas and Prabhat Chandra Ganguli. 3rd ed. Calcutta: Sadharan Brahmo Samaj, 1962.

Colquhoun, Patrick. *A Treatise on the Wealth, Power, and Resources of the British Empire.* London, 1814.

Curiosities of Bristol and Its Neighbourhood: With a Guide, for the Use of Strangers. Bristol, [1854].

De Quincey, Thomas. *Confessions of an English Opium-Eater, Part 1 & 2.* Vol. 2 of *The Works of Thomas De Quincey,* gen. ed. Grevel Lindop. London: Pickering & Chatto, 2000.

———. "Lake Reminiscences, from 1807 to 1830. By the English Opium-Eater. No. IV.— William Wordsworth and Robert Southey." *Tait's Edinburgh Magazine* 6 (July 1839): 453–64.

Derozio, Henry Louis Vivian. *Derozio, Poet of India: The Definitive Edition.* Ed. Rosinka Chaudhuri. New Delhi: Oxford UP, 2008.

———. *The Fakeer of Jungheera, a Metrical Tale; and Other Poems.* Calcutta, 1828.

———. *Poems, by H. L. V. Derozio.* Calcutta, 1827.

———. *Song of the Stormy Petrel: Complete Works of Henry Louis Vivian Derozio.* Ed. Abirlal Mukhopadhyay, Amar Dutta, Adhir Kumar, and Sakti Sadhan Mukhopadhyay. Calcutta: Progressive, 2001.

Dibdin, Thomas Frognall. *Reminiscences of a Literary Life.* 2 vols. London, 1836.

"Dispatches of the Duke of Wellington." *Quarterly Review* 115 (February 1837): 82–107.

Disraeli, Benjamin. *The Bradenham Edition of the Novels and Tales of Benjamin Disraeli.* Ed. Philip Guedalla. 12 vols. London: Peter Davies, 1926–27.

———. *Tales and Sketches by the Right Hon. Benjamin Disraeli, Earl of Beaconsfield K.G.* Ed. J. Logie Robertson. London, 1891.

"Distinction." *Papers, &c. (East India Company) (Second Part.),* vol. 8 (24 November 1812–22 July 1813), paper 7 (14 April 1813), 65.

Drummond, William. *Academical Questions.* London, 1805.

Dubois, Jean Antoine. *Letters on the State of Christianity in India; in which the Conversion of the Hindoos is Considered as Impracticable.* London, 1823.

Duff, Alexander. *India and Indian Missions: Including Sketches of the Gigantic System of Hinduism, both in Theory and Practice.* Edinburgh, 1839.

Dupuis, Charles François. *Origine de tous les cultes, ou Religion universelle.* 7 vols. Paris, 1795.

Dyer, John. John Dyer to John Saffery, 22 May 1817. Reeves R16/4. Angus Library, Regent's Park College, Oxford.

"East Indian's [sic] Meeting." *Calcutta Magazine and Monthly Register* 3 (September 1831): 157–62.

Eichhorn, Johann Gottfried. *Einleitung in das Alte Testament.* 5 vols. Leipzig, 1780–83.

"The English in India." *Calcutta Review* 1 (May–August 1844): 1–41, 290–336.

"English Poetry by a Hindu. Kasiprasad Ghosh." *Asiatic Journal,* n.s., 5 (June 1831): 105–9.

"Establishment of a Native Newspaper, Edited by a Learned Hindoo." *Calcutta Journal* 6, no. 328 (20 December 1821): 518–20.

Evangelical Idolatry: A Sermon. London, 1829.

Evans, John. *The New Guide, or Picture of Bristol, with Historical and Biographical Notices.* 3rd ed. Bristol, 1823.

———. *The Picture of Bristol; or A Guide to Objects of Curiosity and Interest, in Bristol, Clifton, the Hotwells, and their Vicinity; including Biographical Notices of Eminent Natives.* Bristol, 1814.

Faber, George Stanley. *The Origin of Pagan Idolatry Ascertained from Historical Testimony and Circumstantial Evidence.* 3 vols. London, 1816.

Fay, Eliza. *Original Letters from India.* Ed. E. M. Forster. New York: Harcourt, Brace, 1925.

Fhlathúin, Máire ní, ed. *The Poetry of British India, 1780–1905.* 2 vols. London: Pickering & Chatto, 2011.

Fiebig, Frederick. *Panorama of Calcutta Drawn after Nature.* Calcutta, 1847.

Formey, Jean Henri Samuel. *A Concise History of Philosophy and Philosophers.* Glasgow, 1767.

[Foster, John]. "The Curse of Kehama." Pt. 1. *Eclectic Review* 7 (March 1811): 185–205.

———. "The Curse of Kehama." Pt. 2. In Madden, *Robert Southey,* 138–45. Originally published in *Eclectic Review* 7 (April 1811): 334–50.

Fox, William J. "A Discourse on Occasion of the Death of Rajah Rammohun Roy. [1833]." In *Memorial Edition of Collected Works of W. J. Fox,* ed. W. B. Hodgson and H. G. Slack, 3:124–42. 12 vols. London, 1865–68.

Franklin, Michael, ed. *The European Discovery of India: Key Indological Sources of Romanticism.* 6 vols. London: Ganesha, 2001.

Gale, Theophilus. *The Court of the Gentiles; or, a Discourse Touching the Original of Human Literature, both Philologic and Philosophic, from the Scriptures and Jewish Churches.* 4 vols. Oxford, 1669–77.

Gardener, D. *The Original Calcutta Annual Directory and Calendar, for Anno Domini 1812.* Calcutta, [1812–13].

———. *The Original Calcutta Annual Directory and Calendar, for Anno Domini 1813.* Calcutta, [1813–14].

Ghosh, Kasiprasad. "Autobiography of Kasiprasad Ghose." In *Hand-Book of Bengal Missions, in Connnexion with The church of England. Together with an Account of General Educational Efforts in North India.* By the Rev. James Long, 506–10. London, 1848.

———. *The Sháïr; and Other Poems.* Calcutta, 1830.

Gibbes, Phebe. *Hartly House, Calcutta.* Ed. Michael J. Franklin. New Delhi: Oxford UP, 2007.

Gibson, Mary Ellis, ed. *Anglophone Poetry in Colonial India, 1780–1913: A Critical Anthology.* Athens: Ohio UP, 2011.

"The Gospel Messenger. Written in Bengalee by Ram Boshoo, and translated by Mr. Marshman. (Reprinted from the 'Biblical Magazine' for 1802)." *General Baptist Repository, and Missionary Observer* 1, no. 7 (July 1854): 329–31.

Grant, Charles. "Observations On the State of Society among the Asiatic Subjects of

Great Britain, particularly with respect to Morals; and on the means of improving it.—Written chiefly in the Year 1792." Parliamentary Papers, 1812–13, vol. 10, paper 282 (15 June 1813).

Grant, James. *The Great Metropolis*. 2nd ed. 2 vols. New York, 1837.

Guthrie, William. *A New Geographical, Historical, and Commercial Grammar*. London, 1770.

Hamilton, Elizabeth. *Translation of the Letters of a Hindoo Rajah*. Ed. Pamela Perkins and Shannon Russell. Peterborough, ON: Broadview, 1999.

Heber, Reginald. *Narrative of a Journey through the Upper Provinces of India, from Calcutta to Bombay, 1824–1825 . . . and Letters Written in India*. 2 vols. London, 1828.

Henderson, Henry Barkley. *The Bengalee: or, Sketches of Society and Manners in the East*. London, 1829.

Herbert, Edward. *The Antient Religion of the Gentiles, and Causes of their Errors Consider'd*. Trans. William Lewis. London, 1705.

Herder, Johann Gottfried. *Vom Geist der ebräischen Poesie*. 2 vols. Dessau, 1782–83.

Higgins, Godfrey. *Anacalypsis, an Attempt to Draw aside the Veil of the Saitic Isis; or, an Inquiry into the Origin of Languages, Nations, and Religions*. 2 vols. London, 1836.

"Hindoo Liberals." *Asiatic Journal*, n.s., 21 (December 1836): 223–24.

Hindu Holidays, the Festivals of "Devil-Worship;" Ought Christians to Observe Them? Calcutta, 1846.

Holland, John, and James Everett, eds. *Memoirs of the Life and Writings of James Montgomery*. 7 vols. London, 1854–56.

Hope, William. William Hope to John Saffery, 7 December 1818. Reeves R20/10. Angus Library, Regent's Park College, Oxford.

Hume, David. *Dialogues Concerning Natural Religion*. Ed. Martin Bell. Harmondsworth, UK: Penguin, 1990.

———. *Essays, Moral and Political*. 2 vols. Edinburgh, 1741–42.

I'll Consider of It! A Tale, in Three Volumes, in which "Thinks I to Myself" is Partially Considered. 3 vols. London, 1812.

Ivimey, Joseph. *A History of the English Baptists*. 4 vols. London, 1811–30.

Jones, William. "A Discourse on the Institution of a Society, for Inquiring into the History, Civil and Natural, the Antiquities, Arts, Sciences, and Literature, of Asia." *Asiatic Researches* (London) 1 (1799): ix–xvi.

———. *The Letters of Sir William Jones*. Ed. Garland Cannon. 2 vols. Oxford: Oxford UP, 1970.

———, trans. *Sacontalá*. In Franklin, *European Discovery of India*, vol. 3.

———. [Six Hymns to Hindu Deities.] In *Asiatick Miscellany*, vol. 2 of Franklin, *European Discovery of India*.

Keirn, Tim, and Norbert Schürer, eds. *British Encounters with India, 1750–1830: A Sourcebook*. New York: Palgrave, 2011.

Kemble, Frances Ann. *Records of a Girlhood*. 3 vols. London, 1878.

Kennedy, James. *Life and Work in Benares and Kumaon, 1839–1877*. London, 1884.

Khan, Abu Talib. *The Travels of Mirza Abu Taleb Khan*. Ed. Daniel O'Quinn. Peterborough, ON: Broadview, 2008.

Kindersley, Jemima. *Letters from the Island of Teneriffe, Brazil, the Cape of Good Hope, and the East Indies*. London, 1777.

Kipling, Rudyard. *Plain Tales from the Hills*. Ed. Andrew Rutherford. Oxford: Oxford UP, 2009.

Lamb, Charles, and Mary Lamb. *The Works of Charles and Mary Lamb*. Ed. E. V. Lucas. 7 vols. London: Methuen, 1903–5.

Landon, Letitia Elizabeth. *Fisher's Drawing Room Scrap Book; with Poetical Illustrations*. London, 1835.

Le Breton, Anna Letitia. *Memories of Seventy Years*. Ed. Mrs. Herbert Martin. London, 1884.

Lessing, Gotthold Ephraim. "[Editorial commentary on the 'Fragments' of Reimarus, 1777]." In *Philosophical and Theological Writings*, ed. H. B. Nisbet, 61–82. Cambridge: Cambridge UP, 2005.

Lewis, C. B. *The Life of John Thomas, Surgeon of the Earl of Oxford East Indiaman, and First Baptist Missionary to Bengal*. London, 1873.

Lowth, Robert. *Lectures on the Sacred Poetry of the Hebrews*. Trans. G. Gregory. 2 vols. London, 1787.

Macaulay, Thomas Babington. *The Letters of Thomas Babington Macaulay*. Ed. Thomas Pinney. 6 vols. Cambridge: Cambridge UP, 1974–81.

———. "Minute on Indian Education." In *Archives of Empire*, ed. Barbara Harlow and Mia Carter, vol. 1, *From the East India Company to the Suez Canal*, 227–38. Durham, NC: Duke UP, 2003.

Madden, Lionel, ed. *Robert Southey: The Critical Heritage*. London: Routledge, 1972.

Maimbourg, Louis. *The History of Arianism*. 2 vols. London, 1728.

Marshman, John Clarke. *The Life and Times of Carey, Marshman, and Ward*. 2 vols. London, 1859.

Martin, Robert Montgomery. "Rajah Rammohun Roy." *Court Journal* 232 (5 October 1833): 678.

Martineau, Harriet. *Autobiography*. Ed. Linda H. Peterson. Peterborough, ON: Broadview, 2007.

———. *Harriet Martineau's Autobiography with Memorials by Maria Weston Chapman*. 3rd ed. 3 vols. London, 1877.

———. "Sabbath Musings. No. II." *Monthly Repository*, n.s., 5 (1831): 235–39.

Maurice, Thomas. *Indian Antiquities: or, Dissertations, relative to the Ancient Geographical Divisions, the Pure System of Primeval Theology, the Grand Code of Civil Laws, the Original Form of Government, and the Various and Profound Literature of Hindostan. Compared, throughout, with the Religion, Laws, Government, and Literature, of Persia, Egypt, and Greece*. 7 vols. London, 1793–1800.

Mayhew, Henry. *London Labour and the London Poor*. 3 vols. London, 1851.

Middleton, Conyers. *A Free Inquiry into the Miraculous Powers, which are Supposed to have Subsisted in the Christian Church, from the Earliest Ages through Several Successive Centuries*. London, 1749.

Mill, James. *The History of British India*. 3 vols. London, 1817.

Milton, John. *Paradise Lost*. Ed. Gordon Teskey. New York: Norton, 2005.

Minutes of Evidence Taken before the Select Committee on the Affairs of The East India Company. I. Public. House of Commons. 16 August 1832.

Mitchell, Robert. *Plans and Views in Perspective, with Descriptions, of Buildings Erected in England and Scotland: and also an Essay, to Elucidate the Grecian, Roman and Gothic Architecture, Accompanied with Designs*. London, 1801.

Mittra, Peary Chand. *A Biographical Sketch of David Hare*. Calcutta, 1877.

———. *Life of Dewan Ramcomul Sen*. Calcutta, 1880.

"Modern Hindoo Sects." *Asiatic Journal*, n.s., 7 (April 1832): 174–75.

Moor, Edward. *The Hindu Pantheon*. London, 1810.

New Monthly Magazine. Unsigned review, "Poems. By H. L. V. Derozio," 24, no. 87 (March 1828): 104–5.

The Orient Pearl, for 1832. Calcutta, 1832.

The Orient Pearl, for 1834. Calcutta, 1833.

The Orient Pearl, for 1835. Calcutta, 1834.

Owenson, Sydney. *The Missionary: An Indian Tale*. Ed. Julia M. Wright. Peterborough, ON: Broadview, 2002.

Parker, Henry Meredith. *Bole Ponjis. Containing The Tale of the Buccaneer, A Bottle of Red Ink, The Decline and Fall of Ghosts; and Other Ingredients*. 2 vols. Calcutta, 1851.

Patterson [Paterson], J. D. "Of the Origin of the Hindu Religion." *Asiatick Researches* 8 (1805): 44–87.

Peacock, Thomas Love. *Peacock's Four Ages of Poetry*. Ed. H. F. B. Brett-Smith. Oxford: Blackwell, 1967.

Peggs, James. *India's Cries to British Humanity, relative to the Suttee, Infanticide, British Connexion with Idolatry, Ghaut Murders, and Slavery in India*. London, 1830.

Periodical Accounts Relative to the Baptist Missionary Society. Vols. 1–3. Clipstone, UK, 1800–1806.

"Petition of the East Indians to the House of Commons." *Oriental Herald* 23, no. 71 (November 1829): 261–71.

Picart, Bernard, engraver. *The Ceremonies and Religious Customs of the Various Nations of the Known World*. By John Frédéric Bernard, Antoine Augustin Bruzen de la Martinière, et al. 6 vols. London, 1733–39. Originally published as *Ceremonies et coutumes religieuses de tous les peuples du monde*, 8 vols. (Amsterdam, 1723–43).

Porter, J. Scott. *The Growth of the Gospel: A Sermon, Occasioned by the Lamented Death of the Rajah Rammohun Roy; Preached on Sunday, Nov. 10th, 1833, in the Meeting-House of the First Presbyterian Congregation, Belfast*. Belfast, 1833.

Potts, E. Daniel, transcriber. *William Ward's Missionary Journal*. BMS IN/17 (B). Angus Library, Regent's Park College, Oxford.

Prideaux, Humphrey. *The True Nature of Imposture Fully Displayed in the Life of Mahomet. With A Discourse annexed, for the Vindicating of Christianity from this Charge; Offered to the Consideration of the Deists of the present Age*. London, 1697.

Rammohun Roy. *Brahmunical Magazine. The Missionary and the Brahmin*. No. 3. Calcutta, 1821.

———. *The English Works of Raja Rammohun Roy. With an English Translation of "Tuhfatul Muwahhidin."* Ed. Jogendra Chunder Ghose and Eshan Chunder Bose. Bahadurganj, Allahabad: The Panini Office, 1906.

———. *The Precepts of Jesus the Guide to Peace and Happiness, Extracted from the Books of the New Testament Ascribed to the Four Evangelists. With Translations into Sungscrit and Bengalee*. Calcutta, 1820.

———. *The Precepts of Jesus the Guide to Peace and Happiness, Extracted from the Books of the New Testament Ascribed to the Four Evangelists. To which are Added, the First, Second, and Final Appeal to the Christian Public, in Reply to the Observations of Dr. Marshman, of Serampore*. London, 1824.

———. *Translation of an Abridgment of the Vedant, or, Resolution of all the Veds; the Most Celebrated and Revered work of Brahminical Theology: likewise a Translation of the Cena Upanishad, One of the Chapters of the Sama Veda; According to the Gloss of the Celebrated Shancaracharya, establishing the Unity and the Sole Omnipotence of the Supreme Being: and that He Alone is the Object of Worship*. London, 1817.

———— [Ram Doss, pseud.]. *A Vindication of the Incarnation of the Deity, as the Common Basis of Hindooism and Christianity, against the Schismatic Attacks of R. Tytler, Esq., M.D. . . . By Ram Doss.* In Rammohun Roy, *English Works*, 889–908.

"Reflections of a Returned Exile." *Asiatic Journal*, n.s., 22 (January 1837): 65–75.

"The Revd. Krishna Mohun Bonerjee." *India Review*, October 1842, 622–31.

"A Review of Public Instruction in the Bengal Presidency, from 1835–51." *Calcutta Review* 34 (June 1852): 340–86.

[Reynolds, John Hamilton]. *The Fancy: A Selection from the Poetical Remains of the Late Peter Corcoran, of Gray's Inn, Student at Law. With a Brief Memoir of his Life.* London, 1820.

Richardson, David Lester. *Literary Chit-Chat: with Miscellaneous Poems and an Appendix of Prose Papers.* London, 1848.

————. "On Going Home. [Written in India, January, 1835.]." In *Literary Leaves or Prose and Verse Chiefly Written in India*, 1:63–67. 2nd ed. 2 vols. London, 1840.

————, ed. *Selections from the British Poets from the Time of Chaucer to the Present Day with Biographical and Critical Notices.* Calcutta, 1840.

————. *Sonnets, and Other Poems.* London, 1825.

Roberdeau, I. H. T. "Calcutta in 1805." *Calcutta in the 19th Century (Company's Days)*. Ed. P. Thankappan Nair. Calcutta: Firma KLM, 1989. 36–85.

Roberts, Emma. *The East India Voyager, or Ten Minutes Advice to the Outward Bound.* London, 1839.

————. *Oriental Scenes, Dramatic Sketches and Tales, with Other Poems.* Calcutta, 1830.

————. *Scenes and Characteristics of Hindostan, with Sketches of Anglo-Indian Society.* 2nd ed. 2 vols. London, 1837.

————. "Sketches of Indian Society. No. II.—Feminine Employments, Amusements, and Domestic Economy." *Asiatic Journal*, n.s., 10 (February 1833): 105–16.

Rowe, Joshua. Joshua Rowe to John Saffery, 13 November 1805. Reeves R7/8. Angus Library, Regent's Park College, Oxford.

————. Joshua Rowe to John Saffery, 25 December 1815. Reeves R7/37. Angus Library, Regent's Park College, Oxford.

Sandeman, Hugh David. *Selections from Calcutta Gazettes [1806–15] . . . Showing the Political and Social Condition of the English in India upwards of Fifty Years Ago.* Vols. 4–5. Calcutta, 1868–69.

Schlegel, Friedrich. *Über die Sprache und Weisheit der Indier.* Heidelberg, 1808.

Scott, Walter. *Chronicles of the Canongate.* Ed. Claire Lamont. London: Penguin, 2003.

Seton-Karr, W. S. *Selections from Calcutta Gazettes [1798–1805] . . . Showing the Political and Social Condition of the English in India upwards of Fifty Years Ago.* Vol. 3. Calcutta, 1868.

Shelley, Percy Bysshe. *The Complete Poetry of Percy Bysshe Shelley.* Ed. Donald H. Reiman, Neil Fraistat, and Nora Crook. Vol. 3. Baltimore: Johns Hopkins UP, 2012.

————. *The Letters of Percy Bysshe Shelley.* Ed. Frederick L. Jones. 2 vols. Oxford: Clarendon, 1964.

"Sketch of the Great Hindoo Philosopher Rajah Ram-Mohun-Roy." *Alexander's East India Magazine* 1 (May 1831): 557–66.

"A Sketch of the Origin, Rise, and Progress of the Hindoo College." *Calcutta Christian Observer* 1 (June–December 1832): 14–17, 68–76, 115–29.

Slade, Adolphus. *Turkey, Greece and Malta.* 2 vols. London, 1837.

Smith, George. *The Life of William Carey, D.D. Shoemaker and Missionary. Professor of Sanskrit, Bengali, and Marathi in the College of Fort William, Calcutta*. London, 1885.

Smith, Sydney. "Indian Missions." *Edinburgh Review* 11 (January 1808): 340–62; 12 (April 1808): 151–81; 14 (April 1809): 40–50.

"Society in India." *New Monthly Magazine* 22 (March 1828): 224–36; (April 1828): 327–40; (May 1828): 464–72.

Solvyns, Balthazar. *A Collection of Two Hundred and Fifty Coloured Etchings*. Calcutta, 1799.

Southey, Robert. *The Life and Correspondence of Robert Southey*. Ed. Charles Cuthbert Southey. 6 vols. London, 1849–50.

———. *New Letters of Robert Southey*. Ed. Kenneth Curry. 2 vols. New York: Columbia UP, 1965.

———. *Robert Southey: Later Poetical Works, 1811–1838*. Gen. ed. Tim Fulford and Lynda Pratt. 4 vols. London: Pickering & Chatto, 2012.

———. *Robert Southey: Poetical Works, 1793–1810*. Gen. ed. Lynda Pratt. 5 vols. London: Pickering & Chatto, 2004.

———. *Selections from the Letters of Robert Southey*. Ed. John Wood Warter. 4 vols. London, 1856.

Stanhope, Leicester. *Sketch of the History and Influence of the Press in British India*. London, 1823.

Starke, Mariana. *The Widow of Malabar. A Tragedy, in Three Acts*. London, 1791.

Steele, Richard. *The Lucubrations of Isaac Bickerstaff Esq*. 4 vols. London, 1710–11.

Sterne, Laurence. *A Sentimental Journey, and Other Writings*. Ed. Ian Jack and Tim Parnell. Oxford: Oxford UP, 2003.

Stillingfleet, E. W. *On the Character of Idolatry: and on the Propagation of Christianity, in the Eastern Colonial Possessions of Britain: Two Sermons, Written in Obedience to the Royal Mandate, of February 10th; and, to the Archiepiscopal Letter, of May 15th, 1819; with Notes*. Hull, 1819.

Stillingfleet, Edward. *A Discourse Concerning the Idolatry Practised in the Church of Rome*. London, 1671.

Stuart, Charles. *Vindication of the Hindoos from the Aspersions of the Reverend Claudius Buchanan, M.A. with a Refutation of the Arguments Exhibited in his Memoir, on the Expediency of an Ecclesiastical Establishment for British India, and the Ultimate Civilization of the Natives, by their Conversion to Christianity. Also, Remarks on an Address from the Missionaries in Bengal to the Natives in India, Condemning their Errors, and Inviting them to Become Christians. The Whole Tending to Evince the Excellence of the Moral System of the Hindoos, and the Danger of Interfering with their Customs or Religion*. London, 1808.

Sutherland, James. "Sketch of Rammohun Roy, the Celebrated Indian Brahmin." *Parliamentary Review*, 26 July 1834, 1057–70.

Taylor, C. *On Wednesday, October 1, 1806, will be published, (to be continued Monthly), Price Half-a-Crown, [Consisting of Seven Sheets of Letter-press, printed in Octavo, on a fine wove extra royal Paper, large Page with double Columns, so as to contain more Matter than any literary Publication extant.] No. I. of The Literary Panorama*. Advertisement. London, 1806.

Thackeray, William Makepeace. *The Newcomes: Memoirs of a Most Respectable Family*. Ed. D. J. Taylor. London: Everyman, 1994.

———. *Vanity Fair*. Ed. John Carey. London: Penguin, 2001.

Toland, John. *Christianity not Mysterious: or, A Treatise Shewing, That there is nothing in the Gospel Contrary to Reason, Nor Above it: And that no Christian Doctrine can be properly call'd a Mystery*. London, 1696.

Townsend, Meredith, ed. *The Annals of Indian Administration*. Vol. 8. Serampore, 1858.

Triebner, Christopher Frederic. *An Answer to the Pamphlet of G. T. Wloeman*. London, 1799.

"A True Story." *Indicator* 1, no. 40 (12 July 1820): 319–20.

Tytler, Robert. *An Inquiry into the Origin, and Principles of Budaic Sabism, or Adoration addressed to the Almighty, Regarded as the Regenerator of the World; Comprising Observations Serving to Identify the Worship of Buddha with that of Siva, and an Exposition of General Doctrines Inculcated in Hindoo Religion, and other Systems of Idolatry*. Calcutta, 1817.

Volney, C. F. *Les ruines, ou Méditation sur les révolutions des empires*. Paris, 1791.

Warburton, William. *The Divine Legation of Moses Demonstrated, on the Principles of a Religious Deist*. 2 vols. London, 1738–41.

Ward, William. Journals. BMS IN/17 (A). Angus Library, Regent's Park College, Oxford.

———. *A View of the History, Literature, and Mythology, of the Hindoos: Including a Minute Description of their Manners and Customs, and Translations from their Principal Works*. 2nd ed. 2 vols. Serampore, 1815–18.

Wilson, Horace Hayman, trans. *The Mégha Dúta: or Cloud Messenger; A Poem, in the Sanscrit Language; by Cálidása*. Vol. 4 of Franklin, *European Discovery of India*.

Wood, William. *A Series of Twenty-Eight Panoramic Plates of Calcutta, Extending from Chandpaul Ghaut to the End of Chowringhee Road, together with the Hospital, the Two Bridges, and the Fort*. London, 1833.

Wordsworth, William. *The Poetical Works of William Wordsworth*. Ed. E. de Selincourt and Helen Darbishire. 5 vols. Oxford: Clarendon, 1940–49.

W. W. "Reminiscences of the Hindu College." *Calcutta Literary Gazette* 9 (29 March 1834): 189–92.

Secondary Sources

Ackerman, Robert. *The Myth and Ritual School: J. G. Frazer and the Cambridge Ritualists*. New York: Routledge, 2001.

Adorno, Theodor W. *Prisms*. Trans. Samuel Weber and Shierry Weber. 1955. Reprint. London: Neville Spearman, 1967.

Agamben, Giorgio. *Stanzas: Word and Phantasm in Western Culture*. Trans. Ronald L. Martinez. Minneapolis: U of Minnesota P, 1993.

Ahmed, A. F. Salahuddin. "Rammohun Roy and His Contemporaries." In Joshi, *Rammohun Roy and the Process of Modernization in India*, 89–102.

———. *Social Ideas and Social Change in Bengal, 1818–1835*. 2nd ed. Calcutta: Riddhi India, 1976.

Ahmed, Siraj. "Orientalism and the Permanent Fix of War." In Carey and Festa, *Postcolonial Enlightenment*, 167–206.

———. "'An Unlimited Intercourse': Historical Contradictions and Imperial Romance in the Early Nineteenth Century." In *The Containment and Re-deployment of English India*, ed. Daniel J. O'Quinn. Romantic Circles Praxis Series, 2000. www.rc.umd.edu/praxis/containment/ahmed/ahmed.html.

Alavi, Seema, ed. *The Eighteenth Century in India*. Oxford: Oxford UP, 2002.

Altick, Richard. *The Shows of London*. Cambridge, MA: Belknap Press of Harvard UP, 1978.

Anderson, Benedict. *Imagined Communities: Reflections on the Origin and Spread of Nationalism.* 2nd ed. London: Verso, 1991.

―――. *The Spectre of Comparisons: Nationalism, Southeast Asia and the World.* London: Verso, 1998.

Anthony, Frank. *Britain's Betrayal in India: The Story of the Anglo-Indian Community.* Bombay: Allied Publishers, 1969.

Appadurai, Arjun. "Disjuncture and Difference in the Global Cultural Economy." In *Modernity at Large: Cultural Dimensions of Globalization,* 27–47. Minneapolis: U of Minnesota P, 1996.

―――. "Introduction: Commodities and the Politics of Value." In *The Social Life of Things: Commodities in Cultural Perspective,* ed. Arjun Appadurai, 3–63. Cambridge: Cambridge UP, 1986.

Aravamudan, Srinivas. *Enlightenment Orientalism: Resisting the Rise of the Novel.* Chicago: Chicago UP, 2012.

―――. *Guru English: South Asian Religion in a Cosmopolitan Language.* Princeton, NJ: Princeton UP, 2006.

―――. *Tropicopolitans: Colonialism and Agency, 1688–1804.* Durham, NC: Duke UP, 1999.

Asad, Talal. *Formations of the Secular: Christianity, Islam, Modernity.* Stanford: Stanford UP, 2003.

Asad, Talal, and John Dixon. "Translating Europe's Others." In Barker et al., *Europe and Its Others,* 1:170–77.

Bagal, Jogesh C. "The Hindu College." *Modern Review,* July 1955, 55–60; September 1955, 229–34; December 1955, 461–67.

Baillie, Alexander Francis. *The Oriental Club and Hanover Square.* London: Longmans, 1901.

Bal, Mieke. *Double Exposures: The Subject of Cultural Analysis.* London: Routledge, 1996.

Ballantyne, Tony. *Between Colonialism and Diaspora: Sikh Cultural Formations in an Imperial World.* Durham, NC: Duke UP, 2006.

―――. "Empire, Knowledge and Culture: From Proto-Globalization to Modern Globalization." In *Globalization in World History,* ed. A. G. Hopkins, 115–40. London: Pimlico, 2002.

―――. *Orientalism and Race: Aryanism in the British Empire.* Basingstoke, UK: Palgrave, 2002.

Banerjee, Sumanta. *The Parlour and the Streets: Elite and Popular Culture in Nineteenth Century Calcutta.* Calcutta: Seagull Books, 1989.

Bann, Stephen. *The Clothing of Clio.* Cambridge: Cambridge UP, 1984.

Barker, Francis, Peter Hulme, Margaret Iversen, and Diana Loxley, eds. *Europe and Its Others.* 2 vols. Colchester: U of Essex, 1985.

Barns, Margarita. *The Indian Press: A History of the Growth of Public Opinion in India.* London: Allen & Unwin, 1940.

Basham, A. L. "Sophia and the Brahmin." In *East India Company Studies: Papers Presented to Professor Sir Cyril Philips,* ed. Kenneth Ballhatchet and John Harrison, 13–30. Hong Kong: Asian Research Service, 1986.

Bayly, C. A. *The Birth of the Modern World, 1780–1914.* Malden, MA: Blackwell, 2004.

―――. *Empire and Information: Intelligence Gathering and Social Communication in India, 1780–1870.* Cambridge: Cambridge UP, 1996.

————. *Imperial Meridian: The British Empire and the World, 1780–1830.* London: Longman, 1989.

————. "Rammohan Roy and the Advent of Constitutional Liberalism in India, 1800–30." *Modern Intellectual History* 4, no. 1 (2007): 25–41.

————. *Recovering Liberties: Indian Thought in the Age of Liberalism and Empire.* Cambridge: Cambridge UP, 2012.

Beckingham, C. F. "A History of the Royal Asiatic Society, 1823–1973." In *The Royal Asiatic Society: Its History and Treasures,* ed. Stuart Simmonds and Simon Digby, 1–77. Leiden: E. J. Brill, 1979.

Benjamin, Walter. *The Arcades Project.* Ed. Rolf Tiedemann. Trans. Howard Eiland and Kevin McLaughlin. Cambridge, MA: Harvard UP, 1999.

————. *Illuminations.* Ed. Hannah Arendt. Trans. Harry Zohn. New York: Schocken, 1968.

Bennett, Tony. *The Birth of the Museum: History, Theory, Politics.* London: Routledge, 1995.

Bernhardt-Kabisch, Ernest. *Robert Southey.* Boston: Twayne, 1977.

Bewell, Alan. "A 'true story . . . of evils overcome': Sacred Biography, Prophecy, and Colonial Disease in Southey's *Tale of Paraguay.*" *Nineteenth Century Contexts* 26, no. 2 (June 2004): 97–124.

Bhabha, Homi. *The Location of Culture.* London: Routledge, 1994.

Bhadra, Gautam. "The Performer and the Listener: Kathakata in Modern Bengal." *Studies in History* 10, no. 2 (1994): 243–54.

Bloom, Harold. "The Internalization of Quest-Romance." In *Romanticism and Consciousness: Essays in Criticism,* ed. Harold Bloom, 3–23. New York: Norton, 1970.

Bolton, Carol. *Writing the Empire: Robert Southey and Romantic Colonialism.* London: Pickering & Chatto, 2007.

Bosworth, F. *The Baptist College, Bristol: Its History, Students, and Treasures: A Paper, read at the Autumnal Session of the Baptist Union, Held at Bristol, October 15, 1868.* Bristol, 1868.

Bourdieu, Pierre. *Distinction: A Social Critique of the Judgment of Taste.* Trans. Richard Nice. Cambridge, MA: Harvard UP, 1984.

Brown, Bill, ed. *Things.* Chicago: U of Chicago P, 2004.

————. "Thing Theory." *Critical Inquiry* 28, no. 1 (Autumn 2001): 1–22.

Buettner, Elizabeth. *Empire Families: Britons and Late Imperial India.* Oxford: Oxford UP, 2004.

Burton, Antoinette M., ed. *After the Imperial Turn: Thinking with and through the Nation.* Durham, NC: Duke UP, 2003.

————. *At the Heart of the Empire: Indians and the Colonial Encounter in Late-Victorian Britain.* Berkeley: U of California P, 1998.

Butler, Judith. *Bodies That Matter.* New York: Routledge, 1993.

Butler, Marilyn. "Byron and the Empire in the East." In *Byron: Augustan and Romantic,* ed. Andrew Rutherford, 63–81. Basingstoke, UK: Macmillan, 1990.

Carey, Daniel. "Reading Contrapuntally: *Robinson Crusoe,* Slavery, and Postcolonial Theory." In Carey and Festa, *Postcolonial Enlightenment,* 105–36.

Carey, Daniel, and Lynn Festa, eds. *The Postcolonial Enlightenment: Eighteenth-Century Colonialism and Postcolonial Theory.* Oxford: Oxford UP, 2009.

Carnall, Geoffrey. *Robert Southey and His Age: The Development of a Conservative Mind.* Oxford: Clarendon, 1960.

Carpenter, Mary, ed. *The Last Days in England of the Rajah Rammohun Roy.* London, 1866.

Carson, Penelope. *The East India Company and Religion, 1698–1858*. Woodbridge, UK: Boydell, 2012.

Carton, Adrian. *Mixed-Race and Modernity in Colonial India: Changing Concepts of Hybridity across Empires*. New York: Routledge, 2012.

Chakrabarty, Dipesh. *Provincializing Europe: Postcolonial Thought and Historical Difference*. Princeton, NJ: Princeton UP, 2000.

Champion, L. G. *Farthing Rushlight: The Story of Andrew Gifford, 1700–1784*. London: Carey Kingsgate, 1961.

Chanda, Mrinal Kanti. *History of the English Press in Bengal, 1780 to 1857*. Calcutta: K. P. Bagchi, 1987.

Charlesworth, Michael. "Subverting the Command of Place: Panorama and the Romantics." In *Placing and Displacing Romanticism*, ed. Peter J. Kitson, 129–45. Aldershot, UK: Ashgate, 2001.

Chatterjee, Asim Kumar. *The Cult of Skanda-Kārttikeya in Ancient India*. Calcutta: Punthi Pustak, 1970.

Chatterjee, Partha. "Anderson's Utopia." *Diacritics* 29, no. 4 (Winter 1999): 128–34.

———. *The Black Hole of Empire: History of a Global Practice of Power*. Princeton, NJ: Princeton UP, 2012.

———. *Nationalist Thought and the Colonial World: A Derivative Discourse?* London: Zed, 1986.

———. *The Nation and Its Fragments: Colonial and Postcolonial Histories*. Princeton, NJ: Princeton UP, 1993.

Chatterjee, Sunil K. *Ram Ram Basu: Munsi of Rev. William Carey*. Serampore: Serampore College, 2006.

———. *William Carey and Serampore*. 2nd ed. Serampore: printed by author, 2004.

Chattopadhyay, Goutam, ed. *Awakening in Bengal in Early Nineteenth Century (Selected Documents)*. Vol. 1. Calcutta: Progressive, 1965.

———, ed. *Bengal: Early Nineteenth Century (Selected Documents)*. Calcutta: Research India, 1978.

Chattopadhyay, Swati. *Representing Calcutta: Modernity, Nationalism, and the Colonial Uncanny*. Abingdon, UK: Routledge, 2005.

Chaudhuri, Rosinka. "The Dutt Family Album: And Toru Dutt." In Mehrotra, *History of Indian Literature in English*, 53–69.

———. *Freedom and Beef Steaks: Colonial Calcutta Culture*. Hyderabad: Orient Blackswan, 2012.

———. *Gentlemen Poets in Colonial Bengal: Emergent Nationalism and the Orientalist Project*. Calcutta: Seagull Books, 2002.

———. "An Ideology of Indianness: The Construction of Colonial/Communal Stereotypes in the Poems of Henry Derozio." *Studies in History* 20, no. 2 (2004): 168–87.

———. Introduction to *Derozio, Poet of India: The Definitive Edition*, ed. Chaudhuri, xxi–lxxxi. New Delhi: Oxford UP, 2008.

———. "The Politics of Naming: Derozio in Two Formative Moments of Literary and Political Discourse, Calcutta, 1825–31." *Modern Asian Studies* 44, no. 4 (2010): 857–85.

———. " 'Young India: A Bengal Eclogue': Or Meat-Eating, Race, and Reform in a Colonial Poem." *Interventions* 2, no. 3 (2000): 424–41.

Chaudhuri, S. B. "Early English Printers and Publishers in Calcutta." *Bengal: Past and Present* 87 (January–June 1968): 67–77.

Chhabra, G. S. *Advanced Study in the History of Modern India, Volume 1 (1707–1813)*. New Delhi: Sterling, 1971.

Cohn, Bernard. *Colonialism and Its Forms of Knowledge: The British in India*. Princeton, NJ: Princeton UP, 1996.

———. "Representing Authority in Victorian India." In Hobsbawm and Ranger, *Invention of Tradition*, 165–209.

Colebrooke, T. E. *Life of the Honourable Mountstuart Elphinstone*. 2 vols. London, 1884.

Collet, Sophia Dobson. *The Life and Letters of Raja Rammohun Roy*. Ed. Dilip Kumar Biswas and Prabhat Chandra Ganguli. 3rd ed. Calcutta: Sadharan Brahmo Samaj, 1962.

Colley, Linda. *Britons: Forging the Nation, 1707–1837*. London: Pimlico, 1992.

———. *Captives: Britain, Empire, and the World, 1600–1850*. New York: Anchor Books, 2002.

Collingham, Lizzie. *Curry: A Tale of Cooks and Conquerors*. Oxford: Oxford UP, 2006.

Comment, Bernard. *The Panorama*. London: Reaktion Books, 1999.

Coomer, Anita. "H. H. Wilson and the Hindu College (1823–1832)." *Calcutta Historical Journal* 6, no. 1 (1981): 30–59.

Craig, David M. *Robert Southey and Romantic Apostasy: Political Argument in Britain, 1780–1840*. Woodbridge, UK: Boydell, 2007.

Cutmore, Jonathan, ed. *Conservatism and the Quarterly Review: A Critical Analysis*. London: Pickering & Chatto, 2007.

———. "A Plurality of Voices in the *Quarterly Review*." In Cutmore, *Conservatism and the Quarterly Review*, 61–85.

Cutts, Elmer H. "The Background of Macaulay's Minute." *American Historical Review* 58, no. 4 (July 1953): 824–53.

Dalrymple, William. *White Mughals: Love and Betrayal in Eighteenth-Century India*. London: Flamingo, 2003.

Darnton, Robert. "What Is the History of Books?" In *The Book History Reader*, ed. David Finkelstein and Alistair McCleery, 9–26. London: Routledge, 2002.

Das, Harihar. "The Early Indian Visitors to England." *Calcutta Review* 13 (October 1924): 83–114.

Dasgupta, Subrata. *The Bengal Renaissance: Identity and Creativity from Rammohun Roy to Rabindranath Tagore*. New Delhi: Permanent Black, 2007.

Davis, Richard H. *Lives of Indian Images*. Princeton, NJ: Princeton UP, 1997.

De Almeida, Hermione, and George H. Gilpin. *Indian Renaissance: British Romantic Art and the Prospect of India*. Aldershot, UK: Ashgate, 2005.

Debord, Guy. *Society of the Spectacle*. Trans. Ken Knabb. London: Rebel, 2004.

de Certeau, Michel. *The Practice of Everyday Life*. Trans. Steven Rendall. Berkeley: U of California P, 1984.

Derrida, Jacques. "Signature Event Context." In *Limited Inc*, ed. Gerald Graff, trans. Samuel Weber, 1–23. Evanston, IL: Northwestern UP, 1988.

Desmond, Ray. *The India Museum, 1801–1879*. London: India Office Library and Records, 1982.

Dirks, Nicholas B. *The Scandal of Empire: India and the Creation of Imperial Britain*. Cambridge, MA: Harvard UP, 2006.

Dover, Cedric. *Half-Caste*. London: Martin Secker & Warburg, 1937.

Droogers, André. "Syncretism: The Problem of Definition, the Definition of the Problem." In *Dialogue and Syncretism: An Interdisciplinary Approach*, ed. Jerald Gort, Hendrik Vroom, Rein Fernhout, and Anton Wessels, 7–25. Amsterdam: Rodopi, 1989.

Dubbini, Renzo. *Geography of the Gaze: Urban and Rural Vision in Early Modern Europe.* Trans. Lydia G. Cochrane. Chicago: U of Chicago P, 2002.

Dyrness, William A. *Reformed Theology and Visual Culture: The Protestant Imagination from Calvin to Edwards.* Cambridge: Cambridge UP, 2004.

Eaton, Natasha. "Between Mimesis and Alterity: Art, Gift, and Diplomacy in Colonial India, 1770–1800." *Comparative Studies in Society and History* 46, no. 4 (October 2004): 816–44.

Eck, Diana L. *Darśan: Seeing the Divine Image in India.* 3rd ed. New York: Columbia UP, 1998.

Edwards, Thomas. *Henry Derozio, The Eurasian Poet, Teacher, and Journalist.* Calcutta: W. Newman, 1884.

———. "The Press of Calcutta." *Calcutta Review* 77, no. 153 (1883): 58–71.

Ellis, Markman. "'Spectacles within doors': Panoramas of London in the 1790s." *Romanticism* 14, no. 2 (2008): 133–48.

Fabian, Johannes. *Time and the Other: How Anthropology Makes Its Object.* New York: Columbia UP, 1983.

Fallon, Pierre. "Christianity in Bengal." In *Studies in the Bengal Renaissance: In Commemoration of the Birth Centenary of Bipinchandra Pal,* ed. Atulchandra Gupta, 448–59. Calcutta: National Council of Education, 1958.

Faxon, Frederick. *Literary Annuals and Gift Books: A Bibliography, 1823–1903.* Boston: Boston Book Co., 1912.

Festa, Lynn. *Sentimental Figures of Empire in Eighteenth-Century Britain and France.* Baltimore: Johns Hopkins UP, 2006.

Finn, Margot C. "Colonial Gifts: Family Politics and the Exchange of Goods in British India, c. 1780–1820." *Modern Asian Studies* 40, no. 1 (2006): 203–31.

Fisch, Jörg. "A Pamphlet War on Christian Missions in India, 1807–1809." *Journal of Asian History* 19 (1985): 22–70.

Fhlathúin, Máire ní. "India and Women's Poetry of the 1830s: Femininity and the Picturesque in the Poetry of Emma Roberts and Letitia Elizabeth Landon." *Women's Writing* 12, no. 2 (2005): 187–204.

Fisher, Michael. *Counterflows to Colonialism: Indian Travellers and Settlers in Britain, 1600–1857.* New Delhi: Permanent Black, 2004.

———. *The First Indian Author in English: Dean Mahomed (1759–1851) in India, Ireland, and England.* New Delhi: Oxford UP, 1996.

———, ed. *The Travels of Dean Mahomet: An Eighteenth-Century Journey through India.* Berkeley: U of California P, 1997.

Flood, Gavin. *An Introduction to Hinduism.* Cambridge: Cambridge UP, 1996.

Forrest, Denys. *The Oriental: Life Story of a West End Club.* London: B. T. Batsford, 1968.

Foster, William. "British Artists in India." In *The Nineteenth Volume of the Walpole Society, 1930–31,* 1–88. Oxford: Walpole Society, 1931.

Franklin, Michael J. "Cultural Possession, Imperial Control, and Comparative Religion: The Calcutta Perspectives of Sir William Jones and Nathaniel Brassey Halhed." *Yearbook of English Studies* 32 (2002): 1–18.

———. "'Drafts upon Heaven': Robert Southey, *Tapas,* and the 'monstrous fables' of Hinduism and Romanism." *European Romantic Review* 22, no. 2 (April 2011): 257–76.

———. "General Introduction and [Meta]historical Background [Re]presenting 'The palanquins of state; or, broken leaves in a Mughal garden.'" In Franklin, *Romantic Representations of British India,* 1–44.

————. *Orientalist Jones: Sir William Jones, Poet, Lawyer, and Linguist, 1746–1794*. Oxford: Oxford UP, 2011.

————. "'Passion's Empire': Sydney Owenson's 'Indian Venture,' Phoenicianism, Orientalism, and Binarism." *Studies in Romanticism* 45, no. 2 (Summer 2006): 181–97.

————. "Radically Feminizing India: Phebe Gibbes's *Hartly House, Calcutta* (1789) and Sydney Owenson's *The Missionary: An Indian Tale* (1811)." In Franklin, *Romantic Representations of British India*, 154–79.

————, ed. *Romantic Representations of British India*. London: Routledge, 2006.

Freedgood, Elaine. *The Ideas in Things: Fugitive Meaning in the Victorian Novel*. Chicago: U of Chicago P, 2006.

Freitag, Sandria B. Introduction to "Aspects of the 'Public' in Colonial South Asia." Special issue, *South Asia* 14, no. 1 (1991): 1–13.

Friswell, N. C. "The Indian Princess: Helena Bennett." *Asian Affairs* 31, no. 3 (November 2000): 295–302.

Fulford, Tim. "Blessed Bane: Christianity and Colonial Disease in Southey's *Tale of Paraguay*." *Romanticism On the Net* 24 (November 2001). www.erudit.org/revue/ron2001/v/n24/005998ar.html.

————. "Heroic Voyagers and Superstitious Natives: Southey's Imperialist Ideology." *Studies in Travel Writing* 2 (Spring 1998): 46–64.

————. "Pagodas and Pregnant Throes: Orientalism, Millenarianism and Robert Southey." In *Romanticism and Millenarianism*, ed. Tim Fulford, 121–37. New York: Palgrave, 2002.

————. "Plants, Pagodas and Penises: Southey's Oriental Imports." In Pratt, *Robert Southey and the Contexts of English Romanticism*, 187–201.

Fuller, C. J. *The Camphor Flame: Popular Hinduism and Society in India*. Rev. ed. Princeton, NJ: Princeton UP, 1992.

Fuller, Jean Overton. *Shelley: A Biography*. London: Jonathan Cape, 1968.

Galperin, William H. *The Return of the Visible in British Romanticism*. Baltimore: Johns Hopkins UP, 1993.

Gaonkar, Dilip Parameshwar, ed. *Alternative Modernities*. Durham, NC: Duke UP, 2001.

————. "On Alternative Modernities." In Gaonkar, *Alternative Modernities*, 1–23.

Garcia, Humberto. "In the Name of the 'Incestuous Mother': Islam and Excremental Protestantism in De Quincey's Infidel Book." *Journal for Early Modern Cultural Studies* 7, no. 2 (Fall–Winter 2007): 57–87.

Gaskell, Ivan. Review of *On the Museum's Ruins*, by Douglas Crimp, with photographs by Louise Lawler; *The Cultures of Collecting*, edited by John Elsner and Roger Cardinal; and *Museum Culture*, edited by Daniel J. Sherman and Irit Rogoff, *Art Bulletin* 77, no. 4 (December 1995): 673–75.

Gaudio, Michael. *Engraving the Savage: The New World and Techniques of Civilization*. Minneapolis: U of Minnesota P, 2008.

Ghosh, Anindita. "Between Text and Reader: The Experience of Christian Missionaries in Bengal, 1800–50." In *Free Print and Non-Commercial Publishing since 1700*, ed. James Raven, 162–76. Aldershot, UK: Ashgate, 2000.

————. *Power in Print: Popular Publishing and the Politics of Language and Culture in a Colonial Society, 1778–1905*. New Delhi: Oxford UP, 2006.

————. "An Uncertain 'Coming of the Book': Early Print Cultures in Colonial India." *Book History* 6 (2003): 23–55.

Ghosh, Durba. "Another Set of Imperial Turns?" *American Historical Review* 117, no. 3 (June 2012): 772–93.

———. *Sex and the Family in Colonial India: The Making of Empire*. Cambridge: Cambridge UP, 2006.

Gibson, Mary Ellis. *Indian Angles: English Verse in Colonial India from Jones to Tagore*. Athens: Ohio UP, 2011.

Gidal, Eric. *Poetic Exhibitions: Romantic Aesthetics and the Pleasures of the British Museum*. Lewisburg, PA: Bucknell UP, 2001.

Gikandi, Simon. *Maps of Englishness: Writing Identity in the Culture of Colonialism*. New York: Columbia UP, 1996.

Grundy, Isobel. " 'The Barbarous Character We Give Them': White Women Travellers Report on Other Races." *Studies in Eighteenth-Century Culture* 22 (1992): 73–86.

Gupta, Abhijit, and Swapan Chakravorty, eds. *New Word Order: Transnational Themes in Book History*. New Delhi: Worldview, 2011.

———. *Print Areas: Book History in India*. New Delhi: Permanent Black, 2004.

Habermas, Jürgen. *The Structural Transformation of the Public Sphere: An Inquiry into a Category of Bourgeois Society*. Trans. Thomas Burger. Cambridge: MIT Press, 1989.

Halbertal, Moshe, and Avishai Margalit. *Idolatry*. Trans. Naomi Goldblum. Cambridge, MA: Harvard UP, 1992.

Hall, Catherine. *Civilising Subjects: Metropole and Colony in the English Imagination, 1830–1867*. Cambridge: Polity, 2002.

Hall, Catherine, and Sonya Rose. "Introduction: Being at Home with the Empire." In *At Home with the Empire: Metropolitan Culture and the Imperial World*, ed. Catherine Hall and Sonya Rose, 1–31. Cambridge: Cambridge UP, 2006.

Hall, David. *Worlds of Wonder, Days of Judgment: Popular Religious Belief in Early New England*. Cambridge, MA: Harvard UP, 1989.

Hawes, Christopher J. *Poor Relations: The Making of a Eurasian Community in British India, 1773–1833*. Richmond, UK: Curzon, 1996.

Hay, Stephen, ed. *Sources of Indian Tradition: Modern India and Pakistan*. 2nd ed. Vol. 2. New York: Columbia UP, 1988.

Head, Raymond. *The Indian Style*. London: George Allen & Unwin, 1986.

Heidegger, Martin. *What Is a Thing?* Trans. W. B. Barton Jr. and Vera Deutsch. Chicago: Henry Regnery, 1967.

Hobsbawm, Eric, and Terence Ranger, eds. *The Invention of Tradition*. Cambridge: Cambridge UP, 1983.

Howe, Stephen, ed. *The New Imperial Histories Reader*. London: Routledge, 2010.

Howsam, Leslie. *Cheap Bibles: Nineteenth-Century Publishing and the British and Foreign Bible Society*. Cambridge: Cambridge UP, 1991.

Hungerford, Edward B. *Shores of Darkness*. New York: Columbia UP, 1941.

Hunt, Lynn. "The Experience of Revolution." *French Historical Studies* 32, no. 4 (Fall 2009): 671–78.

Hyde, Ralph. *Panoramania! The Art and Entertainment of the "All-Embracing" View*. London: Trefoil, 1988.

Inden, Ronald. *Imagining India*. Cambridge, MA: Blackwell, 1990.

Innes, Fergus. *Oriental Club. Library*. London: Oriental Club, 1978.

Jackson, Eleanor. "From Krishna Pal to Lal Behari Dey: Indian Builders of the Church in England, 1800–1894." In *Converting Colonialism: Visions and Realities in Mission His-*

tory, 1706–1914, ed. Dana L. Robert, 166–205. Grand Rapids, MI: William B. Eerdmans, 2008.

Jameson, Frederic. "The End of Temporality." *Critical Inquiry* 29, no. 4 (Summer 2003): 695–718.

JanMohamed, Abdul R. "Worldliness-Without-World, Homelessness-as-Home: Toward a Definition of the Specular Border Intellectual." In *Edward Said*, ed. Patrick Williams, 1:218–41. 4 vols. London: Sage, 2001.

Janowitz, Anne. *England's Ruins: Poetic Purpose and the National Landscape*. Cambridge, MA: Blackwell, 1990.

Jasanoff, Maya. *Edge of Empire: Lives, Culture, and Conquest in the East, 1750–1850*. New York: Vintage, 2005.

Johnson, Rebecca Carol, Richard Maxwell, and Katie Trumpener. "*The Arabian Nights*, Arab-European Literary Influence, and the Lineages of the Novel." *Modern Language Quarterly* 68, no. 2 (June 2007): 243–79.

Jones, J. Jennifer. "Absorbing Hesitation: Wordsworth and the Theory of the Panorama." *Studies in Romanticism* 45, no. 3 (Fall 2006): 357–75.

Joseph, Betty. *Reading the East India Company, 1720–1840: Colonial Currencies of Gender*. Chicago: U of Chicago P, 2004.

Joshi, V. C., ed. *Rammohun Roy and the Process of Modernization in India*. New Delhi: Vikas, 1975.

Kesavan, B. S. *History of Printing and Publishing in India: A Story of Cultural Re-awakening*. Vol. 1, *South Indian Origins of Printing and Its Efflorescence in Bengal*. New Delhi: National Book Trust, 1985.

Khan, M. Siddiq. "William Carey and the Serampore Books (1800–1834)." *Libri* 11, no. 3 (1961): 197–280.

Killingley, Dermot, trans. *The Only True God: Works on Religion by Rammohun Roy*. Newcastle upon Tyne: Grevatt & Grevatt, 1982.

———. *Rammohun Roy in Hindu and Christian Tradition*. Newcastle upon Tyne: Grevatt & Grevatt, 1993.

———. "Rammohun Roy's Controversies with Hindu Opponents." In *Perspectives on Indian Religion: Papers in Honour of Karel Werner*, ed. Peter Connolly, 144–59. New Delhi: Sri Satguru, 1986.

Klancher, Jon P. *The Making of English Reading Audiences, 1790–1832*. Madison: U of Wisconsin P, 1987.

Koditschek, Theodore. *Liberalism, Imperialism, and the Historical Imagination: Nineteenth-Century Visions of a Greater Britain*. Cambridge: Cambridge UP, 2011.

Kolsky, Elizabeth. "Codification and the Rule of Colonial Difference: Criminal Procedure in British India." *Law and History Review* 23, no. 3 (Fall 2005): 631–83.

Kopf, David. *The Brahmo Samaj and the Shaping of the Modern Indian Mind*. Princeton, NJ: Princeton UP, 1979.

———. *British Orientalism and the Bengal Renaissance: The Dynamics of Indian Modernization, 1773–1835*. Berkeley: U of California P, 1969.

Krishnan, Sanjay. *Reading the Global: Troubling Perspectives on Britain's Empire in Asia*. New York: Columbia UP, 2007.

Krishnaswamy, Revathi. "Postcolonial and Globalization Studies: Connections, Conflicts, Complicities." In *The Postcolonial and the Global*, ed. Revathi Krishnaswamy and John C. Hawley, 2–21. Minneapolis: U of Minnesota P, 2007.

Kuhn, Albert J. "English Deism and the Development of Romantic Mythological Syncretism." *PMLA* 71, no. 5 (December 1956): 1094–1116.

Laurie, W. F. B. *Sketches of Some Distinguished Anglo-Indians. With an Account of Anglo-Indian Periodical Literature.* London, 1875.

Leask, Nigel. *British Romantic Writers and the East: Anxieties of Empire.* Cambridge: Cambridge UP, 1992.

———. *Curiosity and the Aesthetics of Travel Writing, 1770–1840: "From an Antique Land."* Oxford: Oxford UP, 2002.

———. " 'Wandering through Eblis': Absorption and Containment in Romantic Exoticism." In *Romanticism and Colonialism: Writing and Empire, 1780–1830,* ed. Tim Fulford and Peter Kitson, 165–88. Cambridge: Cambridge UP, 1998.

Lillywhite, Bryant. *London Coffee Houses: A Reference Book of Coffee Houses of the Seventeenth, Eighteenth and Nineteenth Centuries.* London: G. Allen & Unwin, 1963.

Little, Bryan. "Calcutta in the Cotswolds." *Transactions of the Bristol and Gloucestershire Archaeological Society* 98 (1980): 5–10.

Llewellyn-Jones, Rosie. *Engaging Scoundrels: True Tales of Old Lucknow.* New Delhi: Oxford UP, 2000.

Logan, Deborah H. *Harriet Martineau, Victorian Imperialism, and the Civilizing Mission.* Farnham, UK: Ashgate, 2010.

Lorenzen, David N. "Who Invented Hinduism?" *Comparative Studies in Society and History* 41, no. 4 (October 1999): 630–59.

Losty, Jeremiah P. *Calcutta, City of Palaces: A Survey of the City in the Days of the East India Company, 1690–1858.* London: British Library, 1990.

Macdonald, D. L., and Anne McWhir, eds. *The Broadview Anthology of Literature of the Revolutionary Period, 1770–1832.* Peterborough, ON: Broadview, 2010.

Mackenzie, John. *Propaganda and Empire: The Manipulation of British Public Opinion, 1880–1960.* Manchester: Manchester UP, 1984.

Madge, E. W. *Henry Derozio, the Eurasian Poet and Reformer.* Calcutta: Herald, 1905.

Majeed, Javed. " 'The Jargon of Indostan': An Exploration of Jargon in Urdu and East India Company English." In *Languages and Jargons: Contributions to a Social History of Language,* ed. Peter Burke and Roy Porter, 182–205. Cambridge, MA: Polity, 1995.

———. *Ungoverned Imaginings: James Mill's "The History of British India" and Orientalism.* Oxford: Oxford UP, 1992.

Majumdar, Surendrachandra, and Gokulnath Dhar, eds. *Presidency College Register.* Calcutta: Bengal Secretariat Book Depot, 1927.

Makdisi, Saree. *Making England Western: Occidentalism, Race, and Imperial Culture.* Chicago: U of Chicago P, forthcoming.

———. *Romantic Imperialism: Universal Empire and the Culture of Modernity.* Cambridge: Cambridge UP, 1998.

Mangamma, J. *Book Printing in India.* Nellore: Bangorey Books, 1975.

Mani, Lata. *Contentious Traditions: The Debate on Sati in Colonial India.* Berkeley: U of California P, 1998.

Manuel, Frank E. *The Eighteenth Century Confronts the Gods.* Cambridge, MA: Harvard UP, 1959.

Marriott, John, and Bhaskar Mukhopadhyay, eds. *Britain in India, 1765–1905.* Vol. 1, *Justice, Police, Law and Order.* London: Pickering & Chatto, 2006.

Marshall, P. J. *Bengal: The British Bridgehead; Eastern India, 1740–1828.* Cambridge: Cambridge UP, 1987.

———. "The British in Asia: Trade to Dominion, 1700–1765." In *The Oxford History of the British Empire*, vol. 2, *The Eighteenth Century*, ed. P. J. Marshall, 487–507. Oxford: Oxford UP, 1998.

———. "British-Indian Connections c. 1780 to c. 1830: The Empire of the Officials." In Franklin, *Romantic Representations of British India*, 45–64.

———. *The Impeachment of Warren Hastings.* Oxford: Oxford UP, 1965.

Marx, Karl. *Capital.* Trans. Ben Fowkes. Vol. 1. London: Lawrence & Wishart, 1977.

McDermott, Rachel Fell. *Revelry, Rivalry, and Longing for the Goddesses of Bengal: The Fortunes of Hindu Festivals.* New York: Columbia UP, 2011.

Mee, Jon. *Conversable Worlds: Literature, Contention, and Community, 1762–1830.* Oxford: Oxford UP, 2011.

———. *Romanticism, Enthusiasm, and Regulation: Poetics and the Policing of Culture in the Romantic Period.* Oxford: Oxford UP, 2003.

Mehrotra, Arvind Krishna, ed. *A History of Indian Literature in English.* London: Hurst, 2003.

Mehta, Uday Singh. *Liberalism and Empire: A Study in Nineteenth-Century British Liberal Thought.* Chicago: U of Chicago P, 1999.

Michaels, Axel. *Hinduism: Past and Present.* Trans. Barbara Harshaw. New Delhi: Orient Longman, 2004.

Mitchell, W. J. T. *What Do Pictures Want? The Lives and Loves of Images.* Chicago: U of Chicago P, 2005.

Moon, Norman S. *Education for Ministry: Bristol Baptist College, 1679–1979.* Bristol: Bristol Baptist College, 1979.

Mukherji, Sajni Kripalani. "The Hindu College: Henry Derozio and Michael Madhusudan Dutt." In Mehrotra, *History of Indian Literature in English*, 41–52.

Mukhopadhyay, Sakti Sadhan, ed. *Derozio: His Background and Cultural Milieu.* Kolkata: Kidderpore College, 2008.

Nechtman, Tillman W. *Nabobs: Empire and Identity in Eighteenth-Century Britain.* Cambridge: Cambridge UP, 2010.

New Statesman. Unsigned capsule review of *Poems by Henry L. V. Derozio*, ed. Bradley-Birt, 24, no. 599 (1924): 26.

Nicholson, Andrew J. *Unifying Hinduism: Philosophy and Identity in Indian Intellectual History.* New York: Columbia UP, 2010.

Niranjana, Tejaswini. *Siting Translation: History, Post-structuralism, and the Colonial Context.* Berkeley: U of California P, 1992.

Nussbaum, Felicity A. *Torrid Zones: Maternity, Sexuality, and Empire in Eighteenth-Century English Narratives.* Baltimore: Johns Hopkins UP, 1995.

Nussbaum, Martha C. "Patriotism and Cosmopolitanism." In *For Love of Country?*, ed. Martha C. Nussbaum, 3–17. Boston: Beacon, 2002.

Oaten, Edward Farley. *A Sketch of Anglo-Indian Literature.* London: Kegan Paul, 1908.

Oettermann, Stephan. *The Panorama: History of a Mass Medium.* New York: Zone Books, 1997.

Ogborn, Miles. *Indian Ink: Script and Print in the Making of the East India Company.* Chicago: U of Chicago P, 2007.

Oleksijczuk, Denise Blake. *The First Panoramas: Visions of British Imperialism.* Minneapolis: U of Minneapolis P, 2011.

O'Quinn, Daniel J. *Staging Governance: Theatrical Imperialism in London, 1770–1800.* Baltimore: Johns Hopkins UP, 2005.

Otto, Peter. "Between the Virtual and the Actual: Robert Barker's Panorama of London and the Multiplication of the Real in Late Eighteenth-Century London." *Romanticism on the Net* 46 (2007). www.erudit.org/revue/ron/2007/v/n46/016130ar.html.

Pannell, Sandra. "From the Poetics of Place to the Politics of Space: Redefining Cultural Landscapes on Damer, Maluku Tenggara." In *The Poetic Power of Place: Comparative Perspectives on Austronesian Ideas of Locality*, ed. Katy Bellingham, Margaret Tyrie, Norma Chin, and Barbara Holloway, 163–72. Canberra: Australian National UEP, 2006.

Pascoe, Judith. *The Hummingbird Cabinet: A Rare and Curious History of Romantic Collectors.* Ithaca, NY: Cornell UP, 2006.

Peck, Walter. "An Essay by Shelley." *TLS*, 27 November 1924, 797.

———. *Shelley: His Life and Work.* 2 vols. Boston: Houghton Mifflin, 1927.

Pennington, Brian. *Was Hinduism Invented? Britons, Indians, and the Colonial Construction of Religion.* Oxford: Oxford UP, 2005.

Piper, Andrew. *Dreaming in Books: The Making of the Bibliographic Imagination in the Romantic Age.* Chicago: U of Chicago P, 2009.

Pitts, Jennifer. *A Turn to Empire: The Rise of Imperial Liberalism in Britain and France.* Princeton, NJ: Princeton UP, 2005.

Pocock, J. G. A. *The Machiavellian Moment: Florentine Political Thought and the Atlantic Republican Tradition.* Princeton, NJ: Princeton UP, 1975.

Porter, Andrew. *Religion versus Empire? British Protestant Missionaries and Overseas Expansion, 1700–1914.* Manchester, UK: Manchester UP, 2004.

Porter, Bernard. *The Absent-Minded Imperialists: Empire, Society, and Culture in Britain.* Oxford: Oxford UP, 2004.

Potts, E. Daniel. *British Baptist Missionaries in India, 1793–1837: The History of Serampore and Its Missions.* Cambridge: Cambridge UP, 1967.

Prakash, Gyan. "The Impossibility of Subaltern History." *Nepantla: Views from South* 1, no. 2 (2000): 287–94.

Pratt, Lynda, ed. *Robert Southey and the Contexts of English Romanticism.* Aldershot, UK: Ashgate, 2006.

———. " 'Where . . . success [is] certain'? Southey the Literary East Indiaman." In Franklin, *Romantic Representations of British India*, 131–53.

Price, Leah. *How to Do Things with Books in Victorian Britain.* Princeton, NJ: Princeton UP, 2012.

Priestman, Martin. *Romantic Atheism: Poetry and Freethought, 1780–1830.* Cambridge: Cambridge UP, 1999.

Priolkar, Anant Kakba. *The Printing Press in India: Its Beginnings and Early Development.* Bombay: Marathi Samshodhana Mandala, 1958.

Pye, Michael. *Syncretism versus Synthesis.* British Association for the Study of Religion Occasional Papers 8 (1993), 2–18.

Rangarajan, Padma. "Imperial Babel: Translation, Exoticism, and the Long Nineteenth Century." Unpublished manuscript.

Ray, Amit. *Negotiating the Modern: Orientalism and Indianness in the Anglophone World.* New York: Routledge, 2007.

Ray, William. *The Logic of Culture: Authority and Identity in the Modern Era.* Oxford: Blackwell, 2001.

Riches, Hugh. *A History of the Oriental Club.* London: Oriental Club, 1998.

Ringgren, Helmer. "The Problems of Syncretism." In *Syncretism*, ed. Sven S. Hartman, 7–14. Stockholm: Almqvist & Wiksell, 1969.

Robbins, Bruce. "Introduction Part 1: Actually Existing Cosmopolitanism." In *Cosmopolitics: Thinking and Feeling beyond the Nation*, ed. Pheng Cheah and Bruce Robbins, 1–19. Minneapolis: U of Minnesota P, 1998.

Roberts, Daniel Sanjiv. "Beneath High Romanticism: 'Southeian' Orientations in De Quincey." In Pratt, *Robert Southey and the Contexts of English Romanticism*, 37–48.

Robertson, Bruce Carlisle. "The English Writings of Raja Rammohan Ray." In Mehrotra, *History of Indian Literature in English*, 27–40.

———. *Raja Rammohan Ray: The Father of Modern India*. New Delhi: Oxford UP, 1995.

Rocher, Rosane, and Ludo Rocher. *The Making of Western Indology: Henry Thomas Colebrooke and the East India Company*. London: Routledge, 2012.

Rosen, Steven J. *Essential Hinduism*. Westport, CT: Praeger, 2006.

Roy, Asim. *The Islamic Syncretistic Tradition in Bengal*. Princeton, NJ: Princeton UP, 1983.

Rudd, Andrew. *Sympathy and India in British Literature, 1770–1830*. New York: Palgrave, 2011.

Rudolph, Kurt. "Synkretismus—vom theologischen Scheltwort zum religionswissenschaftlichen Begriff." In *Humanitas Religiosa: Festschrift für Haralds Biezais*, ed. Liene Neulande, 193–212. Stockholm: Almqvist & Wiksell, 1979.

Saglia, Diego. "Words and Things: Southey's East and the Materiality of Oriental Discourse." In Pratt, *Robert Southey and the Contexts of English Romanticism*, 167–86.

Said, Edward. *Culture and Imperialism*. London: Vintage, 1994.

———. "The Mind of Winter: Reflections on Life in Exile." *Harper's*, September 1984, 49–55.

———. *Orientalism*. New York: Vintage, 1978.

———. "Orientalism Reconsidered." In Barker et al., *Europe and Its Others*, 1:14–27.

———. "Reflections on Exile." In *Reflections on Exile, and Other Essays*, 173–86. Cambridge, MA: Harvard UP, 2000.

Sangupta, Jatindra Chandra. *West Bengal District Gazeteers: West Dinājpur*. Calcutta: State Editor, 1965.

Sankhdher, B. M. *Press, Politics, and Public Opinion in India: Dynamics of Modernization and Social Transformation*. New Delhi: Deep & Deep, 1984.

Sarkar, Nikhil. "Printing and the Spirit of Calcutta." In *Calcutta: The Living City*, ed. Sukanta Chaudhuri, vol. 1, *The Past*, 128–36. Calcutta: Oxford UP, 1990.

Sarkar, Sumit. "The Complexities of Young Bengal." *Nineteenth-Century Studies* (Calcutta) 4 (October 1973): 504–34.

———. *A Critique of Colonial India*. Calcutta: Papyrus, 1985.

Sarkar, Susobhan. *Bengal Renaissance, and Other Essays*. New Delhi: People's Publishing, 1970.

Sassen, Saskia. "Spatialities and Temporalities of the Global: Elements for a Theorization." *Public Culture* 12, no. 1 (Winter 2000): 215–32.

Sastri, Sivanath. *Ramtanu Lahiri: Brahman and Reformer; A History of the Renaissance in Bengal*. Trans. S. K. Lahiri. Ed. Roper Lethbridge. London: Swan Sonnenschein, 1907.

Schwab, Raymond. *The Oriental Renaissance: Europe's Rediscovery of India and the East, 1680–1880*. Trans. Gene Patterson-Black and Victor Reinking. New York: Columbia UP, 1984.

Sen, Amartya. *The Argumentative Indian: Writings on Indian History, Culture and Identity*. New York: Farrar, Straus & Giroux, 2005.

Sen, Asok. "The Bengal Economy and Rammohun Roy." In Joshi, *Rammohun Roy and the Process of Modernization in India*, 103–35.

Sen, Asoka Kumar. "The Derozians and Journalism." *Nineteenth-Century Studies* (Calcutta) 7 (July 1974): 328–47.

Sen, Sudipta. *Distant Sovereignty: National Imperialism and the Origins of British India*. New York: Routledge, 2002.

———. "Imperial Subjects on Trial: On the Legal Identity of Britons in Late Eighteenth-Century India." *Journal of British Studies* 45, no. 3 (July 2006): 532–55.

Sen, Sukumar. "Early Printers and Publishers in Calcutta." *Bengal: Past and Present* 87 (January–June 1968): 59–66.

Shaffer, E. S. *"Kubla Khan" and "The Fall of Jerusalem": The Mythological School in Biblical Criticism and Secular Literature, 1770–1880*. Cambridge: Cambridge UP, 1975.

Shaw, Graham. *Printing in Calcutta to 1800: A Description and Checklist of Printing in Late 18th-Century Calcutta*. London: Bibliographical Society, 1981.

Sherman, Daniel J. "Quatremère/Benjamin/Marx: Art Museums, Aura, and Commodity Fetishism." In *Museum Culture: Histories, Discourses, Spectacles*, ed. Daniel J. Sherman and Irit Rogoff, 123–43. London: Routledge, 1994.

Simmons, Clare. "'Useful and Wasteful Both': Southey's *Thalaba the Destroyer* and the Function of Annotation in the Romantic Oriental Poem." *Genre* 27 (Spring–Summer 1994): 83–104.

Singh, Iqbal. *Rammohun Roy: A Biographical Inquiry into the Making of Modern India*. 3 vols. Bombay: Asia Publishing House, 1983.

Singh, S. B. "Growth of Public Opinion in India (1835–1861)." In *Growth of Public Opinion in India: 19th and Early 20th Centuries (1800–1914)*, ed. Nisith Ranjan Ray, 1–14. Calcutta: Naya Prokash. 1989.

Sinha, Mrinalini. "Britishness, Clubbability, and the Colonial Public Sphere: The Genealogy of an Imperial Institution in Colonial India." *Journal of British Studies* 40, no. 4 (October 2001): 489–521.

Sinha, N. K. "The Hindu College." *Bengal: Past and Present* 87 (January–June 1968): 78–91.

Speck, William. *Robert Southey: Entire Man of Letters*. New Haven: Yale UP, 2006.

———. "Robert Southey's Contribution to the *Quarterly Review*." In Cutmore, *Conservatism and the Quarterly Review*, 165–77.

Spivak, Gayatri Chakravorty. "The Rani of Sirmur: An Essay in Reading the Archives." *History and Theory* 24, no. 3 (1985): 247–72.

Stanley, Brian. *The History of the Baptist Missionary Society, 1792–1992*. Edinburgh: T. & T. Clark, 1992.

Stark, Herbert A., and E. Walter Madge. *East Indian Worthies, Being Memoirs of Distinguished Indo-Europeans*. Calcutta: Cambridge Steam Printing Works, 1892.

Stewart, Susan. *On Longing: Narratives of the Miniature, the Gigantic, the Souvenir, the Collection*. Baltimore: Johns Hopkins UP, 1984.

Stewart, Tony K., and Carl W. Ernst. "Syncretism." In *South Asian Folklore: An Encylopedia*, ed. Margaret A. Mills, Peter J. Claus, and Sarah Diamond, 586–88. New York: Routledge, 2003.

Stietencron, Heinrich von. "Hinduism: On the Proper Use of a Deceptive Term." In *Hinduism Reconsidered*, ed. Günther D. Sontheimer and Hermann Kulke, 11–27. New Delhi: Manohar, 1989.

Stokes, Eric. *The English Utilitarians and India*. Oxford: Clarendon, 1959.

Stoler, Ann Laura, and Frederick Cooper. "Between Metropole and Colony: Rethinking a Research Agenda." In *Tensions of Empire: Colonial Cultures in a Bourgeois World*, ed. Frederick Cooper and Ann Laura Stoler, 1–56. Berkeley: U of California P, 1997.

Storey, Mark. "'A Hold upon Posterity': The Strange Case of Robert Southey." Inaugural lecture delivered at the University of Birmingham, School of English, on 20 February 1992. 1993.

Strachey, John. *India: Its Administration and Progress*. London: Macmillan, 1903.

Strong, Rowan. *Anglicanism and the British Empire, c. 1700–1850*. Oxford: Oxford UP, 2007.

Suleri, Sara. *The Rhetoric of English India*. Chicago: U of Chicago P, 1992.

Sussman, Charlotte. "Epic, Exile, and the Global: Felicia Hemans's *The Forest Sanctuary*." *Nineteenth-Century Literature* 65, no. 4 (March 2011): 481–512.

Sutton, Jean. *Lords of the East: The East India Company and its Ships*. London: Conway Maritime, 1981.

Tamen, Miguel. *Friends of Interpretable Objects*. Cambridge, MA: Harvard UP, 2001.

Taylor, Charles. "Afterword: Apologia pro Libro suo." In Warner, VanAntwerpen, and Calhoun, *Varieties of Secularism in a Secular Age*, 300–21.

———. *A Secular Age*. Cambridge, MA: Belknap Press of Harvard UP, 2007.

———. "Two Theories of Modernity." In Gaonkar, *Alternative Modernities*, 172–96.

Taylor, Clair, ed. *British and American Abolitionists: An Episode in Transatlantic Understanding*. Edinburgh: Edinburgh UP, 1974.

Taylor, David Francis. *Theatres of Opposition: Empire, Revolution, and Richard Brinsley Sheridan*. Oxford: Oxford UP, 2012.

Teltscher, Kate. *India Inscribed: European and British Writing on India, 1600–1800*. New Delhi: Oxford UP, 1995.

Thomas, Nicholas. *Entangled Objects: Exchange, Material Culture, and Colonialism in the Pacific*. Cambridge, MA: Harvard UP, 1991.

———. "Licensed Curiosity: Cook's Pacific Voyages." In *The Cultures of Collecting*, ed. John Elsner and Roger Cardinal, 116–36. London: Reaktion, 1994.

Thomas, Sophie. *Romanticism and Visuality: Fragments, History, Spectacle*. New York: Routledge, 2008.

Thompson, E. P. "Time, Work-Discipline, and Industrial Capitalism." *Past and Present* 3 (December 1967): 56–97.

Travers, Robert. *Ideology and Empire in Eighteenth-Century India: The British in Bengal*. Cambridge: Cambridge UP, 2007.

Trumpener, Katie. *Bardic Nationalism: The Romantic Novel and the British Empire*. Princeton, NJ: Princeton UP, 1997.

Tucker, Herbert. *Epic: Britain's Heroic Muse, 1790–1910*. Oxford: Oxford UP, 2008.

Visram, Rozina. *Asians in Britain: 400 Years of History*. London: Pluto, 2002.

———. *Ayahs, Lascars and Princes: Indians in Briton, 1700–1947*. London: Pluto, 1986.

Viswanathan, Gauri. "Colonialism and the Construction of Hinduism." In *The Blackwell Companion to Hinduism*, ed. Gavin Flood, 23–44. Malden, MA: Blackwell, 2003.

———. *Masks of Conquest: Literary Study and British Rule in India*. New York: Columbia UP, 1989.

———. *Outside the Fold: Conversion, Modernity, and Belief*. Princeton, NJ: Princeton UP, 1998.

Warner, Michael, Jonathan VanAntwerpen, and Craig Calhoun. "Editors' Introduction." In Warner, VanAntwerpen, and Calhoun, *Varieties of Secularism in a Secular Age*, 1–31.

———, eds. *Varieties of Secularism in a Secular Age*. Cambridge, MA: Harvard UP, 2010.

Webb, R. K. *Harriet Martineau: A Radical Victorian*. London: Heinemann, 1960.

Wheeler, Stephen, ed., *Annals of the Oriental Club, 1824–1858*. [London]: privately printed, 1925.

Whelan, Timothy. "A Glance at the 1795 Catalogue of Books in the Library of the Bristol Baptist Academy and Museum." *Baptist Quarterly* 39 (January 2001): 35–38.

White, Daniel E. *Early Romanticism and Religious Dissent*. Cambridge: Cambridge UP, 2006.

Wilcox, Scott. "The Early History of the Panorama." In *Das Panorama in Altötting: Beiträge zu Geschichte und Restaurierung*, ed. Michael Petzet, 9–16. Munich: Bayerisches Landesamt für Denkmalpflege, 1990.

Wilson, Kathleen. "Citizenship, Empire, and Modernity in the English Provinces, c. 1720–90." In *Cultures of Empire: A Reader; Colonizers in Britain and the Empire in the Nineteenth and Twentieth Centuries*, ed. Catherine Hall, 157–86. Manchester, UK: Manchester UP, 2000.

———. "Introduction: Histories, Empires, Modernities." In Wilson, *New Imperial History*, 1–26.

———. *The Island Race: Englishness, Empire and Gender in the Eighteenth Century*. London: Routledge, 2003.

———, ed. *A New Imperial History: Culture, Identity and Modernity in Britain and the Empire, 1660–1840*. Cambridge: Cambridge UP, 2004.

Wood, Gillen D'Arcy. *The Shock of the Real: Romanticism and Visual Culture, 1760–1800*. New York: Palgrave, 2001.

Wright, Julia M. *Ireland, India, and Nationalism in Nineteenth-Century Literature*. Cambridge: Cambridge UP, 2007.

Young, Desmond. *Fountain of the Elephants*. London: Harper, 1959.

Zastoupil, Lynn. *Rammohun Roy and the Making of Victorian Britain*. New York: Palgrave, 2010.

Zemka, Sue. "The Holy Books of Empire: Translations of the British and Foreign Bible Society." In *Macropolitics of Nineteenth-Century Literature: Nationalism, Exoticism, Imperialism*, ed. Jonathan Arac and Harriet Ritvo, 102–37. Philadelphia: U of Pennsylvania P, 1991.

Zoli, Corri. " 'Black Holes' of Calcutta and London: Internal Colonies in Vanity Fair." *Victorian Literature and Culture* 25 (2007): 417–49.

Note: Page numbers in *italics* indicate figures.